IRELAND'S ABBEY THEATRE

IRELAND'S ABBEY THEATRE

A History
1899-1951

★

COMPILED BY
LENNOX ROBINSON

KENNIKAT PRESS, INC./PORT WASHINGTON, N. Y.

IRELAND'S ABBEY THEATRE

First Published in 1951
Reissued in 1968 by Kennikat Press

Library of Congress Catalog Card No:67-27639

Manufactured in the United States of America

FOREWORD

THERE have been many difficulties in writing this History, the chief difficulty being the absence of documents relating to the Theatre's beginning, the years 1899-1904, that is to say the years of the Antient Concert Rooms, the Gaiety Theatre, St. Teresa's Hall, the Camden Street and the Molesworth Halls. It is impossible to find out how much Edward Martyn spent on the Theatre's earliest productions, and it is very difficult to clear up the finances of the first years of the Abbey Theatre. So many prosaic books, Account books and Minutes of meetings, have been destroyed. They seemed rubbish to the destroyer, but they would not have seemed rubbish to the historian. But, here and there, from a reminiscence, I have tried to build up a picture of our early Theatre and make it as authentic as possible. A Secretary of the Theatre said to me once: "I don't know whom I dislike most—you, who tear up everything, or Mr. Gorman, who keeps everything." If the Mister Gorman of sixty years ago had kept all the seemingly worthless notes, how brilliantly they would have coloured this History.

In choosing the illustrations I have tried as far as possible to make them contemporary to the narrative. So, in Chapter Two I have preferred a rather poor early portrait of Lady Gregory by AE (I know of only one other portrait by him), rather than Sir Gerald Festus Kelly's portrait or the Mancini one in Dublin's Municipal Gallery. And, illustrating Chapter One, a young Yeats rather than forty or more years later the noble Augustus John or the equally noble Sean O'Sullivan.

This book is not an appreciation of Ireland's Abbey Theatre, nor is it a criticism. It is a History, and, as far as possible, I have tried to bury my likes and dislikes. I have tried to marshal all the facts, the dates of production, and casts of first productions of plays, making them as accurate as possible and making the book a History which future students may feel confident to quote, but I feel sure that I have made many mistakes in the spelling of Gaelic names.

But, like Doctor Johnson's immortal friend who "tried to be a philosopher but cheerfulness was always breaking in," sometimes in spite of myself gossip and cheerfulness keep breaking in.

ACKNOWLEDGEMENTS

MY first thanks go to the Directors of the Theatre and to our Secretary, Eric Gorman, who have put all their documents at my disposal. It is not their fault that they were not able to give me the facts of the Theatre before it became the Abbey Theatre. Our National Library has been tireless in its help. I particularly want to thank Dr. Richard Best, Mr. O'Connor, and other members of the staff who were very helpful. Mrs. Martin, Seaghan Barlow and Udolphus Wright have contributed valuable personal memories, and Mr. Wright has helped me in many other ways. I particularly thank Major R. C. Gregory, Mrs. A. de Winton and Mrs. C. F. Kennedy, grand-children of Lady Gregory, for permission to quote from her *Journals* and from her book, *Our Irish Theatre*. Others who have contributed to this History are Mrs. W. B. Yeats, James Cousins, C. P. Curran, Gerald Fay, Jack B. Yeats, Sara Payne, Muriel Kelly, and Miss Cullen. Messrs. Whitney, Moore and Keller were the Theatre's financial advisers for many years and Mr. R. N. Keller has allowed me to consult many documents of great interest and value to this book. Two firms of the Theatre's auditors, Messrs. Craig, Gardner and Co. and George Munro and Co., have been very useful in helping me with the financial details of the Theatre. I may have forgotten some other helpers, I am indebted to so many people who by a phrase, a memory, have helped me, and I apologise to them if I have not written down their names.

For the illustrations I must acknowledge debts to the National Gallery of Ireland, for permission to reproduce a drawing of W. B. Yeats; to the Municipal Gallery of Modern Art of Dublin, for the reproduction of Edward Martyn's portrait by kind permission of the Dublin Corporation; to the Tate Gallery of London, for permission to use Walter Sickert's portrait of George Moore; and to Messrs.

Macmillan and Co. and to Augustus John, for the portrait of Sean O'Casey.

Finally, I owe many thanks to my Secretary, Elizabeth Clancy, and to Michael O'Neill who has patiently helped me with the final proofs.

CONTENTS

		PAGE
Foreword		vii
Acknowledgements		ix
List of Illustrations		xiii
Chapter One	The Irish Literary Theatre, 1899	1
Chapter Two	The Irish Literary Theatre, 1900	13
Chapter Three	The Irish Literary Theatre, 1901	20
Chapter Four	W. G. Fay's National Dramatic Society and, later, the Irish National Theatre Society, 1902-1903	25
Chapter Five	1903-1904	32
Chapter Six	The Abbey Theatre, 1904-1909	42
Chapter Seven	1909-1918	83
Chapter Eight	1919-1932	119
Chapter Nine	1932-1950	149
Conclusion		181
Postscript		183
Appendices		
I. Pictures in a Theatre		185

Appendices (*continued*)
- II. Plays in Gaelic 196
- III. Translations 207
- IV. Experimental Theatre 212
- V. Ballets 215

General Index 218

Index of Casts of First Productions 220

Index of Plays referred to in Text 223

LIST OF ILLUSTRATIONS

The Abbey Theatre, Dublin . . . . . . *Frontispiece*

Facing page

W. B. Yeats by J. B. Yeats (1900). *National Gallery, Ireland* . 4
Edward Martyn by Sarah Purser (1900). *Municipal Art Gallery, Dublin* 5
George Moore by Walter Sickert. *Tate Gallery, London* . . . 12
Lady Gregory by AE. (About 1900) 13
Dr. Douglas Hyde by Sarah Purser. *Municipal Art Gallery, Dublin* . 20
William Fay by J. B. Yeats 24
Frank Fay by J. B. Yeats 24-25
J. M. Synge by J. B. Yeats 24-25
Maire Nic Shiubhlaigh by J. B. Yeats 25
Padraic Colum by J. B. Yeats 28
Miss A. E. F. Horniman by J. B. Yeats 40
Interior of Abbey Theatre, Dublin 40-41
Vestibule of Abbey Theatre, Dublin 40-41
Sara Allgood by Robert Gregory 48
Maire O'Neill by J. B. Yeats 49
Arthur Sinclair by Robert Gregory 64
Fred O'Donovan (as "Robert Emmet" in *The Dreamers*) by James Sleator 64-65
Udolphus Wright 64-65
Mrs. Martin 65
Seaghan Barlow 80
Souvenir Programme 81
T. C. Murray 96

Lennox Robinson	97
St. John Ervine (1911)	112
Sean O'Casey by Augustus John	128
George Shiels	129
Brinsley MacNamara by Sean O'Sullivan	144
The Abbey Theatre Company outside the Broadway Theatre, Denver, Colorado, during its tour of America in 1932	156
F. J. McCormick by Sean O'Sullivan	157

CHAPTER ONE

The Irish Literary Theatre, 1899

In making a play the dramatist is always faced with the problem—at what point shall I break into my subject? That problem must have stared Shakespeare in the face when he brooded over *Hamlet*. We never question now the proper moment Shakespeare chose, yet he may have considered cutting into the tangle of those lives earlier, perhaps when Hamlet's father was still alive. Ibsen, in his later plays, was wont to strike in later and later; almost everything of importance has happened before the curtain rises on *Little Eyolf* or *John Gabriel Borkman* or *When We Dead Awaken*. These plays are but the turning-over of warm cinders in extinct volcanoes —but they have been volcanoes. In writing this History of the Abbey Theatre, it might have been proper to hark back to the very important Irish theatre of the seventeenth and eighteenth centuries, to the playwrights, the Farquhars, Goldsmiths, Sheridans, and to a galaxy of Irish actors and actresses, and go on to remind ourselves of our fine nineteenth-century dramatist, Boucicault. But it seemed better, plainer—are those others not written in the text-books?—to start simply with a quotation from Lady Gregory's book *Our Irish Theatre*.

>   I was in London in the beginning of 1898, and I find written, "Yeats and Sir Alfred Lyall to tea, Yeats stayed on. He is very full of play-writing. . . . He, with the aid of Miss Florence Farr, an actress who thinks more of a romantic than of a paying play, is very keen about taking or building a little theatre somewhere in the suburbs to produce romantic drama, his own plays, Edward Martyn's, one of Bridges', and he is trying to stir up Standish O'Grady and Fiona Macleod to write some. He believes there will be a reaction after the realism of Ibsen, and romance will have its turn. He has put a 'great deal of himself' into his own play *The Shadowy Waters* and rather startled me by saying about half his characters have eagle's faces. . . ."
>   One day at Duras (Co. Galway) in 1898, Mr. Edward Martyn, my neighbour, came to see me, bringing with him Mr. Yeats, whom I did not then know very well, though I cared for his work very much and had already, through his directions, been gathering folk-lore. They had lunch with us, but it was a wet day and we could not go out. . . . We sat there through that wet

afternoon, and though I had never been at all interested in theatres, our talk turned on plays. Mr. Martyn had written two. *The Heather Field* and *Maeve*. They had been offered to London managers, and now he thought of trying to have them produced in Germany where there seemed to be more room for new drama than in England. I said it was a pity we had no Irish theatre where such plays could be given. Mr. Yeats said that had always been a dream of his, but he had of late thought it an impossible one, for it could not at first pay its way, and there was no money to be found for such a thing in Ireland.

We went on talking about it, and things seemed to grow possible as we talked, and before the end of the afternoon we had made our plan. We said we would collect money, or rather ask to have a certain sum of money guaranteed. We would then take a Dublin theatre and give a performance of Mr. Martyn's *The Heather Field* and one of Mr. Yeats's own plays, *The Countess Cathleen*. I offered the first guarantee of £25.

A few days after that I was back at Coole, and Mr. Yeats came over from Mr. Martyn's home, Tillyra, and we wrote a formal letter to send out....

Our statement—it seems now a little pompous—began: "We propose to have performed, in Dublin, in the spring of every year certain Celtic and Irish plays, which, whatever be their degree of excellence, will be written with a high ambition, and so build up a Celtic and Irish school of dramatic literature. We hope to find in Ireland an uncorrupted and imaginative audience, trained to listen by its passion for oratory, and believe that our desire to bring upon the stage the deeper thoughts and emotions of Ireland will ensure for us a tolerant welcome, and that freedom to experiment which is not found in the theatres of England, and without which no new movement in art or literature can succeed. We will show that Ireland is not the home of buffoonery and of easy sentiment, as it has been represented, but the home of an ancient idealism. We are confident of the support of all Irish people, who are weary of misrepresentation, in carrying out a work that is outside all the political questions that divide us."

A sum of three hundred pounds was asked for to make the experiment, which was to be carried on for three years. That sum was quickly guaranteed by about fifty people representing every difference in religion and politics, and this only a few years after the Parnell "split," when the questions of politics and religion were very burning ones.

The statement was signed by W. B. Yeats, Edward Martyn and Lady Gregory.

W. B. Yeats was then thirty-three. Born at Sandymount, just outside Dublin, his mother's relations and his boyish recollections were all connected with the West, with County Sligo. His father, bred a barrister, became a very fine painter; he lived in London, so his son's young-man's life was mostly in London in the society of artists, William Morris and his circle, but with long holidays in Sligo. He drew a little himself, but it soon became obvious that his genius lay in poetry. The stage attracted him, and in 1894 a one-act play of his, *The Land of Heart's Desire*, was produced in the Avenue Theatre, London. It served as a curtain-raiser to John Todhunter's *Comedy of Sighs* and Bernard Shaw's *Arms and the Man*. Yeats's *Land of Heart's Desire* was utterly Irish in subject, it was peasant, it was faery, it was "Celtic Twilight" —he himself coined the phrase. Two years before, a much longer play, *The Countess Cathleen*, had been published in England but not produced in a theatre. Yeats had got the story of it from a French source, but he laid the scene in Ireland. Yet it was not vanity, it was not the wish to see his play on the stage that made him join forces that rainy afternoon with Lady Gregory and Edward Martyn, for he dreamed of an Irish National Theatre, a theatre of poetry, a theatre of "ancient idealism" and of noble Irish history. The money for the Irish Literary Theatre was guaranteed by the following:

W. E. H. Lecky
Douglas Hyde
Lord Castletown
George Coffey
Lord Morris
Martin Morris
Lady Gregory
John O'Leary
Maud Gonne
Sir Thomas Moffat
Hon. Emily Lawless
E. J. Gwynn
Jane Barlow
Rt. Hon. C. T. Redington
Count de Basterol
Sir Peter O'Brien
T. W. Lyster
Sir F. W. Burton
Duchess of St. Albans
Viscountess de Vesci
John Dillon
Dr. Kenny
T. M. Healy.

The McDermott
William O'Brien
Judge Boyd
Lord and Lady Ardilaun
Lord Gough
John Pentland Mahaffy
Horace Plunkett
Lord Plunkett
W. P. Coyne
J. G. Barton
T. P. Gill
Mrs. Ross-of-Bladensburg
John Redmond
Earl of Westmeath
Mrs. Fitzgerald
Miss C. Gore-Booth
Flora Shaw
Edith Oldham
George Russell
John Eglinton
James McLoone
C. H. Oldham

Lady Gregory was ten years Yeats's senior in age. She says that she had never been particularly interested in the theatre. She had married a distinguished Irishman—he had been Governor of Ceylon—you see his statue as you enter Colombo harbour—and after his retirement he and his wife lived most of the months of the year in London in the society of political and literary people. His home was Coole Park, County Galway. Lady Gregory had been born a Persse, not many miles away, in a big country house, Roxboro'. The Gregorys' feelings were entirely Irish (Sir William and his forebears had been model landlords) and when he died—he was many years older than she—her thoughts went more and more across the Irish Sea. But, in 1898, she had no ambitions as a writer; she had edited her husband's autobiography, and letters of an ancestor of his, but she had written no original work. But she loved poetry and was particularly attracted by Yeats's poetry; and he had set her gathering Irish folk-lore, and soon she set herself to learn Gaelic.

Edward Martyn was a Catholic Irish landlord, Yeats and Lady Gregory were Protestants. His home, Tillyra, was only a few miles from Lady Gregory's Coole Park. Unlike her, he was deeply interested in the theatre and, like Yeats, he had a play—two plays—he wanted to see performed. He was a disciple of Ibsen, and Yeats hated Ibsen: Yeats was influenced by Maeterlinck and the French and English modern poets; yet both wanted an Irish theatre. Both were passionately Irish, so it was not very difficult for Lady Gregory to blend this oil and vinegar and make them agree that the first performances of the Irish Literary Theatre, for thus it was called, should consist of Edward Martyn's Ibsenitish play *The Heather Field* and Yeats's dreamily poetic play *The Countess Cathleen*.

But suddenly, amazingly, a new figure steps into the picture —George Moore. Yeats had his roots in Sligo, Lady Gregory and Martyn in County Galway, Moore's family home was in Mayo; so they were all Westerns. Moore had left Ireland as a young man (he was born the same year as Lady Gregory, 1852) and had spent most of his years in Paris and London; but now, sickened by the South African War, he longed to

W. B. YEATS

EDWARD MARTYN

scrape the mud of England from his boots and to return to the country of his birth. Also he, like Yeats and Martyn, had a play or two in his head and, what was very valuable and important, he had some practical knowledge of the stage, he had mixed in Paris with players and producers. (Martyn and Yeats were very ignorant of stage-craft, they were to learn this later.) Moore preferred Martyn to Yeats (he knew them both quite slightly); but when, in London—*The Countess Cathleen* and *The Heather Field* were in rehearsal—Martyn said sadly that his play seemed to be going all wrong, but that Yeats's play was moving beautifully, Moore seized the reins, took over the rehearsals, and, after a few weeks' work in London, crossed the Irish Sea with a company of players, and established himself in Dublin for a number of years. He recounts the facts in *Hail and Farewell*, and his subsequent collaborations with Martyn and Yeats. A somewhat different version may be found in Yeats: Lady Gregory contents herself by saying "Mr. George Moore gave excellent help in finding actors, and the plays were rehearsed in London."

All the principal parts were played by English players. May Whitty (afterwards Dame May Whitty) was the Countess; Aleel, her lover, was played by Florence Farr who afterwards used to go on tour with Yeats, accompanying him in his readings on her psaltery. Marcus St. John and Trevor Lowe were the Demons. The performance seems to have been a very satisfactory one from the players' and producers' point of view. The play was not staged in a theatre but in the Antient Concert Rooms, Brunswick Street (now Pearse Street), Dublin, on 8th May 1899. The Antient Concert Rooms is a commodious hall, seating about eight hundred people; the stage is adequate. The hall is now a cinema. Years later, Bernard Shaw lectured there, perhaps his first lecture in Dublin, and recalled how he had heard his mother, a fine singer, singing there in oratorio.

Briefly, the plot of *The Countess Cathleen* is that, in a time of desperate famine in Ireland, demons arrive and buy the starving peasants' souls for gold. The saintly, immaculate Countess Cathleen sells her soul and, by her barter, redeems all the poor people's souls. Yet the Devil and the demons are cheated, for an Angel appears and declares that:

> The light beats down; the gates of pearl are wide;
> And she is passing to the floor of peace.
> And Mary of the seven times wounded heart
> Has kissed her lips and the long blessed hair
> Has fallen on her face; the Light of Lights
> Looks always on the motive, not the deed,
> The Shadow of Shadows on the deed alone.

A rumour ran around that the play was unorthodox. An enemy of Yeats, Frank Hugh O'Donnell, published a pamphlet entitled *Souls for Gold*, which was widely and gratuitously distributed. Cardinal Logue, who had not read the play, said in a letter to the *Daily Nation*:

> Dear Sir,
> You invite my opinion on the play of Mr. Yeats "The Countess Cathleen." All I know of this play is what I could gather from the extracts given in Mr. O'Donnell's pamphlet and your paper. Judging by these extracts, I have no hesitation in saying that an Irish Catholic audience which could patiently sit out such a play must have sadly degenerated, both in religion and patriotism.
> As to the opinions said to have been given by Catholic Divines, no doubt the authors of these opinions will undertake to justify them, but I should not like the task were mine.
> I am, dear Sir,
> Yours faithfully,
> Michael Cardinal Logue.
> Armagh, 9th May 1899.

The Countess Cathleen is a difficult play to stage, but it is reported to have been very adequately presented.

But, if the performance and the play's settings got praise, the play itself met with opposition before its performance. Yeats wrote to Edward Martyn:

> March 22nd. 18 Woburn Bldgs.,
> Upr. Woburn Pce.
>
> My dear Martyn,
> You are wrong about the facts to begin with. Coffey told Gill that he supposed Dr. Molloy would omit what Coffey thought to be the unorthodox passages. Gill, whom I have just seen, heard Dr. Molloy and listened very carefully because of what Coffey had said and assures me that he omitted nothing from the pages selected for him.

Now I am ready to omit or change any passages which you may think objectionable. Taking into consideration the extreme difficulties in which your backing out at this stage will involve Lady Gregory, Yeats, Moore, Gill, the National Literary Society, yourself and myself, and the miserable scandal it will make I think I have the right to ask you to do this. I am entirely convinced that the play contains no passages which can give offence to any Catholic. If you cannot and do not wish me to say certain things cut out these passages, remembering your guarantee and the scandal your withdrawal of it would make, the suspicions this would throw upon the literary movement in Ireland and even upon people like Horace Plunkett who has supported this movement. I am bound to ask you to take the only other course—to submit the matter to an arbitrator, Dr. Barry, Dr. Delaney, Dr. Vaughan, Father Finlay or any other competent and cultivated theologian. I will take out or change any passage objected to by the arbitrator.

Of course I need not remind you that we have very little time to lose.

Yrs.
W. B. Yeats.

Mr. Yeats writes to Dr. Barry, a well-known English man of letters, on 24th March:

Dear Dr. Barry,

I don't know if you have heard of our project of a literary theatre in Dublin, at which two plays already published, were to be performed—"The Heather Field" by Mr. Martyn, and "The Countess Cathleen" by myself. I enclose the list of guarantors that you may see how much interest the project has awakened. It has now been suggested that there are some passages in the latter play which might be objected to by a Catholic audience as not being in harmony with Catholic theology. I do not myself see anything in the play that could give offence, but as the last thing I desire is to give legitimate offence to any of my countrymen I have proposed that your opinion should be asked on the play, in case you would be kind enough to take the trouble of looking through it. The representation of the play has been fixed for the 8th of May and as it would be too late for another to put in its place I have offered to alter or omit any passages that a theologian of so much literary culture as yourself may object to. It never occurred to me that a work of imagination could be expected to have a definite theological basis. One has of necessity to leave out in a work of imagination the reservations and saving clause which one puts into a scientific treatise. I send you a copy of the book by this post and as we have so little time to lose I will ask leave to call on you on Monday to talk over the matter if you can spare me the time. I would not venture to ask this if it was a personal matter but the withdrawal of the play at this late moment would need public explanations that might cause a good deal of ill feeling.

Yrs. sincerely,
W. B. Yeats.

Dr. Barry was emphatic in his praise of the play.

Thirty-three members of the Royal University (later, University College, Dublin) signed a letter stating:

> We are not opposed to a movement for the reform of the stage in Ireland. We should be most ardent supporters of a healthy genuine movement in that direction, but we object to being compromised by such plays as *The Countess Cathleen*.

The signatories included Hugh Kennedy, afterwards Chief-Justice of Ireland, T. M. Kettle, F. Sheehy Skeffington and Seamus Clandillon. Edward Martyn, good Catholic that he was, grew perturbed but stuck by Yeats and Moore. Police appeared at the performance to quell the expected riot but there was little or no disturbance. The students made a dignified protest, but, as Dame May Whitty wrote to me thirty years later, "After a very few minutes of Mr. Yeats's play everyone in the audience was captivated by its beauty and there was no riot at all."

The leading article in the *Irish Times*, 9th May 1899, headed "The Literary Theatre," said that:

> *The Countess Cathleen* is neither a play nor a presentment of either the ideals or actions or motives of Irish men and women. ... *The Countess Cathleen* as performed last night by a company of artists chosen by those accountable for the movement is, in the first place, not *The Countess Cathleen* published by Mr. Yeats, and is consequently not a play. It is without action, without definiteness in the characterisation and without consistency in the dramatic development, without truth in its reflection of Celtic temperament or life, and like all inferior plays it fails to excite the smallest genuine interest. ... *The Countess Cathleen* has no action which could seize and carry on to a climax the interest of an audience; therefore, it is not a good play and in as much as it offends against the tenour of Irish history in regard to Theological connection and against the position of the Irish peasant in face of physical pain, it cannot be considered an Irish play. ... Still less as a Celtic dramatic effort it was not entitled to have serious consideration.

The Dublin *Evening Mail* of 9th May 1899 said:

> Last night *The Countess Cathleen* by W. B. Yeats was performed at the Antient Concert Rooms, and from the success of this initial effort of the Irish Literary Theatre, we may fairly estimate what that institution is likely to be able to accomplish in the future. The house was packed with an enthusiastic audience, and the unanimity of the applause was only broken by some dozen persons, who found something to object to in some of the expressions put into the mouths of the characters of the play. They manifestly took their cue

from an article which appeared in one of our contemporaries, and as will be seen from the analytical criticism of the play which we give below, the expressions to which they took exception were not, in our opinion, entirely above criticism from certain points of view.

When we consider the tremendous disadvantage under which the whole performance laboured, the smallness of the stage, the meagreness of the scenery and other necessary accessories, its success appears all the more surprising and gratifying. Besides the great poetical beauty of the play, one of the chief causes of this was the undoubted ability with which it was acted. All who took part in the performance were excellent. Miss May Whitty, who took the part of Countess Cathleen, has already appeared with distinction before Dublin audiences.

The Prologue, which was specially written for the occasion by Mr. Lionel Johnson, was prettily delivered by Miss Dorothy Paget. The selection was peculiarly happy, in as much as Miss Paget acted as a child with great success in Mr. Yeats's *Land of Heart's Desire* which was produced some years ago by Miss Florence Farr at the Avenue Theatre.

At the end of the performance, in answer to repeated and enthusiastic calls, Mr. Yeats appeared on the stage, and shook hands publicly with Miss May Whitty and Miss Florence Farr.

The *Freeman's Journal*, 9th May 1899, said:

> The presentation of such a play under the conditions described must, of course, make even a greater innovation on the ordinary playgoer's expectations and make success all the more difficult. Themes of this kind have hitherto been to the accompaniment of trembling harmonies and Wagnerian discords. To present them in their literary simplicity is to travel very far indeed from the theatrical conventions of the hour.
>
> In the circumstances the promoters of the Irish Literary Theatre must have had their expectations fulfilled last evening. An audience of between 400 and 500 assembled to witness the presentation of *The Countess Cathleen*. A small organised knot of less than a dozen disorderly boys, who evidently mistook the whole moral significance of the play, cast ridicule upon themselves by hissing the demons under the impression that they were hissing the poet. But the audience, representative of every section of educated opinion in Dublin, was most enthusiastic, recalling the actors and the author again and again and cheering loudly.

The following night, 9th May, in sharp contrast, appeared Edward Martyn's *The Heather Field*.

The *Irish Times*, on 10th May 1899, said:

> In as far as the everyday playgoer is concerned *The Heather Field* will scarcely excite anything like the feelings that it would seem to have produced in Mr. Moore. To many it may appeal as a deep analysis of human nature, as an effort to read into life as it exists round about us mystical and exalted

readings, but to a man who goes to a play to be amused, instructed or initiated into the workings of the mainsprings of human conduct, *The Heather Field* is little likely to be of any assistance. The truth is that, despite Ibsen and his realism, one can scarcely make a drama out of a conversation on a drainage loan advanced by the Board of Works, a wholesale reduction of lands by the Land Commission, and similar topics.

The Heather Field is wearisome because it has no action worthy of the name. Its dialogue is stilted, its characters are not very deftly drawn and its reflection of Irish life is not very convincing.

But the *Evening Mail*, 10th May 1899, said:

The second performance of the Irish Literary Theatre repeated and even emphasised the success of the first. *The Heather Field* is not only a fine literary play, but it is also and even more noticeably, a splendid acting play. Last night at the Antient Concert Rooms a crowded audience bore testimony by their enthusiastic applause to the truth of this fact. Mr. Martyn is to be congratulated on what is, in every sense of the word, a great dramatic triumph. Below we give an analysis and appreciation of the play which was accorded such an enthusiastic ovation. Here we may confine ourselves to the artists, who claim an equal share with the author in the success of the representation.

The chief character in the play is Carden Tyrrell. In the opinion of the audience Mr. Thomas Kingston gave a truly wonderful realism and impressiveness to this part.

And the *Evening Mail* in a leading article on the same date said:

The Heather Field is an interesting play, and it gave almost unqualified satisfaction to the first-nighters, assembled in the Antient Concert Rooms last night. We should omit the word "almost" only that we think the opening dialogues between Carden Tyrrell—first with his bosom friend, Barry Ussher and then with his own brother, Miles Tyrrell—are over elaborated and somewhat tiresome. The author might have remembered Hamlet's "something too much of this" which put a stop to protestations much less offensive than those of Carden and his Horatio. But from that dialogue the interest of the audience increased, and from the time of the wife's entrance on the scene, became enthralling. . . . That interest is not in any degree due to the Irish associations which are supposed to recommend the play to Irish favour.

Another Irish paper said:

The success which attended the experiment of establishing the Irish Literary Theatre when its inaugural play *The Countess Cathleen* was produced on Monday developed into something very nearly approaching a triumph when Mr. Ed. Martyn's drama *The Heather Field* was put on the boards. The audience was again a distinguished one, but not so large as on the previous occasion. On the other hand, there was no hostile element present, a circumstance which gave Mr. Martyn's play an advantage over Mr. Yeats.

The audiences at these two performances were large: there is no record of the expenses, but the guarantee fund of three hundred pounds was never called on, for Edward Martyn met all the losses, if there were losses. He was a generous, wealthy man, Yeats a very poor one, and Lady Gregory a generous, poor woman. Moore had always comfortable means.

Casts of First Productions, 1899

8th May 1899

THE COUNTESS CATHLEEN

A Miracle Play in Four Acts by W. B. Yeats

First Demon	Marcus St. John
Second Demon	Trevor Lowe
(Both disguised as merchants)	
Shemus Rua (a peasant)	Valentine Grace
Teig Rua (his son)	Charles Sefton
Maire Rua (his wife)	Madame San Carolo
Aleel (a bard)	Florence Farr
Oona (Cathleen's nurse)	Anna Mather
Herdsman	Claude Holmes
Gardener	Jack Wilcox
First Peasant	— Walford
Sheogue	Dorothy Paget
Peasant Woman	M. Kelly
Servant	F. E. Wilkinson
and	
The Countess Cathleen	May Whitty

9th May 1899

THE HEATHER FIELD

A Play in Three Acts by Edward Martyn

Barry Ussher (a landowner, student, philosopher, etc.)	Trevor Lowe
Lord Shrule (a neighbouring landowner)	Marcus St. John
Lady Shrule, Lilian, his wife	Anna Mather
Carden Tyrrell	Thomas Kingston
Mrs. Grace Tyrrell (born Desmon, his wife)	May Whitty
Kit (their son, nine years old)	Charles Sefton
Miles Tyrrell (Scholar of Trinity College, Dublin, and brother of Carden)	J. Wilcox
Physicians:	
Doctor Dowling	Claude Holmes
Doctor Roche	F. E. Wilkinson

GEORGE MOORE

[*By courtesy of the Trustees of the Tate Gallery*

LADY GREGORY

CHAPTER TWO

THE IRISH LITERARY THEATRE, 1900

FOR the performances in 1900 the Irish Literary Theatre engaged the Gaiety Theatre, Dublin, for the week of 19th February. This theatre remains practically unchanged in form to the present day. It is a charming theatre of the old-fashioned type, with its Dress Circle and Upper Circle, its Gallery and Boxes. It seats more than a thousand people, it has a commodious stage. The theatre was mainly the home of companies from England playing "drawing-room" plays, in contrast to the much larger Theatre Royal (now a Cinema-Variety theatre). Thus, on occasion, Forbes-Robertson would have a month's season at the Gaiety, playing such plays as *Mice and Men*, and during the same month Beerbohm Tree would be at the Theatre Royal, with a programme of more spectacular drama. At the same time there was a constant succession of melodrama at the Queen's Theatre in Brunswick Street—the street of the Antient Concert Rooms. J. W. Whitebread's Company would perform Boucicault's Irish melodramas, *Arrah-na-Pogue*, *The Colleen Bawn*, and the like, and English companies would perform *The Face at the Window* and *East Lynne*. There were also two excellent music-halls. All these theatres were well patronised. Dublin was, and is, a very theatrically-minded city.

The Irish Literary Theatre's programme must have seemed a very strange one to the patrons of the Gaiety. It consisted of three plays: *The Bending of the Bough* by George Moore, *Maeve* by Edward Martyn, and *The Last Feast of the Fianna* by Alice Milligan. *The Bending of the Bough* is Moore's version of Martyn's play *The Tale of a Town*. Moore had been very disappointed when he read his friend's play and set to work to improve it, but the collaboration did not prove successful. Martyn, in his preface to the published version of his play, states "There was an adaptation of *The Tale of a Town* made by Mr. George Moore with my consent for the Irish Literary Theatre's performance in 1900."

Comparing the two versions it is obvious that Moore's is the better one; yet it is a pallid play, it has no warmth, the women, particularly, are lifeless. It is not dramatic. Its subject is small-town politics, a pull between Irish and English commercial interests, but there is nothing authentically Irish or English in the drawing of the characters. It derives obviously from *An Enemy of the People* and other Ibsen dramas of that type—just as the madness motif in *The Heather Field* derives from Strindberg's *The Father*. Later (1906) William Boyle was to treat the same subject in a *The Tale of a Town*, an excellent rough comedy, *The Eloquent Dempsey*, and Seumas O'Kelly in a moving and subtle play *The Bribe* (1913), and Moore's charwoman in the Town Council's chambers was to be completely outshone by Edward McNulty's two charwomen in *The Lord Mayor* (1914). The Dublin critics gave *The Bending of the Bough* long and respectful notices, but, reading between their lines, it is obvious that the play proved as dull on the stage as it is in the book.

> The piece resembled the Ibsen drama in its working out, but many of the long speeches put into the mouths of Jasper Dean and Ralf Kirwan became most unreal when spoken as dialogue. This was specially noticeable at the commencement of Act III, where these two characters stand apart and, facing the audience, repeat long passage after long passage gazing fixedly at nothing in particular, when they are supposed to be addressing their remarks to each other. This irritating fault of speaking to the house seems to be the rule, instead of the exception, at the Irish Literary Theatre's performances.

The distinguished critic from *The Times* of London, A. B. Walkley, crossed from England to see the play but condemned it heartily, and sums up his long criticism by saying, "In fine, his play is dull and tame and prosaic, and (to borrow the undergraduate's word) 'smug.'" This play and the others in the week's programme were performed by a company of English actors.

Maeve is in two acts. Like *The Bending of the Bough* the subject is Ireland versus England. The modern Irishwoman Maeve is wooed by the Norman Fitzwalter. She hesitates, their natures are not akin, and eventually the long-ago real Queen

Maeve appears and carries off her young namesake to Tir-na-nOg—the Land of the Ever-Young. Though written in bad, unrhymed poetry the play has spirit and action and it seems to have been very much liked by the audience. It is noteworthy that even if Martyn's characters in *The Heather Field* and *Maeve* are not particularly Irish, the landscapes are. *The Heather Field* is obviously Connemara, *Maeve* is the Burren in County Clare. On the other hand, Moore has no landscape, not even that of an Irish country town.

Alice Milligan's play is in very musical prose and contains three lyrics. It was performed as a series of tableaux. Her play was perhaps the first one that took as its subject early Irish history and legend. It was enthusiastically received, but the periodical *The United Irishman* reports the audiences as having been "wretchedly small." The audiences for all the plays during this week seem to have been meagre. The play is one of old age, the twilight of the gods, and it has a touching quality. The *United Irishman* says of it:

> The scene, words and figures were a revelation. It gave us the only glimpse we have seen of what the Ireland of pre-Christian days must have been. There was a richness about the dresses of the women that recollects the old books; a manliness about the men that offered a little idea of the great host whose swords were the sure protection of Eireann. There was a simplicity over all that made the contrast between this theatre and all others at once evident. ... The staging was excellent, and the background exceptionally fine. The primal object of the drama was its translation into Irish. That done, an incalculable service must result.

Comparing the play with *Maeve*, the *Daily Express* says:

> Mr. Martyn follows the school of Ibsen, Miss Milligan reproduces that equivalent to the drama in ancient Gaelic literature—namely the Isheen-Patric Dialogues, which were recited in character by two speakers. If the aim of the Irish Literary Theatre is to create a national drama it is obvious that the development of Miss Milligan's method is the proper road to reach ultimate success. ... It is simply a sketch, but it had charm, particularly for Irish people, which makes up for its deficiencies in dramatic intensity. ... It was curious to see a crowd of spectators, accustomed to the highly spiced vulgarities, applauding with relish a poetical thought or musical passage.

It is difficult, without access to figures, to judge whether the second production of the Irish Literary Theatre was a financial success. The newspaper accounts are contradictory, probably Edward Martyn footed the bill as he did in the case of *The Countess Cathleen*. But on 22nd February a luncheon was given to the members of the Irish Literary Theatre by the Irish National Literary Society in the Gresham Hotel. Douglas Hyde spoke first, then W. B. Yeats, finally George Moore. Moore said:

> I feel I must apologise for appearing before you with a manuscript of a speech in my hand. The sight of a manuscript in the country where oratory flourishes everywhere, in all ranks of society, and in all conditions of intellect, must appear anomalous and absurd. But I am the exception among my gifted countrymen. I have not inherited any gifts of improvisation, and the present is certainly no time for an experiment, for I believe that I have a matter of importance to lay before you. . . . Of the plays which were performed this week I do not intend to speak, and of the plays which the Irish Literary Theatre hopes to produce next year, I only propose to say that a play by Mr. Yeats and myself, entitled *Diarmuid and Grania*, will probably be produced. A more suitable subject than the most popular of our epic stories would hardly be found for a play for the Irish Literary Theatre, and I may say that it would be difficult to name any poet that Ireland has yet produced, more truly elected by his individual and racial genius to interpret the old legend, than the distinguished poet whose contemporary and collaborateur I have the honour to be.
>
> But even if this play should prove to be that dramatic telling of the great story which Ireland has been waiting for these many years, it will not, in my opinion, be the essential point of next year's festival, for next year we have decided to give a play in our own language, the language which, to our great disgrace, we do not understand . . . the performance of plays in our language is part and parcel of the idea which led up to the founding of the Irish Literary Theatre . . . and to emphasise this position, to make it clear to everyone, we are of the opinion that we should give a play in Irish. I would not be understood to mean that the Irish play to be given next year is to stand as a mere sign for our project; it will do this it is true, but it will do a little more than this—it will serve as a flag to lead to the restoration of our language as the literary and poetical language of this country. But before I speak of the necessity of the restoration of our language, I will tell you about the play that we have decided to produce. The play is not one originally written in the Irish language. It is a translation of a play written in the English language, and for this choice I am responsible. Lady Gregory, Mr. Martyn, Mr. Yeats and myself—here I must break off for a moment to say that Lady Gregory will be the one amongst us who will be able to follow the Irish text. She has done what we have not had the industry to do—she has made herself a proficient Irish scholar. Lady Gregory, Mr. Yeats and Mr. Martyn were all equally agreed as to the necessity for producing a play in our original language, but I am responsible for the decision to produce a translation rather than an original play in Irish. . . . I wish our first Irish play to rest on a solid literary

foundation. . . . I wish to present those who read our language with a piece of solid literature, and for this end my choice fell on a play at once simple and literary, *The Land of Heart's Desire*, by Mr. W. B. Yeats. Mr. Yeats was at first averse to the translation of his play. . . . Dr. Douglas Hyde, whose Irish scholarship has passed beyond question, has been pleased to promise to translate the play for us. More on this point I need not say: I will hasten to the essential subject—the subject on which I have come to speak to you—the necessity of the revival of the language if Ireland is to preserve her individuality among nations. It will be conceded to me that the three distinctions are religion, language and law. The distinction of religion Ireland holds secure; for this distinction she has suffered robbery, violence and contumacy, but I do not think I need insist on this point, which is well known to the whole world; and she has struggled no less fiercely for the distinction of law; but for the third distinction, the distinction of language, she has shown less determination and perseverance. Fellow countrymen, the language is slipping into the grave, and if a great national effort be not made at once to save the language it will be unknown in another generation and with it will go much of the character and genius of the Celt. I do not say that without our language we shall become English. I do not say it, though I fear that the distinction of language is, perhaps, the most essential of all distinctions, for it is by means of language that the characteristics of race are preserved. We must return to the language. It is through language that a tradition of thought is preserved, and so it may be said that the language is the very soul of the race. . . .

My fellow countrymen, the language hovers on the verge of the grave, and what you have to remember is that when the language is dead the soul of Cuchullin, which we all share still a little, will have vanished. The restoration of the language is the essential need of the moment. Even if we had a national government it would not be a real national government if the language had perished, for the Celt would have been robbed of his original home. You will be told that these are sentimental reasons—transcendental reasons: even so, a sentimental reason is valid and eternal, and practical reason is merely of the moment, and all that is merely of the moment is superficial and false. You will be told that out of Ireland no one will understand the language, and further that for the practical purpose of earning a livelihood it will be useless. You will be told that for the purpose of Art the language is quite useless, that ancient and Irish literature is merely formless folk-tales and that in modern Irish there is no literature whatsoever. You will be told that, if a genius such as Burns should arise tomorrow among the Irish peasantry and write his great work in Irish, it would remain unread. To this I reply that Ibsen writes in a language which is spoken by very few millions, yet his plays are read all over Europe. The old Irish poems, written in a form no longer spoken, are known to scholars over Europe. There is no such thing as a beautiful unknown page of literature; there is no such thing as a beautiful unknown line of poetry. Were a great work written in Irish tomorrow, in a few years it would have travelled all over Europe. To say that a man's language avails a man nothing except among people who understand his language is like saying that a man's religion avails him nothing except among his co-religionists. A language grows up with the people like a religion, and it is no more possible for a nation to put off its language and do either of these things at the expense of becoming something different. I say that a special language is as essential to a nation as a special style to a writer. . . . And to the objection often urged against the Irish language, that it is not as suitable for literary purposes as the English language, the answer is that the Latin language has become the medium through which only theological ideas are communicated, the English language will become, in the very near future, a language in which nothing except commercial letters will be written. . . .

On the 17th of the next month George Moore wrote to the press as follows:

When the Queen landed at the Cove of Cork the inhabitants with one voice invited her to change the name to Queenstown. It seems to me that it would be well if the inhabitants would now summon a meeting and decide with one voice to change the name of their harbour to whatever was its original Gaelic name. And it would be still more to the point if the Kingstown Corporation would quickly decide to bring back the old name Dun Leary which commemorated the name of an Irish King and which was changed in 1819 to commemorate the name of an English King of whom everyone is ashamed.

Already, there were murmurs of criticism that the plays of the Irish Literary Theatre should not be acted by players from the other side of the Irish Sea. Had not Ireland since the seventeenth century contributed some of the most famous players to the English stage? Could not Ireland in the nineteenth century, in her own plays, act them with her own players? The answer came swiftly after the next and final performance by the Irish Literary Theatre, that of *Diarmuid and Grania* and *The Twisting of the Rope*, in the Gaiety Theatre.

Susan Mitchell's lines come to mind:

I've puffed the Irish language, and puffed the Irish soap;
I've used them on my nephew—with the best results, I hope;
For with this older, dirtier George, I have no heart to cope. . . .

We have reformed the Drama, myself and Yeats allied:
For I took small stock in Martyn, and less in Douglas Hyde;
To bow the knee to rare AE was too much for my pride.

But W. B. was the boy for me—he of the dim, wan clothes;
And—don't let on I said it—not above a bit of a pose;
And they call his writing literature, as everybody knows.

Casts of First Productions, 1900

20th February 1900

THE BENDING OF THE BOUGH

A Comedy in Five Acts by George Moore

Joseph Tench, the Mayor . . Alex Austin
Alderman of the Corporation:
  Jasper Dean . . . . . Percy Lyndal
  Daniel Lawrence . . . W. W. West
  Thomas Ferguson . . John F. Denton
  Valentine Folay . . . Eugene Mayeur
  Ralf Kirwan . . . William Devereux
  James Pollock . . T. Bryant Edwin
  Michael Leech . . . W. F. Rotheram
John Cloran, the Town-
  Clerk . . . . . J. H. Beaumont
George Hardman, Lord Mayor
  of Southaven . . . Blake Adams
Miss Millicent Fell, his niece,
  engaged to marry Alderman
  Dean . . . . . Agnes B. Cahill
Maiden aunts of Alderman Dean:
  Miss Caroline Dean . . Mona Robin
  Miss Arabella Dean . . Annie Hill
Mrs. Pollock, wife and first
  cousin of Alderman Pollock,
  sister of Alderman Leech,
  and cousin of the Deans . Fanny Morris
Mrs. Leech, wife and first
  cousin of Alderman
  Leech, sister of Alder-
  man Pollock, and cousin
  of the Deans . . . Dorothy Hammond
Mr. Macnee, caretaker of
  the Town Hall . . . Franklin Walford

A Parlourmaid at Alderman
  Deans's . . . . . Miss Warren
A waiter at the Hotel . . William P. Kelly
Act 1 . Meeting Hall of the Corporation
Act 2 . Drawing-Room in Jasper Dean's
      House
Act 3 . Same as Act 2
Act 4 . A Room in the principal Hotel
Act 5 . Same as Act 2

22nd February 1900

MAEVE

A Psychological Drama in Two Acts by
      Edward Martyn

Maeve . . . . . Dorothy Hammond
Finola . . . . Agnes Cahill
Peg Inerney . . . . . Helen Robins
The O'Heynes . . . . . Blake Adams
Hugh Fitzwalter (a young
  Englishman) . . . J. Herbert Beaumont

22nd February 1900

THE LAST FEAST OF THE FIANNA

A Play in One Act by Miss Alice Milligan,
  special music by Mrs. Fox Milligan

Niamh . . . . . Dorothy Hammond
Finola . . . . Fanny Morris
Fionn . . . . Bryant Edwin
Oisin . . . . . . Franklin Walford
Caolte Mac Romain . . . . John Dent

CHAPTER THREE

THE IRISH LITERARY THEATRE, 1901

THE third performance of the Irish Literary Theatre took place in the Gaiety Theatre, Dublin, on the 21st October 1901, the plays presented were *Diarmuid and Grania* by W. B. Yeats and George Moore, and *Casadh an tSugain* (The Twisting of the Rope) by Douglas Hyde.

Mr. Frank Benson's Company was imported from England to make the important production of the Yeats-Moore play. Frank Benson (afterwards Sir Frank Benson) was not an actor of the first rank, he could not compare with Irving, nor with Beerbohm Tree, but he was a Shakespearean actor to his finger-tips, and to be a young man in his company meant that you learned your acting, gradually, from tip to toes. His wife was not as good a player—how often actors have been hampered with wives who can act, yet not very well, one thinks of Martin-Harvey, one thinks of Beerbohm Tree. Reading over the cast of *Diarmuid and Grania*, what names there are in it, that for twenty years to come were stars on the English stage! Alfred Brydone, Charles Bibby, Henry Ainley, Harcourt Williams, Matheson Lang, Arthur Whitby, H. O. Nicholson; incidental music was specially written by Dr. (later Sir Edward) Elgar. A few years before his death Yeats asked me to read the play. Since its first performance it had never been repeated. He said, "I think it's better than I remembered it to be." I didn't read it until after his death, but I agreed with him.

It begins with a fine scene, a setting of the banqueting-hall, the Sons of Oisin are arriving—one feels that Moore's sense of the stage is apparent here—then follows a long scene between Grania and her mother. Grania has to be wedded to Finn, whom she has never met, but she has looked once on Diarmuid. There is a certain intensity in the scene, but Diarmuid when he arrives is always pallid. He has his loyalty to

DR. DOUGLAS HYDE

Finn and we can never feel that he loves Grania. It is small wonder that Frank Benson could not make much of the part, no actor could, but Mrs. Benson, it is obvious, even from the friendliest notices, completely failed—the part was originally offered to Mrs. Patrick Campbell. The play is colourful, full of ghosts and hag-ridden people; the last act, painting a wonderful picture of wind and storm, crashing trees, thunder and lightning, reminds one of a Wagnerian opera—Moore's work perhaps? But it is difficult to say, in reading it, where Yeats stops and Moore steps in. It got, one thinks now, unjust criticism, but an English company was struggling with an Irish subject and the players hadn't even made up their minds how to pronounce the Irish names, or to consistently mispronounce them.

Certain papers, the *Leader* noticeably, attacked the play, first because it was performed by an English company, secondly because it was a travesty of an Irish legend. George Moore replied with one of his devastating letters and pointed out, quoting from all the Irish legends, that Grania was unfaithful to Diarmuid, that the blood-potion of comradeship, objected to by the *Leader*, was in the legend, that every incident in the play was backed up by legend. His letter was not answered, but there seems no doubt that the play was a failure in spite of the fact that Lady Cadogan, the vice-reine, and the Lord Mayor of Dublin and many other notabilities were in the audience. It was going to be many more years before anyone of social notability was again in the audience.

George Moore's idea was that the first play to be performed in Gaelic should be an Irish version of Yeats's *The Land of Heart's Desire*. But instead Douglas Hyde wrote a one-act comedy based on an Irish folk-story.

Douglas Hyde was born in 1860, youngest son of the Reverend Arthur Hyde, Frenchpark, Co. Roscommon. He was educated at Trinity College, Dublin, in which he had a most distinguished career. He became President of the Irish National Literary Society in 1894, and President of the Gaelic League in 1893. His life-work was the restoration, the preservation, of Ireland's ancient language. He was non-political; and when, as he thought, in 1915, the Gaelic League was becoming political, he resigned his presidency. In 1938 the Government made him the first President of Ireland, and it was a perfect choice. When his term of office was up, he retired, and died in 1949 at the age of 89. He wrote under the pseudonym of "An Craoibhin Aoibhinn ("The delightful little branch"), and he was known to all his friends as "An Craoibhin."

Lady Gregory, in *Poets and Dreamers*, writes:

> I hold that the beginning of modern Irish drama was in the winter of 1898, at a school feast at Coole, when Douglas Hyde and Miss Norma Borthwick acted in Irish in a Punch and Judy show; and the delighted children went back to tell their parents what grand curses *An Craoibhin* had put on the baby and the policeman. A little time after that, when a play was wanted for our Literary Theatre, Dr. Hyde wrote, and then acted in, *The Twisting of the Rope*, the first Irish play ever given in a Dublin theatre.

If the reception given to *Diarmuid and Grania* was lukewarm—when not definitely hostile—Dr. Hyde's play went with a swing from start to finish, thanks to its excellent plot and the author's (he played the principal part) exuberant acting. Of course such ultra-Irish papers, the *Leader*, for instance, rejoiced in the Gaelic play's success in contrast to the English-acted one. The *Express* only admits that it was "a success of curiosity," but another paper says, "How daintily the old tongue sounded from the lips of the young girls on the stage, and what a grand language it is to swear in, or make love in, Dr. Hyde amply showed. It was acted with a natural tempo and zest that was simply a breath of spring air after the heaviness and monotony of the more ambitious piece." The *Daily Independent* found it "an unqualified success . . . even those who could not interpret the language—and they were many—had good translations of it and could follow the action with interest. The piece is a perfect little gem."

Besides the principal part, Hanrahan, there are four important parts and a crowd of young men and women. They were played by members of the Keating Branch of the Gaelic League in Dublin; their names do not appear on the programme, but it transpires that the heroine, Oona, was played by Miss O'Kennedy, her mother, Maura, by Miss O'Donovan, a neighbour, Sheila, by Miss Sullivan, and Oona's betrothed by Mr. Tadgh O'Donoghue. The *Independent* notes that "the piece was enthusiastically applauded."

A few days before these performances, Yeats had stated that they marked the end of the Irish Literary Theatre, but that it was hoped to start a new movement on somewhat different lines. In its three performances during three years it had produced at least two fine plays, *The Countess Cathleen* and *The Heather Field*, and even the less good plays were helping to lay the foundations of the Irish Theatre; and Douglas Hyde's play definitely laid the foundation-stone of the Gaelic Theatre.

Casts of First Productions, 1901

21st October 1901

DIARMUID AND GRANIA
By George Moore and W. B. Yeats

King Cormac, the High
   King . . . . . . Alfred Brydone
Finn MacCoole, Chief of the
   Fianna . . . . . . Frank Rodney
Diarmuid . . . . . . F. R. Benson
His chief men:
   Goll . . . . Charles Bibby
   Usheen . . . . . . Henry Ainley
   Caoelte . . . E. Harcourt Williams
Spearmen:
   Fergus . . . G. Wallace Johnstone
   Fathna . . . . . Walter Hampden
   Griffan . . . . . . Stuart Edgar
Niall, a head servant . . Matheson Lang
Conan the Bald, one of the
   Fianna . . . . . Arthur Whitby
An Old Man . . . . H. O. Nicholson
A Shepherd . . . . Mr. Owen
A Boy . . . . Ella Tarrant
A Young Man . . . . Joan Mackinlay
Grania, the King's daughter Mrs. F. R. Benson
Laban, an old Druidess . Lucy Franklein

Serving men, Troops of the Fianna, etc.
Act 1 . The Banqueting Hall in Tara
Act 2 . Diarmuid's House
Act 3 . The Wooded Slopes of Ben Bulben
Special music written by Dr. Edward Elgar
Acting Manager for Mr. F. R.
   Benson . . . . . A. Smyth-Pigott
Stage Manager . . . . Leonard Buttress
Assistant Stage Manager . Edward Broadley
Advance Representative . . James Fox
To be followed on Monday, Tuesday and Wednesday evenings by "The Twisting of the Rope" by Douglas Hyde, LL.D.
Cast filled by members of the Gaelic Amateur Dramatic Society.

21st October 1901

THE TWISTING OF THE ROPE
By Douglas Hyde

N.B.—No complete copy of the cast is in existence. Members of the Keating Branch of the Gaelic League took part in it. Douglas Hyde played Hanrahan, Miss O'Kennedy Oona, Miss O'Donovan Maura, Miss Sullivan Sheila. Mr. Tadgh O'Donoghue and Mr. Seamus Heron also took part.

WILLIAM FAY

FRANK FAY

J. M. SYNGE

MAIRE NIC SHIUBHLAIGH

CHAPTER FOUR

W. G. Fay's National Dramatic Society and, later, the Irish National Theatre Society, 1902-1903

In announcing that the third performance of the Irish Literary Theatre was to be its last, Yeats had hinted, without going into details, at a new development. George Moore had been an unexpected incursion into Yeats's and Martyn's theatre in 1899, now a very different incursion was to come, and one which was to mould the Irish National Theatre for the rest of its life. It came in the form of two brothers, Frank and William Fay. In 1891 they had started their theatrical careers with performances in the Dublin Dramatic School, directed by Mrs. J. W. Lacy, wife of a touring manager, at 11 Westland Row, Dublin; Willie Fay became advance agent to the Lacy Company, and in 1898 the brothers formed the Ormonde Dramatic Society. Three years later we hear of W. G. Fay's Comedy Combination playing such farces as *His Lost Legs*, and *The Second*, in the Coffee Palace and in numerous halls in Dublin, and taking short tours into the country, as far away as Dundalk. They engaged many halls, rooms and clubs, in which they taught elocution and stage-craft. They sought out sketches, farces and short plays, which were very carefully rehearsed. In twelve years they devised more than a hundred productions. Among those who worked with the brothers were Dudley Digges, Ernest Vaughan, P. J. Kelly, Marie Walker (Maire Nic Shiubhlaigh) and Sara Allgood.

The Fays were natives of Dublin. W. G. Fay entered Belvedere College at the age of thirteen in September 1886, Frank was educated at Marlborough Street School. The brothers started life with united aims and affections. They loved the theatre with a deep-rooted love and set themselves with concentrated energy and dogged persistence to train themselves and to train others for a theatrical career. The elder brother, Frank, was mostly interested in verse, especially in Shakespeare, Willie was more interested in character and in comedy. But they were performing rather worthless plays, and when it was suggested to them that they might appear in serious, national, Irish plays they leaped at the notion, and for the next six years their work was to be as important to the Irish Theatre as was that of Yeats and his fellow-dramatists.

How exactly Yeats and the Fays came together is not quite clear. It is clear that AE (George Russell) played a very important part—a more important part than Yeats. AE had written, or less than half written, a play on the Deirdre story.

AE (George Russell), born in 1867 in Co. Antrim, was destined to be a very important figure in the Irish Literary Revival: as poet and essayist, and as editor of the *Irish Homestead*, that brilliant periodical which set forth the aims of the I.A.O.S.; and, later, he was editor of the *Irish Statesman*. After *Deirdre*, he never again wrote for the stage; but he always took the liveliest interest in the Irish Theatre, and remained a close friend to Yeats.

AE wrote his *Deirdre* as a one-act play, then he added a second act, later a third act.

About Christmas 1901, at George Coffey's house, 5 Harcourt Terrace, the first and second acts of AE's *Deirdre* were performed. Naoise was played by the author, Fergus by George Coffey, Ainnle by R. I. Best, Buinne by J. H. Cousins, Deirdre by Violet Mervyn (who was really Elizabeth Young), Ella Young was Lavarcam.

I quote now from Dr. Cousins' reminiscences:

> The Fay Company's rehearsals of the full-size *Deirdre* in the Coffee Palace theatre proceeded with growing mastery and enthusiasm. Everybody learned everybody else's part for sheer love of the thing. The lack of a suitable curtain-raiser worried the management. But their worry disappeared when it was whispered that Yeats had had a dream, and had put it into a one-act play, and that Maud Gonne would have the central part. The play *Cathleen ni Houlihan* was read to the company. I shall not in this life forget the thrill of patriotic realisation that went through me at the final lines, after the departure of the "poor old woman" (symbol of Ireland at the end of the eighteenth

century, in which the play was set, and not less symbolical in 1902) when an unsuspecting lad put prophecy into his reply to a question:

> Did you see an old woman going down the path?
> I did not, but I saw a young girl, and she had the walk of a queen.

The plays were given in St. Teresa's Hall, Clarendon Street. The stage was 30 feet by 21 feet, and the hall seated about three hundred people. The plays were a great success, especially in the case of *Cathleen ni Houlihan*, due to Maud Gonne's magnificent acting. The *All-Ireland Review* was grudging in its praise and said:

> Miss Gonne, as Cathleen ni Houlihan, cannot be considered as an actress in the sense of a person who produces a certain effect by means of an illusion in portraying the character created by the author.... No hiding personality, it was just Maud Gonne the well-known Nationalist agitator, addressing not the actors, as is usual in drama, but the audience, speaking to them just as she might in Beresford Place or Phoenix Park, the only difference was that the words were not her own.

After these performances by W. G. Fay's National Dramatic Society the Fays decided to make a permanent society of players, who would produce Irish plays and nothing but Irish plays. It was suggested at first that AE should be president, but the committee preferred Mr. Yeats: and so, on 1st February 1903, the Irish National Theatre Society was founded, its president being W. B. Yeats; vice-presidents, Maud Gonne, Douglas Hyde, George Russell (AE); stage-manager, W. G. Fay; secretary, Fred Ryan.

The following letter to Yeats emphasises the position:

3 Holles Street,
Dublin.
10th August 1902

Dear Sir,

As I believe Mr. Russell has told you, the National Dramatic Society which Mr. Fay organised has been placed on a more definite basis, and has rented a Hall for twelve months, capable of accommodating 200 people. This gives a permanent prospect of carrying on the work and is in every way preferable to spasmodic performances.

At a meeting of the Society held yesterday it was, on the motion of Mr. Russell (AE), unanimously decided to ask you to be President, Mr. George Russell being Vice-President; and as Secretary I was instructed to convey this to you and to inquire if you would kindly honour us by accepting.

When the Hall has been put in order—which I fancy will be in about a week—and when the Company is ready to give performances, we are very anxious that you should "send us off" with a lecture, if at all convenient, in which we could explain our objects, hopes, ambitions, etc. and set out what are our plans and prospects. Personally, if I may say so, I think it absolutely necessary to do this, by way of preface, and of course there is no one who could do it as you. If it is not trespassing I should be glad if you would let me know as to this, so that we could make arrangements. Doubtless Mr. Russell and Mr. Fay have written or will write you on the matter.

    Yours sincerely
      Frederick Ryan
       Secretary Irish Natl. Dramatic Socy.

Perhaps Mr. Ryan had some other hall in mind, or perhaps he was optimistic: at any rate Mr. Fay's Society next appeared in a small hall at 34 Camden Street, it did not hold two hundred people, it could at best hold fifty. The audience sat on benches in an unheated hall. The hall was at the back of a shop—now a post-office and a shop which sells children's clothes and feminine undergarments. The hall is approached by a long dark passage—and now is open to the air: there is no roof, grass grows where the audience used to sit, a granite rock rears itself up in the middle of the auditorium. The stage-space cannot have been more than six feet deep, there was no "back-stage," there were no dressing-rooms; dressing had to be done at the side of the stage. But there a Miss Horniman would come and stitch ugly dresses for *The King's Threshold* and there Lady Gregory would come and there Yeats's play *The Pot of Broth* would be read and thought unsuitable by the Fays.

Lady Gregory wrote her first play, *Twenty-Five*, which was rejected but subsequently produced in the Molesworth Hall next year.

 (To Mr. Yeats from F. J. Fay):
      12 Ormond Road,
       Rathmines,
       26th Sept. 1902

In my brother's opinion "Twenty-Five" would not suit us. He thinks the dialogue excellent, but does not think an Irish peasant, however hard up, would play a stranger for his money like old Michael does, and, even assuming the possibility of that, my brother thinks the card-playing scene too long.

PADRAIC COLUM

Again, he does not approve of card-playing as a means of getting money, and he thinks the play in country districts might incite to emigration, on account of the glowing terms in which America is spoken of. I may say that myself I quite agree with this verdict.

Yours
F. J. Fay.

Lady Gregory's play, *The Rising of the Moon*, was rejected, but admitted at a subsequent meeting of the Society. Years later, the Camden Street Hall was used by Countess de Markievicz as a drilling-hall for her Boy Scouts. The "Black-and-Tans" raided the neighbourhood, but, curiously, didn't touch the Hall. It seems just to have fallen into disrepair, and is now a pleasant ruin. I quote from W. A. Henderson's diary:

> Some future day perhaps visitors will seek out the Camden Street Hall, No. 34 Lower Camden Street, hidden away at the rear of the warehouse. Those who were present on a bitter October night, in a draughty ill-lighted hall and without fire, will not forget the experience—the first performance by the Irish National Theatre Society.
> The hall held about fifty persons. The play was *The Laying of the Foundations* in two Acts by Fred Ryan.
> At 8 o'clock three knocks noted the rising of the curtain. There were many defects; the scenery was poor, and the stage very small. The play did not make amends. It was a drama of municipal wrong-doing and drain-pipes, after the fashion of Ibsen. Then followed *The Pot of Broth*, a poor farce, only bearable by the funny acting and freaks of W. G. Fay. One wonders that Mr. Yeats would put his name to such a production.

The performances in the Camden Street Hall were from 4th to 6th December 1902. The plays performed were *The Laying of the Foundations*, *The Pot of Broth*, concluding with a play in Irish, *Eilis agus an Bhean Deirce*; afterwards the Hall was used as a workshop, a place for stitching clothes and making scenery, until the Company moved to the more commodious premises in the Molesworth Hall.

Mr. F. Ryan's play was first produced by the Irish National Dramatic Company for the Cumann na nGaedeal in the Antient Concert Rooms in October 1902. This play, together with *The Sleep of the King* and *The Racing Lug*—both by Seumas O'Cuisin—produced at the same festival, may be regarded as the earliest plays of the Abbey Theatre "School." These dramatists and the Fay brothers were laying the foundations of the Abbey Theatre. Some years later Mr. Ryan died. Yeats wanted to revive the play, but the manuscript could not be found, though diligent search was made for its recovery.

It seems clear that there were two dominant factors in the Society, first the Fays' delight in drama and then an intense patriotic feeling on the part of the players. Sinn Fein was beginning to stir.

Casts of First Productions, 1902

2nd April 1902

DEIRDRE
A Play in Three Acts by AE

Deirdre	Maire T. Quinn
Lavarcam, her foster-mother, a Druidess	Maire Nic Shiubhlaigh
Fergus	P. J. Kelly
Sons of Fergus:	
Buinne	P. Colum
Illaun	C. Caulfield
The Sons of Usna:	
Ardan	F. Ryan
Ainnle	H. Sproule
Naisi	J. Dudley Digges
Messenger	Brian Callender
Concobar, Ard-rie of Ulla	F. J. Fay

2nd April 1902

CATHLEEN NI HOULIHAN
A Play in One Act by W. B. Yeats

Cathleen ni Houlihan	Maud Gonne
Delia Cahel	Maire Nic Shiubhlaigh
Bridget Gillan	Maire T. Quinn
Patrick Gillan	C. Caulfield
Michael Gillan	J. Dudley Digges
Peter Gillan	W. G. Fay

29th October 1902

THE SLEEP OF THE KING
An Allegory in One Act by Seumas O'Cuisin

Conn, "The Hundred Fighter," High King of Erinn	F. J. Fay
Connla, "Of the Flowing Golden Hair," his son	P. J. Kelly
Fairy Princess	Maire Nic Shiubhlaigh
Coran, a Druid	J. Dudley Digges

29th October 1902

THE LAYING OF THE FOUNDATIONS
A Play in Two Acts by Fred Ryan

Mr. O'Loskin, T.C.	F. J. Fay
Michael, his son	P. J. Kelly
Alderman Farrelly, Chairman of "The New Building Syndicate"	J. Dudley Digges
M. MacFadden, T.C.	P. MacShiubhlaigh
Mr. Nolan, T.C., editor of "The Free Nation"	N. Butler
Mrs. O'Loskin	Maire Nic Shiubhlaigh
Mrs. MacFadden	Honor Lavelle
Eileen, her daughter	Maire T. Quinn

30th October 1902

THE POT OF BROTH
A Farce in One Act by W. B. Yeats

A Beggarman	W. G. Fay
Sibby	Maire T. Quinn
John, her husband	P. J. Kelly

31st October 1902

THE RACING LUG
A One-Act Play of real life in Two Scenes by Seumas O'Cuisin

Johnny, an old fisherman	F. J. Fay
Nancy, his wife	Maire T. Quinn
Bell, their daughter	Maire Nic Shiubhlaigh
Rob, a young fisherman	J. Dudley Digges
Rev. Mr. McMeekin, a young Presbyterian Minister	P. J. Kelly

31st October 1902

EILIS AGUS AN BHEAN DEIRCE
By P. T. MacFhionnlaoich

Eilis	Maire T. Ni Chuinn
Conchubhar (a mac)	Prionnsias MacShiubhlaigh
Maedhbha (Bhean deirce)	Maire Ni Pherols

CHAPTER FIVE

1903-1904

THE Molesworth Hall seats three hundred people, the stage opening is 16 feet by 11 feet, the depth of the stage 12 feet, and the floor space 16 feet by 12 feet, and there were two small dressing-rooms.

On the 14th March 1903 at 8 o'clock the Irish National Theatre Society opened in the Hall with the first production of Yeats's play *The Hour-Glass*, and Lady Gregory's play *Twenty-Five*. Between the plays Yeats lectured on "The Reform of the Theatre." He said:

> They were endeavouring to restore the theatre as an intellectual institution. They would all agree with him that the present commercial theatre was deplorable. It was conducted to suit rich men who wanted to digest their dinners in peace, and therefore it could not well stir any deep tumult of the soul. And as for those who filled the pit and gallery, they were tired out by the day's work, and that not always of a high kind. In these matters one must strike a balance; devote, say, two-thirds of his life to intellectual pursuits and one-third to obtaining the necessary food to go on with. Happily in this country we were not rich, for it was the poor races that had done the great things in art. As for technical things, they must restore to the stage beautiful speech. Great plays were written for actors capable of speaking great things greatly. In Elizabethan times plays were spoken in a solemn, rhythmical delivery, and it was known that Racine had taught his favourite actress by some sort of regulative musical notation. To restore good speech they must simplify acting. Modern actors slurred over the solemnest passages, and strove constantly to attract attention to their bodily movements. According to English ideas of what was known as "business" an actor when not speaking must always be moving his hands or feet or jigging about somewhere in a corner, and so attention was constantly drawn away from the central character. Gesture should be treated rather as a part of decorative art, and the more remote a play was from daily life, the more grave and solemn should the gesture be. As for scenery, it should be inexacting to the eye, so that the great attention might be paid by the ear. For instance, his play had been staged with a monotonous green background, and the chief actor wore a purple garment. In this country we had many opportunities for producing a great drama. We had a stirring history which made men imaginative and ready for risks. Patriotism with us was an idea which laid burdens on a man, while with our English

neighbours it merely increased his comfort and self-admiration, and it was out of the dangerous life that drama had come.

His own dream had always been to treat the old legends so as to put on the stage types of heroic manhood. He wrote in English, for we must speak in the language we think in and write in the language we speak in. And more important than questions of politics or language it was to give new artistic form to beauty and truth, and when that command came to a man he must leave many things to follow it.

The cast of *The Hour-Glass* was as follows:

The Wise Man	J. Dudley Digges
Bridget (his wife)	Maire T. Quinn
His children	Eithne and Padragan Nic Shiubhlaigh
His pupils	P. J. Kelly
	Seamus O'Sullivan
	P. Columb
	P. MacShiubhlaigh
The Angel	Maire Nic Shiubhlaigh
The Fool	F. J. Fay

and the cast of *Twenty-Five*:

Michael Ford (a middle-aged farmer)	W. G. Fay
Kate Ford (his young wife)	Maire Nic Shiubhlaigh
Christie Henderson	P. J. Kelly
A Neighbour	Dora Hackett
Another Neighbour	P. MacShiubhlaigh

On 8th October 1903 Yeats's *The King's Threshold* was performed there for the first time. This was the cast:

King Guaire	P. J. Kelly
The Chamberlain of King Guaire	Seamus O'Sullivan
A Soldier	W. Conroy
A Monk	S. Sheridan-Neill
The Mayor of Kinvara	W. G. Fay
A Cripple	P. Columb
Another Cripple	E. Davis
Aileen	Honor Lavelle
Essa	Dora Melville
Princess Buan	Sara Allgood
Princess Finnhua (her sister)	Doreen Gunning
Fedelm (Seanchan's sweetheart)	Maire Nic Shiubhlaigh
Cian	G. Roberts
Brian	Caitia Nic Chormac
Seanchan (Chief Poet of Ireland)	F. J. Fay
Pupils, Courtiers.	

This production marked a change in Yeats's work, and for many years he turned deliberately to Irish legends, especially to the Cuchulain legend. It also brought into the theatre a new influence, a new genius, J. M. Synge. Yeats had met him in Paris, and had advised him to turn from translating French poetry and to go back to Ireland. His play, *In the Shadow of the Glen*, followed *The King's Threshold*; the cast was as follows:

Dan Burke (farmer and herd)	G. Roberts
Nora Burke (his wife)	Maire Nic Shiubhlaigh
Michael Dara (a young herd)	P. J. Kelly
A Tramp	W. G. Fay

John Millington Synge was the youngest child in a family of eight. Of his parents little need be said. His father was John Hatch Synge, Barrister-at-Law, a modest thoughtful man, who preferred the quiet of home life to any outside amusement. He was the younger son of a large family, born in 1824, and reared at the family seat, Glanmore Castle, Co. Wicklow, and provided for in life by being sent to the Bar (in 1847), a profession for which he was not particularly well suited, but by which, with the help of some private means derived from landed property in Co. Galway, he managed to live quite comfortably. Those of the Synges who took a profession usually went into Holy Orders in the Church of Ireland, and their education and culture were clearly of the type to be found in people long connected with the Church. Synge's mother, Kathleen Traill, was the daughter of the Rev. Robert Traill, D.D., M.R.I.A. (born in 1793), whose excellent translation of Flavius Josephus largely superseded that of William Whiston, and who died in 1847 in the parish of West Schull, Co. Cork, of which he was Rector, from fever contracted during his attempts to help the poor in the great potato famine.

The Synges are a large and well-known County Wicklow family. Yet they are not of pure Irish origin. They are said to be descended from the Millingtons of Millington Hall in Cheshire. The surname Synge was originally a kind of nickname or by-name. According to tradition John Millington, a "Canon" or Precentor of the Chapel Royal, sang so sweetly that King Henry VIII bade him take the name of Sing or Synge. The whole story—which shows that the puzzling name is not to be pronounced *à la française* or like the verb "to singe"—may be an invention which the man's will or some other document would expose; yet a picture of a stained-glass window formerly in Bowden Church, now among the Harleian MSS. (2151, Cheshire Monuments), representing a kneeling Abbot, with the legend "Orate pro bono statu Roberte Millington" (the date being 1382 and the coat of arms the same as that of the Synge or Sing family), goes some little way to confirm the legend. It will be observed that Synge's full name was identically that of his progenitor.

Synge's father died when Synge was quite a small child. His mother, finding herself in somewhat reduced circumstances, came to live at Orwell Park, Rathgar, which was his home until 1890. He received a somewhat desultory education, at which in after life he would sneer with a violent sardonic scorn: he attended classes at private schools in Dublin, and then in Bray. But his health being always very delicate, he was obliged to leave school when about 14 years of age, to read at home with a private tutor till he entered Trinity College, Dublin.

An examination of Synge's early days really does help to establish what may be termed the spiritual continuity of his life. As a lad, Synge was strangely reserved and even unboyish to a certain extent; he shunned rather than desired companionship, he would hardly take part in the games of his age, and he much preferred open-air exercises and solitary rambles in the Dublin mountains to indoor life. In later years he went wandering in strange places, for he was always a sad and lonely man. It was by solitude that he asserted his personality, in the gentle, unromantic manner that was always his. From the very start he was and remained himself, and nothing but himself.

Throughout his youth and early manhood his summer holidays were spent at Tom Riland House, "Uplands," near Annamoe, in Wicklow. Later he developed a strong taste for music. He taught himself to play the flute, but was never good at it. Yet he was very proficient on that primitive instrument, the penny whistle, with which in later years he greatly amused the Aran Islanders. His favourite instruments, however, were the piano and especially the violin. While at Trinity College, Dublin, he secured a good technical knowledge of music, studying under Sir Robert Prescott Stewart at the Royal Irish Academy of Music, Westland Row, where he won a scholarship in counterpoint and harmony. He then thought of taking up music as a profession, and, although he soon gave up the idea, music always remained one of the pastimes in which he most fondly indulged, and it exercised a potent influence on his ability as a playwright.

He travelled a great deal on the Continent; spent part of his time in Paris and part in Ireland, either in Aran or in Dublin and Wicklow, or with his mother and relatives, who had removed in 1890 to 31 Crosthwaite Park, Dun Laoghaire, which was his home until shortly before his death.

It is not known which play of his, *In the Shadow of the Glen*, or *Riders to the Sea*, was written first. They seem to have arrived by the same post. Two masterpieces; *Riders to the Sea* has been played all over the English-speaking world as the greatest one-act tragedy in the modern theatre; in *In the Shadow of the Glen* Synge used the dialect of West Wicklow. This play caused one of the first splits in the Irish National Theatre movement. The idea of a young wife parting from her elderly husband was considered by the *Daily Independent and Nation* as

> nothing more or less than a farcical libel on the character of the average decently reared Irish peasant woman.... At the conclusion of Mr. Synge's work a section of the audience mingled some hissing with the applause which proceeded from the other parts of the house.

(I quote from Dr. Cousins):

> Maud Gonne, Maire Quinn and Dudley Digges left the hall in protest against what they regarded as a decadent intrusion where the inspiration of idealism rather than the down pull of realism was needed.

In *Riders to the Sea* (produced in the Molesworth Hall on 25th January 1904) and in his subsequent great plays Synge used the dialect of West Kerry or Connemara. *Riders to the Sea* subtle, and early rises into lyricism. . . . The play has a curious formal excellence. It preserves absolutely the unity of time, the whole action being compressed into something less than two hours. . . .

No play yet produced in the Abbey Theatre has so gripped and held captive an audience. There have been fuller houses, but never more enthusiastic. What we have been waiting for was a play that should be at once good and popular. Mr. Yeats has proved a little too abstruse, and Mr. Synge a little too bizarre, to get fully down to the hearts of the people. What distinguishes *The Land* and gives it a special value in the development of the Abbey Theatre is its spirit and subject. Mr. Colum has caught up his play out of the mid-current of actual Irish life.

It was five years before Padraic Colum came to his full blossom in *Thomas Muskerry*, but of this play later.

In November 1902 the Irish National Dramatic Society had given a performance in the Antient Concert Rooms (the home of *The Countess Cathleen*) for the Cumann na nGaedeal. (I quote W. G. Fay):

The secretary of the Irish Literary Society, Mr. Stephen Gwynn, happened to be in Dublin at the time, and came to see our show. He was so impressed that, when he returned to London, he persuaded his Society to offer to provide a hall in London for a performance and to pay all our expenses. . . . The Irish Theatre owes an eternal debt of gratitude to Mr. Gwynn. But it was one thing to say we would go to London, and another to be able to go. Not many of us could get free to travel at that time of the year. We had our jobs, and it was far too early for holidays. The most we could hope for was to get a whole Saturday off, and that in the end was how the great affair was managed. It was arranged that on Saturday, 2nd May 1903, we should give an afternoon and an evening performance at the Queen's Gate Hall, South Kensington.

The plays the little company brought to London were *The Hour-Glass*, *Twenty-Five*, *Cathleen ni Houlihan*, *The Pot of Broth* and *The Laying of the Foundations*.

Thanks probably to Stephen Gwynn's and Lady Gregory's efforts, all the great London dramatic critics were present at these modest performances: A. B. Walkley, William Archer, Arthur Symonds, "Michael Field." They gave unstinted praise. They found in the quality of the players and in the strange quality of the plays something unknown, something unique in the modern theatre.

Miss Horniman is certain to have been at those performances. She was no stranger to Yeats, for she had helped to finance the performances at the Avenue Theatre, London, in 1894, when his *The Land of Heart's Desire* and Shaw's *Arms and the Man* were first performed. She had for some years acted as Yeats's secretary. She was born in 1860, and her father, of "Horniman's Teas," Manchester, had considerable wealth. She was interested in painting, and studied at the Slade School under Legros; her other interests were astrology, female suffrage, and the modern theatre. Her interest in the theatre and in Yeats brought her to Dublin in 1903, where she designed and made the costumes for Yeats's *The King's Threshold*. After a performance in the Molesworth Hall, Yeats appeared on the stage and appealed to the small audience for financial help to carry on the work of the Society. He hoped for a small subscription from Miss Horniman; to his astonishment she said, "I will give you a theatre."

W. G. Fay says that the idea was in her mind for some time, and she told him that if shares she had bought in the Hudson's Bay Company boomed she would give Fay and his fellow-workers a theatre. The shares rose and rose, and (I quote from Fay):

> Meanwhile I was always wondering and considering what Miss Horniman would do if her Hudson Bays came up to expectations. About this time there was a bad enough fire in an English theatre, followed by a shocking one, involving great loss of life, at the Iroquois Theatre, Chicago. Local authorities throughout the United Kingdom began to tighten up the theatre regulations, with the result that one of the oldest houses in Dublin had to close down. Attached to a Mechanics' Institute, and hence commonly known as "The Mechanics," this was at one time under the management of that great character actress, Mrs. Glenville, mother of Shaun Glenville. . . . As soon as I heard that the theatre was closed I made it my business to examine it for necessary alterations, and to enquire into what money these would cost. This done, I sent full particulars to Miss Horniman, suggesting that here was our chance. Her answer told us that our luck was in. Hudson Bays having risen well above what she required of them, she came to Dublin at once.

On the 14th January 1904 W. B. Yeats's play *The Shadowy Waters* was produced for the first time in the Molesworth Hall; with it was produced *The Townland of Tamney* by Seumas MacManus. The casts of these plays are appended. Perhaps *The Shadowy Waters* is the least successful of Yeats's verse plays; it should have been made into an opera—and I believe has been played in Athens as such; it should have been a kind of Tristan and Isolde—and Isolde was Irish. But how Yeats hated music and Wagner!

MISS A. E. F. HORNIMAN

INTERIOR OF ABBEY THEATRE

VESTIBULE OF ABBEY THEATRE

Casts of First Productions, 1904

14th January 1904
THE SHADOWY WATERS
By W. B. Yeats

Forgael . . . . F. J. Fay
Aibric . . . . P. J. Kelly
Helmsman . . . . Seamus O'Sullivan
Sailors . G. Roberts, P. MacShiubhlaigh
Dectora . . . . Maire Nic Shiubhlaigh
The prologue will be spoken by Honor Lavelle
Scene—The Deck of a Galley

14th January 1904
THE TOWNLAND OF TAMNEY
A Folk Play in One Act by Seumas MacManus

The Wise Man . . . . . W. J. Fay
Feargal (a bird-catcher)   De Courcy Millar
Conal . . . . G. Roberts
Donal . . . . . P. MacShiubhlaigh
Teague . . . . P. J. Kelly

CHAPTER SIX

THE ABBEY THEATRE, 1904-1909

A THEATRE, the old Theatre Royal Opera House in Abbey Street, built in 1820, had been burned down some years later. The Mechanics' Institute, then situate in Capel Street, acquired the site and built on it their new premises. As well as a small concert-hall, there was a lending-library, a reading-room and a chemical laboratory. The Institute wanted to change the concert-hall into a theatre for letting purposes, but theatres in Ireland require a Patent from the Lord Lieutenant. Such Patents are, naturally, opposed by rival theatres and the Mechanics' did not obtain one. The concert-hall, therefore, could only be used for short sketches or vaudeville shows not lasting more than twenty minutes.

An old actor recalled to me that he used to act in the Mechanics' Theatre. The prices of the seats were sixpence and threepence. There were no dressing-rooms and changes of costumes had to be made in the wings. The performances started at 7 o'clock and continued till 11. Jack B. Yeats, remembering performances at the Mechanics' Theatre, says:

> As to the Mechanics' Theatre . . . I was there a few times. I am sure of nothing except that the people were a grand crew, and I am against any memory about them that might be incorrect. They played two, or three, or more plays, every night (and changed the bill completely in the middle of the week). I saw no Variety entertainment, but each play was shortened up, perhaps to get over the difficulties of the other theatres. They had exciting bills out with the fly-posters. If you could get one of these from one of the old bill-stickers, and if you could get your old hero to talk to yourself, and make notes, you should be able to give this fine old, brave old, body a nice memory.

Finally, as Fay relates, the Corporation Fire Department demanded alterations which the Trustees of the Institute could not afford, and the premises became practically derelict.

Thanks to Fay's enterprise, Miss Horniman agreed to acquire part of the property. The entrance to the Institute was from Lower Abbey Street, but the Corporation demanded new exits, a new stage and new dressing-rooms. Fortunately, separated from the Institute by only one large building, Marlborough Street cut across Abbey Street. The large building extended round the corner into Marlborough Street, and beyond it were vacant premises. By acquiring these premises a second entrance was obtained, which could lead to a vestibule, an office, and two large dressing-rooms. The Marlborough Street premises had formerly been a bank and then, temporarily, the City Morgue. The proposed theatre, therefore, was shaped like an L upside down. In making the necessary alterations some human bones were discovered and murder was suspected, but the caretaker recalled that a few years before they had mislaid a body, "when the time came for the inquest it couldn't be found." The Theatre's connection with a morgue was often in years to come to be made the subject of gibes after the production of some especially gloomy play. It is certainly a little haunted; but what theatre is without its ghost—not only the one that walks on Friday? The new theatre was named The Abbey Theatre.

Miss Horniman did not take over that part of the Institute which housed the library, reading-room, billiard-table and laboratory. From the Marlborough Street entrance there was access to the front seats and to the balcony; from the Abbey Street entrance there was access to the back of the house, to the pit. This arrangement has been left practically unaltered, nor has the original stage been enlarged. Its dimensions are as follows: proscenium-opening 21 feet; curtain-line to back wall, 16 feet 4 inches; width of stage from wall to wall, 40 feet. At first there were two large dressing-rooms; there was no scene-dock, and scenery had to be stored in the wings and properties underneath the stage. On these alterations Miss Horniman spent about £1,300. The year after the Theatre opened—that is to say in 1905—she acquired on the side of the stage opposite to Marlborough Street some old stables. On this site were erected the green-room, the office (afterwards made into a wardrobe-room), a small wardrobe-room, and a rehearsal-room with a stage. Still later, Miss Horniman took in further stables, and made them into a large scene-dock, a paint-room, six dressing-rooms, and a workshop. At the present time there are six dressing-rooms on one side of the stage and three on the other, all with hot and cold water. The seating capacity of the Theatre has varied very little in forty-eight years; it is now 536. The worst features in the theatre are the lack of depth of the stage; a public lane runs behind it, making enlargement impossible; and the balcony being in the shape of a horse-shoe, the upper seats on the side are what the French call "seats for the blind."

The following letter from Miss Horniman to Yeats clarifies her offer:

H.I. Montague Mansions,
London, W.
April 1904.

Dear Mr. Yeats,

 I have great sympathy with the artistic and dramatic aims of the Irish National Theatre Company, as publicly explained by you on various occasions. I am glad to be able to offer you my assistance in your endeavours to establish a theatre in Dublin. I am taking the hall of the Mechanics' Institute in Abbey Street and an adjoining building in Marlborough Street, which I propose to turn into a small theatre with a proper entrance hall, green-room and dressing-rooms. As the Company will not require the hall constantly, I propose to arrange to let it for lectures and entertainments at a rental proportionate to seating capacity.

 The Company can have the building rent-free whenever they want it for rehearsals and performances, except when it is let. The green-room I hope to arrange to be kept for their sole use. They must pay for their own electric light and gas, as well as for the repair of damage done during their occupation. The building will be insured, and any additions to the lighting for special occasions or plays must be permitted by the insurance company formally in writing.

 If any President, Vice-President or member of the Company wants the hall for a lecture, concert or entertainment, the rent must be paid to me as by an ordinary person. If a lecture be given on a dramatic or theatrical subject and the gross receipts go to the Irish National Theatre, then the President, Vice-President or member of the Company can have the hall for nothing. But it must be advertised clearly as being for the sole benefit of the Irish National Theatre pecuniarily as well as in aid of its artistic objects.

 The prices of the seats can be raised, of course, but not lowered, neither by the Irish National Theatre nor by anyone who will hire the hall. This is to prevent cheap entertainments from being given which would lower the letting value of the hall. I hope to be able to arrange to number most of the seats and to sell the tickets beforehand, with a small fee for booking. The entrance to the more expensive seats will be from Marlborough Street, where there will be a cloak-room. The situation being near to the tramway terminus is convenient for people living in any part of Dublin. I shall take every possible means to ensure the safety and convenience of the public. I can only afford to make a very little theatre and it must be quite simple. You all must do the rest to make a powerful and prosperous theatre with a high artistic ideal.

A copy of this letter will be sent to each Vice-President and another to the Stage Manager for the Company.

Yours sincerely,
A. E. F. Horniman.

The Society replied:

Dear Miss Horniman,

We, the undersigned members of the Irish National Theatre Company beg to thank you for the interest you have evinced in the work of the Society and for the aid you propose giving to our future work by securing a permanent Theatre in Abbey Street.

We undertake to abide by all the conditions laid down in your letter to the Company, and to do our utmost to forward the objects of the Society.

The letter was signed by: W. B. Yeats, F. J. Fay, William G. Fay, James S. Starkey, Frank Walker, Udolphus Wright, Miss Garoby, Vera Esposito, Dora L. Annesley, George Roberts, Douglas Hyde, Thomas E. Keohler, Harry F. Norman, Helen S. Laird, G. Russell, Miss Walker, J. M. Synge, Sara Allgood, Frederick Ryan, Padraic Colum.

Miss Horniman was not resident in Ireland. She was, therefore, ineligible as a Patentee, so the Patent was applied for in Lady Gregory's name. Lady Gregory writes: "The other theatres took fright and believed we might interfere with their gains, and there was delay after delay." But at last the enquiry was held before the Privy Council. After a tussle the battle was won and Lady Gregory amongst other things was "enjoined and commanded to gather, entertain, govern, privilege and keep such and so many players" and not to put on the stage any "exhibition of wild beasts or dangerous performances. No women or children to be hung from the flies nor fixed in position from which they cannot release themselves."

The week before the Theatre opened its doors Miss Horniman gave a large tea-party there for her friends. One can imagine how proudly, how justly proudly, she showed them over the premises. True, she had been able to afford "only a very little theatre and it must be quite simple." Little and simple it was, and little it remained: but when the curtain rose on 27th December 1904 it was to prove an epoch-making event in the world of the theatre. There was not a vacant seat, all the notabilities of literary and artistic life in Dublin were present. The programme was a noble one. It began with the first production of Yeats's *On Baile's Strand*, perhaps his most perfect verse-play. Here is the cast:

Cuchullain, a King of Muirthemne	F. J. Fay
Concobar, a High King of Ulster	George Roberts
Daire, a King	Arthur Sinclair
Fintain, a blind man	Seumas O'Sullivan
Barach, a fool	W. G. Fay
A Young Man	P. MacShiubhlaigh

Young Kings and Old Kings: Maire Ni Gharbhaigh, Emma Vernon, Sara Allgood, Doreen Gunning, R. Nash, N. Power, U. Wright, E. Keegan.

The verse-play was followed by Lady Gregory's comedy, *Spreading the News*. She had criticised her first play, *Twenty-Five*, as "a rather sentimental comedy, not very amusing." But her second comedy had no sentiment in it and was tremendously amusing. In one stride she had achieved a small masterpiece. And in the casts of these plays names appear which in years to come were to play large parts in the Theatre's history, Sara Allgood and Arthur Sinclair. Sara had played small parts before, but suddenly, as Mrs. Fallon, she showed herself a mistress of comedy. Later she was going to prove herself equally fine as tragedienne. The cast of the comedy was as follows:

Bartley Fallon	W. G. Fay
Mrs. Fallon	Sara Allgood
Mrs. Tully	Emma Vernon
Mrs. Tarpey	Maire Ni Gharbhaigh
Shawn Early	J. H. Dunne
Tim Casey	George Roberts
James Ryan	Arthur Sinclair
Jack Smith	P. MacShiubhlaigh
A Policeman	R. S. Nash
A Removable Magistrate	F. J. Fay

The Dublin press next day was unanimous in its appreciation. Abridged extracts from the *Irish Times* and the *Freeman's Journal* will serve as samples. Thus, the Unionist *Irish Times*:

> The Irish National Theatre Society made its bow to an expectant audience at the newly acquired theatre in Abbey Street last evening. Those who came, either by invitation or by the simple British method of paying at the door,

were much impressed and delighted by the change wrought externally and internally on the old theatre premises.... The audience was fairly representative of literary and artistic culture and the occasion was an experiment and possibly an epoch-maker, invested with unique interest.... Lady Gregory's play is a tripping little piece founded on a simple idea of modern Irish life, it yields in its short compass abundance of rich comedy. Mr. W. G. Fay who came before the curtain at the close said that the authoress, Lady Gregory, was not able to be present but they would convey to her an assurance of the hearty appreciation of the audience.

And the Nationalist paper said:

> Last night the new theatre which the Irish National Theatre Society has had so generously placed at its service by Miss Horniman was opened under the happiest auspices. There was a crowded and popular audience. Long before the curtain rose the pit and gallery were packed ... there was not a vacant place in the theatre when all the audience had assembled.... There were loud calls for the author of *On Baile's Strand*, when the curtain fell, who did not disguise the pleasure that the reception of the play gave him, made a brief speech expressing his thanks to the audience, and his thanks to the lady to whose spirit and generosity the Society owes its new home. Authors, he said, must be free to choose their own way; but in their pilgrimage towards beauty and truth they require companions by the way.

In the following year (1905) first productions were given of *The Well of the Saints* (J. M. Synge), *Kincora* (Lady Gregory), *The Building Fund* (William Boyle) and *The White Cockade* (Lady Gregory). The casts of these plays are to be found at the end of this chapter.

But rifts were appearing within the lute. Generous Miss Horniman, not content with giving the Society a theatre, was now prepared to pay the players' salaries to the extent of £500 a year. In one sense this was a great boon, since it left Fay and his brother and others free to devote all their time to the Theatre. On the other hand, it turned the Theatre from an enterprise undertaken for love of Ireland and dramatic art into a "commercial" theatre. It was not unnatural that a split should result and Maire Nic Shiubhlaigh resigned. With her went Miss Lavell, Miss Vernon, Miss Garvey, Frank Walker, Seamus O'Sullivan and George Roberts. Miss Horniman's generosity, having regard to her comparatively small wealth, was unbounded; and eventually she gave the Society an annual subsidy of £800, to continue to the date of the expiration of the Patent, six years hence from February 1905. The following letter indicates her intentions:

Hôtel du Cité du Netrio,
Madeleine,
Paris,
Jan. 13th, '06.

Dear Miss Taylor,

Thank you very much for the list. The fact is that I am anxious for educated Dublin people to see for themselves what the plays are like. What is good enough for dons at Oxford and Cambridge is good enough for anybody.

I know perfectly well that people think that the Abbey Theatre is a political "side-show"—if it were, *I* would have nothing to do with it. I expect it will be a long time before I am believed, but I am a patient person. I will send that list to Mr. J. M. Synge (31 Crosthwaite Park, Kingstown) and he will communicate with you if he wants more names, as we may want to save time and I shall be here until the end of next week. His play "Well of the Saints" was produced at the Deutsches Theater, Berlin, last night, I hope that it was successful.

I have taken a ruinous stable next door to the Abbey Theatre, to enlarge behind the scenes, and when I come next I hope to have the pleasure of showing you the alterations and giving you some tea after a performance.

With kind regards,
Yours sincerely,
A. E. F. Horniman.

But by the middle of 1906 the clash of personalities and opinions became evident. In a letter to the Directors, dated 4th July 1906, she writes:

Dear Directors,

I find that our present arrangements in regard to the Abbey Theatre won't work. At Glasgow Mr. Fay spoke to me in a way which made my position very unpleasant. I have come to the conclusion that the whole power of the purse must be in the Directors' hands.

I propose to pay £600 in quarterly payments of £150 to the Directors to be used by them for the following purposes, and what is over to be spent as they think fit.

£500 for salaries.

£100 for the purposes of petty cash as now expended by Mr. Fay. This to begin when you tell me it is necessary.

The cheques from Cramer's to go, as before, towards paying the rents, rates and taxes.

That the Directors should pay the gas and electric light bills, and send me in a bill for what is used by my tenants. This to avoid confusion and forwarding me small accounts. . . . I pay half the cost of such scenery as my tenants

SARA ALLGOOD

MAIRE O'NEILL

might use. Mr. Day's salary for seeing after the business of the Abbey is paid up to the end of September.

That the Directors and I continue to hold to the letters published in "Samhain." The Directors can charge what price they wish for seats, but my business circular holds good in regard to my lets, until I see fit to alter it. I give all refreshment-rights to the Directors. I retain the right to refuse the publication of any play in the "Abbey Theatre Series" which has not been produced by the National Theatre Society.

In case of necessity, I will give further pecuniary assistance, but only for performances at the Abbey Theatre. At Edinburgh the slovenly appearance of the performances had not improved and, with the exception of Miss Allgood, no one took the trouble to act at all. I was present on the Monday and Wednesday evenings, and Wednesday was, if anything, worse than Monday. The two performances I saw in Glasgow after my painful interview with Mr. Fay were as good as those earlier in the week. I have come to the conclusion that I cannot ask the paying public to come to see performances which are liable to become at any moment like those I saw at Edinburgh. I do not advise you to accept the Manchester offer, nor to think of appearing before the general public until the whole company are competent and the management adequate. The way in which details are allowed to vary renders good performances very difficult. I shall not interfere with the Abbey Theatre except at the request of the Directors in the future, and I decline to have anything more to do with the Company until they have all learned to be worthy my troubling about them.

There were to be other clashes later, ending up with her final clash, on the head of myself, in 1909.

During 1906 there were noteworthy first productions of Lady Gregory's *Hyacinth Halvey*, *The Doctor in Spite of Himself*, *The Gaol Gate*, and *The Canavans*. Yeats contributed a revised version of *The Shadowy Waters* and *Deirdre*. William Boyle had in the previous year contributed a half-comic, half-tragic play, *The Building Fund*, a harsh three-act comedy in which the chief character dies at the end of the second act. He followed it now with *The Eloquent Dempsey*, a rather obvious small-town comedy which won the audience's hearts. In the same year came a less good play from his pen, *The Mineral Workers*. These plays were not quite the sort of plays which Yeats and Martyn and Lady Gregory had in their minds when they dreamed of an heroic theatre and a theatre of Ibsen, but they were indubitably Irish. Synge had appeared, sounding a strange, unexpected note, so had Padraic Colum. Yeats and Lady Gregory stood aside and let them say their say. Now Boyle appeared and they let him say his say. They were right. Though Boyle is seldom played today his *Building Fund* and his *Eloquent Dempsey* have an important place in our canon of plays. In *Dempsey*, for almost the first time, he depicted the life of the small Irish town, though George Moore in *The Bending of the Bough* and Fred Ryan in *The Laying of the Foundations* had attempted such a thing, but Moore's play smells of Norway and Fred Ryan's—not knowing it we cannot judge it. Boyle's play owes nothing to Norway, its little intrigues, its minor corruptions, everything so wrong and yet so innocent, make it Irish of the Irish.

William Boyle was an authority on the life and poetry of James Clarence Mangan; in political life he was on terms of intimate friendship with Charles Stewart Parnell and John Redmond; but he will be remembered as the author of *The Eloquent Dempsey* and *The Building Fund*.

From the moment she wrote the last line of *Spreading the News* Lady Gregory began to come into her full strength. She rightly discarded her first little play *Twenty-Five*, but made it a masterpiece years later as *The Jackdaw* (1907). In *Kincora*, in *The White Cockade*, in *The Canavans*, in *Dervorgilla*, she tried and very nearly succeeded in making what she called "Folk-History Plays" popular. They were to be part of the noble Irish theatre she and Yeats had dreamed of. Yeats immensely admired *Kincora* in its rewritten version. *The White Cockade* is a touching play; perhaps it is a little too thinly written. *The Canavans*, if extravagantly produced (and Hugh Hunt thirty years after its first production did it thus), is a delight and *Dervorgilla* is a small masterpiece. Besides these folk-history plays she was putting Molière into Irish country prose. There was *The Doctor in Spite of Himself* (1906), *The Rogueries of Scapin* (1908), *The Miser* (1909), finally *The Would-be Gentleman* (1926). Her translations of Molière into "Kiltartan" dialect have been criticised by the Dublin public, but here is what Gerothwon, Professor of Romance Languages in Dublin University, wrote about them:

> I am frequently asked, in my unfortunate capacity as a *professional* critic of French literature, whether these semi-Irish adaptations of Molière do not

strike me as being in a literary sense somewhat blasphemous. This question I answer most unhesitatingly in the negative—for I see no reason why the main scenes and business of *The Miser*, for instance, which we already find in Roman garb in Plautus; then, again, in Italian garb, in Lorenzino de Medici or Ariosto—just as the main scenes and business of *The Rogueries* are first to be found in Roman garb in Terence's *Formio*, supplemented by a few Italian additions in a farce called *Partalone*—father of a family—should not find a congenial setting in Galway County, or, why not?, in some Dublin metropolitan *Suburban Groove*. In fact you will notice that if I have any fault to find with Lady Gregory's spirited versions it is that they are not altogether and avowedly Irish, Irish in mode of speech, costume and locality. I include speech, for Molière's peasants and servants in particular, speak not academic French, but the dialects of their respective provinces. . . . In plays such as *The Miser* or *The Rogueries* both the plots and the characterisations are so universal, alike in their conception and moral application, that no change of scenery or idiom would impair them, as I think, in the slightest degree. At the same time you will not grudge Mr. Yeats his artistic scrupulousness in reviving for your benefit the traditional business inherited from Molière through an uninterrupted chain of great comedians, his successors in the foremost theatre of France—nor the glowing colours of that rascal Scapin's Italian jacket and stockings.

The Fays, William Fay particularly, were steeped in the traditional theatre of Europe and, in the case of the Molière adaptation, obtained from the Comédie Française copies of the prompt-scripts which had come down unaltered from Molière's day. You crossed then and you recrossed then. Such a bit of "business" was done here and another bit of business was done there. This meticulous, stereotyped production existed for many years in the Abbey Theatre, and *Spreading the News* and *Hyacinth Halvey*, for instance, must be produced with the exact movements and business used on the first night. It is only of late years that we have ventured to break the mould.

At first there was no orchestra, but a year or two later Mr. Arthur Darley formed a small orchestra. Arthur Darley, descendant of our poet George Darley, was a very distinguished musician. He excelled in his traditional Irish airs, he was a beautiful violin player. He went on tour with the Company to England, but disliked being made a show piece, and when he left the Theatre young J. F. Larchet took up his baton. For many, many years to come the little Abbey orchestra was to be one of the features of the evening; indeed there were people who would leave the theatre for what they called "the intervals" (i.e. the plays) and return for what the players did call "the intervals."

The Company spread its wings. In Ireland it visited Wexford, Dundalk, Waterford and Longford; in England, Manchester, Liverpool, Leeds, Oxford, Cambridge, London. Sometimes the tours were very successful, sometimes they just made their expenses, sometimes they lost money; by 1909 Lady Gregory reports that the Theatre had been able to save "a few hundred pounds."

After the defection of Maire Nic Shiubhlaigh and her friends new players appeared. Sara Allgood had made her first startling appearance in *Spreading the News*, and she was quickly followed by her equally brilliant sister Maire O'Neill, and there was Arthur Sinclair and J. M. Kerrigan. Lesser, but almost as important, people were Sydney J. Morgan, U. Wright, J. A. O'Rourke, A. Power, and Seaghan Barlow. By 1907 Fay had built up a company of players comparable in their genre to any company in Europe.

But at the beginning of that year 1907, something which looked like disaster fell on the Theatre—the production of *The Playboy of the Western World*. Synge's plays, with the exception of *Riders to the Sea*, had been disliked by many people from the first; it will be remembered that Maud Gonne and Dudley Digges had walked out of the Molesworth Hall on the first night of *In the Shadow of the Glen*. *The Well of the Saints* had been coldly received. Perhaps it can never be a popular play, George Moore thought it a marvellous script for an opera, and to some people it seems his most beautiful play. Today, when *The Playboy* is almost universally acclaimed the masterpiece it is, it is difficult to understand why its first performance forty years ago should have caused such a storm, such a hurricane of opposition. The subject is an exaggeration and should be taken with a chuckle. The language is never obscene though the word "bloody" is used and a female garment is described as a "shift." The grotesque situation and those few words seem to be the only things to object to—if object you must—yet they caused a riot in the Theatre.

Lady Gregory says:

> I remember Synge bringing the play to us in Dublin.... We were almost bewildered by its abundance and fantasy, but we felt, and Mr. Yeats said very plainly, that there was far too much "bad language." There were too many violent oaths, and the play itself was marred by this. I did not think it was fit to be put on the stage without cutting. It was agreed that it should be cut in rehearsal. A fortnight before its production, Mr. Yeats, thinking I had seen a rehearsal, wrote: "I would like to know how you thought *The Playboy* acted.... Have they cleared many of the objectionable sentences out of it?" I did not, however, see a rehearsal and did not hear the play again until the night of its production, and then I told Synge that the cuts were not enough, that many more should be made. He gave me leave to do this and, in consultation with the players, I took out many phrases which, though in the printed book, have never since that first production been spoken on our stage. I am sorry they were not taken out before it had been played at all, but that is just what happened.

A Dublin newspaper vividly describes what occurred on the occasion of the play's second performance:

> Remarkable scenes were witnessed last evening at the Abbey Theatre during the production of Mr. J. M. Synge's comedy *The Playboy of the Western World*.... On its initial production unfavourable comments were passed on it and at least two of the Dublin critics expressed the opinion that its production was not desirable. The author and management proceeded with the comedy last evening in the presence of an audience of about 300.... At the rise of the curtain there was still no indication that trouble was brewing, but the performance had not proceeded for more than ten minutes when it was obvious that the house was not disposed to a favourable reception of the piece.... The first act was given amidst a scene of great disorder and before its close Mr. W. G. Fay came to the footlights and announced that it was the opinion of those concerned in the production of the comedy that anyone who did not like it would be well advised to leave the building. A crash of disorder was the response and the lusty singing of "The West's Asleep" followed in the interval before the curtain was raised again. Hisses and boos greeted the uprising of the curtain, and the disorder of the gallery and pit prevented anyone in the other parts of the house from hearing what was said on the stage.... Then Mr. Fay amid a storm of hisses came forward and announced that he had sent for the police and under their protection the comedy would be continued to the end. The orchestra played and directly six policemen entered the parterre while three made their way into the balcony. Despite this display of force there was no cessation of noise and the next act was commenced amid scenes of greater disorder. When the curtain was about to fall on the second act Mr. Synge, the author, and Lady Gregory announced to the sergeant in charge of the police that their services were no longer required inside. Forthwith the police withdrew amidst cheers....

The final act was then proceeded with, but no one in the house heard a word of it owing to the din created by the audience, many of whom cried "Sinn Fein," "Sinn Fein Amhain" and "Kill the author." . . . The final curtain fell amid a scene of great disorder.

Yeats was lecturing in Scotland and therefore was not present at the earlier performances—for the play was persisted in. Malone says:

>Every night there were fights in the theatre, and when the police removed the belligerents the fights were continued in the neighbouring streets. There was what amounted to a riot, and by the end of the week nearly five hundred police were required to keep order in the theatre and its precincts. When the curtain fell on the Saturday night amidst "thunders of applause" the play had never been heard in the theatre, it had only been heard *of* in the columns of the newspapers or the gossip in the streets.

Synge was present on the first riotous night and was called on to speak but refused to do so. He was suffering from influenza, and at any rate his was not a nature to fight hooligans.

In contrast Yeats, ever a fighter, arranged a debate in the Theatre on the Monday following the week's performances. The *Evening Mail* thus reports it:

>The fact that there was an entrance charge did not apparently affect the attendance. The principal persons concerned in the opposition to the play were early arrivals, and their supporters were also present in full strength. The clientele who supported Mr. Yeats were hardly represented in the same relative degree, but their lack of numbers, especially when it came to a question of making a demonstration, was compensated for by an apparently irresponsible section who seemed to have come with the sole object of enjoying the prospective fun. . . . The chair was taken by Mr. P. D. Kenny, better known under his literary soubriquet of "Pat." He said he had been asked to take the chair and he was very glad to do so. . . . He outlined the course of the debate. . . . First, the liberty of the Theatre, and next the play itself. The discussion would be as wide and full and as free as possible. (A voice—"The police are at the back.") The Theatre was not a political institution. (Another voice—"It should be a national one.") Groans and hisses and interruptions went on all through his speech.
>
>Mr. Yeats who then came forward on the stage received a very mixed reception. His friends cheered him, but the hissing and groaning predominated, and for a time the air was thick with rival and conflicting cries. . . . He began by saying, as he thought over the last week he was reminded of a previous period, when he had a difference with the public over *The Countess Cathleen*. Then he was attacked with great violence, and a newspaper then his friend was now his enemy, but no man should be cast down by the enmity of an Irish newspaper, or elated by its friendship. He was freer today than he was

then, and he stood now representative of an artistic institution. (Laughter.) On the former occasion his position was complicated. He was President of the Wolfe Tone Association (renewed laughter) and also on that occasion he had called in the police. ("Hear, hear" and groans.) He was there that night to justify himself for having done the same thing.... Before he finished the Chairman had to appeal once or twice for order, and the confusion and noise was general over the house. The Chairman then invited discussion.... The proceedings were then developing into a farce, the speakers without exception being made the butt of all kinds of jocose remarks and shouts having no reference to the subject in hand.... Mr. Yeats replied with difficulty on account of the disorder. He was unable to make himself heard for a considerable time, and then only with constant interruptions.... It was now bordering on half-past eleven; the audience were tired of speeches and their own noisy demonstrations, and it was a relief to everyone when "Pat" left the chair and declared the debate over. The audience went home after a night not so much tinged with rowdyism as with boisterous foolery.

The *Playboy* battle had been fought and won in Dublin, but won only in the sense that its opponents had not been able to stop any performance. No audience, no single member of any audience, had been able to judge the play dispassionately. Such a judgment was obtained when, early in the following summer, the play was presented in a London theatre, the Great Queen Street Theatre. It was immediately recognised as a masterpiece. The play was subsequently performed in Manchester, Oxford, Cambridge and elsewhere, always with notable success, and was, daringly, put on again at the Abbey in 1909. On this occasion there was very little opposition. The battle seemed to be over; the Directors could not foresee 1911 and the U.S.A.

Apart from *The Playboy*, 1907 was a momentous year in the Theatre's history, for in the first month of the next year the Fays left the Abbey. Miss Horniman and Yeats were growing a little dissatisfied. Miss Horniman thought that a producer more professional than Fay should be imported from England, while Yeats thought that a more professional actress than Sara Allgood or her sister should be brought into the Theatre and made a "star." As a result Mr. Iden Payne joined the Company as producer in March, and Miss Darragh crossed the Irish Sea to play Deirdre in Yeats's play of that name. Neither experiment proved a success. Mr. Payne was English, and after producing Maeterlinck's *Interior* and Scawen Blunt's

Fand resigned, to embark on a very distinguished career, first at Miss Horniman's Gaiety Theatre in Manchester, later at the Stratford Shakespeare Memorial Theatre, and later again in universities in U.S.A.

Miss Darragh was Irish, an actress of great ability though perhaps not of the first rank. Her salary was much larger than that of the other ladies in the Company and there was naturally much jealousy, and after *Deirdre* she did not appear again.

It had been W. G. Fay's opinion for some time that there was a lack of discipline amongst the players, and now, after Mr. Payne's brief reign as producer had come to an end, he demanded full powers as Manager and Producer, thinking that the Directors interfered too much. It was a clash of personalities. Yeats immensely admired his work as a comedian, and his brother's as a beautiful speaker of verse, and the comedian brother had contributed so much to Lady Gregory's comedies. But neither she nor Yeats were disposed to let the reins slip from their hands. It is difficult, thirty and more years after, to judge who was most in the right; doubtless there were wrongs on both sides. It is perhaps best to quote briefly from Fay:

> From the first, Frank and I had seen in the National Theatre movement the possibility of a real art movement, and we had been led to believe that the Abbey Directors shared our vision. Miss Horniman certainly did, otherwise she would not have backed the movement with her money, for what was Ireland to her, or she to Ireland? Unfortunately, the lavish encomiums of the English Press had been too heady for our friends, Yeats, Synge, and Augusta Gregory. They imagined we had arrived when we had no more than started. We had a company that could do pleasant plays with an accomplishment and finish that have never been rivalled, much less excelled. But we should have to show much more than that before we could claim to be a real art theatre. We should have to create by degrees a company capable, both in numbers and experience, of performing any type of play, whether low life or high life, whether prose or verse. Frank and I reckoned that this would be a long and hard job—a matter of ten years at least, even with the excellent material we undoubtedly had.
>
> I put these considerations to the Directors, pointing out that it would be idle for me to attempt such a task unless I were given the usual power of a manager and producer. Of course it would be possible to muddle through in the old way, if we were content to potter along with peasant plays, which would mean first stagnation and ultimately, when we found no more pots to boil and no more news to spread, death. But that was not my idea for the

future of the Abbey Theatre. What agitated confabulations the Directors held I know not. All I know is that after a few days Lady Gregory came to me to say that they were not disposed to make any changes, and what was I going to do about it? I did the only thing that was left to me—I resigned on the spot.

It must have been a bitter moment for Fay when he closed the stage-door behind him on 13th January 1908. His connection with the movement had started in 1901, in the Gaiety Theatre, where, though his knowledge of Gaelic was "not extensive," he produced *Casadh an tSugain*. From that time, in St. Teresa's Hall, in Camden and Molesworth Streets, his was the dominant hand on the stage as producer, he and his brother were the chief actors. It seems to have been mainly owing to his persistence and enthusiasm that Miss Horniman created the Abbey Theatre. Due honour is always paid to Yeats and Lady Gregory for their spade-work, perhaps Fay's hard digging is in danger of being overlooked. Yeats wrote thus in *Samhain*:

> We are about to lose our principal actor. William Fay has had enough of it, and we do not wonder, and is going to some other country where his exquisite gift of comedy and his brain teeming with fancy will bring him an audience, fame and a little money. He has worked with us now since 1902 when he formed his Company to carry on the work of the Irish Literary Theatre, and feels that he must leave to another man the long laborious battle. We have his good wishes, and he will return to us if at all possible to play his old parts for some brief season, or seasons, and may possibly join us for a London or American tour. We believe that William Fay is right to go and he will have our good will and good wishes with him, though we have lost in losing him the finest comedian of his kind upon the English-speaking stage.

Arthur Symons, having seen the performance by the little company in London in 1902, writes:

Dear Mr. Fay,

> I have just got your address from Mr. Yeats, and I want to say how much I admired and enjoyed the performance (I only saw the matinée) of your Company. I am no longer writing dramatic criticisms, and thus had no chance of writing about it. But I hope to recur to it some day in the future, when I am saying how acting should be done. I need not tell you how entirely sympathetic I am with your general principles; the quietude and simplicity of the whole thing, the beautiful speaking, and in the case of your brother, a real genius for acting which seems rather an instinct than an art. This means of course he is a true artist. Your own performance of the Fool I thought wholly admirable. Miss Walker has a touch of genuine distinction in her

reticent naturalism, but I did not agree with the Cathleen and one of the scholars was very bad, but I hear he is a new man. It seems to me almost the first time I have ever seen a company in love with the words spoken. I am trying to remember separate details of a performance which delighted me as a whole. There is no doubt you are doing the right thing in the right way. Come over to London again, and teach our public to turn against all the popular actors of London.

Frank Fay many years later reappeared in the Abbey as the Wise Man in *The Hour-Glass*, but William never trod its boards again. The brothers went first to U.S.A. and afterwards to England, where they had busy and successful stage careers. Towards the close of his life Frank settled with his family in Dublin and taught elocution.

Elderly people who saw the Fays in those early days speak of them with a kind of awe. But that awe was to reappear very soon, in the cases of Sara Allgood, Maire O'Neill and Arthur Sinclair. Later still there is awe in connection with Barry Fitzgerald, F. J. McCormick later again—ah, we are too near our contemporaries, it is wiser to stop.

It had been a serious blow to the Theatre when, in 1905, Maire Nic Shiubhlaigh and her friends left, yet their places were quickly filled by players as competent, or often more competent. And the loss of the Fays was not as severely felt as might have been expected. Arthur Sinclair was coming to the height of his power as comedian and as tragedian (one likes to emphasise his tragic quality in such plays as *The Well of the Saints* and *The Pie-Dish*). Maire O'Neill was the original, incomparable, Pegeen Mike in *The Playboy*. We shall have to note in the future at least two swarms from the Abbey hive which seem to leave the combs barren, yet always some queen-bee remains and within a year or two the hive is humming again. Just after the Fays left Fred O'Donovan appeared, the young romantic actor the Theatre so badly needed. He was one of those rare cases, an actor who needed no training, he appeared full-fledged, strong-winged. He was to prove a tower of strength for the next ten years.

But if the battle over *The Playboy* had been won the occurrence grievously affected the Theatre financially. The Pit quickly forgave and forgot; after all, it and other differences of the same kind which were to come after were but "a lover's quarrel," as Lady Gregory named them. But the more expensive seats, the Stalls and Balcony, grew shy and the audiences in Dublin were meagre. Rigid economy and tours to England were necessary to induce ends to meet.

The following year (1908) should be noted for two plays, *The Man Who Missed the Tide* and *The Suburban Groove*. Written by W. F. Casey, they dealt with a phase of Irish life which had not hitherto been touched on—upper middle-class life; in one case that of a country town, in the other that of a Dublin suburb. Though neither of them are plays of the first importance, they are well constructed and very actable, and were immensely enjoyed. They seemed to foretell many and better plays of the same genre from Casey, but he left Ireland and became a journalist, ending up as editor of *The Times* in London.

Also in that year appeared a one-act tragedy, *The Pie-Dish*, by George Fitzmaurice. A three-act comedy by him, *The Country Dressmaker*, had been performed in the previous year. Fitzmaurice is a very individual writer, almost as individual as Synge. His country is Kerry and his dialogue is richly colourful, and sometimes his plots are wildly fantastic. His *Dressmaker* was, and is, very popular, his *Pie-Dish* gave Arthur Sinclair a splendid tragic role.

In 1905 G. B. Shaw had offered the Theatre a new play, *John Bull's Other Island*. The Directors refused it, foolishly we now think, on the ground that there was no one in the Company who could play the Englishman, Broadbent. (The part was magnificently played many years later by that very Irish actor Barry Fitzgerald.) But the Theatre made an *amende* a few years later when the English Censor refused to license *The Shewing-up of Blanco Posnet*. Mr. Shaw offered the play to the Abbey, for the Censor had no jurisdiction in Ireland. The Abbey accepted it and put it into rehearsal (July 1909). I quote Lady Gregory:

> We were without a regular stage-manager at that time and thought to have it produced by one of the members of the Company, but very soon the player who had taken it in charge found the work too heavy and troublesome, and withdrew from the stage-management, though not from taking a part. I had

a letter one morning telling me this, and I left by the next train for Dublin.
... That evening I held a rehearsal, the first I had ever taken quite alone. ...
I began to find an extraordinary interest and excitement in the work. ...

Mr. Yeats had stayed on at Coole at his work, and my letters to him, and letters after that to my son and to Mr. Shaw, will tell what happened through those hot summer days, and of the battle with Dublin Castle, which had taken upon itself to make the writ of the London Censor run at the Abbey....

Thursday, August 12th. At the Theatre this morning, the Secretary told me Whitney and Moore (solicitors) had telephoned that they had had a hint there would be interference with the production of *Blanco Posnet* by the Castle, and would like to see me.

I went to see Dr. Moore. He said a Castle Official, whose name he would not give, had called the day before yesterday and said, "As a friend of Sir Benjamin Whitney, I have come to tell you that if this play is produced it will be a very expensive thing for Miss Horniman." Dr. Moore took this to mean that the Patent would be forfeited. I talked the matter over with him and asked if he would get further information from his friend as to what method they meant to adopt, for I would not risk the immediate forfeiture of the Patent, but would not mind a threat of refusal to give a new Patent, as by that time—1910—perhaps neither the present Lord Lieutenant nor the present Censor would be in office.

Dr. Moore said he would go and see his friend, and at a quarter past two I had a message on the telephone that I had better see the Castle Official before 3 o'clock. I went to the Castle and saw the Official. I said, "Are you going to cut off our heads?" He said, "This is a very serious business; I think you are very ill-advised to think of putting on this play. May I ask how it came about?" I said, "Mr Shaw offered it and we accepted it." He said, "You have put us in a most difficult and disagreeable position by putting on a play to which the English Censor objected." I answered, "We do not take his view of it, and we think it hypocrisy objecting to a fallen woman in homespun on the stage when a fallen woman in satin has been the theme of such a great number of plays that have been passed." He said, "It is not that the Censor objected to; it is the use of certain expressions which may be considered blasphemous. Could not they be left out?" "Then there would be no play. The subject of the play is a man, a horse-thief, shaking his fist at Heaven, and finding afterwards that Heaven is too strong for him. It is the same theme that Milton has taken in Satan's defence in *Paradise Lost*. I consider it a deeply religious, and one could hurt no man, woman, or child. If it had been written by some religious leader, or even by a dramatist considered "safe," nonconformists would admire and approve of it." He said, "We have nothing to do with that, the fact for us is that the Censor has banned it." "Yes, and passed *The Merry Widow* which is to be performed here the same week, and which I have heard is objectionable, and *The Devil* which I saw in London." He said, "We would not have interfered, but what can we do when we see such paragraphs as these?" handing me a cutting from the *Irish Times* headed "Have we a Censor?" I replied, "We have not written or authorised it, as you might see by its being incorrect. I am sole Patentee of the Theatre." He said, "Dublin society will call out against us if we let it go on." "Lord Iveagh has taken six places." "For that play?" "Yes, for that play, and I believe Dublin society is likely to follow Lord Iveagh." He went on, "And Archbishop Walsh may object." I was silent. "It is very hard on the Lord Lieutenant. You should have had more consideration for him." I replied, "We did not know or remember that power rested with him, but it is hard on him, for he can't please everybody." He said, "Will you not give it up?" "What will you do if we go on?" "Either take no notice or take the Patent from you at once." I said, "If you decide to forfeit our Patent, we will not give a public performance; but if we give no performance to be judged by, we shall rest under the slur of having tried to produce something bad and injurious." "We must not provoke public opinion." "We provoked Nationalist public opinion in *The Playboy*, and you did not interfere." "Aye," said he, "exactly so, that was quite different; that had not been banned by the Censor." I said, "Time has justified us, for we have since produced *The Playboy* in Dublin and on tour with success, and it will justify us in the case of this play." "But *Blanco Posnet* is very inferior to *The Playboy*." I said, "Even so, Bernard Shaw has an intellectual position above that of Mr. Synge though he is not above him in imaginative power. He is recognised as an intellectual force, and his work cannot be despised." "Lord Aberdeen will have to decide." "I should like him to know," I said, "that from a business point of view the refusal to allow this play, already announced, to be given would do us a serious injury." He said, "No advertisements have been published." "Yes," I said, "the posters have been out some days, and there is a good deal of booking from England as well as here. We are just beginning to pay our way as a Theatre. We should be able to do so if we got about a dozen more stalls regularly. The people who would take stalls will be frightened off by your action. The continuance of our Theatre at all may depend on what you do now. We are giving a great deal of employment, spending in Dublin over £1,500 a year, and our Company bears the highest possible character." He said, "I know that well." I said, "I know Lord Aberdeen is friendly to our Theatre, though he does not come to it, not liking the colour of our carpets." He said, "He is a supporter of the drama. He was one of Sir Henry Irving's pall-bearers." "When shall we know the decision?" "In a day or two, perhaps tomorrow. You can produce it in Cork, Galway or Waterford. It is only in Dublin the Lord Lieutenant has power." He read from time to time a few lines from the Patent or Act of Parliament before him, "just to get them into your head." The last words he read were, "There must be no profane representation of sacred personages," and that, he said, "applies to Blanco Posnet's representations of the Deity." . . . We then said good-bye.

Friday. 5 o'c. Dr. Moore sent for me at 4 o'clock. I went with W. B. Yeats, who had arrived. The Crown Solicitor at the Castle, Sir B. Whitney's friend, had called and told him the Lord Lieutenant "was entirely opposed to the play being proceeded with and would use every power the law gave him to stop it," and that "it would be much better for us to lay the play aside."

We decided to go on with the performance and let the Patent be forfeited, and if we must die, die gloriously. Yeats was for this course and I agreed. Then I thought it right to let the Permanent Official know my change of intention and W. B. Y. and I went to see him at the Castle. He was very smiling and amiable this time and implored us to save the Lord Lieutenant from his delicate position. He threatened to take away our Patent before the play came on at all, if we persisted in the intention. I said that would give us a fine case. Yeats said he intended to do *Oedipus*, that this also was a censored play, though so unobjectionable to religious minds that it had been performed in the Catholic University of Notre Dame, and that we should be prevented if we announced it now. He replied, "Leave that till the time comes and you needn't draw our attention to it." We said the *Irish Times* might again draw his attention to it. He proposed our having a private performance only. I said, "I had a letter from Mr. Shaw objecting to that course." He moaned, and said, "It is very hard on us. Can you suggest no way out of it?" We answered, "None, except our being left alone." "Oh, Lady Gregory," he said, "appeal to your own commonsense." When I mentioned Shaw's letter, he said, "All Shaw wants is to use the Lord Lieutenant as a whip to lay upon the Censor." Yeats said, "Shaw would use him in that way whatever happens." "I know he will," said the Official. At last he asked if we would get Mr. Shaw to take out the passages he had already offered to take out for the Censor. We agreed to ask him to do this, as we felt the Castle was beaten, as the play even then would still be the one forbidden in England. . . .

Mr. Shaw telegraphed his answer to the demand for cuts:

"The *Nation* article gives particulars of cuts demanded, which I refused as they would have destroyed the religious significance of the play. The line about moral relations is dispensable as they are mentioned in several other places; so it can be cut if the Castle is silly enough to object to such relations being called immoral, but I will cut nothing else. It is an insult to the Lord Lieutenant to ignore him and refer me to the requirements of a subordinate English Official. I will be no party to such indelicacy. Please say I said so if necessary."

August 14. Having received the telegram from Shaw and the *Nation* article, we went to the Castle to see the Official, but only found his secretary, who proposed our going to see him at his house as he has gout and rheumatism and couldn't come to see us. We drove to his house. He proposed our giving a private performance, and we again told him Shaw had forbidden that. I read him the telegram refusing cuts, but he seemed to have forgotten that he had asked for cuts, and repeated his appeal to spare the Lord Lieutenant. . . . He asked if we could make no concession. We said "no," but that if they decided to take away our Patent, we should put off the production till the beginning of our season, end of September, and produce it with *Oedipus*; then they would have to suppress both together. He brightened up and said if we could put it off things would be much easier as the Commission would not be sitting then or the Public be so much interested in the question. I said, "Of course we should have to announce at once that it was in consequence of the threatened action of the Castle we had postponed it." "Oh, you don't really mean that! You would let all the bulls loose. It would be much better not to say anything at all, or say the rehearsals took longer than you expected." "The public announcement will be more to our advantage." "Oh, that is dreadful!" I said, "We did not give in one quarter of an inch to Nationalist Ireland at the *Playboy* time, and we certainly cannot give in one quarter of an inch to the Castle.... We are determined to produce the play. We cannot accept the Censor's decision as applying to Ireland and you must make up your mind what course to take, but we ask to be let know as soon as possible because if we are to be suppressed we must find places for our players, who will be thrown out of work." He threw up his hands and exclaimed, "Oh, my dear lady, but do not speak of such a thing as possible!" "Why?" I asked, "what else have you been threatening all the time?" . . .

On August 15th I had written to the Castle:

"I am obliged to go home tomorrow, so if you have any news for us, will you very kindly let us have it at Coole. We are as you know arranging to produce *Blanco* on Wednesday 25th, as advertised and booked for, unless you serve us with a 'threatening notice,' in which case we shall probably postpone it till September 30th and produce it with the already promised *Oedipus*." . . .

I received the following answer:

"I am sorry you have been obliged to return to Galway. His Excellency, who arrived this morning, regrets that he has missed the opportunity of seeing you and desires me to say that, if you wished an interview with him on Thursday, he would be glad to receive you at the Viceregal Lodge."

We arrived at 2.15 and were met by the Official's secretary who asked us to go to the Viceregal Lodge. Arrived there, another secretary came and asked me to go and see the Lord Lieutenant alone, saying Mr. Yeats could go in later. Alas, I must be discreet and that conversation with the King's representative must not be given to the world, at least by me.... At last he asked us to go on to the Castle and see again a very experienced Official.

We found the Official rather in a temper. He had been trying to hear Lord Aberdeen's account of the interview through the telephone and could not. ... He said Mr. Yeats had stated in the Patent Enquiry, the Abbey was for the production of romantic works. I quoted Parnell, "Who shall set bounds to the march of a Nation?" We told him our Secretary had reported "Very heavy booking, first-class people, very many from the Castle."

As holder of the Patent, I took counsel's opinion on certain legal points, of which the most vital was this:

"Should counsel be of opinion that the Crown will serve notice requiring the play to be discontinued, then counsel will please say what penalty he thinks querist would expose herself to by disregarding the notice of the Crown and continuing the representation?"

The answer to this question was: "If the Theatre ceases to be licensed, as pointed out above, and any performance for gain takes place there, the penalty under the 26 Geo. III, cap. 57, sec. (2) is £300 for each offence, to be recovered in a 'qui tam' action; one half of the £300 going to the Rotunda Hospital, the other half to the informer who sues."

Mr. Yeats and I were just going to a rehearsal at the Abbey on the evening of August 21st when we received a letter from the Castle, telling us that a formal legal document forbidding the performance of the play would reach us immediately. The matter had now become a very grave one. We knew that we should, if we went on and this threat were carried out, lose not only the Patent but that the few hundred pounds that we had been able to save and with which we could have supported our players until they found other work, would be forfeited. This thought made us waver, and very sadly we agreed that we must give up the fight. We did not say a word of this at the Abbey but went on rehearsing. When we left the Theatre and were walking through the lamp-lighted streets, we found that during those two or three hours our minds had come to the same decision, that we have given our word, that at all risks we must keep it, or it would never be trusted again; that we must in no case go back, but must go on at any cost.

We wrote a statement in which we told of the pressure put upon us and the objections made. . . .

"One thing," we ended by saying, "is plain enough, an issue that swallows up all else and makes the merit of Mr. Shaw's play a secondary thing. If our Patent is in danger, it is because the decisions of the English Censor are being brought into Ireland, and because the Lord Lieutenant is about to revive, on what we consider a frivolous pretext, a right not exercised for a hundred and fifty years to forbid, at the Lord Chamberlain's pleasure, any play produced in any Dublin theatre, all these theatres holding their Patents from him.

"We are not concerned with the question of the English Censorship now being fought out in London, but we are very certain that the conditions o the two countries are different, and that we must not, by accepting the English Censor's ruling, give away anything of the liberty of the Irish Theatre of the future. Neither can we accept without protest the revival of the Lord Lieutenant's claim, at the bidding of the Censor or otherwise. The Lord Lieutenant is definitely a political personage, holding office from the party in power, and what would sooner or later grow into a political Censorship cannot be lightly accepted."

Having sent this out for publication, we went on with our rehearsals. . . . We put on *Blanco* on the date announced, the 25th of August. We were anxious to the last, for counsel were of the opinion that if we were stopped, it would be on the clause in the Patent against "any representation which should be deemed or construed immoral," and that if Archbishop Walsh, or Archbishop Peacocke or especially the Head of the Presbyterian Assembly, should say anything which might be "deemed and construed" to condemn the play, the threats made would be carried out. There were fears of a riot also, for newspapers and their posters had kept up the excitement, and there was an immense audience. It was a pity we had not thought in time of putting up our prices. Guineas were offered even for standing-room in the wings.

The play began, and till the end it was received in perfect silence. Perhaps the audience were waiting for the wicked bits to begin. Then, at the end, there was a tremendous burst of cheering, and we knew we had won. Some stranger outside asked what was going on in the Theatre. "They are defying

ARTHUR SINCLAIR

FRED O'DONOVAN

UDOLPHUS WRIGHT

MRS. MARTIN

the Lord Lieutenant," was the answer; and when the crowd heard the cheering they took it up and it went far out through the streets.

Mr. Shaw commented on all this later when the play was published:

> It only remains to say that public performances of *The Shewing-up of Blanco Posnet* are still prohibited by the Lord Chamberlain. An attempt was made to prevent even its performance in Ireland by some indiscreet Castle officials in the absence of the Lord Lieutenant. This attempt gave extraordinary publicity to the production of the play; and every possible effort was made to persuade the Irish public that the performance would be an outrage to their religion, and to provoke a repetition of the rioting that attended the first performance of Synge's *Playboy of the Western World* before the most sensitive and, on provocation, the most turbulent audience in the kingdom. The Directors of the Irish National Theatre, Lady Gregory and Mr. William Butler Yeats, rose to the occasion with inspiriting courage. I am a conciliatory person, and was willing, as I always am, to make every concession in return for having my own way. But Lady Gregory and Mr. Yeats not only would not yield an inch, but insisted, within the due limits of gallant warfare, on taking the field with every circumstance of defiance, and winning the battle with every trophy of victory. Their triumph was as complete as they could have desired.

Synge's name does not appear in this controversy. He had died a few months previously, on 24th March 1909, after a long illness, leaving a three-act play, *Deirdre of the Sorrows*, not quite completed. Though one of the outstanding dramatists of the Abbey, and a Director since its inception, he was not a "man of the theatre." On one occasion he went with the Company to Scotland as travelling manager, but he hated the work and never did such a thing again. He concerned himself deeply with the nature of the plays presented, he hated the realistic drama, the drama of Ibsen and Zola "dealing with the reality of life in joyless and pallid words. On the stage one must have reality, and one must have joy; and that is why the intellectual modern drama has failed, and people have grown sick of the false joy of the musical comedy, that has been given them in place of the rich joy found only in what is superb and wild in reality. In a good play every speech should be as fully flavoured as a nut or an apple."

These words were written in his introduction to *The Playboy* and he seemed to foresee what was coming. Perhaps it was as well that he did not live to see the work of the "Cork realists" and their like. His untimely death, he was only thirty-eight, marked the death of a genius.

As appendices to this Chapter I add three reminiscences by people who have been for many years faithful servants of the Theatre. First, Mrs. Martin, who superintended the cleaning of the Theatre and was a close friend to Lady Gregory. Once, indeed, Lady Gregory complained that one of her friends in the stalls had been bothered by a flea, but Mrs. Martin indignantly replied, "It must have hopped in from the pit." In those long-ago days there was always, in the middle of the performance, in the green-room, a big black teapot, and lashings of bread and butter, and Mrs. Martin poured the tea. It was no party, just for the players, yet sometimes a distinguished visitor would be allowed in. War came, and those little happy parties ceased. Mrs. Martin was a real friend, as always the early workers were friends, as Barney was—the best prompter we ever had, though he once threw down the script of *A Minute's Wait*—the play was shamelessly gagged—saying, "Only the National Library could prompt this." And there are still Mick Judge and Frank Ellis, and I have let some of these friends speak for themselves, hardly altering a word of their reminiscences. Seaghan Barlow had been with the Theatre—well, he will tell you how long. He has been actor, a very good Red Jack Smith in *Spreading the News*, but it is in all other ways that he has shown his genius for the stage. He knows everything in scene-making and prop-making, but, sullen over his cocoa and his Greek, he states he can do nothing. An hour later, everything is done to perfection.

Udolphus Wright has been with the Theatre for almost as many years as Seaghan Barlow and Mrs. Martin. He acted very often in the earliest productions, he knows our Theatre through and through, since he first appeared as a mere helper in Camden Street, then he followed the little Company to Molesworth Hall, then to the Abbey Theatre, and today, February 1950, I have seen Seaghan Barlow and Dossie Wright directing how our new piano should be placed. This is only forty-five years after their first appearance. Mrs. Martin should have been there to clean up, after the boys had made the mess.

Mrs. Martin.

My first engagement for Abbey Theatre was in October 1904, as dressmaker and also to sew canvas for painting the scenery.

I did a lot of that sort of work until the end of December, when I had a letter from Mr. Fay, to be interviewed. I went. Mr. Fay engaged me on a month's trial as caretaker. He explained to me my duties. I and my daughter Rosamund, then only 14 years old, prepared the Theatre for the first performance on 27th December 1904. Cramer Woods did all the booking. Part of my duty was to mind stage-door, take in parcels, etc.

One cold morning, an old lady called and asked if Mr. Fay was in. I said "He will be in at 1.30." I did not admit her. She looked very unusual to my mind. When Mr. Fay arrived he inquired "Has Lady Gregory called." I said not. Then about 6 o'clock all the artists began to come for rehearsal. Another ring at the door. I opened it. To my great surprise it was the same old lady. She went upstairs to where Mr. Fay and all the artists were having tea before starting rehearsal, but only six nights later this old lady came to see the first performance. She was dressed in all her grandeur of satin tea-jacket, her pearl necklace, a gift from Sir Hugh Lane, worth some hundreds of pounds, and her costly diamond rings, and yet so humble; I was taken back a step. This lady was our great benefactor. She gave all her brains and money to bring the Theatre to perfection. Then we had another great lady, Miss Horniman. She was lessee of the Theatre and spared no money to have the Theatre handsomely fitted out. She would come over from London to be present at nearly every first performance. She would also attend the reception given by Lady Gregory after the week's performances. She would smoke a cigar and enjoy a glass of claret-cup made by Lady Gregory's own hands. Miss Horniman subsidised the Theatre for six years, but she withdrew her interest in four years and sold it to Mr. W. B. Yeats and Lady Gregory. They were the only directors at that time.

Then there was room for another director, and Mr. J. M. Synge was made a director, that was three in all. Mr. J. M. Synge was also a writer. He was the author of *The Playboy of the Western World*. He was the author of many other plays.

We had for our first manager Mr. W. G. Fay, and his brother Frank, two very great geniuses. W. G. was a clever comedian, he also produced all the plays, painted the scenery. There was never a more hard-working man, he gave all his time night and day for the Theatre. He was very generous and kind to everyone; although small in stature he was great in character. His brother Mr. Frank Fay would come straight from his office-work and would type the scripts and rehearse, and would spend all his days off teaching elocution and Lady Gregory would ask me "what does Mr. Fay have for dinner?" He would just have a cup of cocoa and a sandwich.

After about six years those two brothers decided to leave the Theatre, and a very great shock to a good many, as they were very popular and the Theatre would never have been in existence only for them; it was a very sad parting.

The next manager Mr. Vaughan, a very nice gentleman. He was very keen on the laundry bills, he would query other bills and would use his axe on the green-room bills, he failed to pay all the bills. He could not make ends meet; however his stay was brief. Next manager Mr. Wilson, a Scottish man, a very generous and good fellow, he produced many plays. Was the author of one play entitled *The Orangeman*. He did not remain long in office. Next manager Mr. St. John Ervine, he did his best, but the Theatre at this time was suffering from a severe criticism from Sinn Fein, they were down on the Theatre and the houses were bad, and the Company went on tour to England and then he retired.

The next manager Mr. Fred O'Donovan, he was one of our best actors; he produced plays, also acted and managed the Theatre. A very good man indeed, he also left and went to England.

Another manager Mr. Nugent Monk. I also thought him outside of the Abbey style of production, more like a ballet or pantomime manager.

Next manager Mr. August Keogh. He was responsible for the production of Mr. G. B. Shaw's plays and put the Theatre going splendidly, as we were after being almost closed down previously. He had two brothers, Leo and Charles, they looked after the front of the house, but his stay was also short.

Next Mr. J. M. Dolan, he was an acting manager. He also taught elocution and produced plays and did very well; a very good gentleman indeed.

Two other artists, they were Maire and Annie Walker. Mr. Yeats called Maire the Virgin actress. He said she possessed Virginal Beauty and Charm. There also was Miss Maureen Delany, Miss Eileen Crowe and Mr. F. J. McCormack, and Miss May Craig, Mr. Walter Starkie and Miss Esposito, and many other gifted actresses which are too numerous to mention.

I remember Mr. Lennox Robinson when he came to the Theatre first, a very tall, kind and peaceful gentleman. Amongst the staff and behind the scenes he was called the Peacemaker. At the parties in the Theatre he would just partake of a little claret-cup. I remember his first play, I think, *The Cross Roads*. I never could forget how thrilled I was at the outstanding performance of Miss Sara Allgood, Mr. Arthur Sinclair and Mr. Fred O'Donovan. Mr. Robinson was twice manager, also producer. He became director after he became manager. He always seemed to get the best from the artist, owing to the gentle easy way of explaining what he required. I little thought at that time he would become my great benefactor in later years. Miss Allgood is now a film star. She was always very great in her parts. Mr. Arthur Sinclair also a clever actor, and would be sure to get the laughs over footlights. Mr. Fred O'Donovan a very great versatile actor, his art also extended to the movies. He had a great ambition to become a film star. In 1918 he played in a film called *Knock-na-Gow*. Another film he also played in, it was called *Rafferty's Rise*. Mr. J. M. Kerrigan played with him in *Rafferty's Rise*, he too had a very great ambition to see himself acting on a screen. They all belonged to the Abbey's happy family. Miss O'Neill another clever girl; apart from her successful stage career she had a fancy for cats. I called her the Cat-Fancier; she had a cat called Black Mike who would absent herself occasionally, and on looking for her we would find her in the hotel window opposite the Theatre, fast asleep.

Mr. J. M. Dolan also acting manager and producer. He also did very well. A reserved kind of gentleman, he would play the part of a priest excellently, he also could be a covey or a lawyer.

Apart from all the great work the Theatre done, there was a good deal of Romances behind the scenes. I could count more than the fingers of my two hands, the lovers who met their future partner in the Theatre, from the directors, managers, artists, even down to the Theatre attendants. I hold many secrets behind the scenes. I won't mention names just now.

Amongst those who hired the Theatre were our Great Leaders of Easter Week 1916. Mr. P. H. Pearse, he and his brother Willie, they produced several plays. I often helped Mrs. Pearse with the stage props.

Also Countess de Markievicz would hire, for her play *The Memory of the Dead*. Her husband, Count de Markievicz, wrote this play and had it copywritten at the Theatre and I waited in the box-office to take the sovereign, which was the Fee, for the copyright. Before the First World War, Count de Markievicz had to return to Russia, as he was a Russian Pole. There was a great send-off party given to him. It was held in the green-room. I remember how sad the Countess was on that night. I never saw him after, until the day of the Countess's funeral.

Seaghan Barlow.

In 1902 I was a member of a club that met in a hall at the back of Walker's newsagent's shop at No. 18 High Street. There I made the acquaintance of the Walkers, and through them I met W. G. Fay, whose Comedy Combination Co. was about this time giving their final performance of *His Lost Legs*, at the old Coffee Palace Hall, in Townsend Street. One night in the Walkers' house, conversation turned on the new dramatic movement and the need for an Irish Theatre. As I knew nothing about it I was merely a listener.

Soon after this, a meeting took place in the hall attached to Walker's shop, and at this meeting the National Dramatic Society was founded. As far as I can remember, the two Fays, Mr. Yeats, and Lady Gregory were present at this meeting. Later on, Frank Walker took me up to No. 34 Camden Street, where rehearsals, etc., were carried on. It was a ramshackle old hall, at the back of a butcher's shop, and you had to dodge past the carcase of a dead sheep to get in through the hall door. I saw Mr. W. G. Fay, Maire Nic Shiubhlaigh, and some others, there.

I went to St. Teresa's Hall, Clarendon Street, to see the first production of *Deirdre* by AE, and *Cathleen ni Houlihan* by W. B. Yeats.

Later on, at supper in the Walkers' house, I met W. G. Fay, and talk came round to the chance of finding a suitable hall to play in. The old Mechanics' Theatre was mentioned, but it had been condemned and closed by the Corporation and the cost of putting it in repair would be too big. So the Molesworth Hall had to be hired until Miss Horniman appeared.

I was often in the Walkers' house at this time, and saw a good deal of the work that was done behind the scenes by Mrs. Walker, who, assisted by Mrs. Martin, made most of the costumes used at that time; they were nearly all made of hessian, as that was the cheapest and most serviceable material for costumes such as were used in *The Hour-Glass, The Shadowy Waters*, etc. In some cases, indeed, hessian was even used for costumes in peasant plays.

The names of Yeats, Lady Gregory and Synge were little known to the general public at that time, and the receipts at the Molesworth Hall were scarcely enough to cover the expense of hiring the hall and carting the scenery, etc., back and forward. For this reason, the utmost economy was necessary in the production of plays. Scenery, costumes, properties, etc., had to be provided at the lowest possible cost, and this condition remained for a long time even after the Abbey Theatre had opened, as Miss Horniman paid only the lighting expenses.

About a month or so before the Theatre was due to open, I went down to what had been the Mechanics' Theatre (I think it was a Saturday afternoon). The builders' men had knocked off work, but I found my way in somehow, and found W. G. Fay and Fred Bryers (the scenic artist) working on the stage, painting scenery that had been made for the opening. As I volunteered to make myself useful, I was at once handed a brush, and left to paint a door while they went out to tea. Later on Fay told me about other things that needed doing. There were a number of large shields and spears to be made for *On Baile's Strand*, as well as a couple of benches, etc. So I began to turn up at the Theatre every evening after my day's work was over, to put in another few hours' work, using mostly scrap timber left behind by the builders.

I had, of course, no knowledge of stage-craft at all at this time, and it was Willie Fay who first taught me, but I soon picked it up, and in fact I was soon able to suggest improved methods of doing certain things.

The shields had to be made of papier-mâché, about which I knew nothing, but Mr. Fay showed me how to make moulds according to his designs, and, when I had the moulds made, to fill them in with the paper. This was a longish job, owing to the numbers of layers of paper I had to fill in, and they took a long time to dry when filled, but we got them all done in time.

In the first twelve months or so the Abbey Company only played for seven nights at the beginning of each month, beginning on Saturday night and running to the following Saturday night, the week always ending with a stage party, the refreshments provided being tea, claret-cup, Gort cake and sandwiches. On one occasion I was pressed into service as cook. Lady Gregory came to me with a basket of eggs and asked me to boil them hard. I didn't know how long one had to boil eggs to make them hard, but to make sure I boiled them for about ten minutes, and when sliced they were hard enough. Another job I got was slicing lemons into a large jug to make claret-cup. These parties were very enjoyable affairs and the Gort cake was great stuff, provided you were careful about the raisin stones. Lady Gregory never forgot to show appreciation of any effort, even when it was not successful. In fact, she was, at times, so lavish in praise that one was inclined to suspect her sincerity.

In the early days of the Theatre there were no rooms beyond the stage on the Custom House side, and all work had to be done either on or underneath the stage. The builders had put in a narrow wooden bridge across the back of the stage to facilitate painting of cloths, but this bridge had been put so high that one could not paint more than the upper six feet of backcloth from it, and the lower half had to be painted on the stage, rolling up the cloth to reach the centre. Willie Fay had asked me if I could lower this bridge so that about two-thirds of the cloth could be done from it, and I had done so, and while I was finishing the job at the fly-rail, he happened to be standing right underneath when I accidentally dropped a hammer and the handle struck him a glancing blow on the head (had it struck him fairly he would have been seriously injured), but he wasn't much hurt, and merely asked if I was trying to kill him!

Some time later, however, he got his own back by sending me down to take the cap off one of the stage plugs, and then pressing his fingers down on the contacts while I was below, which gave me a severe shock.

After the Fays left, Mr. Yeats was for a while quite despondent about the future of the Theatre, and actually discussed with his sister the possibility of finding a job for me. Lady Gregory, however, was more optimistic, and after some discussion it was arranged to carry on, with Sara Allgood as coach and producer, under the direction of Lady Gregory and Yeats and (in the case of his own plays) J. M. Synge, Joseph O'Rourke stage manager, and myself as carpenter and scene-painter. Robert Gregory had gone to Paris for his art studies, and the directors had decided to produce *The Well of the Saints* in the autumn with a proper setting; it had already been done, but only with such scenery as we could at the time afford. Mr. Synge went to London to get designs by Mr. Ricketts. When he returned they were handed over to me, and I felt a bit nervous when I saw what I was expected to do. But Mr. Ricketts had sent very clear and definite instructions about the painting and I had plenty of time, so I did my best, and when the sets were finished Lady Gregory was so pleased with them that she wrote to Robert in Paris about them, and on his return some months later the first thing he did was to call at the Abbey to see the scenery I had painted. She also wrote to tell the Fays in America about it.

After this I was trusted to carry out designs by all sorts of people, and was left to my own devices. Robert Gregory had designed settings for his mother's play *The Image*, and when I had the scenery made and ready for painting he came up to Dublin to do it, I assisting him; when we were about half-way through the work, it happened that Tramore races were on, and when he came in that day he wasn't dressed for work. He said, "Seaghan, you can do stones better than me, I'm going to Tramore races!" and off he went. But next day (or the day after) Lady Gregory came up to the paint-room, as I was working on the wings which showed the tops of wind-swept trees. After watching me for a minute or so, she said, "Give me the brush, Seaghan." I handed her the brush I was using and she then showed me how the strokes I had been making should be drawn upwards, and not downwards, as I had been making them. She asked me, had I taken any drawing lessons, and I told her I hadn't, only the ordinary school sort. She said, "You ought to." But my wages at the time didn't run to drawing lessons, so I had to do without. Frank Fay and I had many arguments as to who should have the stage, as he would come along with a pupil to coach when I would be engaged in rather noisy work, and I had no other place to work. The result was usually a hot argument. On one occasion, after one of these, Willie Fay said to me, "Tell him you'll sack him, Seaghan, if he's not careful!"

We could not afford at that time to spend much on scenery, and many of our settings consisted of curtains made of hessian and dyed in the Theatre. This dyeing was a messy job when dealing with large quantities of hessian. I remember we got a large galvanised bath and dipped the hessian in it, and from that into another full of water, then draining each piece as best we could, and finally hanging them up to dry. We had clothes-lines all over the place; but it worked.

The builders had put in two great beams, one each side of the stage, stretching from back to front, and carrying wing grooves. These beams prevented us from using cloths wider than 21 feet, and I had suggested their removal, and was engaged on the job the morning Miss Violet Darragh arrived.

I was sitting astride the beam, removing bolts and dropping them on the stage as I did so, but taking care, of course, that they would not strike anyone passing below. Just as I dropped one, however, Miss Darragh passed underneath, and looking up at me she said, "Oh, I suppose *I* don't matter!" Mr. Yeats, coming fast after her, called up to me, "Seaghan, save them for the orchestra!"

On one occasion I was working in the paint-room, when Lady Gregory came in to speak to me about something. I had been smoking my pipe, and I at once left it down on the table to answer her, but she said, "Go on smoking your pipe, Seaghan, I like to see a man smoking."

Shortly after this she was returning to Gort for the Christmas, and before she left she came into the Theatre and handed me a large bar of tobacco, saying, "There's a smoke for Christmas, Seaghan," and told me that if it wasn't what I liked, I could change it for my favourite brand at the shop.

It had been arranged that the Company should give a performance at Dundalk Town Hall on St. Patrick's Night, 1906. So having loaded up the scenery, baggage, etc., at Amiens Street Station the evening before, I left by the 6.30 train that morning and got to Dundalk at 8.20. The first thing I had to do was to go and get breakfast; and then I went off to find a carter to convey the scenery from the station to the hall. Having found the carter I had to stop with him till he went to fetch a load of stones from the quarry and deliver them, after that he would be mine. This wasted an hour or more of my time, so that it was near midday before I eventually got the scenery and effects to the hall, and, with no help but that of the carter, managed to get it all inside.

I tried to find some idle labourer who wanted a day's work, but nobody wanted to work on St. Patrick's Day. So I had to set to by myself, fitting up the scenery; I had got a backcloth and borders hung up, but when it came to flying the cottage ceiling, I was unable to pull it up by myself, I was too tired, so as it was past one o'clock I knocked off for lunch.

After lunch and a rest, I went back to the hall and pulled up the ceiling, and I had the stage set for *Cathleen ni Houlihan* when the company arrived about 3 o'clock.

We played *Cathleen* and *The Eloquent Dempsey*, and the scene-changing, etc., was all done by W. G. Fay, Ambrose Power, Dossie Wright and myself.

The crowd outside the window in *The Eloquent Dempsey* consisted of Ambrose Power and me, but we had a fairly good audience and both plays went very well.

After the show I had to get all the stuff out again and back to the station, but this time I had the help of Ambrose Power and one or two others; but when I got to the station I found it in darkness, and nobody but an old night man, who, instead of helping to load the truck, grumbled and abused me for dragging a man out to work on St. Patrick's Day.

Miss Horniman had arranged a week's visit to England to take in three cities, Manchester, Liverpool and Leeds. We gave two performances at each place. We carried no scenery and only the essential props and costumes, playing plays like *Cathleen*, *The Building Fund*, *Spreading the News*, and *The Shadow of the Glen*. Arthur Darley came with us and played during the intervals. We were put up in hotels, and after the show each night we used to sit up till about 2 a.m. in the coffee-room listening to Mr. Darley's stories and violin-playing. Later on, we went on tour in England for five weeks, under the management of Mr. Waring.

We opened at Her Majesty's Theatre at Cardiff in Wales, and had a moderately good week; when we were leaving the theatre after the matinee on the Saturday, there was a large crowd of young women students waiting outside the stage door to get autographs; that was the first, and almost the only time anyone has asked for mine, but I wrote it in Irish just because I was in Wales. From Cardiff we jumped to Glasgow, leaving Cardiff at 11.45 Saturday night. We were travelling all Saturday night and most of Sunday, getting into Glasgow about 3.45 Sunday afternoon, thoroughly tired and fed up with train travel. We played at the King's Theatre, Glasgow, but the business was bad. An unfortunate incident occurred at the end of our Glasgow week. Arthur Darley and Dossie Wright shared one dressing-room, and, on going to the room to change after the show, they found that their pockets had been picked; two sovereigns had been taken from Mr. Darley's waistcoat pocket, and a valuable gold watch from Mr. Wright's. The management and the police were notified, but we had to leave Glasgow on the Sunday morning and they heard no more about their property. It was a serious loss to Mr. Wright, particularly, for apart from being gold the watch had a sentimental value.

Our next stop on this tour was Newcastle-on-Tyne, and here also, apart from the Irish people, our audiences were small. Another big jump to Edinburgh, where we played at the Lyceum Theatre, and had at any rate intelligent audiences, even if they were not numerous.

At Edinburgh we came up against an instance of stupidity in the case of a fireman.

In all Howard and Wyndham's theatres there were regulations prohibiting the use of naked lights on the stage, and we always had to get special permission to use candles in *The Shadow of the Glen*. In Edinburgh we were only allowed to use the one in the window, and the fireman was told to stand by; and so he did, complete with bucket of water, wet blanket on his arm, sponge filled with water, brass helmet and all. He stood at the back behind the cottage window, stooping down every now and again all throughout the play to look in through the window, which was supposed to be looking out on the Wicklow Hills!

From Edinburgh we went to Aberdeen, and had another week of poor houses.

After Aberdeen, Hull, where we had a good many Irish in the audience, but the houses were not much bigger, and then back to the Abbey again. This was our first actual tour, and it must have been arranged for publicity, for it could scarcely have paid even if the houses were much better than they were, owing to the long railway jumps and the amount spent on billing. Lady Gregory, Mr. Yeats, and Mr. Synge accompanied us on this tour.

Joe O'Rourke and I took the scenery back to the Abbey, and on the following Tuesday we loaded up a small fit-up frame and sets of small scenery that had been made for playing in small halls, and went to Longford, where we were to open on Wednesday night in St. Joseph's Hall.

St. Joseph's was a small hall, with a stage so small that we could barely manage to fix up the fit-up frame, and the contrast between it and the big theatres we had been playing in England made it seem even smaller.

At one side of the stage was a small door leading to the auditorium and from this a narrow stair led up to the stage. When we were playing *Riders to the Sea*, I had to stand on the stairs, balancing the stretcher on the handrail, while the dead man got on to it, then the first bearer took his place in front, and, as he entered the cottage, I would guide the stretcher along the handrail into the hands of the second man.

There was some kind of exhibition in Galway, and Lady Gregory made arrangements for the Company to give performances there. We carried nothing but costumes and small props.

When we got to Galway we found that the "theatre" where we were to play was an old galvanised iron shed close to the station. It had been fitted with wooden benches for the audience to sit on, and a small stage of planks on barrels. We had no scenery, but the walls of the stage were covered with hessian. We played short pieces like *Cathleen, The Pot of Broth* and *Spreading the News*, and, as there was no provision for dressing in the hall, we had to dress and make up in an empty house on the other side of the road.

Joe O'Rourke and I had come across made up for *Spreading the News*, and we knocked at the side door of the shed to get in. After knocking for a while Lady Gregory opened the door a few inches and said, "Go away, my good man, go round to the other door." Then we explained who we were, and recognising our accents she let us in. In the costumes we had on she had mistaken us for two of the "locals."

At the show of *Spreading the News* a funny thing happened. Lady Gregory had invited two young men, weavers from Aran, who had no English and had never seen a play, to the show, and somebody explained the plays to them, but when it came to the part in *Spreading the News* where W. G. Fay and I were arrested and handcuffed, they had to be restrained from leaving their seats and coming on to the stage to rescue us!

The houses were so poor at many of the earlier performances in the Abbey that on one occasion Mr. Yeats invited those in the pit and balcony to come together in the stalls, for the sake of comfort and sociability.

On another occasion he invited any member of the audience who cared for music during the interval to play the piano, as we had no orchestra.

We had arranged to play in the Town Hall, Waterford, but on arriving there we found there was no means of getting the scenery into the hall, except by carrying it in through the front doors and over the seats, and lifting it up on to the stage. The front doors, however, were too small to enable us to get in the houses we used for Mr. Quirke and Mrs. Delane in *Hyacinth Halvey*, and the only place we could leave them was in the fire station close by.

But we had to have a substitute, as we were doing the play that night. We managed a makeshift for Quirke's house, but Mrs. Delane's house had to have an upper window, and we were at a loss, until the caretaker told us there was an old piece that had once been used in the balcony-scene in *Romeo and Juliet*. We got it out, dusted it, and set it up, although it was very old and shaky, and that night Mrs. Delane appeared on Juliet's balcony; I don't think Lady Gregory was there.

When Lady Gregory's *Kincora* was first produced, an Irish piper was engaged to march back and forward round the balcony in costume, playing Irish airs.

The first orchestra was a trio, consisting of George Hillis, piano, Henry McCarthy, violinist, and a flute player whose name I don't remember.

Mr. Yeats had a habit of interrupting actors in the middle of a speech, which was rather trying. On one occasion, after several of these interruptions, Frank Fay lost his temper and asked him how he expected him to deliver his line properly, when he didn't know what he was talking about!

On another occasion, when Mr. Wright had been making experiments with an arc-lamp, to get an effect Mr. Yeats wanted, and had tried one medium after another in vain, suddenly Mr. Yeats called up from the stalls, "That's it, Wright, that's it; what is that?" "Oh, it's the bloody gelatine gone on fire!" said Dossie.

At another rehearsal, he wanted the shadow of a cat thrown on to a pillar at the side of the stage. We had cut cardboard silhouettes and tried holding them in various positions in front of the lamp, but without success, then Dossie tried a new adjustment of the lamp itself. As he stood in front of the lamp Mr. Yeats called up, "That's not bad, Wright." It was the back of Dossie's head!

All of us on the staff were very sorry when the Fays left, and on the night W. G. and his wife were leaving for England, I went down to the boat to say goodbye. Mrs. Martin was there also, and Jack Keegan; I cannot remember if Tommy Allgood was there.

Jack Keegan was the boy who used to look after the boiler, and do props, etc.; and in later years he became a very useful property-man. He was killed in France in 1916. Tommy Allgood is now in a Cistercian Monastery. While the Fays were still at the Abbey, I think about 1906, Mr. Yeats brought Mr. Ben Iden Payne to the Theatre, and he remained for about six months, but he was not popular with the players. While Mr. Payne was at the Abbey, he produced Maeterlinck's *Interior*, and, I think, Yeats's *Shadowy Waters*.

About the beginning of 1909, Mr. Norreys Connell (Conal O'Riordan) came to the Abbey as manager and producer, and he was one of the most courteous and considerate men I have ever met, always cheerful, and painstaking at rehearsals, polite to everyone; although he could be sarcastic when necessary.

He remained at the Abbey for about eight months, during which time he produced two of his own plays, *An Imaginary Conversation* and *Time*. While we were on a visit to Cork, he wrote a letter of advice to the players, to be read by Mr. Henderson, who was the secretary at that time, and the reading was very unfavourably received by the members of the Company. Soon after Mr. Norreys Connell left the Abbey.

Mr. Wright.

Soon after I became articled to a firm of electrical engineers, I was told one day after knocking about the firm's shop to go to a large building at 8 o'clock in the morning and there I would meet the foreman. The building happened to be the Eye and Ear Hospital, Adelaide Road. I arrived in due course at the appointed hour and asked where I would find the Electrical Foreman. A 60 feet perpendicular ladder was pointed out to me, and I was told if I went up that I would find him on the top floor, which I managed to do with fear and trembling. I then found the foreman who happened to be W. G. Fay. From the start we got on very well together, during the continuance of that particular contract and many others. It wasn't long before we got talking of other things besides electrical work, and—after he had listened to some of my stories of stealing out at night down the country (in the small town of Carrick-on-Suir) to see dramatic shows, the stage being the side of a caravan let down and the auditorium a canvas tent—he asked me would I like to come round and see a rehearsal of some plays which were about to be presented at the Molesworth Hall. Of course I jumped at the opportunity. The rehearsal room in those days was the Camden Hall. There I met the members of the Company.

Strange to say, I just can't remember what the first rehearsal I saw was—I think it was Lady Gregory's *Twenty-Five*. All the people were very nice to me, and for the first production in the Molesworth Hall I just made myself generally useful on the stage. During these rehearsals there were a great many people came in and sat round the gas stove until long after I had to leave to get home. They were AE, the Rt. Hon. W. F. Bailey—of course W. B. Yeats, George Moore, Edward Martyn, and James Joyce on a few occasions. I then remember W. G. telling me that I was to be a pupil in *The King's Threshold*, and that I had been elected a member of the Irish National Literary Society unanimously. Soon after that we were introduced to a tall stately lady, whom I always thought rather austere, and that was Miss A. E. F. Horniman. She had come over in connection with the dressing of *The King's Threshold*, and immediately took our measurements for the costumes, a few of which are still to be found in our wardrobe. It was not very long after this that we were told Miss Horniman was going to build us a Theatre, and from then on till the Abbey was opened, we saw quite a great deal of her. Though she was, as I said, not very approachable to the members of the Company—at least so it seemed to me

—I only saw her lose her temper once during a rehearsal of one of Yeats's plays, for which she had also made the costumes; which did not seem to please Mr. Yeats too well, and during the rehearsal his mind seemed to be wandering from the play, and in those days he always carried a black stick which at this time he was swinging to and fro, so much that it got on Miss Horniman's nerves—so much that she exclaimed, "For goodness sake, Willie! stop swinging that stick, or leave the rehearsal!"

Casts of First Productions, 1905-1908

4th February 1905
THE WELL OF THE SAINTS

A Play in Three Acts by J. M. Synge

Martin Doul, a blind man	W. G. Fay
Mary Doul, his wife	Emma Vernon
Timmy, a smith	George Roberts
Molly Byrne	Sara Allgood
Bride	Maire Nic Shiubhlaigh
Mat Simon	P. MacShiubhlaigh
A Wandering Friar	F. J. Fay
Girls and Men	

Scenery by Pamela Coleman Smith and another

25th March 1905
KINCORA

A Play in Three Acts by Lady Gregory

Brian of the Tributes, King of Munster, afterwards High King	F. J. Fay
Murrough, his son	George Roberts
Malachi, High King of Ireland	A. Power
Gormleith, his wife, afterwards wife of Brian	Maire Nic Shiubhlaigh
Sitric, her son by Olaf of the Danes	P. MacShiubhlaigh
Maelmora, her brother, King of Leinster	Seamus O'Sullivan
Brian's servants:	
Brennain	Arthur Sinclair
Derrick	W. G. Fay
Rury, Malachi's servant	J. H. Dunne
Phelan, Maelmora's servant	U. Wright
Maire, Brennain's daughter	Maire Ni Gharbhaigh
Aoibhell, a woman of the Sidhe	Sara Allgood
Brodar	R. Nash
A Dane	U. Wright

Scenery and Costumes by Robert Gregory

25th April 1905
THE BUILDING FUND

A Comedy in Three Acts by William Boyle

Mrs. Grogan, a miserly old woman	Emma Vernon
Shan Grogan, her son, another miser	W. G. Fay
Sheila O'Dwyer, her granddaughter	Sara Allgood
Michael O'Callaghan, an elderly farmer	F. J. Fay
Dan MacSweeny, a young farmer	Arthur Sinclair

9th December 1905
THE WHITE COCKADE

A Comedy in Three Acts by Lady Gregory

Patrick Sarsfield, Earl of Lucan	F. J. Fay
King James II	Arthur Sinclair
Carter, Secretary to King James	J. H. Dunne
A Poor Lady	Maire Nic Shiubhlaigh
Matt Kelleher, an Inn-keeper at Duncannon	W. G. Fay
Mary Kelleher, his wife	Sara Allgood
Owen Kelleher, his son	P. MacShiubhlaigh
French Sailors:	Walter S. Magee and Edward Keegan
1st Williamite	A. Power
2nd Williamite	U. Wright
Williamite Captain	M. Butler

20th January 1906
THE ELOQUENT DEMPSEY

A Comedy in Three Acts by William Boyle

Jeremiah Dempsey, publican and grocer, County Councillor for Cloghermore	W. G. Fay
Mrs. Catherine Dempsey	Sara Allgood
Mary Kate, his daughter	Brigit O'Dempsey
Dr. Bunbury, J.P.	F. J. Fay
Captain McNamara, J.P.	Arthur Sinclair
Mike Flanagan, a working man	J. H. Dunne
Brian O'Neill, in love with Mary Kate	U. Wright

A HISTORY, 1899-1951

19th February 1906

HYACINTH HALVEY
A Comedy in One Act by Lady Gregory

Hyacinth Halvey	F. J. Fay
James Quirke	W. G. Fay
Fardy Farrell	Arthur Sinclair
Sergeant Carden	Walter Magee
Mrs. Delane	Sara Allgood
Miss Joyce	Brigit O'Dempsey

16th April 1906

THE DOCTOR IN SPITE OF HIMSELF
A Farce in Three Acts by Molière
Adapted by Lady Gregory

Sganarelle	W. G. Fay
Martha, his wife	Sara Allgood
Robert, his neighbour	Arthur Sinclair
Valere, servant of Geronte	A. Power
Luke, the same	U. Wright
Geronte, father of Lucy	F. J. Fay
Jacqueline, nurse at Geronte's and wife of Luke	Maire O'Neill
Lucy, daughter of Geronte	Brigit O'Dempsey
Leeane, Lucy's lover	Arthur Sinclair

20th October 1906

THE GAOL GATE
A Tragedy in One Act by Lady Gregory

Mary Cahel, an old woman	Sara Allgood
Mary Cuchin, her daughter-in-law	Maire O'Neill
The Gate-Keeper	F. J. Fay

20th October 1906

THE MINERAL WORKERS
A Play in Three Acts by William Boyle

Sir Thomas Musgrove	Arthur Sinclair
Mrs. Walton, his sister	Sara Allgood
Stephen J. O'Reilly	F. J. Fay
Dan Fogarty, a farmer	W. G. Fay
Ned Mulroy, a farmer	A. Power
Mary, his wife	Alice O'Sullivan
Patrick, his son	U. Wright
Kitty, his daughter	Maire O'Neill
Uncle Bartle	J. A. O'Rourke
Mr. Casey, P.L.G.	H. Young
Dick, an engine driver	J. Barlow

24th November 1906

DEIRDRE
A Play in Verse by W. B. Yeats

Concobar	J. M. Kerrigan
Fergus	Arthur Sinclair
Naisi	F. J. Fay
Messenger	U. Wright
Executioner	A. Power
First Musician	Sara Allgood
Second Musician	Maire O'Neill
Third Musician	Brigit O'Dempsey
Deirdre	Miss Darragh

Scenery by Robert Gregory

24th November 1906

THE CANAVANS
A Comedy in Three Acts by Lady Gregory

Peter Canavan, a miller	W. G. Fay
Antony Canavan, his brother	J. A. O'Rourke
Captain Headley, his cousin	Arthur Sinclair
Widow Greely	Brigit O'Dempsey
Widow Deeny	Maire O'Neill

26th January 1907

THE PLAYBOY OF THE WESTERN WORLD
A Comedy in Three Acts by J. M. Synge

Christopher Mahon	W. G. Fay
Old Mahon, his father, a squatter	A. Power
Michael James Flaherty (called "Michael James"), a Publican	Arthur Sinclair
Margaret Flaherty (called "Pegeen Mike"), his daughter	Maire O'Neill
Shawn Keogh, her second cousin, a young farmer	F. J. Fay
Small farmers:	
Philly O'Cullen	J. A. O'Rourke
Jimmy Farrell	J. M. Kerrigan
Widow Quin	Sara Allgood
Sara Tansey	Brigit O'Dempsey
Susan Brady	Alice O'Sullivan
Honor Blake	May Craig
Peasants	U. Wright, Harry Young

23rd February 1907
THE JACKDAW
A Comedy in One Act by Lady Gregory
Joseph Nestor	F. J. Fay
Michael Cooney	W. G. Fay
Mrs. Broderick	Sara Allgood
Tommy Nally	Arthur Sinclair
Sibby Fahy	Brigit O'Dempsey
Timothy Ward	J. M. Kerrigan

9th March 1907
THE RISING OF THE MOON
A Play in One Act by Lady Gregory
Ballad Singer	W. J. Fay
Policeman X	J. A. O'Rourke
Policeman B	J. M. Kerrigan
Policeman Z	Arthur Sinclair

(List as given in original programme)

1st April 1907
THE EYES OF THE BLIND
A Play in One Act by Miss W. M. Letts
Mrs. Doyne	Maire O'Neill
Theresa Doyne	Brigit O'Dempsey
Lawrence Shaughnessy	W. G. Fay
Blind Phelim, a beggar	F. J. Fay

3rd April 1907
THE POORHOUSE
A Comedy in One Act by Lady Gregory
and Dr. Douglas Hyde
Colum	W. G. Fay
Paudeen	Arthur Sinclair
The Matron	Maire O'Neill
A Country Woman	Brigit O'Dempsey

20th April 1907
FAND
A Play in Verse, in Two Acts,
by Wilfrid Scawen Blunt
Cuchulain	F. J. Fay
Conchubar	Arthur Sinclair
Laeg, Cuchulain's charioteer	J. M. Kerrigan
Friends to Cuchulain:	
Laeghaire	Ernest Vaughan
Lugaid	J. A. O'Rourke
Emer, Cuchulain's wife	Sara Allgood
Fand, a fairy wife to Manannan	Maire O'Neill
Eithne, a poetess, beloved of Cuchulain	Maire Ni Gharbhaigh
Attendants	Brigit O'Dempsey, Annie Allgood

The music to the songs was composed by Arthur Darley

3rd October 1907
THE COUNTRY DRESSMAKER
A Comedy in Three Acts by
George Fitzmaurice
Julia Shea, a country dressmaker	Sara Allgood
Norry Shea, her mother	Brigit O'Dempsey
Matt Dillane, their next-door neighbour	F. J. Fay
Min, his daughter	Maire O'Neill
Pats Connor, a returned American	J. M. Kerrigan
Edmund Normyle	J. A. O'Rourke
Michael Clohesy, a strong farmer	Arthur Sinclair
Maryanne, his wife	Maire O'Neill
Their daughters:	
Babe	Eileen O'Doherty
Ellie	Cathleen Mullamphy
Jack, their son	T. J. Fox
Luke Quilter, the man from the Mountains	W. G. Fay

31st October 1907
DERVORGILLA
A Tragedy in One Act by Lady Gregory
Dervorgilla, once Queen of Breffney	Sara Allgood
Flann, an old servant	F. J. Fay
Mona, his wife	Maire O'Neill
Owen	J. M. Kerrigan
Mamie	Brigit O'Dempsey
Other young men and girls: Arthur Sinclair, J. A. O'Rourke, Cathleen Mullamphy	
Wandering Songmaker or Jester	W. G. Fay

21st November 1907
THE UNICORN FROM THE STARS
A Play in Three Acts by W. B. Yeats
and Lady Gregory
Father John	Ernest Vaughan
Thomas Hearne, a coachbuilder	Arthur Sinclair
Andrew Hearne, brother of Thomas	J. A. O'Rourke
Martin Hearne, nephew of Thomas	F. J. Fay
Johnny Bacach, a beggar	W. G. Fay
Paudeen	J. M. Kerrigan
Biddy Lally	Maire O'Neill
Nanny	Brigit O'Dempsey

SEAGHAN BARLOW

SOUVENIR PROGRAMME

A HISTORY, 1899–1951

13th February 1908

THE MAN WHO MISSED THE TIDE

A Play in Three Acts by W. F. Casey

Dr. Gerald Quinn . . .	Arthur Sinclair
James Walsh	Fred O'Donovan
Martin Kelly	J. M. Kerrigan
Mrs. Gerald Quinn, Moira	Sara Allgood
Sheila Kennedy, her sister.	Maire O'Neill
A Housemaid . . .	Eileen O'Doherty
A Barmaid	Eileen O'Doherty

13th February 1908

THE PIPER

An Unended Argument in One Act by Norreys Connell

The Piper	Sara Allgood
Larry the Talker . . .	J. M. Kerrigan
Black Mike	Ambrose Power
Tim the Trimmer . .	J. A. O'Rourke
Pat Dennehy . . .	Sydney J. Morgan
Captain Talbot . . .	Arthur Sinclair
An English Ensign . .	U. Wright

Soldiers: Stuart Hamilton, T. J. Fox, Harry Young
Rebels: Fred O'Donovan, J. J. Seymour, D. Robinson, Harry O'Neill

19th March 1908

THE PIE-DISH

A Play by George Fitzmaurice

Leum Donoghue . . .	Arthur Sinclair
Daughters to Leum:	
Margaret	Sara Allgood
Johanna	Maire O'Neill
Sons to Margaret:	
Eugene	J. A. O'Rourke
Jack	Sydney Morgan
Father Troy. . . .	J. M. Kerrigan

19th March 1908

THE GOLDEN HELMET

A Heroic Farce by W. B. Yeats

Cuchulain	J. M. Kerrigan
Conal	Arthur Sinclair
Leagerie.	Fred O'Donovan
Laeg, Cuchulain's charioteer	Sydney Morgan
Emer, wife of Cuchulain .	Sara Allgood
Conal's wife	Maire O'Neill
Leagerie's wife . . .	Eileen O'Doherty
Red Man	Ambrose Power

Scullions and Horseboys and Blackmen: S. Hamilton, T. J. Fox, U. Wright, D. Robinson, T. O'Neill, J. A. O'Rourke, P. Kearney

4th April 1908

THE ROGUERIES OF SCAPIN

(Les Fourberies de Scapin) Lady Gregory's adaptation of Molière's Comedy in Three Acts

Argante, father of Octave and Zerbinette	Sydney Morgan
Geronte, father of Leandre and Hyacinthe . . .	J. A. O'Rourke
Octave, in love with Hyacinthe	Fred O'Donovan
Leandre, in love with Zerbinette	J. M. Kerrigan
Zerbinette	Maire O'Neill
Hyacinthe . . .	Maire Ni Gharbhaigh
Scapin, valet of Leandre .	Arthur Sinclair
Silvestre, valet of Octave .	Ambrose Power
Nerine, nurse of Hyacinthe	Eileen O'Doherty
Carle	Stuart Hamilton
Two Porters . .	T. J. Fox, D. Robinson

20th April 1908

THE WORKHOUSE WARD

A Comedy in One Act by Lady Gregory

Mike MacInerney . . .	Arthur Sinclair
Michael Miskell . . .	Fred O'Donovan
Mrs. Donohoe, a countrywoman	Maire O'Neill

29th May 1908

First Production by the Abbey Company of

THE SCHEMING LIEUTENANT

A Farce by Richard Brinsley Sheridan

Lieutenant O'Connor . .	J. M. Kerrigan
Doctor Rosy	Fred O'Donovan
Justice Credulous . . .	Arthur Sinclair
Sergeant Trounce . . .	Sydney Morgan
Corporal Flint	J. A. O'Rourke
Lauretta	Maire O'Neill
Mrs. Bridget Credulous .	Sara Allgood

Soldiers: Ambrose Power, Stuart Hamilton, U. Wright, Eileen O'Doherty

F

1st October 1908

THE SUBURBAN GROOVE
A Mild Satire in Three Acts by W. F. Casey

Dick Dalton	J. M. Kerrigan
James O'Connor	Fred O'Donovan
Mrs. James O'Connor	Sara Allgood
Their son and daughter:	
Jack O'Connor	U. Wright
Una O'Connor	Maire O'Neill
Claude Callan	Arthur Sinclair

8th October 1908

THE CLANCY NAME
A Tragedy in One Act by S. L. Robinson

Mrs. Clancy	Sara Allgood
John Clancy, her son	Arthur Sinclair
Mrs. Spillane	Maire O'Neill
Eugene Roche	Fred O'Donovan
Jerry Brien	J. A. O'Rourke
Mary Brien	Eileen O'Doherty
Father Murphy	J. M. Kerrigan
Michael Dempsey	Sydney J. Morgan

15th October 1908

WHEN THE DAWN IS COME
A Tragedy in Three Acts by Thomas MacDonagh

The Seven acting as Captains of the Irish Insurgent Army, and Members of the Council of Ireland:

Thurough MacKieran	J. M. Kerrigan
Hugh MacOscar	Sydney J. Morgan
Reamonn O'Sullivan	Arthur Sinclair
Father John Joyce	Eric Gorman
Alexander Walker	Fred O'Donovan
Rory MacMahon	Ambrose Power
Patrick Ryan	U. Wright
Ita MacOscar, daughter of Hugh, Member of the Council of Ireland	Sara Allgood
Sheela O'Hara, Member of the Council	Maire O'Neill
Connor O'Gatry, a ballad singer, a spy	J. A. O'Rourke
MacEamonn, a spy	J. H. Dunne
Irish Soldiers as Guards:	G. H. Fitzgerald, Maurice McCall

CHAPTER SEVEN
1909-1918

It seemed a wise breaking-up of the material of this book to make the previous chapter end with the death of Synge and the departure of the Fays. In a very real sense these events did mark the End of a Chapter in the Theatre's history, for, following Synge's death, a new school of dramatists was to appear, a school of young realists, and new players were to take the place of the Fays and the players who had played with them were further to develop their art.

One has got to try to find an explanation, a reason, for the realistic dramatists. Why these "three Cork dramatists," as Yeats called T. C. Murray, R. J. Ray and myself? Why did this ugly school suddenly raise its head? Perhaps the realist movement was a reply to the romantic, poetical, historical theatre Yeats and Martyn and Lady Gregory dreamed of. The Irish Renaissance (it seems too portentous a term but it has been used many times, so let's stick to it) owed its birth, strange to say, from a *débâcle*—the downfall of Parnell. Ireland for nearly a hundred years had been politically-minded; there were three great questions to solve, Catholic Emancipation, the Land Question, political Independence from England —in the eighteen-seventies they named it "Home Rule." But there was a minority, and we must not forget it, who wanted to cut every connecting rope with England. The Parnell crash came in 1892 and made Ireland politically divided. It seemed almost certain that no political progress could be made for forty years, it would take these years or more than that time for the wounds to be licked clean. It was then that certain young men and women in Ireland realised that their country, in seeking for material gains, had lost sight of more spiritual things. And so the young enthusiasts set to work. The Gaelic language was on the point of extinction, therefore the Gaelic League must be formed to blow the dying embers.

The Irish Texts Society must be formed to reprint old manuscripts and to prove that the old Gaelic sagas were not just dull and bawdy but were full of human story and a love of nature, a love of birds and beasts and flowers. Poetry flowed up, like fountains in a garden, like streams at the end of a lawn. AE, Yeats, Katherine Tynan, Seamus O'Sullivan, Padraic Colum and many another. And drama flowed up, again Yeats, Synge, Colum, Lady Gregory. Their thought about Ireland was romantical. Ireland was "A young girl with the walk of a queen," "'Twas the dream of a God."

> And the mould of His hand,
> That you shook 'neath His stroke,
> That you trembled and broke
> To this beautiful land.
>
> He made you all fair,
> You in purple and gold,
> You in silver and green,
> Till no eye that has seen
> Without love can behold.

We young men, a generation later than Yeats, later than Katherine Tynan, later than Seamus O'Sullivan, didn't see her as a queen, didn't see her all fair in purple and gold, we loved her as truly as Yeats and Dora Shorter and the rest—maybe we loved her more deeply, but just because we loved her so deeply her faults were clear to us. Perhaps we realists saw her faults too clearly, perhaps we saw her too often as a grasping, middle-aged hag. She was avaricious, she was mean, for family pride she would force a son into the Church against his will, she would commit arson, she would lie, she would cheat, she would murder and yet we would write all our terrible words about her out of our love.

We hadn't the genius of Synge, his genius of combining poetry of speech with humdrum facts, and, of course, we hadn't the poetry of Yeats.

My one-act play, *The Clancy Name* (1908), set the pace. It was violently attacked in the press:

The *Freeman's Journal* said:

> Last night a new play, one called by the distinctly picturesque title of *The Clancy Name*, by S. L. Robinson, was produced at the Abbey Theatre

and proved a most fatal fiasco.... The idea of the play is that an Irish peasant commits a foul murder; his mother, by no means concerned about the barbarity of his crime, is anxious to prevent him giving himself up to the police, and to urge him to marry a peasant girl and to clear the Clancy name. Has it come to this, that acceptance to the ranks of writers at the Abbey Theatre is subject to the writer blackguarding his countrymen and countrywomen, setting up a shocking and ruthless picture of the methods and characteristics and making the Irish actors and actresses play parts which they know to be worse than travesties of their countrymen and countrywomen?

... Now that a Judge is occasionally sitting to hear pressing motions, one can see no just reason why a representative member of the distinctive family whose name has been so flagrantly mentioned in connection with this so-called play should not apply at once for an injunction to stop the further perpetration of a libel on the good house of Clancy, and, if possible, for the ultimate determination as to the fate of the author, referred in the usual way to the worthy sub-sheriff of the city.

I followed it six months later with a play in two Acts and a Prologue, *The Cross Roads*. The inspired performances by Sara Allgood, Arthur Sinclair, Fred O'Donovan, J. M. Kerrigan and Maire O'Neill made this play an outstanding event.

S. L. Robinson (I afterwards called myself Lennox Robinson on Yeats's suggestion, for Yeats said Robinson was such a common name) was born in Douglas, Cork, in 1886. My education was meagre. I have since *The Cross Roads* written many plays and biographies and autobiographies, and edited *The Golden Treasury of Irish Verse* and produced a hundred plays by other authors. In various capacities I have been connected with the Abbey Theatre for over forty years.

My first production in the Theatre was a revival of William Boyle's *The Eloquent Dempsey*. I thought it a commonplace play and was much more excited in producing, in early May 1910, Padraic Colum's *Thomas Muskerry*, probably the best play Colum has yet written: a realistic workhouse play, beautifully played by Arthur Sinclair, Sara Allgood and Maire O'Neill, Sydney J. Morgan and all the others.

It was announced for Thursday, Friday and Saturday nights and a matinée, the 5th, 6th, and 7th May 1910, but, rather unexpectedly, the King of England, Edward VII, died late on Friday night: his death put me into a difficulty. One of the Directors, Mr. Yeats, was in France, the other Director, Lady Gregory, was in County Galway. My dilemma (I was young and inexperienced) need not be dwelt on too heavily, but it had certain repercussions, best summed up in the letter to Yeats from me dated in January of the next year:

> You have asked me to tell you exactly what happened on May 7th last. I read in the morning papers of the King's death, but I never thought of the effect it would have on the theatres and places of amusement. However about 11.15 our secretary came to my rooms and told me that he heard that the other theatres in Dublin were closing and asked me what we should do. I knew that the Abbey Theatre had been carried on from the beginning as a purely artistic venture, I knew that its policy was to ignore politics, and I thought that if we closed we would be throwing ourselves definitely on one political side and that we should remain open taking no notice of a circumstance that had no significance to the arts. However I decided to leave the matter to Lady Gregory and wired to her as follows:
>
> "Theatres closing here. What am I to do? I think we should remain open but leave decision to you."
>
> This was handed in ten minutes before twelve. I then went to the Theatre and waited for a reply; none came, and I decided to go on with the matinée. Lady Gregory's answer desiring the Theatre to be closed came in the course of the afternoon—in the interval before the last act of the play we were performing.
>
> "Should close through courtesy. A. Gregory."
>
> It was too late to stop the matinée then, and the good audience encouraged me to think that little criticism would be passed on our having remained open. It was too late to put notices in the evening papers cancelling the night performances and if there was any crime in having played we had already committed it.

Miss Horniman's repercussion to my action was immediate and emphatic. She wired to Lady Gregory on the 10th of May: "Opening last Saturday was disgraceful. Performance on day of funeral would be political and would stop subsidy automatically." She demanded my dismissal.

The subsidy in any case would have ended in nine months' time, but the Directors were not willing to serve up their manager's head on a charger, and eventually the matter was submitted for arbitration to Mr. Scott, the editor of the *Manchester Guardian*. Miss Horniman had established her distinguished Gaiety Theatre in Manchester, and the dramatic critics of the *Guardian*, C. E. Montague and G. H. Mair, the best in England, had always shown themselves very appreciative of the Abbey Theatre's work, so there could be little bias.

The *Manchester Guardian* gave its decision in the Theatre's favour. Miss Horniman, therefore, owed the Theatre half a year's subsidy, £400, but the Theatre waived its claim to the money. I tried to make amends, and when the Secretary left did the Secretary's work as well as my own with no increase of salary. But with that occurrence Miss Horniman's connection with the Theatre ceased. The Directors, Lady Gregory and W. B. Yeats, wrote to her on 4th May 1911:

> We have just had Mr. Scott's award. We wish at once to say that remembering all your generosity in the past it was never our intention to press the legal point against you. If with all the facts before you you still cannot accept the integrity of our action, we cannot accept the money and the matter is at an end.

It is not difficult to appraise Miss Horniman's services to the Irish Theatre, but it is a little difficult to estimate the kind of person she was. That she had a great admiration for the young Yeats's work is certain; she helped, with her money, to have his first play put on the stage in London, *The Land of Heart's Desire* in 1894, and she probably loved him for himself —they were much of the same age. But, apart from Yeats, she genuinely loved the Theatre; the Theatre of the 1890's. She loved not only the plays of Ibsen and Yeats and Shaw but also the plays of the young English dramatists; indeed she made them, and established in 1907 the Gaiety Theatre in Manchester which was to be for many years the most distinguished theatre in England, outside London. But before she made her Manchester theatre she was designing and stitching costumes for *The King's Threshold* in a shabby street in Dublin. Charles Ricketts was years later to design noble costumes for this play. Miss Horniman's designs were heavy and German and coarse, but they were designed and stitched in her love for the drama and for Yeats's work.

From almost the first there seems to have been a clash between two temperaments, the English and the Irish one. Miss Horniman was a Lancashire business-woman, she was proud of the fact, she was proud of Horniman's Teas. She loved art, loved the theatre, yet, if she didn't expect great value for her money, she wanted, at least, efficiency. Arnold Bennett and his Five Towns springs to mind. Miss Horniman was a little like Bennett's Anna.

The historian of the Theatre has read many, many letters from Miss Horniman to the Directors and to her Dublin lawyers. There is never, on her part, a suspicion of meanness, if anything, the desire is to be over-generous, but gradually, thanks to Yeats, Lady Gregory and Fay, she becomes more and more set aside from the Theatre she had financed.

Perhaps J. M. Hone is right when he says in his Yeats Biography that she and Lady Gregory fought for Yeats and that Lady Gregory won.

> Maud Gonne, who had watched with mild amusement the struggle for Yeats between Lady Gregory and Miss Horniman, dates Lady Gregory's triumph from the trip to Italy: "They should have been allies," she says in her memoirs, "for both stood for art for art's sake . . . (but) they both liked Willie too well . . . Miss Horniman brought back Italian plaques to decorate the Abbey but Lady Gregory carried off Willie to visit the Italian towns where they were made."

The curtain-line of the first act of *The Playboy* comes to mind (as if spoken by Yeats): "Two fine women fighting for the likes of me!" Miss Horniman wrote in red ink on yellow paper in a meticulous hand, and Synge declared he used to grow faintly ill when he saw the yellow envelope in his morning's post, he could never appreciate daffodils afterwards. Lady Gregory, one suspects, looked on her as a parvenue, but she had money, not a great deal, but she could be used.

This seems a fairly honest portrait, sketched by a person who never met her. But then, in the Theatre's vestibule, hangs a painting which seems to destroy the portrait the historian has tried to depict.

Of the five fine portraits that hang there J. B. Yeats's one of her is the loveliest. She dreams down, she doesn't glare, she is no Lancashire hussie, no old maid who has made money out of her father's tea. The face is spiritual, the beautiful hands are pale and delicate. Lady Gregory in her portrait (not by Yeats) does glare with her mantilla and the great jewel on her bosom. Bring those two women out of their frames, match them each to each in front of the box-office, and there is no shadow of doubt as to who will win. There is a press photograph—of course not as sensitive as the Yeats portrait—of her in 1909. The thought-brooding eyes, the lovely delicate hands, the mannish dress: a pen is in her hand, she is meditating—she is writing a cheque—for the Abbey Theatre?—for the Manchester Gaiety?—but the caption reads, "I wonder how many I's there are in similar." Her contribution to that Christmas Souvenir of the Gaiety Theatre (1909) is a long quotation from Marcus Aurelius.

A Dublin paper, the *Evening Telegraph*, writing on the first day of November in 1910, seems very adequately to sum up the case:

> The fairy godmother of the Irish Dramatic Movement parts with the Abbey today. Miss A. E. F. Horniman, whose generous help turned Irish school of drama and acting into the undoubted success it now is, relinquishes her hold on it today on the expiration of the six years' Patent granted to her for the Abbey Theatre, which she brought into being. Tomorrow Lady Gregory takes over the reins of patentee for the Theatre's new lease of life for 21 years to come. It should not be forgotten that were it not for the aid given to the dramatic movement in its infancy by Miss Horniman the Irish drama and the Irish acting world would have never grown into the healthy existence they both now enjoy.
>
> Miss Horniman was truly a fairy godmother to the present drama movement in Ireland. Her generous monetary help was the wand that waved it into the proud position it now holds in the eyes of the artistic world, and we here in Ireland should not forget the fairy.
>
> A chance visit made by Miss Horniman to some of the plays produced by the little Company brought together by the Fays on one of these one-day visits to London made Miss Horniman imagine that she discovered in their simple art the bud of something that might blossom with care into an artistic creation, and as she had money at her command, as well as the love of the beautiful strongly developed within her, she there and then decided to take the Irish play and players under her wing and provide a little Theatre in Dublin, and endowed same for them. Thus the Abbey Theatre—like an Aladdin Palace—came into being, and up to today it has been endowed by this disinterested artistic English lady, who must have spent over £13,000 in building up the Irish dramatic movement into the really fine achievement it has become under her generosity.
>
> Though financing the Abbey since its inception to the present moment, she never in any way dictated to the Directors what was to be played on the Abbey stage, and yet, when the Directors made mistakes in judgment now and again, she was wholehearted enough to take sides with them.
>
> In the first years of the Abbey's existence she spared no trouble nor expense

to achieve success for her dramatic movement in Ireland, and often displayed her artistic taste and skill in designing costumes for many of Mr. W. B. Yeats's poetic plays and some of Lady Gregory's, including *Kincora*. In fact, in those days the Abbey and its doings were the dream child of her fancy, but Dublin all along closed its eyes to the lady whose fine artistic instinct on things dramatic was slowly but surely making our city one of the really artistic centres of the world. She was ignored altogether; and yet she continued to supply the capital by which it were possible to make such a movement a thing of actuality and importance as the Abbey and its performances have become of late.

It was not so with Manchester where she started a Repertory Theatre some few seasons ago, and the University a few months since conferred upon her an Honorary Degree for her great services to the Drama.

We in Dublin, up to the present, never as much as said "Thank you" to her for all she has done for us. Is this a fair specimen of Irish hospitality, to a stranger who fostered our actors and plays until they have unquestionably become a part of the artistic centres of the world over? ...

When the history of the new era of drama in Ireland comes to be written, Miss A. E. F. Horniman, the generous English lady who willingly parted with her money to raise it into a sturdy and epoch-making achievement, will, we sincerely hope, be niched in her proper place—the lady whose artistic instinct scented out the late crop that lay fallow in Ireland for the want of funds to work it. Our Drama loses the best friend it ever had in parting with Miss Horniman today.

As realistic dramatists, very quickly R. J. Ray and T. C. Murray overtopped me. Ray's plays have never been published and are undeservedly overlooked. Some day *The White Feather* (1909), *The Casting-out of Martin Whelan* (1910), *The Gombeen Man* (1913), will be revived and shown to be the powerful realistic plays that they are.

R. J. Ray (his real name was Brophy) was a journalist, his first job being on the *Kilkenny Journal* about 1890. He was only a boy then. Later he joined the staff of the *Cork Constitution*. That paper's offices were wrecked during the Civil War, and the proprietors went to Dublin and took over the *Evening Mail*. Soon after, Ray got on the sub-editorial staff of the *Independent*. Some years afterwards he collapsed and died on one of Dublin's streets.

But then T. C. Murray sailed, without an effort, into the front rank of the Theatre's dramatists. Like some players, Fred O'Donovan, F. J. McCormick, Patrick Carolan, Murray never seemed to have had to learn his craft, his genius just happened. I remember that when we were at a loss for a new play I persuaded Yeats to let me put *Little Eyolf* into rehearsal. Yeats consented. He disliked Ibsen but found poetic quality in this play of Ibsen's. I started happily to work on it, but Murray's *Birthright* came along, and *Eyolf* had to be shelved. *Birthright* was a perfect piece of art, as perfect as a Chopin prelude.

T. C. Murray was born in Macroom, Co. Cork, in 1873. He was a teacher-student in St. Patrick's College, Dublin, from 1891 to 1893, and was appointed head master of the Inchicore Model Schools in 1915. His first play, *Birthright*, was produced at the Abbey Theatre in 1910. This was followed by *Maurice Harte, Spring, Aftermath, The Pipe in the Fields, Autumn Fire, Michaelmas Eve, The Blind Wolf, Illumination*, and other plays. In April 1949 the National University of Ireland conferred on him the honorary degree of Doctor of Letters.

Quickly followed St. John Ervine with his *Magnanimous Lover* in 1910; strange to say we shrank from the subject, but a few months later came *Mixed Marriage*, and there was no hesitation about the production of that play in 1911, and *The Magnanimous Lover* followed in 1912.

St. John Ervine was born in Ballymacarrett, a shipyard suburb of Belfast, on the 28th December 1883, and after three years in an Insurance office emigrated to London at the age of seventeen.

Never, perhaps, since the first years at the Abbey, when the Fays were at the height of their fame, had there been such a company, such plays, such success.

Let us pause for a moment to consider money matters and other facts regarding the management of the Abbey. To begin with, it must be stated that the Directors never received any money from the Theatre *qua* Directors, nor do they to this day. Under the Articles of Association they are not allowed to take any money. Years later, when I was made manager and producer, counsel's opinion was sought, and it was decided that it was not improper for me to be paid for those services.

Until 1910 no fees were paid to dramatists, then Harley Granville-Barker drew up a scale of fees which held good for many years; any alteration made subsequently was made in the author's favour.

Until 1916 the Company played only three days a week: Thursday, Friday, and a matinée and evening performance on Saturday. The prices of the seats were:

> Stalls 3s., Balcony (reserved) 2s., Front Pit 1s., Pit 6d.; or, 8 one-shilling vouchers for 6s., or 8 two-shilling vouchers for 12s., or 8 three-shilling Stalls vouchers for 20s.

These were reduced in 1915 to:

> Front Stalls 3s., Back Stalls 2s., Balcony (reserved) 1s. 6d., Ordinary Balcony 1s., Front of Pit 1s., Back of Pit 6d.

The Company rehearsed from 11 to 1.30 and again from 3 to 5 p.m. When there was a dress rehearsal or when players were required who were in business, the rehearsals were held from 8 to 10 p.m. As to salaries, I quote Udolphus Wright:

> At the opening nobody was paid. The first person to go on salary was W. G. Fay. I don't think his salary was more than £3 a week. Frank Fay was not getting salary until some time afterwards. Then Frank Fay and Sara Allgood started at about £1. Then O'Rourke and myself did not get anything until we came right in to the Theatre. When we were on tour I would get a tour allowance, which was £1 a week, plus my home salary, that was about £2. Arthur Sinclair came about that time and was getting about 30s. Sydney Morgan was getting £1 and they went up gradually to about £2, 10s., and when I came in permanently—about 1908—I started with £2 a week. The highest salary at that time was £3 a week and on tour one got £1 for lodging and when the Company went to London they got 7s. 6d. extra. When we were on tour, Sara Allgood, Sydney Morgan, J. O'Rourke, J. M. Kerrigan, Fred O'Donovan, Maire O'Neill and myself usually stayed in the same "digs." We used to divide the bill at the end of the week. It never came to more than 15s. each for the week, and was usually 11s. or 12s. each. This included all meals.
>
> At first the people who came in to walk on got nothing, and then eventually they got 10s. a week.

On certain occasions "Professional" matinées were held on Fridays, when some distinguished players were appearing in other Dublin theatres: Sir John Martin-Harvey and his wife, for instance—always such warm friends to the Theatre—Sir Johnston Forbes-Robertson and his wife, Sir Frank and Lady Benson and Mrs. Brown-Potter, these are names one remembers as having come to these special matinées, with, of course, their supporting companies.

The Patent for the Theatre had to be renewed. In November of 1910 Lady Gregory and Yeats applied for a twenty-one years' renewal. There was on this occasion (though the Theatre Royal and the Gaiety Theatre were represented) no professional opposition, but Mr. Dudley White appeared for The Theatre of Ireland. The *Evening Telegraph*, 26th November 1910, reports:

> Today in the Law Room, Dublin Castle, the Hon. the Solicitor-General sat to hear an application by Lady Gregory and Mr. W. B. Yeats for a Patent for the Abbey Theatre. Mr. J. Day (instructed by Messrs. Whitney and Moore) appeared for the applicants. . . .
>
> Mr. John Linehan (instructed by Mr. M. J. Kelly, Chief Crown Solicitor) represented the Crown.
>
> Mr. Day explained the assistance which Miss Horniman had given to the Abbey Theatre, but now that the Patent was on the point of expiring she thought the public ought to take their share of the responsibility. The Theatre had never paid, and Miss Horniman now proposed to hand over to the applicants her Patent on payment of £1,000. That proposal had been accepted. Lady Gregory and Mr. Yeats proposed to raise £5,000, and already £2,000 had been subscribed. Three very well known gentlemen in Civil Service circles, Mr. W. F. Bailey, Mr. Bourke and Mr. Hanson, were prepared to act as Trustees of this fund. The Memorandum agreed to by all parties provided that the new Patent should be for 21 years, and should authorise the production of all acknowledged masterpieces of dramatic literature of the eighteenth century and earlier. . . .
>
> Mr. White said he appeared for The Theatre of Ireland which had no habitation, but its objects were similar to those of the promoters of the Abbey Theatre, Mr. Edward Martyn, Mr. George Russell, etc. They were completely in intellectual sympathy with the Abbey Theatre. There ought to be a provision in the Patent that The Theatre of Ireland should have the right to get 18 days in the year to produce their plays in the Abbey and get 40 per cent. of the receipts. . . .
>
> Mr. Day said the application was most audacious and Miss Horniman was so much opposed to this Theatre of Ireland that she would not allow them to use their theatre on any terms. . . .
>
> Mr. George Nesbitt was then examined on behalf of The Theatre of Ireland, and said none of the actors were paid; they were all amateurs. They did not differ in any way from the Abbey Theatre, except that they performed their plays in Irish. He did not object to the Patent, but he asked

that 18 days should be reserved for The Theatre of Ireland during the year....

The Patent was granted.

A word must be said about The Theatre of Ireland. It sprung out of the resignation of Maire Nic Shiubhlaigh and her friends in 1905. There was every reason for them to leave the Theatre and to continue to be amateur actors, and perhaps to be more patriotic than the players they had left behind. Unfortunately, they never justified their endeavour. It is difficult to remember any performance of theirs which had outstanding distinction, but shortly after the renewal of the Patent, in May 1912 Thomas MacDonagh has the idea of making a more important Theatre of Ireland, and he writes thus to W. G. Fay:

> I was delighted to get your letter this morning and to see from it that further consideration has not made you foresee any new difficulties. . . .
>
> In the first place Mr. Plunkett and I are of opinion that the new theatre should pay you £150 for the year. Mr. Darley has not yet given us his decision, but he thinks that right too. . . .
>
> Then, with you here, we shall proceed to look for our players. If he does not come in as director, we must try to get someone else. But I hope he will join in. . . . There are outside causes that may keep him out, but for himself he is sufficiently in sympathy with our objects, for one thing, in being instrumental in bringing you back to Dublin for another, and in having an opportunity of doing something for music in the theatre for a third, to take a hand. . . .
>
> By keeping the matter private I by no means mean that we should say or publish nothing of the affair till we were ready for public performance. That would be impossible and unnecessary, I think. I meant, till we were ourselves complete and could avoid suggestions and useless criticism. If Darley consents tomorrow, I think we shall at once have to bring a fairly large number of people into our confidence, guarantors and possible players. We are thinking of getting twenty or more people to give £10 each to start the thing. They would all have to know. But we will not give them right of election or appointment. Darley, Plunkett and I shall then be directors, you manager or actor manager. . . .
>
> About plays, I do not think we would want ever to play Abbey plays, to duplicate Abbey work. I think we ought to surpass their acting. . . . About players, frankly I would prefer to have young unspoiled people. Men and women have young, spring-like enthusiasm for a thing like the drama only once in their lives. If they take the tide, as you did, they ripen to summer and autumn, if not—well, they cannot have a second spring. X— had been a dismal failure these past years. When you taught her, she did good things.

Then when left to herself she went off and off. I am sure it would be far easier work to begin with another girl of twenty, such as she was ten years ago, than to try to galvanize her into the same thing again. She is, I fear, incapable of the kind of young enthusiasm that we shall want. Her brother Y— is still worse than she, and brings an air of casualness with him. He has ruined thing after thing by not learning his lines. . . .

From what I have seen of them at work, I think that M—, F—, Y—, except P—, who is with the Abbey, are hopeless in anything which demands punctuality and efficiency. . . . They are all friends of all of us, and they will all be friends of our theatre, but I think they are incompetent for the work we have to do. I write all this in order to be perfectly explicit as to my views. I am by no means laying down the law. I know you will understand. . . .

For many years it had been the Directors' wish to cross the Atlantic and show the Theatre's work to the sea-divided Gaels. By constantly playing in Dublin and with frequent visits to England means could be just met—but only just. A trip to America might prove a small fortune; by 1910 "a few hundred of pounds" (Lady Gregory's words) had been saved and the venture might be contemplated, if some agent could be found to guarantee the tour against loss. Messrs. Liebler were found, who proved to be the most understanding, generous agents, but the little Company, they were only fifteen, were not going out to affluent salaries, the "stars" received £10 a week, and the lesser stars sunk down to £4 a week. The tour originally was only for three months, but it was so successful that Messrs. Liebler kept it on for another three months, and almost doubled the subsidy, and the salaries were increased accordingly. They opened a new theatre in Boston, the Plymouth Theatre, on 23rd September 1911. The programme was T. C. Murray's *Birthright*, *The Shadow of the Glen*, and *Hyacinth Halvey*.

Boston is dominated by the Irish and the Irish Company thought they were paying a visit to friends. Instead, the friends hailed them with brickbats; no, not quite with brickbats on the appearance of Murray's play, the bats, the potatoes and the watches were to be reserved for *The Playboy* in Boston a few weeks later, in New York, in Chicago, in Philadelphia.

But we must try to see the Irish-American point of view; only two generations before, the fathers and mothers of the people who threw brickbats had been forced to emigrate from

Ireland. They crossed to America, almost illiterate, with hardly a penny in their pockets. The men set themselves to work, perhaps at first as navvies on the streets, later as policemen, later—the ladder is being climbed with swiftness and sagacity—to politics. Soon Tammany Hall dominates New York, something similar dominates Boston; by the time the second generation is born, American Ireland has a gold chain across its chest and a big bank-roll. It is significant that the Irish emigrant, unlike the Scandinavians or Germans, never turned American farmer. Ireland had given him enough of the potato and the oats and the cabbage patch. But there is a memory behind, a memory of Ireland which has come down from a silver-haired Irish grandmother. She came out on the emigrant ship and she remembers the lovely Irish scenery, the winding lane, the turf fire. She has forgotten, after sixty years (and small blame to her), the poverty, the hunger and the cold. She sees Ireland, and so does her man, through a mist of sentiment. Her children, if they go to a play by Dion Boucicault, see Chauncey Alcott playing a broth of a boy, swaggering round the stage in immaculate white breeches; the colleen, Mollie O'Flynn, looks lovely in a little plaid shawl; her uncle, with his clay pipe stuck in his hat, is a bit of a rascal but still a good old type, and the old white-haired mother crouches over the fire and some old song is sung and there is the Wicked Landlord in the background and always the Informer.

This was the Ireland that Irish-Americans dreamed of till 1911, and then, smashing their dream, came T. C. Murray's *Birthright*. Here is no cottage with the roses round the door, no Wicked Landlord, no loving old mother, just a stark, ugly tragedy played between father, mother, and two sons. There is not even a love-affair in the play. As bad, or worse, was to follow. The word had been sent from Ireland that *The Playboy* must be shouted down, but the puzzle for the patriots in Boston and New York was, at what line should the shout be started? But shout they did.

Watches and potatoes were thrown at the stage in New York, and the first act of *The Playboy* was inaudible and had to be played again. Lady Gregory crouched behind the fire encouraging the players and I helped the police to throw

T. C. MURRAY

LENNOX ROBINSON

the disturbers down the marble staircase of the Maxine Elliot Theatre.

But things got more serious in Philadelphia some weeks later, when the whole cast of *The Playboy* was arrested for performing "immoral or indecent plays." I quote Lady Gregory: "Our accuser is a liquor-dealer."

I put up the following "Call" on 18th January 1912:

> The Cast of *The Playboy* to appear before Magistrate James A. Carey at 633 Walnut Street, Philadelphia.

(Lady Gregory):

> Yesterday, Friday morning, we attended the Magistrates' Court at nine o'clock. The liquor-seller, our prosecutor, was the first witness. He had stayed only till Shawneen's "coat of a Christian man" was left in Michael James's hands. He made a disturbance then and was turned out, but was able to find as much indecency even in that conversation as would demoralise a monastery. His brother, a priest, had stayed all through, and found we had committed every sin mentioned in the Act. Another witness swore that sentences were used in the play and that he had heard them, though they are not either in book nor play....
>
> Our actors were furious. Kerrigan tried hard to keep from breaking out and risking all when the priest was attacking his (that is Shawn Keogh's) character and intentions. At last he called out, "My God!" and the Magistrate said, "If that man interrupts the Court again, turn him out," forgetting that he was speaking of a prisoner at the bar! Indeed, as the prosecutors grew excited, the trial of the Irish Players seemed to be forgotten, and it became the trial of Christy Mahon for the attempted murder of his father....
>
> The dramatic event was the arrival of Quinn while a witness was being examined. We had got leave from the Judge for him to cross-examine, and the witness had to confess that the people of Ireland do use the name of God at other times than in blessing or thanking those who have been kind to them, and in gratitude or prayer, as he had at first asserted upon oath. Also when he based his attack on indecency by quoting the "poacher's love," spoken of by Christy, he was made to admit that, a few sentences earlier, marriage had been spoken of, "in a fortnight's time when the banns will be called." Whether this made it more or less moral, he was not asked to say. He called the play "libidinous."
>
> J. Q. asked one witness if anything immoral had happened on the stage, and he answered "Not while the curtain was up!" I think it was the same witness who said, "A theatre is no place for a sense of humour." The players beamed and the audience enjoyed themselves, and then when the Director of Public Safety was called, and said he and his wife had enjoyed the play very much and had seen nothing to shock anybody, the enemy had received, as Quinn said, "a knock-out blow." He made a very fine speech then.

A lot of people have been expressing sympathy. A young man from the University, who had been bringing a bodyguard for me on the riot nights, has just been to say good-bye, and told me the students are going to hold an indignation meeting. The Drama League, six hundred strong, has so far done or said nothing, though it is supposed to have sent out a bulletin endorsing the favourable opinion of Boston upon our plays, a week after we came here, not having had time to form an opinion of its own. Can you imagine their allowing such a thing to happen here as the arrest of a company of artists engaged in producing a masterpiece, and at such hands!...

The Company are in a state of fury, but they adore John Quinn, and his name will pass into folk-lore like those stories of O'Connell suddenly appearing at trials. He spoke splendidly, with fire and full knowledge. You will see what he said about the witnesses in the *North American* and even Robinson says he "came like an angel."

The battle over *The Playboy* raged all through the tour, which lasted from September 1911 to March 1912. It was conducted throughout with courage and enterprise by Lady Gregory, she won every fight—yet without very much liking the play she was fighting for, but, as in the case of *Blanco Posnet*, freedom of thought, freedom of the Theatre was the thing that mattered. The fight is old history, it can be read in detail in her book *Our Irish Theatre*. On subsequent tours to U.S.A. in 1913 and 1914 the fight had to be waged again but the opponents were getting a little weary. Then the 1914-18 War intervened and America was not visited until 1932. By this time a new generation of Irish-Americans had been born, Chauncey Alcott and Boucicault meant nothing to them, instead they rejoiced and took pride in Synge, Yeats, Murray, Gregory and O'Casey. The first tour was a big financial success, the second tour was not quite so good financially, and the third tour lost money.

The 1914 American tour lost a little money, I resigned as Manager in June, and then, in August, war broke out. The next ten years were, in some respects, to prove the grimmest ten years financially in the Theatre's history. The principal players, Sara Allgood, Arthur Sinclair, and their like, were able to command salaries in England which the Irish Theatre could not afford. Two years after the outbreak of war in August 1914 came the Irish Insurrection, April 1916.

It has been noted that after the performances of the Irish Literary Society, Mr. Fay's Company and the Irish National

Theatre Society were concerned as much with National things as with theatrical ones. That fact has been emphasised to me time and time again by some early players, Mary Quinn for instance, and it should be recorded. Certain definite "rebel" plays are to be noted, *Cathleen ni Houlihan* by Yeats:

> " One night I had a dream, almost as clear as a vision, of a cottage where there was well-being and firelight and talk of marriage, and into the midst of that cottage there came an old woman. She was Ireland herself, that Cathleen ni Houlihan, for whom so many songs have been sung, and for whose sake so many have gone to their death. I thought that if I could write this out as a little play I could make others see my dream as I had seen it."

> ... All that I have said and done,
> Now that I am old and ill,
> Turns into a question till
> I lie awake night after night
> And never get the answers right.
> Did that play of mine send out
> Certain men the English shot?

and *The Rising of the Moon*. The Theatre was wont to borrow policemen's uniforms from Dublin Castle for use in this play, but after 1916 permission was refused.

But the production of two plays, neither of them of the first importance, should be noted; the first is Thomas MacDonagh's *When the Dawn is Come* (1908). He was born in Cloughjordan, Co. Tipperary in 1878, the son of a Roscommon teacher at Rockwell College, and went to teach at St. Kiernan's in Kilkenny. He helped Pearse to found St. Enda's School in 1908. With Edward Martyn and Joseph Plunkett he founded The Irish Theatre in Hardwicke Street in 1914. He was a member of the Provisional Committee of the Irish Volunteers at the inaugural meeting, November 1913, in command of Jacob's factory 1916, and was executed 3rd May 1916. The second play, produced thirteen years later (1921), is Terence MacSwiney's *The Revolutionist*. Both plays are prophetic, MacDonagh's of the Rising in 1916, MacSwiney's of his own noble, tragic death.

It has been reported that the little printing-press on which the Proclamation of the Republic of Ireland was printed was, after the printing, hidden somewhere in the Abbey Theatre. I made, years after, searches and enquiries, but could not verify the fact. I wish I could have found that historic little press.

A good friend of the Theatre, W. F. Bailey, brought Sir John Maxwell to the Green-room one evening in the spring of 1916. Sir John, in charge of the English garrison in Ireland, had been responsible for the execution of sixteen of the people who signed the Republic's Proclamation. Bailey had the most friendly intentions, but when Sir John came into the Green-room, the players very quietly left it.

During these four years, 1914-18, not very many great plays were being written. Perhaps the only ones to be noted are, in 1915, Lady Gregory's *Shanwalla*, a strange, moving play, out of her vein and stupidly neglected; St. John Ervine's masterpiece, *John Ferguson*; my *The Dreamers*. But, in 1916, J. Augustus Keogh became the Theatre's producer. He knew Bernard Shaw's plays through and through, he had acted in them, he had produced them, and now, for the first time since the production of *Blanco Posnet*, the Irish Theatre saw the plays of one of Ireland's greatest dramatists. They even saw the rejected *John Bull's Other Island*. From September 1916 to March 1917 six great Shaw plays were presented. There were less important plays, pleasant comedies by Bernard Duffy and, in December 1916, *The Whiteheaded Boy* by myself.

In 1918 there came a fine one-act play by Lady Gregory, *Hanrahan's Oath*; T. C. Murray's moving one-act tragedy *Spring*; and my pseudo-Parnellite play, *The Lost Leader*.

But in spite of a few good plays the Theatre was in the doldrums. If not sinking, the ship seemed in a very water-logged condition, and suddenly, without much warning, the most important members of the Company deserted. They were Fred O'Donovan and Christine Hayden.

There had been other flights from the hive; Maire Nic Shiubhlaigh and her swarm in 1905, the Fays in 1908, Sara Allgood, etc., in 1914. Except in the last case the flights seemed to give room for new wings to expand, but the O'Donovan flight in 1918 left the Theatre almost bankrupt of talent.

Arthur Shields, a young player, stepped into the breach. (He should have played in *Cathleen ni Houlihan*, on Easter

Monday, 1916, but, going to work at the Theatre, found he had to shoulder a rifle and take up his post in the Post Office, and from there proceed to an internment camp in Wales.) But there was a new play, a new dramatist, there were rags and tatters of a Company, the Theatre was not yet twenty years old. It had had a wonderful youth, surely its life was not yet over.

Casts of First Productions, 1909-1918

21st January 1909
THE MISER

Lady Gregory's adaptation, Molière's Comedy in Five Acts

L'Avare (The Miser) originally played 9th September 1668

Harpagon, father to Cleante, in love with Marianne	Arthur Sinclair
Cleante, Harpagon's son, lover to Marianne	Fred O'Donovan
Valere, son to Anselme and lover to Elise	J. M. Kerrigan
Anselme, father to Valere and Marianne	U. Wright
Master Simon, broker	S. J. Morgan
Master Jacques, cook and coachman to Harpagon	J. A. O'Rourke
La Fleche, valet to Cleante	Eric Gorman
Lackeys to Harpagon:	
Brindavoine	U. Wright
La Merluche	Richard Boyd
Commissionaire	S. J. Morgan
Clerk	F. J. Harford
Elise, daughter to Harpagon	Eileen O'Doherty
Marianne, daughter to Anselme	Maire O'Neill
Frosine, an intriguing woman	Sara Allgood

11th March 1909
STEPHEN GREY

A Dream and an Incident in One Act by D. L. Kelleher

Stephen Grey, former schoolmaster of Bawnamore	Fred O'Donovan
Margaret Mary O'Neill, his worshipper, called Maggie May	Maire O'Neill
Small farmers:	
Mrs. N. O'Neill, her mother	Elaine Wodrow
Mike O'Neill, her father	S. J. Morgan
Ellen, household servant	Eileen O'Doherty
Stephen Swanton, widower, vinter of Bawnamore Cross	Arthur Sinclair
Father Canavan, a young curate	J. A. O'Rourke
Dan Sullivan, a neighbour's son	J. M. Kerrigan

1st April 1909
THE CROSS ROADS

A Play in a Prologue and Two Acts by S. L. Robinson

Prologue

James O'Reilly	Sydney J. Morgan
Sydney Doyle	Eric Gorman
Brian Connor	Fred O'Donovan
Henry Balke	J. A. O'Rourke
Ellen McCarthy	Sara Allgood

Play

Ellen McCarthy	Sara Allgood
Mrs. McCarthy, her mother	Maire O'Neill
Mrs. Desmond	Eileen O'Doherty
Mike Dempsey	J. M. Kerrigan
Tom Dempsey, his son	Arthur Sinclair
Brian Connor	Fred O'Donovan

1st April 1909
TIME

A Passing Phantasy by Norreys Connell

A Young Painter	J. M. Kerrigan
A Young Girl	Maire O'Neill
An Old Man	Norreys Connell

29th April 1909

First Production by the Abbey Company of

THE GLITTERING GATE

A Play in One Act by Lord Dunsany

Jim, formerly a burglar, since hanged	Fred O'Donovan
Bill, also a burglar, since shot	Norreys Connell

13th May 1909
AN IMAGINARY CONVERSATION

In One Act by Norreys Connell

Tom Moore	J. M. Kerrigan
Robert Emmet	Fred O'Donovan
Kate Moore	Sara Allgood

A HISTORY, 1899–1951

25th August 1909

THE SHEWING-UP OF BLANCO POSNET

A Sermon in Crude Melodrama by G. Bernard Shaw

Babsy	Eileen O'Doherty
Lottie	Cathleen Mullamphy
Hannah	Sheila O'Sullivan
Jessie	Mary Nairn
Emma	Annie O'Hynes
Elder Daniels	Arthur Sinclair
Blanco Posnet	Fred O'Donovan
Strapper Kemp	J. M. Kerrigan
Feemy Evans	Sara Allgood
Sheriff Kemp	Sydney J. Morgan
Foreman of Jury	J. A. O'Rourke
Nestor, a juryman	A. J. Goulden
The Woman	Maire O'Neill
Waggoner Joe	Eric Gorman

Jurymen, Boys, etc.: U. Wright, J. Dunne, J. Fitzgerald, H. Harford, J. Downes, Hugh Barden, P. Murphy, J. O'Brien, etc.

16th September 1909

THE WHITE FEATHER

A Play in Three Acts by R. J. Ray

Martin Kearney, publican and shopkeeper	J. A. O'Rourke
William Pat McCarthy, an estate bailiff	Sydney J. Morgan
James Cassidy, a cattle dealer	J. M. Kerrigan
Michael John Dillon, a farmer	Arthur Sinclair
Mrs. Margaret Dillon, his mother	Eileen O'Doherty
Sergeant Barton, R.I.C.	G. H. Fitzgerald
Mrs. Brady, wife of a small farmer	Maire O'Neill
Warder A	Fred O'Donovan
Warder B	A. J. Goulden
Governor of County Gaol	Eric Gorman

14th October 1909

THE CHALLENGE

A Play in One Act by W. M. Letts

Charles Caulfield	Arthur Sinclair
James Buchanan	Fred O'Donovan
Terence, a butler	J. A. O'Rourke

11th November 1909

THE IMAGE

A Comedy in Three Acts by Lady Gregory "Secretum Meum Mihi"

Thomas Coppinger, a stone cutter	Arthur Sinclair
Mary Coppinger, his wife	Sara Allgood
Malachi Naughton, a Mountainy Man	Fred O'Donovan
Brian Hosty, a small farmer	Sydney J. Morgan
Darby Costello, a seaweed-gatherer	J. M. Kerrigan
Peggy Mahon, an old midwife	Maire O'Neill
Peter Mannion, a carrier	J. A. O'Rourke

13th January 1910

DEIRDRE OF THE SORROWS

A Play in Three Acts by the late J. M. Synge

Lavarcham	Sara Allgood
Old Woman	Eileen O'Doherty
Owen	J. A. O'Rourke
Conchubor	Arthur Sinclair
Fergus	Sydney J. Morgan
Deirdre	Maire O'Neill
Naisi	Fred O'Donovan
Brothers of Naisi:	
Ainnle	J. M. Kerrigan
Ardan	John Carrick
Two Soldiers	Ambrose Power, Harry Young

10th February 1910

THE GREEN HELMET

A Play in Ballad Metre by W. B. Yeats founded on The Golden Helmet

Cuchulain	J. M. Kerrigan
Conall	Arthur Sinclair
Laegaire	Fred O'Donovan
Laeg, Cuchulain's charioteer	Sydney J. Morgan
Emer, wife of Cuchulain	Sara Allgood
Conal's Wife	Maire O'Neill
Leagerie's Wife	Eithne Magee
Red Man	Ambrose Power

Scullions, Horse Boys and Blackmen: Eric Gorman, J. A. O'Rourke, John Carrick, F. R. Harford, T. Moloney, T. Durkin, P. Byrne

24th February 1910

MIRANDOLINA (La Locandiera)

A Comedy in Three Acts translated and adapted from the Italian of Goldoni by Lady Gregory

Captain Ripafratta . . .	Fred O'Donovan
Marquis of Forlipopli . .	Arthur Sinclair
Count of Albafiorita . .	J. M. Kerrigan
Mirandolina, an inn-keeper	Maire O'Neill
Strolling players:	
Ortensia	Eileen O'Doherty
Dejanira	Eithne Magee
Fabrizio, servant at the inn	J. A. O'Rourke
The Captain's Servant	Sydney J. Morgan

3rd March 1910

THE TRAVELLING MAN

A Miracle Play by Lady Gregory

A Mother	Sara Allgood
A Child	Elinor Moore
A Travelling Man . . .	Fred O'Donovan

5th May 1910

THOMAS MUSKERRY

A Play in Three Acts by Padraic Colum

Christy Clarke, a boy reared in the workhouse	U. Wright
Felix Tournour, the porter at workhouse lodge	Sydney J. Morgan
Myles Gorman, a blind piper	Fred O'Donovan
Thomas Muskerry, the master of Garrisowen workhouse	Arthur Sinclair
Albert Crilly, his grandson	Eric Gorman
Crofton Crilly, his son-in-law	J. M. Kerrigan
Mrs. Crilly, his daughter .	Sara Allgood
Anna Crilly, his granddaughter	Maire O'Neill
James Scollard	J. A. O'Rourke
Paupers in workhouse:	
Mickie Cripes . . .	F. R. Harford
Thomas Shanley . .	Ambrose Power
An Old Man . . .	J. M. Kerrigan

Produced by S. L. Robinson

19th May 1910

HARVEST

A Play in Three Acts by S. L. Robinson

Jack Hurley	Fred O'Donovan
Mildred, married to Jack .	Sara Allgood
Bridget Twomey, a neighbour	Eileen O'Doherty
Maggie Hannigan . . .	Eithne Magee
Timothy Hurley . . .	J. A. O'Rourke
Maurice Hurley . . .	J. M. Kerrigan
William Lordan, a retired schoomaster	Arthur Sinclair
Mary Hurley	Maire O'Neill

Produced by the Author

29th September 1910

THE CASTING-OUT OF MARTIN WHELAN

A Play in Three Acts by R. J. Ray

Mrs. Kirby	Sara Allgood
William Kirby, her son .	Fred Harford
James Kirby, his father .	Sydney J. Morgan
Ned Mooney, a pig-buyer .	Arthur Sinclair
Peter Barton, a farmer . .	J. M. Kerrigan
Ellen Barton, his daughter	Maire O'Neill
Martin Whelan, an Australian	Fred O'Donovan
Mrs. Pender, a servant .	Eileen O'Doherty
Mikeen Whip-the-Wind, a fool	J. A. O'Rourke
Denis Barton . . .	Brinsley MacNamara
Peasants: Eric Gorman, U. Wright, J. H. Dunne, R. Jameson, Harry Young	

Produced by the Author

27th October 1910

BIRTHRIGHT

A Play in Two Acts by T. C. Murray

Dan Hegarty	J. A. O'Rourke
Maura Morrissey . . .	Eileen O'Doherty
Bat Morrissey . . .	Sydney J. Morgan
Frank Harrington, a schoolmaster	J. M. Kerrigan
Shane Morrissey . . .	Arthur Sinclair
Hugh Morrissey . . .	Fred O'Donovan

Produced by the Author

A HISTORY, 1899–1951

10th November 1910

THE FULL MOON
A Comedy in One Act by Lady Gregory

Bartley Fallon	Arthur Sinclair
Shawn Early	J. A. O'Rourke
Hyacinth Halvey	Fred O'Donovan
Mrs. Broderick	Sara Allgood
Peter Tannon	Sydney J. Morgan
Miss Joyce (All Sane)	Eileen O'Doherty
Cracked Mary	Maire O'Neill
Davideen, an innocent, her brother	J. M. Kerrigan

Produced by the Author

24th November 1910

First Production by the Abbey Company of
THE SHUILER'S CHILD
A Tragedy in Two Acts by Seumas O'Kelly

Tim O'Halloran	Sydney J. Morgan
Mrs. Finnessy	Sheila O'Sullivan
Nannie O'Hea	Eileen O'Doherty
Phil Woods	Felix Hughes
Moll Woods, a Shuiler	Maire Nic Shiubhlaigh
Miss Cecilia Stoney	Eithne Magee
Andy O'Hea	Fred O'Donovan

1st December 1910

COATS
A Comedy in One Act by Lady Gregory

Hazel, editor of Champion	J. M. Kerrigan
Mineog, editor of Tribune	Arthur Sinclair
John, a waiter	J. A. O'Rourke

12th January 1911

THE DELIVERER
A Tragic Comedy by Lady Gregory

Dan	Arthur Sinclair
Ard	Fred O'Donovan
Malachi	J. A. O'Rourke
Dan's Wife	Maire O'Neill
Malachi's Wife	Sara Allgood
Ard's Wife	Maire Nic Shiubhlaigh
A Steward	Sydney J. Morgan
King's Nursling	J. M. Kerrigan
An Officer	Brinsley MacNamara

Produced by the Author

26th January 1911

KING ARGIMENES AND THE UNKNOWN WARRIOR
A Play in Two Acts by Lord Dunsany

King Argimenes	Fred O'Donovan
Zarb, a slave, born of slaves	J. M. Kerrigan
An Old Slave	Fred Harford
A Young Slave	Brinsley MacNamara
A Prophet	J. A. O'Rourke
The King's Overseer	Ambrose Power
King Darniak	Arthur Sinclair
Queens of King Darniak:	
Queen Atharlia	Sara Allgood
Queen Oxara	Maeve O'Donnell
Queen Caharfa	Maire O'Neill
Queen Thragolind	Maire Nic Shiubhlaigh
The Idol Guard	Sydney J. Morgan
The Servant of the King's Dog	Eric Gorman
An Attendant	R. Jameson

Produced by S. L. Robinson

16th February 1911

First Production by the Abbey Company of
THE LAND OF HEART'S DESIRE
A Play in One Act by W. B. Yeats

Bridget Bruin	Eileen O'Doherty
Shawn Bruin	Fred O'Donovan
Maurteen Bruin	J. M. Kerrigan
Father Hart	Arthur Sinclair
Maire Bruin	Sara Allgood
A Faery	Maire O'Neill

Produced by S. L. Robinson

30th March 1911

MIXED MARRIAGE
A Play in Four Acts by St. John Ervine

John Rainey	Arthur Sinclair
Mrs. Rainey	Maire O'Neill
Tom Rainey	U. Wright
Nora Murray	Maire Nic Shiubhlaigh
Hugh Rainey	J. M. Kerrigan
Michael O'Hara	J. A. O'Rourke

Produced by Lennox Robinson

16th November 1911

First Production by the Abbey Company of
THE INTERLUDE OF YOUTH
An Old Morality

Charity	Belle Johnston
Youth	Nugent Monck
Riot	Jack Martin
Pride	Charles Power
Luxury	Nora Desmond
Humility	Violet McCarthy

Produced by Nugent Monck

16th November 1911

First Production by the Abbey Company of
THE MARRIAGE
A Play in One Act by Douglas Hyde
Translated from the Irish by Lady Gregory

Martin	Charles Power
Mary	F. M. Salkeld
Blind Fiddler	Michael Conniffe
Old Farmer	A. Patrick Wilson
Middle-aged Woman	R. Leech
Fair Young Man	W. J. Manser
Grey-haired Man	J. McCabe
Two Girls	Mona Shiel, M. Perolze
Young Man	J. R. Burke
Miser	Patrick Murphy

Produced by Nugent Monck

23rd November 1911

First Production by the Abbey Company of
THE SECOND SHEPHERD'S PLAY

First Shepherd	S. Grenville Darling
Second Shepherd	George St. John
Third Shepherd	Farrell Pelly
Mac	A. Patrick Wilson
Gabriel	W. J. Manser
Gill	Mary Roberts

Produced by Nugent Monck

7th December 1911
RED TURF
A Play in One Act by Rutherford Mayne

Martin Burke	J. R. Burke
Mary Burke	Maire O'Neill
Michael Flanagan	Patrick Murphy
Michael Flanagan, the younger	Charles Power
John Heffernan	Farrell Pelly

Produced by Nugent Monck

4th January 1912

First Production by the Abbey Company of
THE ANNUNCIATION

Mary	Nell Byrne
St. Joseph	Nugent Monck
Gabriel	Charles Power

Produced by Nugent Monck

4th January 1912

First Production by the Abbey Company of
THE FLIGHT INTO EGYPT

Mary	Nell Byrne
St. Joseph	Nugent Monck
Gabriel	Charles Power

Produced by Nugent Monck

11th January 1912
MACDARAGH'S WIFE
A Play in One Act by Lady Gregory

First Hag	Mary Roberts
Second Hag	Helena Moloney
Macdaragh	Philip Guiry

Sheepshearers: Messrs. Conniffe, George St. John, Farrell Pelly, Patrick Murphy, A. P. Wilson, J. R. Burke

Produced by Nugent Monck

15th February 1912
AN TINCEAR AGUS AN T-SIDHEOG
Le Dubhglas de hIde

An tSidheog	Nell Ni Bhrion
An Tincear	Cathal Paor
Fear Og	Micheal Ua Coinnibh
Feilmeoir	Philib MacGaoraidh
Bean Og	Una Ni Conchubhar

Sidheogha: Una Nic Shiubhlaigh, G. Ni Muiris, Maire Ni hAodha, M. Ni Ghallcobhair, E. Ni Cathmhaoil, C. Ni Riain, Una Ni Leigh, Mildred Connmhaigh, T. Bairead, F. Peallai, A. Misteal, A. P. Mac Liam, H. Hutchinson, S. Mac Eoin

Produced by Nugent Monck

A HISTORY, 1899–1951 107

29th February 1912

First Production by the Abbey Company of
THE WORLDE AND THE CHYLDE

The Worlde	Patrick Murphy
The Mother	Una Nic Shiubhlaigh
The Chylde	Felix Hughes
Manhood	Nugent Monck
Conscience	A. Patrick Wilson
Folly	Philip Guiry
Perseverance	Charles Power
Pride	Ethel Fletcher
Covetousness	Maidha Gallagher
Wrath	Kathleen O'Brien
Envy	Mary Roberts
Indolence	Nell Byrne
Gluttony	G. Laird
Luxury	Mona O'Beirne
Page	P. Goodwin

Produced by Nugent Monck

28th March 1912

FAMILY FAILING

A Comedy in Three Acts by William Boyle

Maria Donnelly	Eileen O'Doherty
Nelty, a servant	Kathleen Drago
Dominic Donnelly, Maria's brother	Arthur Sinclair
Joe Donnelly, her younger brother	Sydney J. Morgan
Tom Carragher, a neighbour	J. M. Kerrigan
Mrs. Carragher, his wife	Cathleen Nesbitt
Robert Donnelly, Dominic's uncle	Fred O'Donovan
Francy Niel, a rural carrier	M. J. Dolan

Produced by Lennox Robinson

11th April 1912

PATRIOTS

A Play in Three Acts by Lennox Robinson

James O'Mahoney	Sydney J. Morgan
Ann Nugent	Sara Allgood
Rose Nugent, her child	Kathleen Drago
Mrs. Sullivan	Eileen O'Doherty
Ann's brothers:	
Bob	Arthur Sinclair
Harry	J. A. O'Rourke
Willie Sullivan	C. Power
James Nugent	Fred O'Donovan
Father Kearney	J. M. Kerrigan
Dan Sullivan	Philip Guiry
Jim Powell	J. M. Kerrigan
Two Young Men:	U. Wright, Philip Guiry

Produced by the Author

15th April 1912

JUDGEMENT

A Play in Two Acts by Joseph Campbell

Owen Ban	H. E. Hutchinson
Nabla, his wife	Nell Byrne
John Gilla Carr	J. G. St. John
Parry Cam Aosta, a very old man	Philip Guiry
Colum Johnston	A. P. Wilson
Peter	T. Barrett
Kate Kinsella, a midwife	Mona O'Beirne
Peg Straw, a strolling woman	Mary Galway
The Stranger	G. R. Burke
Father John	Charles Power

Produced by Lennox Robinson

20th June 1912

At Royal Court Theatre, London

MAURICE HARTE

A Play in Two Acts by T. C. Murray

Mrs. O'Connor	Eileen O'Doherty
Ellen Harte	Sara Allgood
Maurice Harte	Fred O'Donovan
Father Mangan	Sydney J. Morgan
Michael Harte	Arthur Sinclair
Owen Harte	J. A. O'Rourke
Peter Managan	U. Wright

Produced by Lennox Robinson

4th July 1912

At Royal Court Theatre, London

THE BOGIE MAN

A Comedy in One Act by Lady Gregory

Chimney Sweeps:
Taig O'Harragha	J. M. Kerrigan
Darby Melody	J. A. O'Rourke

Produced by Lennox Robinson

17th October 1912

THE MAGNANIMOUS LOVER

A Play in One Act by St. John Ervine

Samuel Hinde, a grocer	J. A. O'Rourke
Mrs. Cather	Mona O'Beirne
William Cather, her husband, a shoemaker	Sydney J. Morgan
Henry Hinde	J. M. Kerrigan
Maggie Cather	Maire O'Neill

Produced by Lennox Robinson

21st November 1912

DAMER'S GOLD

A Comedy in Two Acts by Lady Gregory

Delia Hessian	Sara Allgood
Staffy Kirwan, her brother	Sydney J. Morgan
Ralph Hessian, Delia's husband	J. M. Kerrigan
Patrick Kirwan (called Damer), Delia's and Staffy's brother	Arthur Sinclair
Simon Niland, their nephew	U. Wright

Produced by Lennox Robinson

26th December 1912

A LITTLE CHRISTMAS MIRACLE

A Play in One Act by E. Hamilton Moore

Bridget Cassidy	Helena Moloney
Daniel Byrne	Philip Guiry
Michael O'Halloran	Patrick Murphy
Larry Sullivan	Michael Conniffe
The Captain	Farrell Pelly
The Strange Woman	Nell Byrne

Produced by Lennox Robinson

23rd January 1913

THE DEAN OF ST. PATRICK'S

A Play in Four Acts by G. Sidney Paternoster

Patrick, servant to Dr. Swift	Michael Conniffe
Sweetheart	Helena Moloney
Mistress Esther Johnston (Stella)	Nell Byrne
Mrs. Dingley	Nora Desmond
Dr. Jonathan Swift	Patrick Murphy
His Grace the Archbishop of Dublin	George St. John
Mr. Joseph Addison	Farrell Pelly
Mrs. Van Homrigh	Ettie Fletcher
Mistress Anne Long	Una O'Connor
Mistress Hester Van Homrigh (Vanessa)	Ann Coppinger
Mrs. Touchet	Nell Stewart
First Lady	Kathleen O'Brien
Second Lady	Betty King
Henry St. John, Viscount Bolingbroke	Philip Guiry
Royal Servant	Thomas Barrett
Mr. Congreve	A. Patrick Wilson
His Grace The Duke of Ormond	Charles Power
Dr. John Arbuthnot, the Queen's Physician	Eric Gorman
Robert Harley, Earl of Oxford	Sean Connolly

Produced by Lennox Robinson

13th March 1913

THE CUCKOO'S NEST

A Comedy in Three Acts by John Guinan

Nora Flanaghan	Peggy Buttimer
Peg Galvin, her first cousin	Nell Stewart
Farmers:	
Phil Dolan	Michael Conniffe
Luke Muldowney	Philip Guiry
Nancy Kennedy	Helena Moloney
Hugh Loughnane, a labourer	Farrell Pelly

Produced by Lennox Robinson

10th April 1913

THE HOME-COMING

A Play in One Act by Gertrude Robins

Ivan Loweski	Philip Guiry
Stefan	Sean Connolly
Paul Loweski	Farrell Pelly
Catherine Loweski	Helena Moloney

Produced by Lennox Robinson

A HISTORY, 1899–1951

24th April 1913

BROKEN FAITH

A Play in Two Acts by S. R. Day and
   G. D. Cummins

Mrs. Gara	Una O'Connor
Bridget Gara, her daughter-in-law	Nora Desmond
Dan Hourihan	Michael Conniffe
Michael Gara	Farrell Pelly
Mikeen	Laurance Byrne
Timothy Coll	Philip Guiry
A Policeman	Charles Power

Produced by Lennox Robinson

24th April 1913

THE MAGIC GLASSES

A Play in One Act by George Fitzmaurice

Maineen Shanahan . .	Helena Moloney
Padden Shanahan . . .	George St. John
Mr. Quille	Philip Guiry
Jaymony Shanahan . .	Charles Power
Aunt Jug	Una O'Connor
Aunt Mary	E. Stewart

Produced by Lennox Robinson

17th May 1913

THE POST OFFICE

A Play in Two Acts by Rabindranath Tagore

Madhav	Philip Guiry
Doctor	Charles Power
Gaffer	Michael Conniffe
Amal, Madhav's adopted child	Lilian Jago
Dairyman	Farrell Pelly
Watchman	H. E. Hutchinson
Headman	James Duffy
Sudha	Nell Stewart
Boys: Desmond Murphy, Owen Clarke, Horace Jennings	
King's Herald	Thomas Barrett
King's Physician . . .	Sean Connolly

Produced by Lennox Robinson

The Scene, composed of Gordon Craig Screens, arranged by J. F. Barlow.

30th June 1913

At Royal Court Theatre, London

THE GOMBEEN MAN

A Play in Three Acts by R. J. Ray

Michael Myers, clerk to Stephen Kiniry . . .	J. M. Kerrigan
Richard Kiniry, son of Stephen Kiniry . . .	Fred O'Donovan
Roger Connors	J. A. O'Rourke
William Naughton, a shopkeeper	Philip Guiry
Mrs. Naughton, his wife .	Eileen O'Doherty
Stephen Kiniry, a Gombeen Man	Arthur Sinclair
Martin Shinnick, a farmer	Sydney J. Morgan
Mrs. Kiniry, his daughter .	Sara Allgood

Produced by Lennox Robinson

11th September 1913

SOVEREIGN LOVE

A Comedy in One Act by T. C. Murray

Donal Kearney, a farmer .	J. M. Kerrigan
His daughters:	
Ellen	Ann Coppinger
Katty	Eithne Magee
Maurice O'Brien, their uncle .	Philip Guiry
Mrs. Hickey, hostess of the "Granuaile"	Helena Moloney
Charles O'Donnell, another farmer	Sydney J. Morgan
David, his son	Charles Power
Tom Daly, cousin to David	Michael Conniffe
Andy Hyde, a returned Yank .	Farrell Pelly

Produced by Lennox Robinson

2nd October 1913

THE MINE LAND

A Comedy in Three Acts by Joseph Connolly

Matta Lynn	Sydney J. Morgan
Jane Lynn, his wife . .	Una O'Connor
Barney O'Hara	Philip Guiry
Burnett, president of the Geological Society . .	Charles Power
Members of the Geological Society:	
Lavelle	H. E. Hutchinson
Hardy	George St. John
Annie McKendry . . .	Eithne Magee
Alec Liddell, his son . .	Farrell Pelly
William Liddell . . .	H. E. Hutchinson
Charlie McCrea . . .	Sean Connolly

Produced by Lennox Robinson

16th October 1913
MY LORD
A Play in One Act by Mrs. Bart Kennedy

My Lord . . . . . Arthur Sinclair
Dermot, an old huntsman, My
 Lord's foster-brother . J. A. O'Rourke
Tenants:
 Curran . . . . . . Philip Guiry
 O'Grady . . . . . Sydney J. Morgan
 Malone . . . . . J. M. Kerrigan
 Nurse . . . . . . Helena Moloney
Other Tenants

Produced by Lennox Robinson

20th November 1913
THE CRITICS
Or A New Play at the Abbey Theatre
Being A Little Morality for the Press
by St. John Ervine

Dramatic Critics:
 Mr. Barbary . . . . J. M. Kerrigan
 Mr. Quacks . . . . Fred O'Donovan
 Mr. Quartz . . . . Sydney J. Morgan
 Mr. Bawlawney . . . Arther Sinclair
An Attendant . . . . H. E. Hutchinson

The Scene is laid in the Vestibule of the Abbey Theatre

Produced by Lennox Robinson

16th December 1913
DUTY
A Comedy in One Act by Seumas O'Brien

Padna Sweeny . . . . J. A. O'Rourke
Micus Goggin . . . . J. M. Kerrigan
Mrs. Cotter . . . . Una O'Connor
Head Constable Mulligan,
 R.I.C.. . . . . . Arthur Sinclair
Sergeant Dooley, R.I.C. . Fred O'Donovan
Constable Huggins, R.I.C. Sydney J. Morgan

Produced by Lennox Robinson

18th December 1913
THE BRIBE
A Play in Three Acts by Seumas O'Kelly

Mrs. Diamond . . . . Nora Desmond
Mary Kirwan . . . . Kathleen Drago
Mrs. Kirwan . . . . Eileen O'Doherty
John Kirwan . . . . Arthur Sinclair
Dr. Luke Diamond . . Fred O'Donovan

Dr. Power O'Connor . . Sydney J. Morgan
Dr. Jack Power O'Connor . Philip Guiry
Mr. Toomey . . . . H. E. Hutchinson
A Pauper . . . . . Michael Conniffe
Mrs. Cooney . . . . Eithne Magee
Poor Law Guardians: J. M. Kerrigan, J. A. O'Rourke, U. Wright, A. Patrick Wilson, Farrell Pelly, etc.

Produced by Lennox Robinson

29th January 1914
DAVID MAHONY
A Play in Three Acts by Victor O'D. Power

Norrie Burke . . . . Eithne Magee
Peggy Hegarty . . . . Kathleen Drago
David Mahony . . . . H. E. Hutchinson
Flurry Mahony . . . . Philip Guiry
The Widow Mahony . . Nora Desmond

Produced by Lennox Robinson

13th March 1914
THE ORANGEMAN
A Comedy in One Act by St. John Ervine

John McClurg . . . A. Patrick Wilson
Jessie McClurg . . Cathleen MacCarthy
Andy Haneron . . . . Sean Connolly
Tom McClurg . . . . Thomas O'Neill

Produced by A. Patrick Wilson

13th March 1914
THE LORD MAYOR
A Comedy in Three Acts by Edward McNulty

Charwomen:
 Mrs. Murphy . . . Sheila O'Sullivan
 Mrs. Moloney . . . Maura O'Byrne
Gaffney, a solicitor Reginald Montgomery
Kelly, his clerk .. . . Michael Hayes
O'Brien, an ironmonger, afterwards Lord Mayor . . Sean Connolly
Mrs. O'Brien, his wife . Maureen Delany
Moira O'Brien, his
 daughter. . . Cathleen MacCarthy
Creditors:
 Scanlon . . . . . Michael Conniffe
 Doherty . . . . . Edward Reardon
 Mrs. Moran . . . . Ethel Fletcher
Mr. Butterfield . . . Arthur Shields
Lackey . . . . . . Thomas O'Neill
Creditors: Messrs. J. Conniffe, J. McEntee, T. L. Christopher and Geo. Harold.

Produced by A. Patrick Wilson

A HISTORY, 1899–1951   111

2nd April 1914
KINSHIP
A Play in One Act by J. Bernard McCarthy

The Widow Connell . .	Nora Shannon
Hugh Connell	Sean Connolly
Mike Connell	Shawn Joyce
Bride Cassidy . .	Cathleen MacCarthy
Jim Twomey	Michael Conniffe
Sergeant Desmond . . .	Brick Noels

Produced by A. Patrick Wilson

13th April 1914
THE COBBLER
A Play in One Act by A. Patrick Wilson

A Cobbler	A. Patrick Wilson
A Ploughman . . .	Sean Connolly
A Farmer	Thomas O'Neill
A Village Gossip .	Cathleen MacCarthy
A Schoolmaster . . .	Arthur Shields
A Schoolboy	Felix Hughes

Produced by A. Patrick Wilson

4th June 1914
At Royal Court Theatre, London
THE SUPPLANTER
A Play in Three Acts by J. Bernard McCarthy

Ellie Cassidy	Eithne Magee
Mrs. Keegan . . .	Eileen O'Doherty
Widow Flynn . . .	Ann Coppinger
John O'Connor . .	Sydney J. Morgan
Phil Keegan . . .	Fred O'Donovan
Pad Saunders	Philip Guiry

Produced by Lennox Robinson

27th August 1914
A MINUTE'S WAIT
A Comedy in One Act by Martin J. McHugh

Barney Domigan . . .	Arthur Sinclair
Christy Domigan . . .	Philip Guiry
Mrs. Falsey	Nora Desmond
Mary Ann McMahon .	Eithne Magee
Andy Rourke	Fred O'Donovan
Pat Morrissey . . .	J. A. O'Rourke
Jim O'Brien	S. J. Morgan
Tom Kinsella . . .	J. M. Kerrigan
Mrs. Kinsella . . .	Ann Coppinger
The Puckawn	
The Crowd	

Produced by A. Patrick Wilson

9th September 1914
THE DARK HOUR
A Comedy in One Act by R. A. Christie

William Finlay	J. M. Kerrigan
Jane Finlay	Nora Desmond
Samuel James . . .	H. E. Hutchinson
Willie Davis	Philip Guiry
Mary Davis	Eithne Magee
Rachael McDowell . .	Ann Coppinger
Wandering Danny .	Sydney J. Morgan

Produced by A. Patrick Wilson

23rd September 1914
THE CROSSING
A Play in One Act by Con O'Leary

William Fenton . . .	Arthur Sinclair
Mary the Roads . . .	Nora Desmond
Matthew the Rhymes .	J. M. Kerrigan
Thomas Fenton . . .	Fred O'Donovan

Produced by A. Patrick Wilson

30th September 1914
THE PRODIGAL
A Play in Four Acts by Walter Riddall

Samuel Walker	Arthur Sinclair
Sarah Walker	Nora Desmond
Helen Walker	Eithne Magee
George Walker	H. E. Hutchinson
Stanley Walker . . .	Fred O'Donovan
Rev. Hugh Chapman . .	Philip Guiry
Billy Bradley	J. M. Kerrigan
Lizzie Bradley	Kathleen Drago
John Evans	S. J. Morgan
Maggie	Ann Coppinger

Produced by A. Patrick Wilson

13th October 1914
THE COBWEB
A Play in One Act by F. Jay

Secretary Cooke . . .	Arthur Sinclair
Kate Caraher . . .	Eithne Magee
Eustace Hyme	Philip Guiry
Leonard McNally . . .	Sean Connolly
Dr. Trevor	Eric Gorman
Slippoon	H. E. Hutchinson
Pinlock	Michael Conniffe

Produced by A. Patrick Wilson

20th October 1914

THE JUG OF SORROW

A Comedy in One Act by W. P. Ryan

Patsy	Sydney J. Morgan
Syve	Ann Coppinger
Peg	Kathleen Drago
Donal	Philip Guiry
Seumas	J. M. Kerrigan
Nora	Eithne Magee
Father Eamonn	Fred O'Donovan

Produced by A. Patrick Wilson

3rd November 1914

THE SLOUGH

A Play in Three Acts by A. Patrick Wilson

Peter Hanlon	Arthur Sinclair
Mary Hanlon	Maura O'Byrne
Annie Hanlon	Kathleen Drago
Peg Hanlon	Eithne Magee
Jack Hanlon	Philip Guiry
Edward Kelly	H. E. Hutchinson
Margaret Kelly	Nora Desmond
Tom Robinson	Fred O'Donovan
Jake Allen	A. Patrick Wilson
Joe Moran	J. F. Barlow
Jim Crocker	Sydney J. Morgan
Tim Daly	J. A. O'Rourke
Bill Nolan	J. M. Kerrigan
Pete Riley	Michael Conniffe
Matt Taylor	Thomas O'Neill

Produced by the Author

26th December 1914

First Production by the Abbey Company of

THE CRITIC

A Comedy in Three Acts
by R. Brinsley Sheridan

Mr. Puff	Arthur Sinclair
Mr. Dangle	Fred O'Donovan
Mr. Sneer	Philip Guiry
Sir Fateful Flagiary	J. M. Kerrigan
Mrs. Dangle	Nora Desmond
Signor Pasticcio Ritornello	Eric Gorman
The Singers	The Rafter Brothers
The Prompter	H. E. Hutchinson
The Master Carpenter	J. F. Barlow
Assistant Carpenter	Thomas O'Neill
The Property Man	George St. John

CHARACTERS OF THE TRAGEDY

Lord Burleigh	J. R. St. Rich
Governor of Tilbury Fort	Sydney J. Morgan
Earl of Leicester	Sean Connolly
Sir Christopher Hatton	J. H. Dunne
Sir Walter Raleigh	J. A. O'Rourke
Master of the Horse	U. Wright
Don Ferolo Whiskerandos	J. M. Kerrigan
Beefeater	Michael Conniffe
Justice	Edward Reardon
Son	Charles Power
Constable	Arthur Shields
Justice's Lady	Maureen Delany
Tilburina	Ann Coppinger
Confidante	Sheila O'Sullivan
First Niece	Eithne Magee
Second Niece	Cathleen MacCarthy
First Sentinel	J. Eustace
Second Sentinel	W. Shields

Produced by A. Patrick Wilson

27th January 1915

BY WORD OF MOUTH

A Comedy in One Act by F. C. Moore
and W. P. Flanagan

Cyranus P. Blaine	J. M. Kerrigan
Hank Morgan	Sydney J. Morgan
Deacon Ezra Simmons	Arthur Sinclair
Fidelia	Ann Coppinger

Produced by A. Patrick Wilson

10th February 1915

THE DREAMERS

A Play in Three Acts by Lennox Robinson

John Brady	Arthur Sinclair
Robert Brady	A. Patrick Wilson
Martin Brady	U. Wright
Robert Emmet	Fred O'Donovan
Lacey	Eric Gorman
Sarah Curran	Sara Allgood
Henry Howley	J. M. Kerrigan
Thomas Freyne	James Smith
McCartney	Sean Connolly
Hannay	H. E. Hutchinson
Morrissey	J. M. Kerrigan
Trenaghan	Philip Guiry
Peter Freyne	George St. John
Roche	J. A. O'Rourke
Mulligan	William Shields
Julia	Kathleen Drago
Jerry	Thomas O'Neill
Jim	J. F. Barlow
Peter Flynn	Sydney J. Morgan
Felix Rourke	J. M. Kerrigan
Larry ⎱ Con ⎰	Sean Connolly
Mickey	Michael Conniffe
Kate	Sheila O'Sullivan

ST. JOHN ERVINE

Mary . . . . . Cathleen MacCarthy
Quigley . . . . Eric Gorman
Phillips . . . . Fred Harford
Mike. . . . . . . J. A. O'Rourke
Mangan . . . . . . Sean Connolly
Mrs. Dillon . . . . Ann Coppinger
Mrs. Palmer . . . . Helena Moloney
Jane Curran . . . . Nora Desmond
Major Sirr . . . . . . Philip Guiry
Jones. . . . . . . H. E. Hutchinson
Other men: Arthur Shields, Edward Reardon, Jack Dunne

Produced by A. Patrick Wilson

5th April 1915
THE BARGAIN
A Play in Three Acts by William Crone

William John McComb . Sydney J. Morgan
Tom McComb . . . . . Philip Guiry
Andy Simpson . . . J. A. O'Rourke
Mary Simpson . . . Cathleen MacCarthy
Jane Simpson . . . . Helena Moloney
James Simpson . . . H. E. Hutchinson
Annie Harvey . . . . Eithne Magee
Sarah . . . . Kathleen Drago

Produced by A. Patrick Wilson

5th April 1915
THE PHILOSOPHER
A Comedy in One Act by Martin J. McHugh

Dan McInerney, a shop-
 keeper. . . . . . Arthur Sinclair
Michael Donnellan, his
 friend . . . . . J. A. O'Rourke
John Magrath . . . J. M. Kerrigan
Mr. Honan, solicitor . . Sean Connolly
Mr. Sullivan, auctioneer . Fred O'Donovan
Tom Burke . . . . Sydney J. Morgan
Joe Minogue . . . H. E. Hutchinson
Sergeant Duffy, R.I.C. . . Philip Guiry

Produced by A. Patrick Wilson

8th April 1915
SHANWALLA
A Play in Three Acts by Lady Gregory

Lawrence Scarry, a stable-
 man . . . . . . H. E. Hutchinson
Hubert Darcy, his master Sydney J. Morgan
Bride Scarry, his wife . . Kathleen Drago
Owen Conery, a blind
 beggar. . . . . . J. M. Kerrigan
Pat O'Malley . . . Fred O'Donovan
James Brogan . . . . Arthur Sinclair

First Girl . . . . . . Eithne Magee
Second Girl . . . . . Ann Coppinger
Head Constable . . . J. A. O'Rourke
First Policeman . . . Michael Conniffe
Second Policeman . . . . Philip Guiry
A Boy . . . . . . Thomas O'Neill

Produced by A. Patrick Wilson

30th November 1915
JOHN FERGUSON
A Tragedy in Four Acts by St. John Ervine

John Ferguson, a farmer . Sydney J. Morgan
Sarah Ferguson, his wife . Nora Desmond
Hannah Ferguson, his daughter Nora Close
James Caesar, a grocer . J. M. Kerrigan
Henry Witherow, a miller Arthur Sinclair
Sam Mawhinney, a post-
 man . . . . . . J. A. O'Rourke
"Clutie" John Magrath, a
 beggar. . . . . . . Philip Guiry
Andreas Ferguson, John
 Ferguson's son . . . Fred O'Donovan
Sergeant Kernaghan,
 R.I.C. . . . . . . H. E. Hutchinson
Two Constables . . A. Shields, D. Kelly
A Crowd of men and women

Produced by the Author

4th January 1916
FRATERNITY
A Satire in One Act by Bernard Duffy

John Timley, President of a
 Branch of the Modern
 Order of Milesians . . Arthur Sinclair
Tom Carrivan, Secretary of
 the Branch . . . . Sydney J. Morgan
James Dulvey . . . . J. A. O'Rourke
Francis Herrissey . . . J. M. Kerrigan
Edward Doonan . . . H. E. Hutchinson
Peter Larrigan . . . . . Jack Dunne
Patrick Morohan . . . . Fred Harford
Jim Hooligan . . . . Edward Reardon
J. F. Moore, a landowner . Fred O'Donovan

Produced by St. John Ervine

8th February 1916
THE COINER
A Comedy in One Act by Bernard Duffy

James Canatt . . . . J. A. O'Rourke
Catherine Canatt . . . Joan Fitzmaurice
John Canatt. . . . . H. E. Hutchinson
Tom McClippon . . . J. M. Kerrigan
A Police Sergeant . . . Sydney J. Morgan

Produced by St. John Ervine

28th March 1916

THE PLOUGH-LIFTERS

A New Comedy in Two Acts by John Guinan

Kieran Coghlan	J. A. O'Rourke
Esther Coghlan	Nora Desmond
Shawn Dooley	Fred O'Donovan
Christy Doran	J. M. Kerrigan
Lacky Meara	Arthur Shields
Garry Rigney	Arthur Sinclair
Jerry Foley	Sydney J. Morgan
Winny Foley	Kathleen Murphy

Produced by St. John Ervine

25th September 1916

First Production by the Abbey Company of

JOHN BULL'S OTHER ISLAND

G. Bernard Shaw's Irish Play: Specially written for this Theatre

Tim Haffigan	H. G. Condron
Broadbent	J. M. Kerrigan
Hodson	J. M. S. Carré
Larry Doyle	Louis O'Connor
Father Keegan	Fred O'Donovan
Patsey	Arthur Bonass
Nora	Irene Kelly
Father Dempsey	Peter Nolan
Corney Doyle	Charles McSwiggan
Aunt Judy	Sive Allen
Matt	Eric Gorman
Barney Doyle	Ambrose Power

Produced by J. Augustus Keogh

9th October 1916

First Production by the Abbey Company of

WIDOWERS' HOUSES

A Play in Three Acts by G. Bernard Shaw

Mr. William De Burgh Cokane	J. M. Kerrigan
Dr. Harry Trench	Earle Grey
Waiter	Arthur Shields
Mr. Sartorius	Fred O'Donovan
Miss Blanche Sartorius	Violet McCarthy
Porter	U. Wright
Lickcheese	J. Augustus Keogh
Maid	Betty King

Produced by J. Augustus Keogh

16th October 1916

First Production by the Abbey Company of

ARMS AND THE MAN

An Anti-Romantic Comedy by G. Bernard Shaw

Raina Petkoff	May Craig
Catherine Petkoff	Maureen Delany
Louka	Irene Kelly
Captain Bluntshli	Fred O'Donovan
Officer	Arthur Shields
Nicola	Peter Nolan
Major Paul Ketkoff	J. M. Carre
Major Sergius Saranoff	Louis O'Connor

Produced by J. Augustus Keogh

25th October 1916

NIC

A Comedy in Three Acts by William Boyle

Peter O'Carroll	Peter Nolan
Mrs. O'Carroll	Maureen Delany
Bessy O'Carroll	Irene Kelly
John O'Carroll	C. Cruise O'Reilly
Nicholas O'Carroll (Nic)	Ambrose Power
Mr. Corcoran	Fred O'Donovan
Miss McNeil	May Craig

Produced by J. Augustus Keogh

15th November 1916

PARTITION

A Political Skit by D. C. Maher

"Molly" Kelly	Maureen Delany
"Bridgie" Kelly	Irene Kelly
"Jamsie" Kelly	Master McCann
"Andy" Kelly	Fred O'Donovan
"Iggy" Murphy	C. Cruise O'Reilly
"Long" Reilly	Arthur Shields
Mrs. McCloone	Sheila O'Sullivan
"Maggie" McGee	Mary Sheridan
Bennett	Hubert McGuire
Donnelly	Peter Nolan
Sergeant McIlweeney	Louis O'Connor
Home Rule Constable	Charles Saurin
Ulster Sergeant	Michael Orr
Ulster Constable	Fred Harford
Cornet Players, Neighbours, etc.	

Produced by J. Augustus Keogh

A HISTORY, 1899–1951

11th December 1916

THE COUNTER CHARM

A Comedy in One Act by Bernard Duffy

Aloysius Kinsella . .	J. Augustus Keogh
Nora Kinsella	Irene Kelly
Joe Hegarty . . .	Chas. C. O'Reilly
Mrs. Mulvey	Sheila O'Sullivan
Mrs. Hegarty	Maureen Delany

Produced by J. Augustus Keogh

13th December 1916

THE WHITEHEADED BOY

A Comedy in Three Acts by Lennox Robinson

Mrs. Geohegan . .	Eileen O'Doherty
George	Breffni O'Rorke
Peter	Arthur Shields
Katie	Dorothy Lynd
Baby	Maureen Delany
Jane	May Craig
Denis	Fred O'Donovan
Donogh Brosnan	Peter Nolan
John Duffy . . .	Chas. C. O'Reilly
Delia	Irene Kelly
Aunt Helen	Maire O'Neill
Hannah	Sheila O'Sullivan

Produced by J. Augustus Keogh

17th January 1917

TOMMY TOM TOM

A Comedy in One Act by Martin J. McHugh

Tom Droney	Peter Nolan
Tom Tom Droney . . .	Chas. C. O'Reilly
Tommy Tom Tom . .	Fred O'Donovan
Mrs. Lafferty	Maureen Delany
Kate Lafferty	Irene Kelly
Mad Molly	Dorothy Lynd

Produced by J. Augustus Keogh

22nd January 1917

CRUSADERS

A Play in Two Acts by Bernard McCarthy

Father Tom Moran, a young priest	Fred O'Donovan
Steve Moran, his father	J. Augustus Keogh
Kate Moran, his mother	Eileen O'Doherty
Tessie, his sister . . .	Irene Kelly
Pat, his brother . . .	Arthur Shields
Rev. Canon Kelly, P.P. . .	Peter Nolan
Rev. Mr. Roycroft . . .	Earle Gray
Edward Sheedy	Louis O'Connor
Michael Hayes	Eric Gorman
Barney Doyle	Barry Fitzgerald
Mr. Hammon	Fred Harford
Thade Mulligan	Frank Fay
Reporter	J. M. Carré

Produced by J. Augustus Keogh

2nd February 1917

FOX AND GEESE

A Farcical Comedy in Three Acts
by S. R. Day and G. D. Cummins

Katie Downey	May Craig
Timothy James	Peter Nolan
John Fitzgibbon . . .	Louis O'Connor
May Fitzgibbon	Irene Kelly
Malachi Phelan . . .	Fred O'Donovan
Biddy Maguire . . .	Maureen Delany
Maurice Downey . . .	Arthur Shields

Produced by J. Augustus Keogh

26th February 1917

First Production by the Abbey Company of

MAN AND SUPERMAN

A Comedy and a Philosophy
by G. Bernard Shaw

Roebuck Ramsden . .	C. Haviland Burke
The Maid	Irene Kelly
Mr. Octavius Robinson .	Louis O'Connor
Mr. John Tanner . . .	Fred O'Donovan
Miss Ann Whitefield . .	Maire O'Neill
Mrs. Whitefield . . .	Maureen Delany
Miss Ramsden	Cathleen Bourke
Violet Robinson . .	Valentine Erskine
Henry Straker	J. M. Carré
Hector Malone	Earle Grey
Old Malone	Peter Nolan

Produced by J. Augustus Keogh

12th March 1917

First Production by the Abbey Company of

THE INCA OF PERUSALEM

An almost Historical Comedietta in One Act
and a Prologue, by a Fellow of the Royal
Society of Literature

Prologue

The Archdeacon . .	C. Haviland Burke
Ermyntrude	Maire O'Neill

Play

The Manager . . .	Louis O'Connor
The Princess . . .	Valentine Erskine
Ermyntrude	Maire O'Neill
The Waiter	J. M. Carré
The Inca	Fred O'Donovan

26th March 1917

First Production by the Abbey Company of
THE DOCTOR'S DILEMMA

A Tragedy in Five Acts by G. Bernard Shaw

Emmy	Mrs. F. J. Fay
Redpenny	Arthur Shields
Sir Colenso Ridgeon	Earle Grey
Schutzmacher	Fred Harford
Sir Patrick Cullen	Peter Nolan
Cutler Walpole	Louis O'Connor
Sir Ralph Bloomfield Bonington	C. Haviland Burke
Dr. Blenkinsop	J. M. Carré
Mrs. Dubedat	Maire O'Neill
Louis Dubedat	Fred O'Donovan
The Maid	Valentine Erskine
The Newspaper Man	Barry Fitzgerald
The Secretary	Arthur Shields

Produced by J. Augustus Keogh

25th April 1917

THE STRONG HAND

A Play in Two Acts by R. J. Ray

Michael John Dillon, a farmer	Fred O'Donovan
Mrs. Margaret Dillon his mother	Maureen Delany
Eileen, his little daughter	Irene Kelly
Thade Kearney, publican and shopkeeper	Eric Gorman
William McCarthy, an estate bailiff	Arthur Shields
James Cassidy, a horse dealer	Donald O'Kelly
Mrs. Brady, wife of a small farmer	Dorothy Lynd
Father Brandon	Peter Nolan

Produced by J. Augustus Keogh

24th September 1917

THE PARNELLITE

A Play in Three Acts by Seumas O'Kelly

Stephen O'Moore, a farmer	Fred O'Donovan
Gerald O'Moore, his brother	Arthur Shields
Lila O'Moore, his sister	Maureen Delany
Father Hugh Barret, a parish priest	Peter Nolan
Ellen Barret, his sister	Irene Kelly
Major Heatherley, a Removable Magistrate	Eric Gorman
Mr. Oliver, a solicitor	Louis O'Connor
Mr. Murtagh, Clerk of a Petty Court	Fred Harford

Produced by Fred O'Donovan

30th October 1917

THE BACAC

A Tragedy in One Act by John Barnewall

Ann Keeffe	Margaret Nicholls
John Collier	Arthur Shields
Mary Collier	Irene Kelly
Terence Brennan	Louis O'Connor
Tom Sheridan	Peter Nolan
Julia Scully	Maureen Delany

Produced by Fred O'Donovan

13th November 1917

THE SPOILING OF WILSON

A Play in One Act by R. J. Purcell

Sir Richard Steele, Chairman of Steele Bros. Contractors	Peter Nolan
Henry Wilson, Dept. Manager	Eric Gorman
Thomas Costello, Confidential Clerk	Fred O'Donovan
Annie Costello, his wife	Maureen Delany
Miss Flora Devine	Irene Kelly
Crissie Carney, servant	Dorothy Lynd
Policeman	Arthur Shields
Carman	P. McDonald

Produced by Fred O'Donovan

20th November 1917

FRIENDS

A Play in One Act by Hubert Farjeon

Dan Donaghan, an undertaker	Arthur Shields
John O'Flaherty, a doctor	Peter Nolan
Father Murphy	Louis O'Connor
Villagers	

Produced by Fred O'Donovan

11th December 1917

BLIGHT (The tragedy of Dublin)

A Play in Three Acts by A. and O.

Stanislaus Tully, a labouring man	Fred O'Donovan
Mrs. Mary Foley, his sister	May Craig
Jimmy, her crippled son	Michael MacLiammoir
Lily, her daughter	Irene Kelly
Mrs. Maxwell-Knox, a district visitor	Margaret Nicholls
Mrs. Larrisey, a neighbour	Maureen Delany
Mr. Bannerman, landlord of tenement	Maurice Esmonde

A HISTORY, 1899–1951

Larrisey, a cabman . . . P. J. McDonnell
A Labourer . . . . . Barry Fitzgerald
Medical Dick . . . . Arthur Shields
Medical Davy . . . Clement Carrick
Charwoman . . . . Dorothy Lynd
Members of the Board of the
   Townsend Sanatorium:
   Mr. Norris-Coote . . . Eric Gorman
   Mr. Tisdall-Townley . . Fred Harford
   Mr. Morphy . . . . Peter Nolan
   Mr. McWhirter . . Hubert McGuire
   Mr. Tumulty . . . Louis O'Connor
George Foley, a discharged
   soldier . . . . . Bryan Herbert

Produced by Fred O'Donovan

8th January 1918
SPRING

A Play in One Act by T. C. Murray

Andreesh, an aged man . Fred O'Donovan
Shuvawn, his sister, very
   old too . . . . Margaret Nicholls
Seumas, his son . . . Peter Nolan
Jude, his son's wife . . . May Craig
Nora, their little daughter . . Irene Kelly

Produced by Fred O'Donovan

22nd January 1918
WHEN LOVE CAME OVER THE HILLS

A Tragic-Comedy in One Act by
W. R. Fearon and Roy Nesbitt

Kathleen O'Connor . . . May Craig
Mrs. Dempsey . . . . Maureen Delany
Mollie O'Connor, Kathleen's
   niece . . . . . . Irene Kelly
A Tramp . . . . . Barry Fitzgerald

Produced by Fred O'Donovan

29th January 1918
HANRAHAN'S OATH

A Comedy in One Act by Lady Gregory

Mary Gillis . . . . . Maureen Delany
Margaret Rooney . . . May Craig
Owen Hanrahan . . . Fred O'Donovan
Coey . . . . . . Arthur Shields
Mrs. Coey . . . . Christine Hayden
Michael Feeney . . . . Peter Nolan

Produced by Fred O'Donovan

19th February 1918
THE LOST LEADER

A Play in Three Acts by Lennox Robinson

Augustus Smith . . . . Eric Gorman
Lucius Lenihan . . . Fred O'Donovan
Mary Lenihan, his niece . . May Craig
Dr. James Powell-Harper . W. Earle Grey
Frank Ormsby . . . . Louis O'Connor
Kate Buckley . . . . Maureen Delany
Peter Cooney, J.P. . . . Peter Nolan
James Clancy . . . . Hubert McGuire
Major John White, J.P. . . Fred Harford
Michael O'Connor . . . Bryan Herbert
Tomas Houlihan . . . Arthur Shields
Long John Flavin . . . Maurice Esmonde
Other Men: Barry Fitzgerald, P. J. McDonnell, etc.

Produced by Fred O'Donovan

12th March 1918
ALIENS

A Play in One Act by Rose MacKenna

Mary Lynch, a widow . Maureen Delany
Fergus Lynch, her son . Arthur Shields
Kathleen Lynch, her daughter . Irene Kelly
Patrick Kane, a shopkeeper Louis O'Connor
Con Foley, an old fisherman . Fred Harford

Produced by Fred O'Donovan

28th May 1918
A LITTLE BIT OF YOUTH

A Comedy in One Act by Christian Callister

Mrs Harman, a widow Margaret Nicholls
Matthew Harman, 45-year-
   old son . . . . . Louis O'Connor
Her Nieces:
   Ethel Riley . . . . . May Craig
   Edith Martin . . . Irene Kelly
Norah McGill, their friend Christine Hayden
Hudson, an old serving man . Fred Harford

Produced by Fred O'Donovan

16th September 1918
SABLE AND GOLD

A Play in Three Acts by Maurice Dalton

John Parke, Manager of the
   Cork Branch of the Com-
   mercial Bank . . . Peter Nolan
Ann Parke, his wife . . Maureen Delany
Gregory Parke, their son . Fred O'Donovan
Eileen Parke, their daughter . May Craig
Friends of the Parke family:
   Paul Keller . . . . Louis O'Connor
   Agnes O'Neill . . . . Una Bourke

Produced by Fred O'Donovan

12th November 1918

THE GRABBER

A Play in Three Acts by Edward F. Barrett

John Foley	Fred O'Donovan
Ellen Foley, his wife . .	Maureen Delany
Mary Foley, his daughter .	Muriel Munro
William Foley, his son . .	F. J. McCormick
Pats Wall	Peter Nolan
Bryan Wall, his son . .	Arthur Shields
Constable Mulcahy . . .	Fred Harford
Constable Duffy . . .	Hubert McGuire

Produced by Fred O'Donovan

17th December 1918

ATONEMENT

A Play in Three Acts by Dorothy Macardle

Mrs. Farrahar . . .	Margaret Nicholls
Shawn Farraher . . .	Fred O'Donovan
Bridie Farraher . . .	Columba O'Carroll
Daniel Huggard	Fred Harford
Donagh Huggard . . .	Arthur Shields
Father MacCarthy . . .	Peter Nolan

Produced by Fred O'Donovan

CHAPTER EIGHT

1919-1932

GREAT plays create great players, contrariwise great players make mediocre plays seem great, Shakespeare created Kean (who played him in "flashes of lightning"), and Garrick and Mrs. Siddons and many others, down to Henry Irving, Ellen Terry, Forbes-Robertson, Beerbohm Tree, Martin-Harvey, John Gielgud and Laurence Olivier. On the other hand, great players often prefer to play and uplift the second-rate. Mrs. Patrick Campbell could make the tawdry seem sublime. Eleonore Duse, though she played the plays of her lover Gabriel d'Annunzio and, towards the end, the great Ibsen, really preferred plays of the genre of *La Dame aux Camélias*.

The Irish Theatre by 1918 had accumulated a heritage of great plays collected over a very short space of years, the plays of Yeats, Synge, Gregory, Murray and others. After Fred O'Donovan and others left in 1918, there still remained a few competent players in the Theatre, and young Arthur Shields pulled them together and made a good production of a new play by a new author.

Those Yeats, Synge, Gregory, Murray, Robinson plays, and others, had become almost classics, had been played again and again by actors and actresses of genius. Was there to be no "rise" in the stream, no ripple on the lake?

The "rise" came in the March of 1919 with Brinsley MacNamara's first play, *The Rebellion in Ballycullen*. Arthur Shields produced this with a competent cast. In the same year a new Lady Gregory appeared. She had in 1904 created her comedies and tragedies of Kiltartan (and put a new word into our Anglo-Irish dictionary). She had made her Folk-History Plays, she had adapted Molière, but now she was to write her Wonder Plays, whose scenes are laid half-way between Clare–Galway and Fairyland. The best of these three plays is *The Dragon* (1919), almost as good is *Aristotle's Bellows* (1921), slightly less good is *The Golden Apple* (1920).

These are plays for children of all ages from seven to seventy, and if Shakespeare evoked great players, these plays of Lady Gregory called forth genius in actress and actor; Barry Fitzgerald's first great part was as the sleepy King in *The Dragon*, Maureen Delany's as his Queen.

But the narrative must be broken for a moment to speak of the financial position of the Theatre. True, by 1918 the European War was over, but the Anglo-Irish War had begun, had indeed begun in Easter Week, 1916. From 1918 to 1921 it grew more and more intensified; with the coming of the "Black-and-Tans" in 1920, the fight on both sides became brutal. The arts are always susceptible to politics, sometimes they lay on them a dead hand, and thus it was in Dublin in the autumn and spring of 1920-21. There was a curfew in Dublin which moved back from midnight to ten o'clock, then to nine, and finally to eight. And that put the theatres out of business. From their businesses men and women scuttled home to save themselves from being caught in an ambush.

There was a dreadful day in the spring of 1921 when the Company had to be dismissed by me; there was a faint hope that the Theatre might open for Horse-Show Week. One actor, F. J. McCormick, sold all his books to keep himself alive; an actress, Maureen Delany (with tears running down her cheeks), declared she would willingly play the part she hated most (it happened to be in a play by myself), if only the doors of the Theatre might remain open.

But if politics can lay a dead hand on the arts they can often stimulate them. I am thinking of the family Cynipidae: in an oak-tree or in a rose-tree this poisonous fly inserts its egg and the tree responds by surrounding the egg with a growth of twigs; and, whence, the oak-apple, the gall.

And so, from the tragic wars of 1916 and the wars that continued till 1923 came the first three great plays of Sean O'Casey, born in Dublin in March 1884.

Sean O'Casey was in succession builder's labourer, railway labourer, and general labourer. His first play was *The Shadow of a Gunman* (1923), his second, *Juno and the "Paycock"*

(1924), thirdly, *The Plough and the Stars* (1926). Later plays are *The Star Turns Red* (1940), *Red Roses For Me* (1943), *Purple Dust* (1945), *Oak Leaves and Lavender* (1946), *Cock-a-doodle Dandy* (1949); and other plays are certain to follow. He has published three notable books of autobiography. But it must not be thought that the Theatre depended entirely on these new playwrights; older ones—apart from Lady Gregory—were continuing to write; Yeats's *The Player Queen* appeared in 1919, it had already been played in London.

My *The Round Table* appeared in January 1922, and a little play, *Crabbed Youth and Age*, at the end of that year.

It must be noted that at the end of 1918 the Dublin Drama League was founded. Its purpose was to perform plays of international repute, it did not interest itself in Irish plays, indeed in its ten years' existence it only produced three plays by Irish authors, two by Lord Dunsany and one by Bernard Shaw. Instead, it introduced Dublin to the work of Pirandello, Sierra, the Quinteros, Lenormand, Eugene O'Neill, d'Annunzio, *et al.*; the League's performances were held in the Abbey Theatre on Sunday and Monday nights and they eventually became very important Theatre functions, every seat in the Theatre was occupied. Most of the players were Abbey players, and many of the plays passed into the Abbey repertoire. The League ceased to exist in 1928, exactly ten years after its birth. Hilton Edwards and Michael MacLiammoir arrived with their plays and their ideas. The League had prepared a path for them, had perhaps inspired a dramatist or two, notably Denis Johnston, and the League, not being a money-making concern, gladly stepped aside to make room for the Edwards-MacLiammoir Company.

Those two early great plays of O'Casey, *The Shadow of a Gunman* and *Juno and the "Paycock,"* saved the Theatre from bankruptcy, but the Theatre was equally aided by an Ulster dramatist, George Shiels. His first play appeared a month after Brinsley MacNamara's second play. It was a small play, *Bedmates*, followed at the end of that year by another slightly longer play, *Insurance Money*, but then, in 1922, came a full-length play, *Paul Twyning*, and from that time to the day of his death George Shiels never ceased to be a dramatist of very considerable importance. Sean O'Casey, George Shiels and Brinsley MacNamara were the three new pillars who supported the Theatre during those dreadful years between 1918 and 1924.

George Shiels is the Thomas Moore of the Irish Theatre. Moore is often despised by the intellectuals, but yet in the hearts of Irish men and women he is their national poet. They have small use for Ferguson and Mangan and Yeats. Moore with his melodies has no peer. Very often Shiels could be too sentimental in his plots and would sacrifice everything for a happy ending, on the other hand he could be as harsh as Synge, as he proved in *The Rugged Path* (1940) and *The Summit* (1941) and *The Passing Day* (1936). It is interesting to note that *The Rugged Path* has had the longest run in our Theatre.

In an earlier chapter I have mentioned Thomas MacDonagh's prophetic play, *When the Dawn is Come*; equally prophetic, almost autobiographical, was the Theatre's production of *The Revolutionist* by Terence MacSwiney in the February of 1921. MacSwiney, Lord Mayor of Cork, had undertaken a hunger strike in England lasting 74 days. This play had been published some years before. It was so pertinent to the situation that the Abbey was determined to produce it, though the country was in the teeth of the "Black-and-Tans" war. There was excitement at the dress-rehearsal. The American Consul and his wife were present. I was producing the play, not an easy one to produce because of the many changes of scene, and, going behind-stage, I was met by a couple of lads with revolvers sagging from their hands, who said that I couldn't pass. I said "Nonsense!" and pushed them aside. Their only object was to prevent an English paper, which had sneered at MacSwiney's hunger strike, from getting a photograph of the rehearsal. The English photographer surrendered his camera in terror and the incident closed, but the American Consul and his wife left the theatre very quickly before the end of the rehearsal, perhaps afraid that they might be involved in an international incident.

The years between 1918 and 1921 were dreadful, for they were years full of dread: the dread of a theatre having to close its doors and throw its players on the streets. But in the grim year, 1921, English and Irish friends in London came to the Theatre's help and J. B. Fagan arranged four lectures in his beautiful house in Chelsea. Mr. Yeats, on 5th May, lectured on "The Irish Theatre," on the 12th, Lady Gregory on "Making a Play," on the 19th, Mr. St. John Ervine on "The Theatre in America," and on the 26th, Mr. Bernard Shaw on "The Spur of the Moment."

"The Spur of the Moment" was, in fact, the first two acts of *Back to Methuselah*, which had not yet been produced or published and which Mr. Shaw read brilliantly.

In addition to the lectures J. B. Fagan gave a special matinée at the Ambassadors Theatre of *The Whiteheaded Boy*, which was then in the middle of a very successful run.

I quote from Lady Gregory's journals:

> May 27 [1921]. G. B. S. yesterday gave his lecture for the Abbey and read two acts of his new play *Back to Methuselah*, and some of the audience were pleased, others would have liked a continuation of his lecture better. Lady Gough fell asleep. The play read well, the bit about the feeding on the heavenly manna very fine, and Dr. Monro's idea is in the phrase "Imagine to create." To-day I have been to Lady Orpen to ask if Orpen would do a poster for the matinée.
>
> We have made: Lectures, £175, 4s. 8d. (but expenses of Lectures, about £30, will come out of this), Matinée £84, 11s. 7d. W. B. Yeats's Reading £39, Donations £172, 13s. 4d. In all £471, 9s. 7d. But I think anyhow we shall be able to pay our £500 debt to the bank.
>
> June 12. Yesterday by second post a letter from Lady Ardilaun with her cheque for £500! How like a Guinness! So the Abbey is safe for a long time, I hope for ever! Such a joy. Lecture misery [her own misery in having to lecture] and matinée fuss wasn't thrown away—we shouldn't have had this without it.

Perhaps it is worth recording what the Theatre said in advertising these Lectures:

> The Abbey Theatre is the fruit of seed sowed more than twenty years ago by Mr. W. B. Yeats and others when they founded in 1898 the Irish Literary Theatre. It owed much in its early days to the genius of the brothers Fay and to the generosity of Miss Horniman, who acquired the lease of the Abbey Theatre, rebuilt it, and from 1904 to 1910 assisted the company of players by an annual subsidy. To this Theatre we owe the discovery of the dramatic gifts of Synge, Lady Gregory, Padraic Colum, T. C. Murray, St. John Ervine and many other playwrights; to it we owe the evolution of a school of natural

acting and the art of Sara Allgood, Maire O'Neill, Arthur Sinclair, Fred O'Donovan and J. M. Kerrigan; its players have appeared in all the English-speaking countries of the world, and its plays have gone into the repertory of every art theatre in Europe. It has created a distinctive Irish drama and a distinctive school of Irish acting, and has inspired imitators all through Ireland. Belfast has its own "Ulster Literary Theatre," and Cork its "Munster Players," and there is not a town of any size in Ireland now without its local company of amateur players.

Its work is well known in England. Before the war it paid annual visits to the Court Theatre in London and to Oxford, Cambridge, Manchester, Liverpool, etc. More recently some of its most famous players have been appearing in London in *The Whiteheaded Boy*.

When Miss Horniman's subsidy ceased the Abbey Theatre—like any other theatre—had to pay its way or die. Being a repertory theatre it could never make a great deal of money by the long run of a successful play, it could never accumulate a large capital. But for ten years, from 1910 to 1920, it managed just to pay its way.

A year ago the Curfew order was put into force in Dublin. First it began at midnight, then at ten o'clock, then at nine, finally at eight. In face of this no theatre could continue to exist. There was always the hope that the Curfew order would be revoked, and the Directors naturally were anxious to keep the Theatre open as long as possible, and not to disband the company they had been training for years; but during the year they have lost nearly £1,000, and they can no longer continue to risk the bankruptcy of the Theatre. This debt has got to be paid.

If the Abbey Theatre were dying of inanition, of a lack of players or playwrights, it were better it should die at once; but no one who knows its work of recent years doubts its vigour. We are confident of the future if we are helped now through these dark days. If the Abbey Theatre dies the whole art of the theatre will have suffered a loss, and we confidently appeal to all friends of the theatre for help.

But, by June 1921, the dread of the Theatre's future seemed to be appeased. There was a truce declared between Ireland and England, the Abbey Theatre could breathe again though the Treaty was not agreed on till the last day of that year.

But it was nearly a bankrupt Theatre. True, the actual property was of considerable value, but the wardrobe and the scenery had grown poorer and shabbier through all the years since 1916. Lady Gregory and Yeats, having held the flag high for more than twenty years, thought, after the Free State was established in 1921, that it should be handed over as a present to the Irish Government.

Lady Gregory writes in her Journals:

Dec. 19 [1923]. A letter from Yeats about giving over the Abbey or rather putting it under the new Government, but I don't agree with him that they would leave it in any way under our control, or subsidise it unless it was entirely theirs, and I am for giving it up altogether, if they will have it. But they may prefer a larger one.

Jan. 11 [1924]. Dublin. I came up yesterday in time for first performance of Murray's *Aftermath*. Lennox Robinson met me at the Broadstone and came to tea. He had lunched with Desmond Fitzgerald and had spoken about turning over the Abbey to a National Government, said we had thought of doing so in Redmond's time, and had heard they were now going to establish one. Fitzgerald said there was no idea of taking the Gaiety or doing anything on a large scale, that he hadn't heard of any definite plan and that of course the Abbey is the National Theatre of Ireland.

Perhaps the Directors had grown a little tired of their work. They had carried the flag for the best part of twenty years, they were very willing that it should be handed to a younger generation. And so they wrote to President Cosgrave on 27th June 1924 as follows:

Dear President Cosgrave,

We have carried on our work at the Abbey Theatre for nearly twenty years and we may claim to have created a school of Irish dramatists and a school of Irish acting that has brought honour to our country. We have carried on our work in spite of the European War—which killed every repertory theatre in England save one—and in spite of the English war in Ireland. We do not claim to have done so unaided, at certain times we have had to appeal for help to friends in Ireland and England but always in times of stress we have said to our friends and to each other, "We must hold the Theatre together that we may offer it to the Irish Nation when Ireland achieves her independence." That, for many years, has been our determination. We believe that a Theatre which does not depend for its existence on the caprice of the public can play a great part in the education of a nation, can be—like the Comédie Française—one of the nation's glories, and we are aware that all civilised governments except those of English-speaking nations and Venezuela—possess their State Theatre.

In that belief we now offer the Abbey Theatre, its entire contents, scenery and wardrobe and the property it owns to the Irish Nation.

We do not pretend that our gift is of great value counted as money. Like others in Ireland we, who were once rich, are now poor; nevertheless the value of the property is not inconsiderable and there is some value in a tradition of fine work finely done.

We offer the Theatre without conditions or restrictions. We resign our Directorship. It is for the Irish Government, should they accept our offer, to determine the method of carrying on our work—whether they will ask us to go on for a little longer or whether they will at once accept entire control. By tradition and accomplishment our Theatre has become the National Theatre of Ireland, it should no longer be in the possession of private individuals, it should belong to the State. Having created it and fostered it through twenty years we believe we can now confidently trust it to the Irish Nation.

(signed) Augusta Gregory.
W. B. Yeats.

But the Government by the middle of 1924 was faced as the result of the Civil War with at least four major problems, Land, Finance, Law, Local Government. It naturally shrank from creating, in addition to these great tasks, a National Theatre.

Mr. Ernest Blythe (then Minister of Finance) has written to me:

> With reference to the point about the origin of the Government subsidy, President Cosgrave took no interest in the Abbey. In fact as far as I can remember it was his boast that he had never been to a performance in it in his life. He knew, however, that I had always had an interest in the Abbey and when the letter signed by Lady Gregory and Yeats arrived, he referred it to me and I received a deputation which came to Government Buildings. I may say that, personally, I thought the offer to give the Theatre to the Government was more tactical than serious [It was a perfectly serious offer. L. R.], and that in fact it was only an emphatic way of asking for a subvention, but in any case I should not for a moment have thought that the Government should accept an offer of the Theatre. I had visions of questions being asked in the Dail as to why particular lines were allowed to remain in a certain play, as to why the work of one dramatist had been accepted while the work of a more moral and patriotic dramatist had been rejected! As to why a particular actress had been given a part which could have been much more competently played by Miss So-and-so, etc. etc.
>
> I thought, however, that there should be no difficulty in giving a small annual grant to the Theatre to make it possible to carry on in changed circumstances. I rang Desmond Fitzgerald on the point and he agreed. Consequently, when I met the deputation I practically promised that a grant would be given. I mentioned the matter at the next meeting of the Government and no objection was raised.

Eight hundred and fifty pounds was voted as an annual subsidy (in succeeding years the subsidy was increased and increased but never to an exaggerated figure) and so the little Abbey Theatre, Dublin, became the first State-subsidised Theatre in the English-speaking world.

After eight years (1916-24) of increasing poverty the

Theatre was now able to pay its players salaries somewhat appropriate to their merits, it was able to replenish its shabby wardrobe and to build new scenery. And there came in quick succession a series of new and deservedly popular plays: Sean O'Casey's *The Plough and the Stars* (1926), numerous comedies by George Shiels, T. C. Murray's *Autumn Fire* (1924), Brinsley MacNamara's *Look at the Heffernans!* (1926). These fine plays evoked fine players and by 1931 the Company's work was comparable with, in fact it often surpassed, that of the days of the Fays, of Arthur Sinclair and the Allgood sisters.

Confident of their repertory, confident of their players, in October 1931 the Company sailed for the United States and Canada. Irish-America had not seen the Abbey players since 1914 when it still disliked *The Playboy* and the realistic dramatists, but in sixteen years a new generation had grown which gloried in the work of Synge and O'Casey, and the tour, which lasted for more than six months, was an almost unbroken success. West to Vancouver, south to New Orleans, twenty-six of the United States were visited. The visit was repeated the following year.

Casts of First Productions, 1919-1932

11th March 1919

THE REBELLION IN BALLYCULLEN
A Play in Three Acts by Brinsley MacNamara

Alan Forde, a young author	Arthur Shields
Esther Forde, his sister . .	Irene Kelly
Anne Forde, his mother .	Helena Moloney
Peter Forde, his father · .	Eric Gorman
Gilachrist O'Hanlon, his friend	Peter Nolan
Maureen Harman, his other friend . . .	Cathleen Murphy

Produced by Arthur Shields

21st April 1919

THE DRAGON
A Wonder Play in Three Acts
by Lady Gregory

The King	Barry Fitzgerald
The Queen	Mary Sheridan
The Princess Nuala . .	Eithne Magee
The Dall Glic (The Blind Wiseman)	Peter Nolan
The Nurse	Maureen Delany
The Prince of the Marshes	J. Hugh Nagle
Nanus, King of Sorcha .	Arthur Shields
Fintan, the Astrologer .	F. J. McCormick
Taig	Eric Gorman
Sibby, Taig's mother . .	Florence Marks
The Dragon	Seaghan Barlow
The Porter	Stephen Casey
The Gatekeeper . . .	Hubert McGuire
Two Aunts of the Prince of the Marshes	Dymphna Daly, Esme Ward

Produced by Lennox Robinson

4th August 1919

BRADY
A Comedy in Two Acts
by Mrs. Theodore Maynard

Tom Brady, of Upper Kilmines	Barry Fitzgerald
Polly Brady, his step-sister .	Esme Ward
Ursula Gwynne	Una Burke
Mrs. Lacy	Helena Moloney
Mrs. Smith	Maureen Delany
Dominic Tully, of Lower Kilmines	F. J. McCormick

Produced by Lennox Robinson

19th August 1919

First Production by the Abbey Company of
THE FIDDLER'S HOUSE
A Play in Three Acts by Padraic Colum

Conn Hourican, a fiddler	Pol Ua Fearghail
Maire Hourican, his daughter .	May Craig
Anne Hourican, a younger daughter .	Margaret Nicholls
Brian MacConnell, a young farmer	Arthur Shields
James Moynihan, a farmer's son	Hugh Nagle

Produced by Lennox Robinson

19th August 1919

A SERIOUS THING
A Play in One Act by Gideon Ousley

A Centurion	Philip Guiry
First Roman Soldier . .	F. J. McCormick
Second Roman Soldier .	Arthur Shields
Lazarus	Hugh Nagle
A Voice	

Produced by Lennox Robinson

2nd September 1919

First Production by the Abbey Company of
A NIGHT AT AN INN
A Play in One Act by Lord Dunsany

A. E. Scott Fortescue . . .	Philip Guiry
William Jones . . .	F. J. McCormick
Albert Thomas	Eric Gorman
Jacob Smith	Arthur Shields
First Priest of Lkesh	
Second Priest of Lkesh	
Third Priest of Lkesh	
The Stranger	

Produced by Arthur Shields

2nd September 1919

THE SAINT
A Play in Two Scenes by Desmond Fitzgerald

Blanaid	Eithne MaGee
John of the Ships	Peter Nolan
Lasareena	Maureen Delany
Breed	Margaret Nicholls
The "Shameful" Monk .	Arthur Shields
Monks: J. Hugh Nagle and R. C. Murray	
Men and Women: Helena Moloney, Una Burke, P. J. McDonald, Hubert McGuire	

Produced by Lennox Robinson

SEAN O'CASEY

GEORGE SHIELS

30th September 1919

THE LABOUR LEADER

A Play in Three Acts by Daniel Corkery

Tim Murphy, Representative of Coal Porters on Strike Committee	Hugh Nagle
John Clarke, Representative of Workmen's Federation on Committee	George St. John
Mrs. Donovan	Margaret Nicholls
John Dampsey, Chairman of Strike Committee	Peter Nolan
Dan O'Reilly, coal porter	M. J. Dolan
Jack O'Donoghue, quay labourer	W. Fitzgerald
Battie Donovan, caretaker of Quaymen's Union Hall	Hubert McGuire
Phil Kennedy, member of Strike Committee	F. J. McCormick
David Lombard, Secretary of Quaymen's Union	Paul Farrell
James O'Sullivan	Eric Gorman
Mrs. Tobin	Maureen Delany
Caretaker of Athenaeum Hall	M. J. Dolan
Quay Labourers and Workmen: Bryan Herbert, R. C. Murray, A. Quinn, etc. etc.	

Produced by Lennox Robinson

7th October 1919

MEADOWSWEET

A Comedy in One Act by Seumas O'Kelly

Johnny Claffey	Arthur Shields
Maria Dempsey	Maureen Delany
Kevin Monahan	Peter Nolan
Luke Tierney	Hubert McGuire

Produced by Arthur Shields

14th October 1919

QUEER ONES

A Play in One Act by Con O'Leary

Mary Hogan	May Craig
Peter Devoy	F. J. McCormick
An Old Priest	Michael Dolan

Produced by Lennox Robinson

4th November 1919

First Production by the Abbey Company of

ANDROCLES AND THE LION

A Play in a Prologue and Two Acts by G. Bernard Shaw

The Lion	Bryan Herbert
Androcles	J. Hugh Nagle
Megaera, his wife	Maureen Delany
The Centurion	J. G. St. John
The Captain	Arthur Shields
Lavinia	Christine Hayden
Lentulus	A. G. Douglas
Metellus	Fred Harford
Apintho	Michael J. Dolan
Ferrovius	Ambrose Power
The Slave Driver	Hubert McGuire
The Call Boy	G. Rock
Secutor	T. Quinn
Retiarius	R. C. Murray
The Editor of the Gladiators	Peter Nolan
The Menagerie Keeper	Barry Fitzgerald
The Emperor	F. J. McCormick
Christians: May Craig, Una Burke, E. Bingham, Gerald Thomas, H. L. Corrigan, J. D. Brennan, etc. etc.	
Soldiers, Slaves, etc.	

Produced by Lennox Robinson. Scenes by Seaghan Barlow.

25th November 1919

THE ENCHANTED TROUSERS

A Play in One Act by Gideon Ousley

Humphrey Heavy, an unemployed actor	Peter Nolan
Andrew Heavy, his brother, a National school teacher	Arthur Shields
Mrs. Heavy, their mother	Christine Hayden
Official 1	Michael J. Dolan
Official 1^2	Bryan Herbert
Official 1^3	J. J. Lynch
Official $\sqrt{1}$, their secretary	J. Hugh Nagle
Pile, an English invalid suffering from pre-war shock	Philip Guiry
Arthur	Eric Gorman

Produced by Lennox Robinson

9th December 1919

THE PLAYER QUEEN

A Play in Two Scenes by W. B. Yeats

1st Old Man	Barry Fitzgerald
2nd Old Man	Philip Guiry
Septimus	Arthur Shields
3rd Old Man	R. C. Murray
Old Woman	Maureen Delany
Happy Tom	Peter Nolan
Peter of the Purple Pelican	T. Quinn
Citizens: Bryan Herbert, J. J. Lynch, R. C. Murray, Philip Guiry, etc.	
Tapster	F. J. McCormick
Countrymen: Hugh Nagle, J. G. St. John, P. J. McDonnell, etc.	
Big Countryman	Ambrose Power
Old Beggar	Michael J. Dolan
Prime Minister	Eric Gorman
Nona	May Craig
Players: Margaret Nicholls, Barry Fitzgerald, Bryan Herbert, J. J. Lynch, P. J. McDonnell, etc.	
Queen	Shena Tyreconnell
Decima	Christine Hayden
Stage Manager	Philip Guiry
Bishop	Peter Nolan

Produced by Lennox Robinson. Scenes designed by Lennox Robinson and painted by Seaghan Barlow.

6th January 1920

THE GOLDEN APPLE

A Play in Three Acts by Lady Gregory

The King	Peter Nolan
Rury, his son	F. J. McCormick
The Doctor	Eric Gorman
Simon the Steward	Barry Fitzgerald
The Witch	Christine Hayden
Pampogue, her daughter	Esme Ward
The Giant	Hugh Nagle
Bridget, his wife	Maureen Delany
The Cook	Michael Dolan
The Barber	Bryan Herbert
The Gardener	Arthur Shields
Muireann, the Enchanted Princess	Eithne Magee
Strangers, Servants, etc.: J. J. Lynch, T. Quinn, Jas. Mahon, H. L. Corrigan, P. Kirwan, J. D. Brennan, etc.	

10th February 1920

First Production by the Abbey Company of
THE DEVIL'S DISCIPLE

A Melodrama in Three Acts
by G. Bernard Shaw

Mrs. Dudgeon	Christine Hayden
Essie	Sheila O'Grady
Christy Dudgeon	Philip Guiry
Anthony Anderson	Peter Nolan
Mrs. Anderson	May Craig
Lawyer Hawkins	Michael Dolan
William Dudgeon	Hubert McGuire
Mrs. William Dudgeon	Una Burke
Titus Dudgeon	H. L. Corrigan
Mrs. Titus Dudgeon	Maureen Delany
Richard Dudgeon	Arthur Shields
The Sergeant	J. J. Lynch
Major Swinton	Eric Gorman
General Burgoyne	F. J. McCormick
The Chaplain	George St. John
The Executioner	Ambrose Power
Officers, Soldiers and Townsfolk	

Produced by Lennox Robinson

19th February 1920

THE DEAMAN IN THE HOUSE

A Play in Two Scenes by F. Barrington

Michael Dwyer, an old farmer	Michael J. Dolan
Norah Dwyer, his eldest daughter	May Craig
Maureen Dwyer, his younger daughter	Christine Hayden
Bridget Delany, a servant	Maureen Delany
Denny Dolan	F. J. McCormick
Pat Cooney	J. Hugh Nagle

Produced by Lennox Robinson

27th April 1920

First Production by the Abbey Company of
THE GOOD-NATUR'D MAN

A Comedy in Five Acts by Oliver Goldsmith

Sir William Honeywood	Peter Nolan
Jarvis	Michael J. Dolan
Mr. Honeywood, Sir William's nephew	Arthur Shields
Butler	W. Fitzgerald
Mr. Croaker	F. J. McCormick
Mrs. Croaker	Maureen Delany
Miss Richland, Mr. Croaker's ward	Christine Hayden

A HISTORY, 1899–1951

Leontine, Mr. Croaker's son . J. J. Lynch
Olivia . . . . . . Kathleen Murphy
Garnet, a maid . . . . . . May Craig
Dubardieu, Lofty's servant. H. L. Corrigan
Mr. Lofty . . . . Eric Gorman
Bailiff . . . . George St. John
Follower . . . . P. Kirwan
Landlady. . . . . . . Esme Ward
Postboy . . . . W. Fitzgerald

Produced by Lennox Robinson

4th May 1920

THE YELLOW BITTERN

A Play in One Act by Daniel Corkery

Shawn McDonnell . . . Peter Nolan
Nora O'Neill, his married
  daughter . . . . . Cathleen Murphy
Hugh McAleenan . , . Arthur Shields
Sheela Gallagher . . . Maureen Delany
Cahal Bwee MacElgunn . Michael J. Dolan
Father Walsh . . . . F. J. McCormick

Produced by Lennox Robinson

24th May 1920

First Production by the Abbey Company of

THE TENTS OF THE ARABS

A Play in Two Acts by Lord Dunsany

Camel-drivers:
  The King . . . . F. J. McCormick
  Bel-Narb . . . . T. Quinn
  Aoob . . . . . . Barry Fitzgerald
The Chamberlain . . . . Eric Gorman
Zabra, a notable . . . Hubert McGuire
Enzarza, a gipsy of the
  desert . . . . . . Cathleen Murphy

Produced by Lennox Robinson

7th September 1920

THE DRIFTERS

A Play in Two Acts
by Frank Hugh O'Donnell

Martin Keane, a well-to-do
  farmer . . . . . . Peter Nolan
John Quirk, his neigh-
  bour . . . . . . F. J. McCormick
Eddie Keane, nephew of
  Martin . . . . Michael J. Dolan
Sarah Keane, Martin's sister . May Craig

Moll Donovan, a cousin of
  the Keanes' . . . . Christine Hayden
Mabel Shields, a lady friend
  of Eddie's . . . . Margot Brunton
Bridget, servant to the Keane
  family . . . . . Maureen Delany

Produced by Lennox Robinson

21st September 1920

A ROYAL ALLIANCE

A Comedy in One Act by Fergus O'Nolan

Corby, a tinker . . . . Barry Fitzgerald
Mag, his wife . . . . Maureen Delany
Drimin, their daughter . Kathleen Fortune
Steve King, a fish-hawker. F. J. McCormick

Produced by Lennox Robinson

5th October 1920

THE SERF

A Play in Two Acts by Stephen Morgan

Charles Drennan, a National
  teacher . . . . . Michael J. Dolan
Margaret Drennan, his
  wife . . . . . . Maureen Delany
Jack Sheridan, his brother-in-
  law, a journalist . . . Eric Gorman
Father Harold, parish priest
  of Coolglash . . . . F. J. McCormick
Mrs. Anne Vaughan, his sister . May Craig
Father Owens, curate to
  Father Harold . . . Joseph A. Hand
Michael Holland, a farmer . Peter Nolan
Seumas Barry, another
  farmer . . . . . Barry Fitzgerald
Mrs. Darby, a village char-
  woman . . . . . Agnese O'Higgins

Produced by Lennox Robinson

12th October 1920

THE ISLAND OF SAINTS AND HOW TO GET OUT OF IT

A Small Piece for the Times
by St. John Ervine

John Cairns, a cobbler . . . Peter Nolan
Ellen Cairns, his wife . . Maureen Delany
Johnnie Cairns, his son . . . T. Quinn
Robert McGrum, a
  millionaire . . . . F. J. McCormick

Produced by Lennox Robinson

30th November 1920
THE LAND FOR THE PEOPLE
A Play in Three Acts by Brinsley MacNamara

Conor Cooney, a County Meath grazier	Peter Nolan
Thomas Broderick, his father-in-law	Eric Gorman
Martha Cooney, his daughter	Gertrude Murphy
Eugene Cooney, his son	Tony Quinn
Hanna Cooney, his wife	Helena Moloney
Johnton Cooney, his brother	Barry Fitzgerald
Brigid Brien, an old servant	Esme Ward
Shaun Glynn, a leader of the people	F. J. McCormick
Andrew Dhrum, another leader of the people	Michael J. Dolan
Jane Dhrum, his daughter, another servant in the house of Conor Cooney	Una Burke
Isaac Robinson, an elderly solicitor	H. L. Corrigan

27th December 1920
CANDLE AND CRIB
A Nativity Play in One Act by K. F. Purdon

Michael Moloney	Peter Nolan
Mrs. Moloney, his wife	Christine Hayden
Art Moloney, their son	Tony Quinn
Delia Moloney, Art's wife	Gertrude Murphy

6th January 1921
BEDMATES
A Comedy in One Act by George Shiels

Pius Kelly, a ragman	Barry Fitzgerald
Andrew Riddle, another ragman	Tony Quinn
Bertie Smith, an English thimble-rigger	Michael J. Dolan
Molly Swan, a doss-house landlady	Maureen Delany

24th February 1921
THE REVOLUTIONIST
A Play in Five Acts by Terence J. MacSwiney

Mrs. Sullivan, Hugh O'Neill's landlady	Maureen Delany
John Mangan, a successful merchant	Barry Fitzgerald
Father O'Connor, C.C.	Michael J. Dolan
Hugh O'Neill, a clerk	F. J. McCormick
Con Sheehan, a small contractor	Peter Nolan
Doyle, a law clerk	Maurice Esmonde
Nora Mangan, daughter of John Mangan	Gertrude Murphy
Fan O'Byrne, engaged to Con Sheehan	Christine Hayden
Dr. Foley, a dispensary doctor	Alan Duncan
Father O'Hanlon, Administrator	Eric Gorman
Mackay, a civil servant	P. Kirwan
Bennett, a reporter	J. Lynch
Maher, a compositor	G. J. Fallon
Kiely, an agent	V. Young
Rohan, a teacher	Hubert McGuire
Keane, a student	Tony Quinn
Lawlor, a shop assistant	U. Wright
Servants, followers, etc.:	J. Barlow, P. MacDonnell, J. McCarthy, M. Gogarty

17th March 1921
ARISTOTLE'S BELLOWS
A Wonder Play in Three Acts by Lady Gregory

The Mother	Maureen Delany
Celia, her daughter	Gertrude Murphy
Conan, her stepson	Barry Fitzgerald
Timothy, her serving man	F. J. McCormick
Neighbours:	
Rock	Peter Nolan
Flannery	Michael J. Dolan
First Cat	Seaghan Barlow
Second Cat	P. Kirwan

8th November 1921
THE COURTING OF MARY DOYLE
A Comedy in Three Acts by Edward McNulty

Mary Doyle, general servant at the Kierans'	Florence Marks
John William Rattigan, a bootmaker	Michael J. Dolan
Jessie Kieran, daughter of Mr. and Mrs. Kieran	Eileen Crowe
Herbert Tisdall, a bank clerk	Tony Quinn
Mrs. Kieran	Annie Kirby
Terence Kieran, shopkeeper, hardware and groceries	Barry Fitzgerald
Peter Carmody, a butcher	Peter Nolan
Townspeople	

A HISTORY, 1899–1951

15th November 1921
THE PIPER OF TAVRAN
A Play in One Act by Bernard Duffy

The Bishop	Peter Nolan
The Abbot	J. A. Hand
Brother Anselm	V. Young
Brother Lucas	Gabriel J. Fallon
A Lay Brother	Matt Connolly
Donagh O'Grady, the Piper of Tavran	P. Kirwan
A Messenger	Tony Quinn
Friars: P. J. Carolan, J. H. Nagle, etc. etc.	

Produced by Michael J. Dolan

13th December 1921
INSURANCE MONEY
A Comedy in Three Acts by George Shiels

Richard Moone, a farmer	Peter Nolan
Tam Erwin, his servant man	Gabriel J. Fallon
Ann Lilly, his servant girl	Eileen O'Kelly
Thomas Hayes, an insurance man	Tony Quinn
Myles O'Donnegan, a tinker	Michael J. Dolan
Sheila O'Donnegan, his wife	Eileen Crowe

Produced by Lennox Robinson

10th January 1922
AFTERMATH
A Play in Three Acts by T. C. Murray

Mrs. O'Regan	Florence Marks
Myles O'Regan, her son	P. J. Carolan
Grace Sheridan, a teacher	Eileen Crowe
Mrs. Dillon, her sister	May Craig
Mrs. Hogan	Maire Sweeney
Mary Hogan, her niece	Eileen O'Kelly
Dr. Hugh Manning	Gabriel J. Fallon
Hannah Geary	Helena Moloney
Mrs. McCarthy, a villager	Annie Kirby

Produced by Lennox Robinson

31st January 1922
THE ROUND TABLE
A Comic Tragedy in Three Acts by Lennox Robinson

Mrs. Drennan	Helena Moloney
Her children:	
De Courcy Drennan	Barry Fitzgerald
Daisy Drennan	Eileen Crowe
Bee Drennan	Eileen O'Kelly
Jonty Drennan	J. Hugh Nagle
Miss Williams-Williams	May Craig
Christopher Pegum	P. J. Carolan
Mrs. Pegum, his mother	Esme Ward
Miss Pegum, his aunt	Annie Kirby
Philip Flahive	Michael J. Dolan
Fan Franks	Dorothy Lynd
A Woman	Beatrice Elvery
Tom Breen	Tony Quinn
Two Men	Peter Nolan, Gabriel J. Fallon
An elderly woman	Maire Sweeney
A Porter	Patrick Kirwan

Produced by the Author

9th March 1922
First Production by the Abbey Company of
THE MAN OF DESTINY
A Trifle in One Act by G. Bernard Shaw

General Napoleon Bonaparte	P. J. Carolan
Giuseppe Grandi	Michael J. Dolan
The Lieutenant	Tony Quinn
The Strange Lady	Eileen Crowe

Produced by Lennox Robinson

6th April 1922
ANN KAVANAGH
A Play in One Act by Dorothy Macardle

Miles Kavanagh	P. J. Carolan
Ann, his wife	May Craig
Stephen, his brother	Tony Quinn
Of the Insurgent Army:	
Redmond	M. Connolly
Ryan	Gabriel J. Fallon
Doyle	Walter Dillon
Moran	Maurice Esmond
A Fugitive	

Produced by Lennox Robinson

6th April 1922
THE YOUNG MAN FROM RATHMINES
A Play in One Act by M. M. Brennan

Mr. Dowd, a labouring man	Michael J. Dolan
Mrs. Dowd, his wife	Mai Neville
Mary, their daughter	Crissie Byrne
Mrs. Sullivan, a neighbour	Sheila Murray
Barney Reilly, suitor for the hand of Mary	Tony Quinn
George Jackson, the young man from Rathmines	Gabriel J. Fallon

Produced by Lennox Robinson

29th August 1922

THE MORAL LAW

A Play in One Act by R. J. Ray

John Shannon, ex-Head
  Constable, R.I.C. . . . Michael J. Dolan
Mrs. Shannon, his wife . . Helena Moloney
Michael Shannon, their son . P. J. Carolan
Sergeant Bullen, R.I.C. . . Maurice Esmonde
A Military Captain . . . Eric Gorman
Two Soldiers P. J. McDonnell, W. O'Hara

5th September 1922

A LEPRECAUN IN THE TENEMENT

A Play in One Act by M. M. Brennan

Mr. Reilly, a labouring
  man . . . . Barry Fitzgerald
Mrs. Reilly . . . . . . Sheila Murray
Alice Kate, their daughter . Eileen Crowe
Mickey Reilly, their son . . Tony Quinn
The Widow Murphy, a neigh-
  bour . . . . May Craig

Produced by Lennox Robinson

3rd October 1922

PAUL TWYNING

A Comedy in Three Acts by George Shiels

Paul Twyning, a tramp-
  plasterer . . . . . Barry Fitzgerald
James Deegan, a farmer and
  magistrate . . . . Gabriel J. Fallon
Dan Deegan, his son . . Michael J. Dolan
Patrick Deegan, another son,
  a publican . . . . . P. J. Carolan
Mrs. Deegan, Patrick Deegan's
  wife . . . . May Craig
Jim Deegan, their son . . . Tony Quinn
Denis M'Gothigan, a farmer . Eric Gorman
Rose M'Gothigan, his
  daughter . . . . . Eileen Crowe
Daisy Mullen, a returned
  American . . . Christine Hayden
Mr. O'Hagan, a solicitor . . Peter Nolan

Produced by Lennox Robinson

24th October 1922

GRASSHOPPER

A Play in Four Acts by Padraic Colum and
E. Washburn Freund

Founded on a Play by Keyserling

Michael Dempsey . . . Gabriel J. Fallon
Anne Dempsey, his wife . . Aoife Taafe
Maeve Dempsey, his sister . . May Craig
Bridget . . . . . . Christine Hayden
Sheila . . . . Eileen Crowe
Thady . . . . P. J. Carolan
Matt O'Connor . . . Maurice Esmonde
Judy . . . . Eileen O'Kelly
Jillin . . . . Sheila Murray
Father Myles . . . . Michael J. Dolan
Sara . . . . Kathleen Fortune
Johanna . . . . . . Irene Murphy
Tracey Nowlan . . . . Tony Quinn
Thomas Bacach . . Michael J. Dolan
Bat Croskerry . . . . M. Connolly
Mark Brogan . . . . P. J. Carolan
Eamon Hynes . . . . M. McCarthy
Murty Lynott . . . Clement Kenny
Mrs. Gilsenin . . . . Sheila Murray
Old Catty . . . . . Lini Doran

Produced by Lennox Robinson

14th November 1922

CRABBED YOUTH AND AGE

A Little Comedy by Lennox Robinson

Mrs. Swan . . . . Helena Moloney
Her daughters:
  Minnie Swan . . . Christine Hayden
  Eileen Swan . . . . . May Craig
  Dolly Swan . . . . Eileen Crowe
Gerald Booth . . . Gabriel J. Fallon
Charlie Duncan . . . . P. J. Carolan
Tommy Mims . . . . Tony Quinn

Produced by Lennox Robinson

9th January 1923

THE LONG ROAD TO GARRANBRAHER

A Play in One Act by J. Bernard McCarthy

Captain Peter Hanley, a
  retired mariner . . . Michael J. Dolan
Jude, his wife . . . . Eileen O'Kelly
Dan, their son . . . . F. J. McCormick
Marcus Coyle, their son-in-
  law . . . . Tony Quinn
Seumas Doran, a sailor . . P. J. Carolan
Mrs. O'Brien, a dealer . Christine Hayden
Maura Mulligan, a neighbour May Craig

A HISTORY, 1899–1951 135

8th March 1923

'TWIXT THE GILTINANS AND
THE CARMODYS
A Comedy in One Act by George Fitzmaurice

Bileen Twomey . . .	Arthur Shields
Shuvawn, his aunt . .	Eileen O'Kelly
Old Jane	. May Craig
Michael Clancy . . .	. Michael J. Dolan
Bridie Giltinan . . .	. Eileen Crowe
Mrs. Giltinan	Maureen Delany
Simon Giltinan . . .	. F. J. McCormick
Madge Carmody . .	Gertrude Murphy
Mrs. Carmody . . .	. Christine Hayden
Jamesie Carmody . .	. Peter Nolan

Produced by Lennox Robinson

2nd April 1923

First Production by the Abbey Company of
SHE STOOPS TO CONQUER
A Comedy by Oliver Goldsmith

Sir Charles Marlow .	. Maurice Esmonde
Young Marlow, his son .	Arthur Shields
Hardcastle	. Michael J. Dolan
Mrs. Hardcastle . . .	. Maureen Delany
Miss Hardcastle, their daughter	. Eileen Crowe
Tony Lumpkin	. Barry Fitzgerald
Hastings	. F. J. McCormick
Miss Neville	. Christine Hayden
Diggory	. Gabriel J. Fallon
Pimple	. . May Craig
Landlord	. P. J. Carolan

Servants and Shabby Fellows: G. Lavelle, P. J. McDonnell, Seaghan Barlow, Tony Quinn, J. Finn, J. Bunyan, W. O'Hara, etc. etc.

Produced by Lennox Robinson

12th April 1923

THE SHADOW OF A GUNMAN
A Tragedy in Two Acts by Sean O'Casey

Residents in the tenement:

Donal Davoren . . .	Arthur Shields
Seumas Shields, a pedlar.	F. J. McCormick
Tommy Owens . . .	. Michael J. Dolan
Adolphus Grigson . .	. P. J. Carolan
Mrs. Grigson	. May Craig
Minnie Powell . .	Gertrude Murphy
Mr. Mulligan, the landlord	. Eric Gorman
Mr. Maguire	. G. V. Lavelle

Residents of an adjoining tenement:

Mrs. Henderson . .	. Christine Hayden
Mr. Gallogher . . .	. Gabriel J. Fallon
An Auxiliary	. Tony Quinn

Produced by Lennox Robinson

3rd September 1923

APARTMENTS
A Comedy in One Act by Fand O'Grady

Mrs. MacCarthy, a boarding-house keeper	. Sara Allgood
Michael MacCarthy, her husband	. Michael J. Dolan

Her daughters:

Geraldine MacCarthy	Gertrude Murphy
Maude MacCarthy . .	Irene Murphy

Boarders at Mrs. MacCarthy's:

Mr. Kiernan, a teacher.	Arthur Shields
Mr. O'Flaherty, a student	F. J. McCormick
Miss O'Rourke, a teacher .	Pearl Moore
Mrs. Quinn, a lodger . . .	Eileen Crowe

Produced by Lennox Robinson

1st October 1923

CATHLEEN LISTENS IN
A Phantasy in One Act by Sean O'Casey

Meehawl O'Houlihan, the man of the house . .	. F. J. McCormick
Sheela O'Houlihan, the woman of the house .	Maureen Delany
Kathleen, their daughter .	. Eileen Crowe
Thomas Thornton, a neighbour	. Barry Fitzgerald
Jimmy, a workman . .	. Michael J. Dolan
The Man in the Kilts .	. Gabriel J. Fallon
The Free-Stater . . .	. Arthur Shields
The Republican . . .	. Tony Quinn
The Business Man . .	. . U. Wright
The Farmer	. Maurice Esmonde
The Doctor	. Eric Gorman
The Man with the Big Drum .	Peter Nolan
Two Men .	Walter Dillon, P. J. Carolan

Produced by Lennox Robinson

27th November 1923

THE GLORIOUS UNCERTAINTY
A Comedy in Three Acts
by Brinsley MacNamara

Gabriel Cunneen . . .	. P. J. Carolan
Julia Cunneen, his wife . .	. Sara Allgood
Susie Cunneen, their daughter	Eileen Crowe
Sam Price	. Barry Fitzgerald
Simon Swords . . .	. Michael J. Dolan
Mortimer Clyne . . .	. Peter Nolan
Andy Whelehan .	. F. J. McCormick
Montagu-Smith Willoughby	. Arthur Shields
Sylvester Seery	Gabriel J. Fallon

Produced by Lennox Robinson

26th December 1923
FIRST AID
A Play in One Act by George Shiels

Nora, an old woman	Eileen Crowe
Shawn Egan, a neighbour	Arthur Shields
Padraig Harte, another neighbour	Tony Quinn
Eileen Harte, his sister	Maureen Delany
Drogheda Moore, a ragman	F. J. McCormick
Tommy Moody, a Belfast man, dealer in Kerry Blues	Michael J. Dolan

Produced by Michael J. Dolan

31st December 1923
THE OLD WOMAN REMEMBERS
A Poem by Lady Gregory
Spoken by Sara Allgood

19th February 1924
NEVER THE TIME AND THE PLACE
A Little Comedy in One Act
by Lennox Robinson

Mrs. Mooney, a middle-aged woman	Maureen Delany
Mrs. Sheep, a widow of forty	Sara Allgood
Mrs. Fitzsimons, a young widow	Eileen Crowe
Rogerigo Callanan, a young policeman	Arthur Shields

Produced by Lennox Robinson

3rd March 1924
JUNO AND THE "PAYCOCK"
A Tragedy in Three Acts by Sean O'Casey
Residents in the Tenement:

"Captain" Jack Boyle	Barry Fitzgerald
"Juno" Boyle, his wife	Sara Allgood
Johnny Boyle, their son	Arthur Shields
Mary Boyle, their daughter	Eileen Crowe
"Joxer" Daly	F. J. McCormick
Mrs. Maisie Madigan	Maureen Delany
"Needle" Nugent, a tailor	Michael J. Dolan
Mrs. Tancred	Christine Hayden
Jerry Devine	P. J. Carolan
Charlie Bentham, a school teacher	Gabriel J. Fallon
First Irregular	Maurice Esmonde
Second Irregular	Michael J. Dolan
First Furniture Remover	Peter Nolan
Second Furniture Remover	Tony Quinn
Coal-block Vendor	Tony Quinn
Sewing-machine Man	Peter Nolan
Two Neighbours:	Eileen O'Kelly, Irene Murphy

Produced by Michael J. Dolan

15th April 1924
THE STORY BROUGHT BY BRIGIT
A Passion Play in Three Acts
by Lady Gregory

Joel, a boy from the mountains	Arthur Shields
Daniel, a tramp	Michael J. Dolan
Marcus, a sergeant of Pilate's guard	Maurice Esmonde
Silas, a scribe in Caiaphas' employment	Barry Fitzgerald
Pilate, the Roman Governor	F. J. McCormick
Judas Iscariot	Eric Gorman
St. John	P. J. Carolan
St. Brigit	Christine Hayden
First Woman	Sara Allgood
Second Woman	Maureen Delany
Third Woman	Eileen O'Kelly
First Man	Peter Nolan
Second Man	Bernard Swan
First Soldier	Gabriel J. Fallon
Second Soldier	F. J. McCormick
Third Soldier	Tony Quinn
A Young Scribe	Gabriel J. Fallon
An Egyptian Nurse	May Craig
The Mother	
Christ	

Produced by Michael J. Dolan

12th May 1924
THE RETRIEVERS
A Comedy in Three Acts by George Shiels

Peter Duat, a walking doctor	Michael J. Dolan
Grace Duat, his wife	Shelah Richards
Steve Maguire	Arthur Shields
Sally Scullion, his housekeeper	Sara Allgood
Mrs. Snider, his American aunt	Ria Mooney
Reub Snider, her husband	F. J. McCormick
John Dollas	P. J. Carolan
Mrs. Dollas, his wife	Maureen Delany
Maurya Dollas, their daughter	May Craig
Joe Kiernan, an apprentice lawyer	Peter Nolan
Pat Hacket	Tony Quinn
Dan Mulgrew, Peace Officer	Gabriel J. Fallon

Produced by Michael J. Dolan

A HISTORY, 1899–1951

8th September 1924
AUTUMN FIRE
A Play in Three Acts by T. C. Murray

Owen Keegan, a farmer	Michael J. Dolan
Ellen, his daughter	Sara Allgood
Michael, his son	Arthur Shields
Morgan, his brother	Barry Fitzgerald
Mrs. Desmond, a cottager	Maureen Delany
Nancy, her daughter	Eileen Crowe
Tom Furlong	F. J. McCormick
Molly Hurley	Helen Cullen

Produced by Michael J. Dolan

29th September 1924
NANNIE'S NIGHT OUT
A Comedy in One Act by Sean O'Casey

Mrs. Polly Pender, proprietress of the Laburnum dairy	Maureen Delany
Sweet on Polly:	
Oul Johnny, a lodger	Barry Fitzgerald
Oul Jimmy	Michael J. Dolan
Oul Joe	Gabriel J. Fallon
Irish Nannie, a young Spunker	Sara Allgood
Robert, Nannie's son	Gerald Breen
A Ballad Singer	F. J. McCormick
A Young Man	Arthur Shields
A Young Girl	Eileen Crowe

Crowd: Seaghan Barlow, F. Ellis, W. O'Hara, M. Judge

Produced by Michael J. Dolan

9th December 1924
THE PASSING
A Tragedy in Vignette by Kenneth Sarr

Nann, a dying street-walker	Sara Allgood
Jimmie, her son, an idiot	Michael J. Dolan

Produced by Michael J. Dolan

22nd December 1924
OLD MAG
A Christmas Play in One Act by Kenneth Sarr

Old Mag, a hawker	Maureen Delany
Terry, her son, a sailor	P. J. Carolan

Women: May Craig, Joan Sullivan, Dolly Lynd, Eileen O'Kelly, Norma Joyce
Sailors: Gabriel J. Fallon, Tony Quinn, Tom Moran, F. J. McCormick

Produced by Michael J. Dolan

24th February 1925
THE OLD MAN
A Play in Two Acts by Dorothy Macardle

Cornelius Sheridan	Barry Fitzgerald
Pauline Sheridan, his granddaughter	Joyce Chancellor
Robert Emmet Sheridan, his grandson	Tony Quinn
David	Eric Gorman
Hugh	Peter Nolan
Joe	Desmond Finn
John	Walter Dillon
Michael	M. J. Scott
Tom	Michael J. Dolan
Nick	Arthur Shields
M'Crae	U. Wright
M'Guire	P. J. Carolan

Produced by Michael J. Dolan

17th March 1925
ANTI-CHRIST
A Commentary in Five Scenes by Frank Hugh O'Donnell

SCENE 1
A Room in Murphy and Nixon's flat

John Boles, ex-Captain of an Infantry Regiment	Michael J. Dolan
Oscar Murphy, chief leader writer of the party organ of the "Saints"	Arthur Shields
Frederick Nixon, chief leader writer of the party organ of the "Scholars"	F. J. McCormick
Pamela Fortescue, Boles's fiancée	Shelah Richards

SCENE 2
A Room in John Boles's house

Pamela Fortescue	Shelah Richards
John Boles	Michael J. Dolan
John Desmond	Walter Dillon
Alfred Sanderson	Tony Quinn
John Drysdale, V.C.	Arthur Shields
Grahame Belton	Barry Fitzgerald
Captain Millar, war companion of Boles	P. J. Carolan

Other Men: Desmond Finn, W. O'Hara, Tom Moran

Scene 3

A London Side Street

Sandwichmen:
Bill	P. J. Carolan
Tom	Tony Quinn
Mike	Desmond Finn
Alf	Walter Dillon
Pat	Barry Fitzgerald
Joe	W. O'Hara
Arthur	Tom Moran
Policeman	Peter Nolan
Newsboy	John O'Neill

Scene 4

Bachup's Study

Cecil Graham, Bachup's Private Secretary	Peter Nolan
Mr. Bachup, the Chief of State	Eric Gorman
General Dingby, Commander of Home Defence Forces	F. J. McCormick
Mr. Burhslip, Minister for Internal Affairs	M. J. Scott
Manservant	Desmond Finn
Maidservant	May Craig

Scene 5

John Drysdale's Drawing-room

Maude Plumer	Joyce Chancellor
Dolly Drysdale	May Craig
Alf Pollehoff	Barry Fitzgerald
George Drysdale	P. J. Carolan
Joe Giddings	Tony Quinn
John Drysdale	Arthur Shields

Produced by Michael J. Dolan

31st March 1925

PORTRAIT

In Two Sittings by Lennox Robinson

Maggie Barnado	Sara Allgood
Peter Brandon	Arthur Shields
Mrs. Barnado	Maureen Delany
Mr. Barnado	Barry Fitzgerald
Mrs. Chambers (Mary)	Joan Sullivan
Charlie Brandon	Tony Quinn
Tom Hughes	P. J. Carolan
Mrs. Brandon	May Craig

Produced by the Author

21st April 1925

First Production by the Abbey Company of

FANNY'S FIRST PLAY

A Play in Three Acts by G. Bernard Shaw

Mrs. Gilbey	Maureen Delany
Mr. Gilbey	Michael J. Dolan
Juggins	Arthur Sinclair
Miss Dora Delaney	Sara Allgood
Mrs. Knox	Christine Hayden
Mr. Knox	P. J. Carolan
Margaret Knox	Shelah Richards
Monsieur Dunallet	F. J. McCormick
Bobby Gilbey	Michael Scott

Produced by Lennox Robinson

14th September 1925

PROFESSOR TIM

A Comedy in Three Acts by George Shiels

John Scally, a farmer	Eric Gorman
Mrs. Scally, his wife	Sara Allgood
Peggy Scally, their daughter	Eileen Crowe
Professor Tim, Mrs. Scally's brother	F. J. McCormick
James Kilroy, a Rural Councillor	Peter Nolan
Mrs. Kilroy, his wife	Christine Hayden
Joseph Kilroy, their son	Barry Fitzgerald
Hugh O'Cahan, a sporting farmer	P. J. Carolan
Paddy Kinney, his groom	Arthur Shields
Moll Flannagan, his housekeeper	Maureen Delany
Mr. Allison, an auctioneer	J. Stephenson

Produced by Michael J. Dolan

12th October 1925

THE WHITE BLACKBIRD

A Play in Three Acts by Lennox Robinson

Mrs. Naynoe	Lini Doran
Mr. Naynoe	Michael J. Dolan
Molly	Ria Mooney
Violet	Maeve McMurrough
Tinker	Arthur Shields
Bella	Shelah Richards
William	F. J. McCormick
Connie	Eileen Crowe

Produced by the Author

A HISTORY, 1899–1951

4th January 1926

THE WOULD-BE GENTLEMAN

An Entertainment in Two Acts by Molière translated and adapted by Lady Gregory

Mr. Jordain	Barry Fitzgerald
Mrs. Jordain	Maureen Delany
Lucile, their daughter	Shelah Richards
Nicola, a maidservant	Eileen Crowe
Cleonte, in love with Lucille	Arthur Shields
Coviel, servant to Cleonte	Tony Quinn
Dorante, a Count	Michael J. Dolan
Dorimene, a Marchioness	May Craig
Music Master	P. J. Carolan
Dancing Master	M. J. Scott
Fencing Master	John S. Breen
Philosophy Master	F. J. McCormick
Master Tailor	Gabriel J. Fallon
Journeyman Tailor	G. M. Hayes
Footmen: Tom Moran, J. Finn	
Musicians: J. Stephenson, Walter Dillon, G. Green	
Dancers: P. Martin, J. Symington, F. Hodgskinson	

8th February 1926

THE PLOUGH AND THE STARS

A Tragedy in Four Acts by Sean O'Casey

Commandant Jack Clitheroe, of the Irish Citizen Army	F. J. McCormick
Nora Clitheroe, his wife	Shelah Richards
Peter Flynn, Nora's uncle	Eric Gorman
The Young Covey, Clitheroe's cousin	Michael J. Dolan
Fluther Good	Barry Fitzgerald
Bessie Burgess	Maureen Delany
Mrs. Gogan, a charwoman	May Craig
Mollser, her consumptive daughter	Kitty Curling
Captain Brennan, of the I.C.A.	Gabriel J. Fallon
Lieut. Langon, of the Irish Volunteers	Arthur Shields
Rosie Redmond	Ria Mooney
A Barman	P. J. Carolan
A Woman	Eileen Crowe
The Voice	J. Stephenson
Corporal Stoddard, of the Wiltshires	P. J. Carolan
Sergeant Tinley, of the Wiltshires	J. Stephenson

Produced by Lennox Robinson

12th April 1926

LOOK AT THE HEFFERNANS!

A Comedy in Three Acts by Brinsley MacNamara

Festus Darby	F. J. McCormick
James Heffernan	Michael J. Dolan
Paul Heffernan, his brother	Barry Fitzgerald
James's children:	
Marks Heffernan	P. J. Carolan
Alice Heffernan	Ria Mooney
Sydney Heffernan	Tony Quinn
Marcella Molloy	Eileen Crowe
Ignatius Crinnion	Gabriel J. Fallon
Mabel Scally	Beatrice Toal
Roseanne Rooney	Shelah Richards
Tessie Malone	Alice Kelly

Produced by Lennox Robinson

16th August 1926

MR. MURPHY'S ISLAND

A Comedy of 1921 in Two Acts by Elizabeth Harte

Dick	Arthur Shields
Jimmy	P. J. Carolan
Brian Prendergast	F. J. McCormick
General Sir Percival Bude	M. J. Dolan
Finola Bude	Eileen Crowe
Mary Ellen	Maureen Delany
Sergeant of Black-and-Tans	T. Moran
First Black-and-Tan	Peter Nolan
Second Black-and-Tan	J. Stephenson
Third Black-and-Tan	Tony Quinn
Workmen, Servant and Black-and-Tans: Walter Dillon, M. Judge, F. Ellis, etc.	

Produced by Lennox Robinson

6th September 1926

THE BIG HOUSE

Four Scenes in its Life by Lennox Robinson

Atkins	P. J. Carolan
Rev. Henry Brown	Michael J. Dolan
Captain Montgomery Despard	F. J. McCormick
Kate Alcock	Shelah Richards
St. Leger Alcock	Barry Fitzgerald
Vandaleur O'Neill	Tony Quinn
Mrs. Alcock	Eileen Crowe
Annie Daly	Ria Mooney
Three Young Men: Arthur Shields, J. Stephenson, Walter Dillon	

Produced by the Author

8th November 1926

First Production by the Abbey Company of
THE IMPORTANCE OF BEING EARNEST
A Trivial Comedy for Serious People
by Oscar Wilde

Lane . . . . Michael J. Dolan
Algernon Moncrieff . . . Arthur Shields
John Worthing, J.P. . . . F. J. McCormick
Lady Bracknell . . . . Maureen Delany
Hon. Gwendolen Fairfax . . Eileen Crowe
Miss Prism . . . . May Craig
Cecily Cardew . . . Shelah Richards
Rev. Frederick Chasuble,
   D.D. . . . . . . Barry Fitzgerald
Merriman, butler . . . . P. J. Carolan
   Second Scene by Miss Norah McGuinness
   Produced by Lennox Robinson

7th December 1926
OEDIPUS THE KING
By Sophocles
Prose version by W. B. Yeats

Oedipus . . . . F. J. McCormick
Jocasta, his wife . . . . Eileen Crowe
Creon, his wife's brother . Barry Fitzgerald
Priest . . . . Eric Gorman
Teresius . . . . Michael J. Dolan
Boy . . . . D. Breen
First Messenger . . . Arthur Shields
Herdsman . . . . Gabriel J. Fallon
Second Messenger . . . . P. J. Carolan
Nurse . . . . May Craig
Children (Antigone and Ismene):
    Raymond and Edna Fardy
Servants: Tony Quinn, Michael Scott,
   C. Haughton
Leader of the Chorus . . . J. Stephenson
Chorus: Peter Nolan, Walter Dillon, T.
   Moran, M. Finn, D. Williams
   Produced by Lennox Robinson

24th January 1927
First Production by the Abbey Company of
TRIFLES
A Play in One Act by Susan Glaspell

George Henderson, County
   Attorney . . . . . F. J. McCormick
Henry Peter, Sheriff . . . Tony Quinn
Lewis Hale, a neighbouring
   farmer . . . . . . M. J. Dolan
Mrs. Peters . . . . . . May Craig
Mrs. Hale . . . . . . Eileen Crowe
   Produced by P. J. Carolan

24th January 1927
First Production by the Abbey Company of
THE EMPEROR JONES
A Play in Eight Scenes by Eugene O'Neill

An old Native Woman . . . May Craig
Henry Smithers, a trader . John Stephenson
Brutus Jones, Emperor   Rutherford Mayne
The Little Formless Fears   —
Jeff . . . . Arthur Shields
Three Negro Convicts: Edgar Keating, C.
   Williams, C. T. Culhane
The Prison Guard . . . . Tony Quinn
The Planters: Maureen Delany, Shelah
   Richards, W. Scott, H. D.
   Walshe, T. O'Connell
The Auctioneer . . . . P. J. Carolan
The Slaves: Edgar Keating, May Craig,
   G. Burke-Kennedy
The Singing Negroes: Edgar Keating, C. T.
   Culhane, C. Williams, T. Kennedy
The Witch Doctor . . Michael Scott
Lem . . . . Arthur Shields
Three Soldiers, adherents of Lem: C. Williams,
   Edgar Keating, C. T. Culhane

Produced by Lennox Robinson. The Forest
Scenes by D. Travers Smith.

14th March 1927
SANCHO'S MASTER
A Play in Three Acts by Lady Gregory

The Housekeeper . . . Maureen Delany
Sampson Carasco, a notary . J. Stephenson
Sancho Panza . . . . Barry Fitzgerald
Don Quixote . . . . F. J. McCormick
Muleteers: M. Finn, Michael Scott, T.
   Moran, F. Ellis
Prison Guard . . . . . Peter Nolan
Prisoners: Gabriel J. Fallon, Walter Dillon,
   Arthur Shields, W. O'Hara, M. Judge
The Duchess . . . . Shelah Richards
Her Duenna . . . . . . May Craig
The Duke . . . . . . P. J. Carolan
A Boy . . . . . . Edward Raymond
A Barber . . . . . Michael J. Dolan
A Trumpeter . . . . Seaghan Barlow
A Veiled Lady . . . . Eileen Crowe
Two Girls . . Ria Mooney, Kitty Curling
Servants . . Gabriel J. Fallon, M. Finn
Chancellor . . . . T. Moran
Attendant . . . . . . Peter Nolan
Two Pages: Michael Scott, Edward Raymond

   Produced by Lennox Robinson

A HISTORY, 1899–1951

5th April 1927

PARTED
A Tragedy in One Act by M. C. Madden

Tom Morris, a farmer	. Michael J. Dolan
Mary Morris, his wife	. . . May Craig
Jim Morris, their son .	. F. J. McCormick
Bat Lonergan, a farmer	. . P. J. Carolan
Molly Lonergan, his daughter	Shelah Richards
Lar Downey, a neighbour .	Michael Scott

Produced by Arthur Shields

9th May 1927

DAVE
A Play in One Act by Lady Gregory

Nicholas O'Cahan . .	. Michael J. Dolan
Kate O'Cahan . . .	Maureen Delany
Timothy Loughlin . .	. P. J. Carolan
Josephine Loughlin . .	. K. Curling

16th May 1927

BLACK OLIVER
A Play in One Act by John Guinan

Giolle Na Naomh . . .	Arthur Shields
Fear Gan Ainm . .	. F. J. McCormick
Skelp	Gabriel J. Fallon

Produced by Lennox Robinson

22nd August 1927

THE DRAPIER LETTERS
A Play in One Act by Arthur Power

Mary-Bridget	Shelah Richards
Mrs. Cafferty, her mother	. Eileen Crowe
Mrs. Kate	. May Craig
Sally O'Gorman . . .	Maureen Delany
Biddy	Aoife Taaffe
An English Officer . . .	P. J. Carolan
Privates Thomson and Smith:	T. Moran, M. Scott
Robert Blakeley, Dean Swift's servant	Peter Nolan

Produced by Arthur Shields

12th September 1927

First Production of W. B. Yeats's version of
OEDIPUS AT COLONUS
By Sophocles

Oedipus . . .	. F. J. McCormick
His daughters:	
Antigone	Shelah Richards
Ismene	K. Curling
Polyneices, his son . .	. Gabriel J. Fallon
Theseus, King of Athens	. Michael J. Dolan
Creon, King of Thebes (brother-in-law of Oedipus)	. Barry Fitzgerald
A Stranger	. Arthur Shields
A Messenger	. P. J. Carolan
Leader of the Chorus . .	. J. Stephenson

Chorus: Peter Nolan, Walter Dillon, T. Moran, M. Finn, M. Scott
Servants and Soldiers: U. Wright, C. Culhane, G. Green, J. Breen, P. Raymond, W. J. Scott

Produced by Lennox Robinson

3rd October 1927

THE PIPE IN THE FIELDS
A Play in One Act by T. C. Murray

Martin Keville	. P. J. Carolan
Nora, his wife . . .	. Eileen Crowe
Peter, their son . .	. F. J. McCormick
Father Moore . . .	. Michael J. Dolan
Mrs. Carolan . . .	. Maureen Delany
A Dancer	. Ginette Waddell

Produced by Lennox Robinson

24th October 1927

First Production by the Abbey Company of
CAESAR AND CLEOPATRA
A History by G. Bernard Shaw

Belzanor	. Barry Fitzgerald
The Persian	. Gilbert Green
The Sentinel	. . M. Finn
Bel Affris	. . M. Scott
Ftatateeta	. Maureen Delany
Caesar	. F. J. McCormick
Cleopatra	. Shelah Richards
Pothinus	. Gabriel J. Fallon
Theodotus	. Michael J. Dolan
Ptolemy	Edward Raymond
Achillas	. Tom Moran
Rufio	. J. Stephenson
Brittanus	. Eric Gorman
Lucius Septimius . . .	. P. J. Carolan
Centurion	. Peter Nolan
Wounded Roman Soldier .	. Walter Dillon
Apollodorus	Arthur Shields
Iras	. May Craig
Charmian	. Eileen Crowe
Girl	. K. Curling
Major-Domo	. U. Wright
Priest	. Walter Dillon

Soldiers, Slaves, etc.
Scenery and Costumes by D. Travers Smith

29th November 1927
CARTNEY AND KEVNEY
A Comedy in Three Acts by George Shiels

Dick Cartney	Barry Fitzgerald
Maud Cartney	Eileen Crowe
Old Cartney	Eric Gorman
Felix Kevney	P. J. Carolan
Mrs. Kevney	Maureen Delany
Harry Kevney	F. J. McCormick
Dr. Palmer	Gabriel J. Fallon
Mr. Petrie	Peter Nolan
Mr. Hartnett	John Stephenson
Miss Denny	May Craig
Dooney	Michael J. Dolan

Produced by Arthur Shields

6th March 1928
THE MASTER
A Play in Three Acts by Brinsley MacNamara

Madge Leonard	Eileen Crowe
Father Andrew Cunningham, P.P.	Michael J. Dolan
Anne Clinton	May Craig
James Clinton	F. J. McCormick
Jane Garland	Gertrude Quinn
Michael Clinton	Arthur Shields
Walter Murphy	Eric Gorman
Jasper Branagan	P. J. Carolan
Eugene Hapenny	Walter Dillon
Lawrence Darby	Peter Nolan
Bedelia Jordan	Christine Hayden
Alexander Simons	J. Stephenson
"The Comic"	Michael Clarke
Shamesey Monaghan	T. Moran
Liza Daly	Maureen Delany

Produced by Lennox Robinson

30th April 1928
THE BLIND WOLF
A Play in Three Acts by T. C. Murray

Peter Karavoe, a Hungarian peasant	Michael J. Dolan
Marina, his wife	Eileen Crowe
Franz, their son	F. J. McCormick
Elizabeth, their son's wife	May Craig
Little Ilma, their granddaughter	Kitty Curling
Sandor Tompa, an innkeeper	P. J. Carolan
Christina, his wife	Maureen Delany
Gregory Berzsenyi, a musician	J. Stephenson
A Serving Boy	Michael Scott

Produced by Arthur Shields

16th July 1928
BEFORE MIDNIGHT
A Tragedy in One Act by Gerald Brosnan

Patrick Francis Kiley, known as "Shocks," a shell-shocked ex-soldier	F. J. McCormick
"Knacker" Kenner, a citizen of the underworld	Michael J. Dolan
Detective Long, of City C.I.D.	P. J. Carolan
Street Hawkers:	
Joe Mason	Barry Fitzgerald
Mike Bannon	Michael Scott
Amey, an outcast	Ria Mooney
A Civic Guard	Arthur Shields
Another Detective	Thomas Marshall

Produced by Lennox Robinson

27th August 1928
FULL MEASURE
A Play in Two Acts by Kathleen O'Brennan

Batty Quinlan, a shopkeeper	P. J. Carolan
Derby Quinlan, his wife	Maureen Delany
Ellen, a shop assistant	Kate Curling
Father Jurley	J. Stephenson
Nora Murtagh	Sara Allgood
Dan Murtagh, her son	Arthur Shields
Peggy Murtagh, her daughter	Eileen Crowe
Jinny Sullivan	Deirdre McAuliffe
Martin O'Grady	Peter Nolan
Tadgh Mahony	Eric Gorman
Timmy Foley	F. J. McCormick
Maurice O'Grady, Martin's son	Michael Scott
Patsy Riordan	Michael J. Dolan
Micky Sheehan	Barry Fitzgerald
Villagers: T. Moran, Walter Dillon, May Craig, Michael Clarke	

Produced by Lennox Robinson. Scene of the Second Act by D. Travers Smith.

22nd October 1928
THE FAR-OFF HILLS
A Comedy in Three Acts by Lennox Robinson

Patrick Clancy	P. J. Carolan
His daughters:	
Marian	Eileen Crowe
Dorothea ("Ducky")	Kate Curling
Anna ("Pet")	Shelah Richards
Oliver O'Shaughnessy	Barry Fitzgerald
Dick Delany	Michael J. Dolan

A HISTORY, 1899-1951

Harold Mahony . . . F. J. McCormick
Susie Tynan . . . . Maureen Delany
Pierce Hegarty . . . . Arthur Shields
Ellen Nolan . . . . May Craig
Produced by Arthur Shields

26th November 1928

First Production by the Abbey Company of
KING LEAR
By William Shakespeare

Lear, King of Britain . . F. J. McCormick
King of France . . . . . . T. Moran
Duke of Burgundy . . . . T. Marshall
Duke of Cornwall . . . . Fred Johnson
Duke of Albany . . . . James West
Earl of Kent . . . . . J. Stephenson
Edgar, son to Gloucester . . . L. Elyan
Edmund, bastard son to
  Gloucester . . . . Arthur Shields
Fool . . . . Michael J. Dolan
Oswald, steward to Goneril . Michael Scott
Doctor . . . . R. Charles
Captain . . . . J. Winter
Old Man . . . . U. Wright
Herald . . . . M. J. Clarke
Servant . . . . M. Finn
Daughters to Lear:
  Goneril . . . . . . Eileen Crowe
  Regan . . . . . Hester Plunkett
  Cordelia . . . . . Shelah Richards
Produced by Denis Johnston

5th March 1929
MOUNTAIN DEW
A Play in Three Acts by George Shiels

Henry Moylen, an old
  stiller . . . . . Michael J. Dolan
Mrs. Moylen, his wife . . . May Craig
His daughters:
  Anna Moylen . . . . Eileen Crowe
  Tessie Moylen . . . . May Bonass
Mike Duddy, a farmer . Barry Fitzgerald
Mrs. Duddy, his mother . Maureen Delany
Kate Duddy, his sister . Hindle Mallard
Brian Mulvenna . . . F. J. McCormick
Mark Malone . . . . . P. J. Carolan
Two Policemen . T. Moran, J. Winter
Produced by Arthur Shields

13th August 1929
FIGHTING THE WAVES
A Ballet Play by W. B. Yeats

Cuchullain . . . . . Michael J. Dolan
Emer, his wife . . . . . Meriel Moore
Eithne Inguba . . . . Shelah Richards

Fand . . . . Ninette de Valois
Singer . . . . J. Stevenson
Ghost of Cuchullain . . Hedley Briggs
Waves: Chris Sheehan, Mai Kiernan, Cepta
  Cullen, Doreen Cuthbert, Margaret
  Horgan, Thelma Murphy

Produced by Lennox Robinson. Music by
George Anthiel. Costumes and Curtain by
D. Travers Smith. Masks by Hildo Krop.
Choreography by Ninette de Valois. Conducted by J. F. Larchet.

10th September 1929
THE WOMAN
A Play in Three Acts by Margaret O'Leary

John O'Hara, a farmer . . P. J. Carolan
Mrs. O'Hara, his wife . . Maureen Delany
Maurice, their son . . . Arthur Shields
James Deasy, brother of
  Mrs. O'Hara . . . Michael J. Dolan
Brothers-in-law of Maurice:
  Jer Murnane . . . F. J. McCormick
  Tim Murnane . . . Michael Clarke
Kitty Doyle, a neighbour . . May Bonass
Mrs. Dunn . . . . May Craig
William Dunn, her son . John Stephenson
Ellen Dunn, her daughter . . Eileen Crowe
A Stranger . . . . . . Denis O'Dea
Produced by Lennox Robinson

8th October 1929
EVER THE TWAIN
A Comedy in Three Acts by Lennox Robinson

Chesterfield Wragsdale . F. J. McCormick
Vivienne Waters . . . . Meriel Moore
Edwin Salmon . . . . Arthur Shields
Udolphus . . . . . . P. J. Carolan
Nicholas Brice . . . . Michael J. Dolan
Michael Love . . Michael MacLiammoir
Molly O'Sullivan . . . Frolie Mulhern
Mrs. Gordon P. Beck . . Christine Hayden
Gordon P. Beck . . . . . Eric Gorman
Birdie Cummins . . . . . Eileen Crowe
Carl Svenson . . . . . Michael Scott
George Jackson . W. J. Roderick Rafter
George Brown . . . . . R. V. Rafter
Alexander Johnson . . . C. L. Rafter
Septimus Lee . . . . E. Russell Rafter
Many Ladies
Henri Leprevost . . . A. J. Leventhal
Ed. . . . . Joseph Linnane

Produced by the Author. Scenery for Acts I and II by D. Travers Smith. Spirituals arranged by J. F. Larchet.

29th October 1929

First Production by the Abbey Company of

THE GODS OF THE MOUNTAIN

A Play in Three Acts by Lord Dunsany

Beggars:
Agmar	F. J. McCormick
Than	P. J. Carolan
Oogno	Denis O'Dea
Slag	Michael Clarke
Mlan	T. Moran
Ulf	Fred Johnson
A Thief	Michael J. Dolan
Illanaun	J. B. O'Mahony
Oorander	Michael Scott
Akmos	U. Wright

Citizens: M. Finn, J. Linnane, R. Reynolds, C. H. Pilkington, J. Stephenson, Eric Gorman
Dromedary Men: Peter Nolan, F. Ellis
Women: Christine Hayden, May Craig, Mai Neville

Produced by Arthur Shields

31st December 1929

DARK ISLE

A Play in Three Acts by Gerald Brosnan

Dan O'Neale	Michael J. Dolan
Michael O'Neale, his son (Captain in I.R.A.)	Denis O'Dea
Father Clennel, British ex-Army Chaplain	F. J. McCormick
Una Cahill	Dodo Carroll
James Gannon, a local publican	P. J. Carolan
Kate Gannon, his wife	Eileen Crowe
Shiela Gannon, his daughter	Gertrude Quinn
Jimmy Gannon, his son	Fred Johnson
Matt Harkness	Arthur Shields
Patsy Daily	J. Stephenson
Mary Daily, Patsy's wife and O'Neale's servant	Maureen Delany

Produced by Lennox Robinson

28th January 1930

PETER

A Comedy, in a Prologue, Three Acts and an Epilogue, by Rutherford Mayne

Peter Grahame	Arthur Shields
Charley Prendergast	Denis O'Dea
Billy Stephens	Fred Johnson
Rosie	Gertrude Quinn
Sam Partridge	F. J. McCormick
Mrs. Anne McCleery	Maureen Delany
Mr. John McCleery	Eric Gorman
Tom	Barry Fitzgerald
Mr. S. Nelson Scott	P. J. Carolan
Buttons	P. Farrell
Young Man	Thomas Linnane
Young Lady	Frolie Mulhern
Colonel Blake	Michael Scott
Mrs. Blake	Meriel Moore
Joan Blake	Eileen Crowe

The Blue Room Girls: Sara Patrick, Cepta Cullen, Doreen Cuthbert, Chris Sheehan

Produced by Lennox Robinson

18th March 1930

THE REAPERS

A Play in Three Acts by Teresa Deevy

Ted Doherty	Denis O'Dea
Lena Doherty	Shelah Richards
Paul Barden	F. J. McCormick
Patricia Doherty	Eileen Crowe
Ada Doherty	May Craig
Jack Doherty	Arthur Shields
Officer	Michael J. Dolan
First Young Man	Fred Johnson
Second Young Man	J. Winter
Two Soldiers	P. J. Carolan, U. Wright

Produced by Lennox Robinson

19th April 1930

THE NEW GOSSOON

A Comedy in Three Acts by George Shiels

Ellen Cary, a farmer	Maureen Delany
Luke Cary, her son	Denis O'Dea
Peter Cary, his uncle	Michael J. Dolan
Ned Shay, the servant man	P. J. Carolan
Mag Kehoe, the servant girl	Frolie Mulhern
Rabit Hamil, a poacher	F. J. McCormick
Sally Hamil, his daughter	Eileen Crowe
John Henly, a corn-miller	Arthur Shields
Biddy Henly, his daughter	Shelah Richards

Produced by Arthur Shields

BRINSLEY MACNAMARA

A HISTORY, 1899–1951

15th September 1930

LET THE CREDIT GO

A Play in Four Acts by Bryan Cooper

Tom McGoldrick	J. Winter
Maurice Kennedy	J. Stephenson
Digby Reid	John Barton
Frank Williamson	Denis O'Dea
Marguerite Moloney	Eileen Crowe
Mrs. Moloney	Maureen Delany
Mr. Kelly	Eric Gorman
Michael Moloney	Michael J. Dolan
Bridgie Dillon	Shelah Richards
Mr. Enright	Arthur Shields
Supt. Flanagan	F. J. McCormick
Inspector Carroll	Fred Johnson
Sergeant Dempsey	P. J. Carolan

Produced by Lennox Robinson

17th November 1930

THE WORDS UPON THE WINDOW PANE

A Play in One Act by W. B. Yeats

Miss McKenna	Shelah Richards
Dr. Trench	P. J. Carolan
John Corbet	Arthur Shields
Cornelius Pattison	Michael J. Dolan
Abraham Johnson	F. J. McCormick
Mrs. Mallet	Eileen Crowe
Mrs. Henderson	May Craig

Produced by Lennox Robinson

6th January 1931

THE CRITIC

or A Tragedy Rehearsed

A Dramatic Piece in Three Acts by Richard Brinsley Sheridan

Modernised by Lennox Robinson

Mr. Dangle	Michael J. Dolan
Mrs. Dangle	Maureen Delany
A Servant	Frolie Mulhern
Mr. Sneer	Fred Johnson
Mr. Plagiary	Arthur Shields
An Interpreter	John Barton
Signora Pasticcio Ritornello	Christine Hayden
Anna	Geraldine Byrne
Nella	Jill Gregory
Mr. Puff	F. J. McCormick
Stage Manager	P. J. Carolan

Characters in "The Spanish Armada" in the order of appearance:

Sir Christopher Hatton	Eric Gorman
Sir Walter Raleigh	Barry Fitzgerald
The Earl of Leicester	J. Stevenson
The Governor of Tilbury Fort	Thomas Moran
The Master of the Horse	U. Wright
A Knight	Denis O'Dea
Two Sentinels: Michael Finn, Michael Clarke	
Tilburina	Eileen Crowe
Confidante	May Craig
Don Ferola Whiskerandos	Arthur Shields
Justice	John Barton
A Constable	Michael Finn
Justice's Lady	Christine Hayden
Son	Denis O'Dea
Relations: U. Wright, Michael Clarke, W. O'Gorman, Pat C. Cahill	
Beefeater	J. Winter
Lord Burleigh	J. Stevenson
Two Nieces	Frolie Mulhern, Gertie Quinn
The Thames	Noel de la Rue
Thames' Banks: Geraldine Byrne, Jill Gregory	
The Ballet: Chris Sheehan, Doreen Cuthbert, Cepta Cullen, Thelma Murphy, V. Wynburne, Noel de la Rue	

Produced by Lennox Robinson. Choreography by Sara Patrick. Music arranged by J. F. Larchet. Ballet costumes and backcloth by D. Travers Smith.

9th February 1931

THE RUNE OF HEALING

A Tragedy in Three Acts by John Guinan

Rody Meara	Michael J. Dolan
Julia Meara	Maureen Delany
Delia Meara	Shelah Richards
Felix Fagan	Arthur Shields
Dudley Fagan	F. J. McCormick
Becky Fagan	May Craig

Produced by Lennox Robinson

23rd February 1931

PETER THE LIAR

A Play in One Act by André Leprevost

Peter Doyle	John Stephenson
First Rebel	T. Moran
Second Rebel	Denis O'Dea
A Nameless Man	Michael Clarke
Maggie Doyle	Maureen Delany
Mary O'Flynn	Frolie Mulhern
Sheila	Shelah Richards
Peter Flanagan	P. J. Carolan

Produced by Lennox Robinson

9th March 1931
MONEY
A Play in Two Acts by Hugh P. Quinn

Mrs. McConachy	May Craig
Mickey, her husband	Michael J. Dolan
Aggie, her daughter	Kate Curling
"Ducksy" Duggan	Denis O'Dea
Sam Meehan, an insurance agent	P. J. Carolan
Mr. Blaney, a grocer	F. J. McCormick
Bella McCann	Maureen Delany
Rosy O'Grady	Frolie Mulhern
Liza	Shelah Richards

Produced by Arthur Shields

27th April 1931
THE MOON IN THE YELLOW RIVER
A Play in Three Acts by "E. W. Tocher"
(Denis Johnston)

Agnes	Maureen Delany
Blanaid	Shelah Richards
Tausch	Fred Johnson
Aunt Columba	Eileen Crowe
George	Arthur Shields
Capt. Potts	Michael J. Dolan
Dobelle	F. J. McCormick
Willie	U. Wright
Darrell Blake	Denis O'Dea
Commandant Lanagan	P. J. Carolan

Produced by Lennox Robinson

8th June 1931
First Production by the Abbey Company of
THE ADMIRABLE BASHVILLE
Being the novel *Cashel Byron's Profession* done into a Stage Play in Three Acts and in Blank Verse by G. Bernard Shaw

Lydia Carew	Eileen Crowe
Cashel Byron	Arthur Shields
Bob Mellish	P. J. Carolan
Lucian Webber	F. J. McCormick
Bashville	Denis O'Dea
Cetewayo	Rutherford Mayne
Lord Worthington	T. Moran
Paradise	V. B. Wynburne
Master of the Revels	J. Linnane
Policeman	Fred Johnson
Adelaide Byron	Maureen Delany
Native Chiefs, Constables, etc.:	
U. Wright, J. Winter, M. Clarke	

Produced by Lennox Robinson

7th July 1931
SCRAP
A Play in One Act by J. A. O'Brennan

Ned Tobin, a working man:	Michael J. Dolan
Kate Tobin, his wife	May Craig
Billy Tobin, their son	Fred Johnson
A Young Man	Denis O'Dea

Produced by Arthur Shields

24th August 1931
A DISCIPLE
A Comedy in One Act by Teresa Deevy

Mrs. Maher	May Craig
Ellie Irwin	Kate Curling
Stacia Claremorris	Maureen Delany
Mrs. Glitteron	Eileen Crowe
Mr. Glitteron	Barry Fitzgerald
Jack the Scalp	Denis O'Dea
A Detective	P. J. Carolan

Produced by Lennox Robinson

21st September 1931
THE CAT AND THE MOON
A Play in One Act by W. B. Yeats

Blind Man	Michael J. Dolan
Lame Man	W. O'Gorman
Singer	Joseph O'Neill
Flautist	T. Browne
Zither	Julia Gray
Drum	Muriel Kelly

Produced by Michael J. Dolan. Music by J. F. Larchet

6th December 1931
THE DREAMING OF THE BONES
A Play in One Act by W. B. Yeats

Young Man	W. O'Gorman
Stranger	J. Stephenson
Girl	Nesta Brooking
Singer	Joseph O'Neill
Flautist	T. Browne
Zither	Julia Gray
Drum	Doreen Cuthbert

Produced by U. Wright. Music by J. F. Larchet.

A HISTORY, 1899-1951

27th June 1932
MICHAELMAS EVE
A Play in Three Acts by T. C. Murray
Moll Garvey	Eileen Crowe
Hugh Kearns	Arthur Shields
Mrs. Kearns	Maureen Delany
Mary Keating	May Craig
Terry Donegan	Michael J. Dolan
Dan Garvey	P. J. Carolan

Produced by Lennox Robinson

25th July 1932
ALL'S OVER, THEN
A Play in Three Acts by Lennox Robinson
Maggie	Shelah Richards
Henry	Barry Fitzgerald
Julia	Ria Mooney
Eleanore	Eileen Crowe
Doctor Beoson	F. J. McCormick
Arthur	Arthur Shields

Produced by the Author

15th August 1932
THINGS THAT ARE CAESAR'S
A Tragedy in Three Acts
by Paul Vincent Carroll
Peter Hardy, an ex-schoolmaster	Michael J. Dolan
Julia Hardy, his wife, proprietress of "The Royal Arms"	Maureen Delany
Alice Brady, a shop-assistant	Ria Mooney
Phil Noonan	Barry Fitzgerald
Terence Noonan, his son	Denis O'Dea
Doctor Downey	P. J. Carolan
Eilish Hardy	Kate Curling
Rev. Father Duffy	F. J. McCormick
Josephine Noonan, Phil's wife	May Craig

Produced by Lennox Robinson

12th September 1932
TEMPORAL POWERS
A Play in Three Acts by Teresa Deevy
Min Donovan	Eileen Crowe
Michael, her husband	F. J. McCormick
Moses Barron	Arthur Shields
Lizzie Brennan	Ria Mooney
Daisy Barron	Maureen Delany
Maggie Cooney	May Craig
Ned, her husband	P. J. Carolan
Jim Slattery	Denis O'Dea
Father O'Brien	Michael J. Dolan

Produced by Lennox Robinson

17th October 1932
THE MATING OF SHAN M'GHIE
A Play in Three Acts by T. H. Stafford
Shan M'Ghie	W. O'Gorman
Rosa M'Ghie, his wife	Dorothy Clement
Anne M'Ghie, his sister	Ann Clery
Laurence (Larry) Bain	Gerard Kelly
Neighbours:	
Peter Burke	Gearoid O'Lochlainn
Judy Burke, his wife	Gertrude Quinn
Barney Ryan	T. Moran
Biddy Ryan, his wife	Bel Johnston
Railway Porters:	
Terry	M. Clarke
Doyne	G. Hogan
Brigit, a servant	Evelyn O'Driscoll
Pat, a farm hand	T. Marshall

Produced by Lennox Robinson

24th October 1932
VIGIL
A Play in One Act by A. P. Fanning
Soldiers of the I.R.A.:	
A Poet	Fred Johnson
A Farmer	T. Moran
A Boy	Cyril Cusack
Soldiers of the F.S. Army:	
An Officer	M. Clarke
A Captain	Joseph Linnane
A Sergeant	J. Winter
A Corporal	W. O'Gorman
A Priest	Ernest W. Nesbitt

Produced by Lennox Robinson

7th November 1932
THE BIG SWEEP
A Comedy in Three Acts by M. M. Brennan
Gerald O'Grady, last of an impoverished line	T. W. Purefoy
Michael Rooney, retired country shopkeeper	Don Barry
Dermot Sullivan, junior grade civil servant	Joseph Linnane
Miss De Lacy, music teacher	Christine Hayden
Mrs. Hayden, boarding-house keeper	Bel Johnston
Kitty Hayden, her step-daughter	Dorothy Clement
Pat Burke, her brother	W. O'Gorman

Produced by Lennox Robinson

14th November 1932

SHERIDAN'S MILLS

A Comedy in Three Acts by Norman Webb

Teresa Sheridan	Hester Plunket
Her children:	
David	Rex Mackey
Martin	R. C. Jones
Isobel	Una O'Connor
Her step-children:	
George	Fred Johnson
Valentine	J. Winter
Sis	Gertrude Quinn
Susan, George's wife	Dorothy Casey
Dennis Pennefeather	V. B. Wynburne

21st November 1932

WRACK

A Play in Six Scenes by Peadar O'Donnell

Brigid Boyle	Ann Clery
Hughie Boyle	W. O'Gorman
Mary Jim	Dorothy Casey
Fanny Brian	Christine Hayden
Kitty Cormac	Bel Johnston
Paddy Cormac	Joseph Linnane
Johnny Anthon	Fred Johnson
Corney	Eric Gorman

Other Men: Rex Mackey, Michael Clarke, J. Winter

Produced by Lennox Robinson

CHAPTER NINE

1932-1950

CHANGES were taking place, new blood was flowing into the Theatre's veins. Young dramatists were appearing to take their place in line with the old brigade. One names these dramatists chronologically, not in order of their importance: Denis Johnston (1931), Paul Vincent Carroll (1932), Francis Stuart (1933), Frank O'Connor and Hugh Hunt (1937), Andrew Ganly (1938), Frank Carney (1939), Louis D'Alton (1939), Elizabeth Connor (1940), Roger McHugh (1941), Mervyn Wall (1941), Austin Clarke (1941), Robert Farren (1943), Gerard Healy (1943), Joseph Tomelty (1944), Ralph Kennedy (1944), Walter Macken (1946), M. J. Molloy (1946), John Coulter (1948), Seamus Byrne (1950).

Some of the older dramatists were still doing important work. Rutherford Mayne, who had been mainly connected with the Ulster Literary Theatre, contributed his noble *Bridgehead* in 1934, Brinsley MacNamara his fine tragedy *Margaret Gillan* a year previously. In 1936 appears St. John Ervine's delightful comedy *Boyd's Shop*, and in 1941 *Friends and Relations*. My *Drama at Inish* appeared in 1933 and my *Church Street* in 1934, and *Forget-Me-Not* in 1941 and *The Lucky Finger* in 1948, and nearly every year there would be a new play by George Shiels. The young dramatists differed from the older ones; they owed little to Synge or to Yeats or to Lady Gregory. If realists, and they often were, they were not of the school of the Cork peasant realism.

The Directorate was changing. I had become a Director in 1923, Lady Gregory died in 1932 at the age of eighty. Her health had been slowly failing and for the last few years of her life she had not taken a very active part in the Theatre's affairs. Yeats wanted new, young blood on the Board of Directors, and so F. R. Higgins was appointed a Director in April 1935, Frank O'Connor in the following October, and Ernest Blythe

Board in the same year. Frank O'Connor resigned and Higgins died in 1941. Higgins had been ...g Director and after his death Ernest Blythe took ...c. In 1940 Robert Farren joined the Board.

Ernest Blythe is an enthusiast for Gaelic and his presence as Managing Director led immediately to many productions of plays in our native language. He has kindly supplied me with the following paragraphs:

The original objects of the Irish Literary Theatre included the production of plays in the Irish language and that object is mentioned in the Articles of Association of the Irish National Theatre Society Ltd. The first play ever written in Irish was Dr. Douglas Hyde's *Casadh an tSugain* (The Twisting of the Rope), and it was produced by the Irish Literary Theatre on 21st October 1901. It is a rather naïve but charming little piece, which was probably intended by its author for production by amateur groups in the rural areas. In the following year, on 31st October, a second play in Irish, called *Eilis agus an Bhean Deirce* (Alice and the Beggarwoman), was performed. It was by Peadar Mac Ginley, who thirty years afterwards was one of Dr. Hyde's successors as President of the Gaelic League. A third production in Irish took place in the Abbey Theatre on 15th January 1912. The play was *An Tincear agus an tSidheog* (The Tinker and the Fairy). This was not, however, the first production of *An Tincear agus an tSidheog*. It had been played in the Gaiety Theatre in 1903 under the general supervision of George Moore, with Douglas Hyde and Sinead Ni Fhlannagain (now Mrs. de Valera) in the two principal parts. After the Abbey production of *The Tinker and the Fairy* there was an interval of twenty-six years before another play in the Irish language was performed by the Abbey Company. On 9th May 1938 there was a revival of *The Twisting of the Rope*. At the time there was no Irish-speaking actress in the Theatre capable of taking the part of the girl Una, and Brid Ni Loinsigh, who has since become one of the Abbey's leading actresses, was brought in from an amateur society to play the part. The 1938 production of *The Twisting of the Rope* was the result of a resolution to which the Directors came early in 1938 that the performance of Irish plays in the future, as well as being one of the Theatre's objects, should become a regular feature of its work. A prize of £50 for a one-act play in Irish was advertised and a very large number of entries were received. Of the competition plays three were selected for production. The first two— which divided the prize—were *Baintighearna an Ghorta* (Our Lady of the Famine) by Seamus Wilmot, and *Donnchadh Ruadh* by Seamus O hAodha. They were produced on 12th December 1938 and 15th May 1939 respectively. Difficulties in casting plays in Irish and disturbances caused by the outbreak of the war led to a pause in the production of plays in Irish. On 22nd February 1942, however, the third one-act play selected from those entered for the 1938 competition, *Gloine an Impire* (The Emperor's Glass) by Traolach O'Rafferty was performed, together with *Cach*, a translation of the mediaeval morality play *Everyman*. In May 1942 the Government asked that the Abbey Theatre should take over the work of An Comhar Dramaiochta, the Drama Co-Operative, a body which for some years had been receiving a small annual subsidy from the Exchequer to aid in the production of plays in Irish. A new committee of An Comhar Dramaiochta, including representatives of the Abbey Theatre, was established and became the medium through which the Government grant for dramatic work in Irish was transmitted to the Abbey. The first performance under the new arrangement took place on 29th November 1942 when *An Stoirm*, a translation of Alexander Ostrovsky's play *The Storm*, was successfully staged. Since that date nine original plays in Irish, together with eighteen translations, eleven of them full-length plays and seven of them one-act plays, have been performed in Irish.

On 26th December 1945 an event took place which was an innovation in the work of the Abbey Theatre—Pantomime entirely in the Irish language was performed. Although the Directors would not regard Pantomime in English as being a suitable activity for the Theatre, they considered, having regard to all the facts of Irish life and to the national policy—enshrined in the Constitution and endorsed by successive Governments—of fostering the Irish language, that the Abbey Theatre ought to undertake Pantomime in Irish. The 1945 Pantomime was based on the same folk tale as Lady Gregory used in her *Golden Apple*. Being entirely experimental, it was billed for six performances only. For the first two or three nights audiences were small. Then there came a sudden rush of booking and it was announced that the Pantomime would be continued for three extra nights. Inside the next couple of days, however, it had to be announced that the run of the Pantomime would continue for some time. Actually 43 performances were given, and the entertainment could have been continued much longer but that with the small seating capacity of the Abbey it was impossible to cover the weekly expense of the large cast and extra stage hands needed for a Pantomime and the subsidy which the Comhar Dramaiochta Committee could afford to give was exhausted. It was noticed that the Pantomime was attended mainly by people of the younger generation who had learned Irish at school, and that, while almost every night people who wanted seats in the cheaper parts of the house were turned away from the door, the dearest seats were practically never sold out. Each year since 1945 a Pantomime entirely in Irish has been performed, and though there was a falling off in interest in the third year, when the first novelty of the entertainment had worn off, the attendance has since been mounting towards the highest level.

Since 1942 when the production of plays in Irish, in conjunction with the Comhar Dramaiochta, was undertaken, it has been the policy of the Theatre not to take on any new junior players who are not able to perform both in Irish and in English. Once or twice, however, a promising player who when he first applied could not do the work expected of him in Irish, has been helped to spend a period in an Irish-speaking district and has afterwards been accepted as a member of the Company.

Yeats died in 1939. New faces on the Board had given him freedom from the Abbey and time to devote himself to his own work. His and Lady Gregory's death brought the great triumvirate to an end. Through thick and thin, through rich years and lean years, through three wars—1914-18, the Anglo-Irish War and our Civil War—they had never flagged in their care for the Theatre. Perhaps there were years before, Yeats came back to live in Ireland when he was not very interested in the Abbey's affairs, but Lady Gregory until a year or two before her death kept her hand firmly on the tiller. In a moment of crisis—and there were many small crises—Coole, grandchildren, family affairs would be all thrust aside and she would take the next train from County Galway to advise, encourage and admonish.

In all these years the Directors had made surprisingly few mistakes in their choice of plays and players. The rejections of *John Bull's Other Island* and of Sean O'Casey's *The Silver Tassie* were doubtless errors of judgement, but in both cases subsequent productions made belated amends.

For too many years I had produced most of the plays at the Theatre, assisted from time to time by Arthur Shields, Michael Dolan and Udolphus Wright. In 1935 Hugh Hunt came over as producer, ably helped by Tanya Moiseiwitsch as painter of scenery and designer of costumes. He left the Theatre in October 1938. The Theatre, though often cramped for money, had always been eager to employ fine scenic artists. In early years Charles Ricketts had designed beautiful dresses for *The King's Threshold*, Gordon Craig had given us his screens, Robert Gregory had made the scenes for *Deirdre of the Sorrows*, Jack Yeats had designed a scene for *The King's Threshold*, Hildo Krop had brought his masks from Holland. Later Dorothy Travers-Smith and Norah McGuinness did many productions; Sean Keating, now President of our Royal Hibernian Academy, made a notable, colourful production of *The Playboy*. For a few months Blandon Peake and James Bould came across from England and gave startling productions of *Macbeth*, Molière's *School for Wives*, Schnitzler's *Gallant Cassian*, and Lady Gregory's *The Canavans*, and from 1941 until August 1946 Frank Dermody made many productions, so did Carl Bonn. Ria Mooney was appointed Producer in 1948.

But in the earlier years Seaghan Barlow's name crops up time and time again as designer and painter of scenery. He has only been with the Theatre for forty-four years, but he is beginning to know his way about.

The years were piling up, 1899-1909, 1909-1919, 1919-1929, and from then to the close of this History. The plays were piling up, almost to an embarrassing degree, and audiences were beginning to complain that they weren't allowed to see the old masterpieces, the Synges, the Yeats, the Lady Gregorys, because they were crowded out by the younger dramatists, the O'Caseys, the Shiels and the MacNamaras. On the other hand, the very young dramatists felt that it was difficult to get a look-in—these giants held the stage. The Directors were conscious of this situation. When Miss Horniman made the Theatre in 1904 she did not acquire that part of the Mechanics' Institute which consisted of a basement, a library and a billiard-room. The Mechanics' as an Institute ceased to exist and about twenty years later the Theatre acquired the premises. The basement was used as a store-room, the ground-floor was made a pit café and the large first-floor room was made into a little theatre. It was decorated in peacock colours, dark-green, dark-blue and a touch of gold; the auditorium was raked and its very comfortable seats held exactly a hundred people. We named it "The Peacock Theatre." The stage is very small, on one side there is practically no "off-stage" space, the other side is more adequate, the lighting equipment is excellent. There is a scene-dock and on the upper storey two large dressing-rooms with hot and cold water. The little theatre was opened in November 1925 with a performance by the New Players; it made history when in the autumn of 1928 Hilton Edwards and Michael MacLiammoir opened their career in Dublin with a performance on this tiny stage of *Peer Gynt*. After a number of productions there they moved to the Gate Theatre and proceeded to go from strength to strength. The lower room was soon abandoned as a café and became the home of the School of Acting. Later our School of Ballet used the upper rooms. For nine months in the year the little

Peacock is used by amateur or semi-amateur societies. It has justified itself. Mr. C. P. Curran has allowed me to quote what he wrote in the *Irish Statesman* on the occasion of its opening:

The Peacock Spreads His Tail

> This week makes a date of some note in Dublin dramatic history. More particularly since the foundation of the Drama League, many people feel that the Abbey Theatre has been more and more content to play for safety and to leave it to others to risk those brilliant defeats which are more to the living theatre than box-office successes. For many years the Abbey Theatre fought a hard fight on slender resources, and found courage the better part of discretion. It is now older, and no one can fairly call it a reckless protest against the commercial theatre. If it is not a commercial theatre with an artistic conscience, it is, at any rate, an art theatre with an eye on a reserve fund. It has aged sufficiently to feel the apprehensions of middle age and, perhaps, an uneasy sense of undischarged responsibilities. In these circumstances it has set up the Peacock, a well-appointed little space where ginger groups may function and youth may have its fling. The Peacock has no company attached to it, nor is it a junior partner of the Abbey. It is as if the Abbey wishes to found a dynasty, but put the child out to nurse. Its first nurses are the New Players, a by-product of the Drama League, and their aim is to build up a regular company of sufficient merit to secure the existence of a true experimental theatre in Dublin. I hope they will succeed, but the circumstances of their proposal suggest that the Abbey in its present generation of actors is surrendering the initiative in experimental work. I hope the new theatre will not be found to be the handkerchief behind which the old firm will comfortably settle down to drowse and even the Drama League to take an odd nap.

In April 1937 our Experimental Theatre was started under Miss Ria Mooney's direction.

She said in April 1937:

> About ten or fifteen years ago, there was much talk in Abbey Theatre circles about the establishing of an Experimental Theatre for the production of plays by Irish Authors whose work was considered not suitable or not sufficiently advanced technically for production on the Abbey stage, and yet was of sufficiently high standard to merit public presentation.
>
> When I was given charge of the School of Acting two years ago, I hoped eventually to find among the students enough talent to establish such a theatre; a theatre that would encourage young Irish playwrights, develop Irish Producers and scenic designers, and give experience to acting talent which would eventually find its way on to the Abbey stage.
>
> Plans for the establishment of an Experimental Theatre were given a more definite outline when, a couple of months ago, one of our senior students, Mr. Cecil Ford, came to me with a scheme for forming the students into a

Theatrical Society for the production of plays—established plays by foreign authors.... My plans for the establishing of an Experimental Theatre on the lines already mentioned were accepted unanimously at a General Meeting of the students and eventually approved by the Abbey Board of Directors, which is giving us every consideration.

The students are financing the experiment themselves. Each student is a shareholder in the Society, his weekly contribution—a very small one—constituting a share. They produce the plays themselves, they design their own sets, make and paint their own scenery and, when necessary, make their own stage clothes. They run the box-office, the pit café, and show people to their seats. The Directors of the Abbey choose the plays and give them the Theatre free, and to make sure that productions are of a certain standard Mr. Hunt and I may use our right of veto over the productions. The students are otherwise free to control and manage their own affairs.

The names of the plays and the casts of the plays produced by our Experimental Theatre can be found in Appendix IV. With a few exceptions, they are not impressive. But the Theatre has never been guilty of quenching young talent. Every play which is submitted to the Theatre is read by two people: firstly by an old Director of the Theatre, secondly by a younger man, a playwright but not officially connected with the Theatre. Ninety per cent. of the plays are worthless and go no farther than these two readers; if there seems to be any worth in a play it goes to the other Directors. The Theatre is always seeking for a new masterpiece, a new Synge, a new O'Casey.

The Abbey's vestibule is small but distinguished. Sarah Purser's green glass windows, William Morris pattern, are beautiful in their quiet way. In 1916 a bullet found its way through one of them but did no damage, so no repairs were necessary. What makes the vestibule distinguished are the portraits that hang on its walls. Visitors stare and stare at them, and why should they not? They are all painted by distinguished artists and are of distinguished players.

A few years ago I wrote a little brochure called "Pictures in a Theatre." I reprint it in Appendix I. The occurrence is imaginary, Brendan O'Neill never existed—but I must make a correction, a tragic correction. Lady Gregory's portrait does not hang over the fireplace, she is opposite on the other side of the hall. Over the fireplace hangs Cecil Salkeld's grand composite portrait of F. J. McCormick which Mr. Salkeld calls "The

Empty Throne." There have been many great actors in the Abbey, the Fay brothers, Arthur Sinclair, Fred O'Donovan, Barry Fitzgerald, and others, but never in my recollection such a versatile actor as McCormick. Cecil Salkeld's picture emphasises his versatility—here is Lear, McCormick himself, "Odd Man Out," Burgoyne, Joxer Daly, Jack Clitheroe in *The Plough and The Stars*, "Hungry Hill," "A Saint in a Hurry," the Miller in *The Canavans*, Maurice; and Oedipus. But Mr. Salkeld hadn't room on the canvas for another twenty parts, some important, some tiny. McCormick's untimely death in April 1947 was a shattering blow to our Theatre. Little known outside Ireland and the U.S.A., it was the passing of a player who was the peer of Kean, Salvini, Irving and any other great actor you care to think of.

THE ABBEY THEATRE COMPANY
At the Broadway Theatre, Denver, Colorado, 1932

Left to Right: Fred Johnson, Harry Leeg, Denis Sullivan, May Craig, Barry Fitzgerald, Maureen Delany, E. White, Arthur Shields, Eileen Crowe, F. J. McCormick, Kate Curling, P. J. Carolan, M. J. Dolan, Shelah Richards, Denis O'Dea

F. J. McCORMICK

Casts of First Productions, 1933-1950

6th February 1933
DRAMA AT INISH
An Exaggeration in Three Acts
by Lennox Robinson

John Twohig, proprietor of the Seaview Hotel	W. O'Gorman
Annie Twohig, his wife	Ann Clery
Lizzie Twohig, his sister	Christine Hayden
Eddie Twohig, his son	Joseph Linnane
Peter Hurley, T.C.	Eric Gorman
Christine Lambert	Gladys Maher
Hector de la Mare	Paul Farrell
Constance Constantia	Elizabeth Potter
Helena, a servant	Nora O'Mahony
Michael, the boots	Rex Mackey
John Hegarty, a reporter	Fred Johnson
Tom Mooney, a Civic Guard	J. Winter
William Slattery, L.P.S.I.	Don Barry

Produced by the Author

13th March 1933
MEN CROWD ME ROUND
A Play in Three Acts by Francis Stuart

Gemma Statick	Shelah Richards
Waiter	Rex Mackey
Lady Irma Allets	Muriel Loughridge
Humbert Tariff	Barry Harte
Barrel-organ Man	Fred Johnson
Peadar Considine	W. O'Gorman
Mick McGrath	J. Winter
Waiter	Michael Clarke
Osbert Allets	Tom Purefoy
Lord David Cossells	A. J. Leventhal
Liam Hegarty	Joseph Linnane
Dave Malone	Fred Johnson
Garry Moylan	Michael Clarke
Jones	Denis Murray

Produced by Lennox Robinson. Scenery by D. Travers Smith.

17th July 1933
MARGARET GILLAN
A Play in Three Acts by Brinsley MacNamara

Margaret Gillan	May Craig
Rose Leonard	Ria Mooney
Esther Gillan	Kate Curling
Michael Taafe	Denis O'Dea
Ellen Ledwidge	Eileen Crowe
Master Growney	Barry Fitzgerald
John Briody	F. J. McCormick

Produced by Arthur Shields

25th July 1933
THE DRINKING-HORN
A Ballet by Arthur Duff

The Elf	Vera Bryans
The Knight of the Well	Robert Francis
The Flute Player	Bartholomew Lynch
Dancers: Christine Kane, Mabel Rockett, Marjorie Pearce, Eileen Mayne, Fanny O'Meara, Tess Dillon Kelly	
The Youth	Toni Repetto-Butler
The Girl	Jill Gregory

21st August 1933
THE JEZEBEL
A Play in One Act by J. K. Montgomery

Mathew White, a farmer	Michael J. Dolan
Jane, his wife	Eileen Crowe
Mary, their daughter	Kate Curling
Esther Black, a neighbour	May Craig
Rab Jamieson, a young farmer	Denis O'Dea

25th September 1933
1920
A Play in Three Acts by Frank X. O'Leary

Joan Kelleher	May Craig
Gertie Kelleher, her niece	Nora O'Mahony
Art O'Kane	Denis O'Dea
Mrs. Harte	Maureen Delany
Miss O'Grady	Eileen Crowe
Gerard P. M. Hunter, District Inspector, R.I.C.	F. J. McCormick
Sergeant Brady, R.I.C.	P. J. Carolan
Constable Cronin, R.I.C.	Arthur Shields
Thady O'Reilly, postman at Kilduff P.O	Barry Fitzgerald
William Flynn, postman at Kilduff P.O.	U. Wright
Shawn Moynihan	Michael J. Dolan
Father Casey	Eric Gorman
Liz Ann	Frolie Mulhern

Produced by Arthur Shields

13th November 1933
GROGAN AND THE FERRET
A Comedy in Three Acts by George Shiels

John Byrne	P. J. Carolan
Miss Hatty	Eileen Crowe
Felix Grogan	F. J. McCormick
Fred Byrne	Denis O'Dea
Mrs. Byrne	Maureen Delany
Blakes	Michael J. Dolan
Mr. Dobbin	Arthur Shields
Paddy Grogan	Barry Fitzgerald
Rose	May Craig

Produced by Arthur Shields

26th December 1933
First Production by the Abbey Company of
YOU NEVER CAN TELL
A Comedy in Four Acts by G. Bernard Shaw

Mr. Valentine	Arthur Shields
Miss Dolly Clandon	Shelah Richards
A Maid	May Craig
Philip Clandon	Denis O'Dea
Mrs. Lanfrey Clandon	Maureen Delany
Miss Gloria Clandon	Eileen Crowe
Fergus Crampton	P. J. Carolan
Finch Mc Comas	F. J. McCormick
A Waiter	Barry Fitzgerald
Another Waiter	Michael J. Dolan
Walter Bohun, Q.C.	J. Winter

Produced by Lennox Robinson

5th February 1934
THE MARRIAGE PACKET
A Play in Three Acts by Arthur Power

Festus King	Michael J. Dolan
Oona King	Eileen Crowe
Simon Cavanagh	Denis O'Dea
Mrs. King	May Craig
Joe Mulligan	Fred Johnson
Ganger Joyce	P. J. Carolan
Mrs. Joyce	Christine Hayden
Daisy Heany	Frolie Mulhern
A Postman	Joseph Linnane
Sarah Ward	Maureen Delany
Tom Costello	F. J. McCormick
Kathleen	Una O'Connor
Mrs. Cready	Ann Clery

Produced by Lennox Robinson

16th April 1934
First Production by the Abbey Company of
DAYS WITHOUT END
A Play in Four Acts by Eugene O'Neill

John	F. J. McCormick
Loving	Arthur Shields
William Eliot	P. J. Carolan
Father Matthew Baird	Michael J. Dolan
Elsa, John Loving's wife	Eileen Crowe
Margaret	Maureen Delany
Lucy Hillman	Shelah Richards
Dr. Herbert Stillwell	Barry Fitzgerald
Nurse	May Craig

Produced by Lennox Robinson

21st May 1934
CHURCH STREET
A Play in One Act by Lennox Robinson

Joseph Riordan, Manager of the National Bank, Knock	Barry Fitzgerald
Kate Riordan, his wife	Maureen Delany
Hugh, their eldest son	Arthur Shields
Jack, another son	Joseph O'Neill
Mollie, Jack's wife	Jennifer Davidson
Aunt Moll, Joseph Riordan's aunt	Eileen Crowe
Mrs. De Lacy	Christine Hayden
Miss Pettigrew, her sister	May Craig
Sallie Long	Shelah Richards
Jim Daly	F. J. McCormick
Honor Bewley	Ann Clery
The Evoked Hugh	Denis O'Dea
Doctor Smith	Michael J. Dolan
Nurse Smith	Frolie Mulhern
A Clergyman	P. J. Carolan

Produced by the Author

18th June 1934
BRIDGEHEAD
A Play in Three Acts by Rutherford Mayne

Stephen Moore	F. J. McCormick
Martin	Arthur Shields
Hugh O'Neill	Denis O'Dea
Mrs. Marcus Morrissey	Maureen Delany
Inari Gosuki	Michael J. Dolan
Dermot Barrington	Tom Purefoy
Cecily Barrington	Eileen Crowe
John Kearney	Eric Gorman
Dan Dolan	Barry Fitzgerald
Maurice Mockler	P. J. Carolan
Michael Morrissey	W. O'Gorman
Philip Watersley	Joseph Linnane

Produced by Lennox Robinson

A HISTORY, 1899–1951

9th July 1934

First Production by the Abbey Company of
ON THE ROCKS
A Play in Two Acts by G. Bernard Shaw

Sir Arthur Chavender, Prime Minister	F. J. McCormick
Hilda Hanways	Gertrude Quinn
Sir Broadfoot Basham	Arthur Shields
Flavia Chavender	Frolie Mulhern
Lady Chavender	Maureen Delany
David Chavender	Cecil Brock
Thomas Humphries	Fred Johnson
Viscount Barking	Denis O'Dea
Miss Aloysius Brollikins	Eileen Crowe
Alderman Blee	J. Winter
Mr. Hipney	Barry Fitzgerald
The Lady	Elizabeth Young
Sir Dexter Rightside	P. J. Carolan
Admiral Sir Bemrose Hotspot	Michael J. Dolan
Mr. Glen Morrison	Denis Carey
Sir Jafna Pandrawath	Eric Gorman
The Duke of Doomsday	Tom Purefoy

Produced by Lennox Robinson

30th July 1934

THE RESURRECTION
A Play in One Act by W. B. Yeats

The Hebrew	A. J. Leventhal
The Greek	Denis Carey
The Syrian	J. Winter
The Christ	Liam Gaffney

Musicians: Michael J. Dolan, Robert Irwin

30th July 1934

THE KING OF THE GREAT CLOCK TOWER
A Play in One Act by W. B. Yeats

The King	F. J. McCormick
The Queen	Ninette de Valois
The Stranger	Denis O'Dea
1st Musician	Robert Irwin
2nd Musician	Joseph O'Neill

The two plays produced by Lennox Robinson. The Music for Mr. Yeats's plays has been written by Arthur Duff; George Atkinson, R.H.A., has made the masks; D. Travers Smith has designed the dresses for the last play.

1st October 1934

PARNELL OF AVONDALE
A Play in Three Acts by W. R. Fearon

ACT I: 1880-81

Anna Steele	Christine Hayden
Mary	Nora O'Mahony
William Henry O'Shea, M.P.	Gearoid O'Lochlainn
The O'Gorman Mahon, M.P.	J. Winter
Kate O'Shea	Ria Mooney
Charles Stewart Parnell, M.P.	Denis Carey
Ellen	Ann Clery
Valet	William Charles

ACT II: 1890

Mary	Nora O'Mahony
Ellen	Ann Clery
Anna Steele	Christine Hayden
Kate O'Shea	Ria Mooney
Charles Stewart Parnell, M.P.	Denis Carey
Sir W. V. Harcourt, M.P.	A. J. Leventhal
John Morley, M.P.	C. H. Pilkington
W. E. Gladstone, M.P.	Eric Gorman
Parnellites:	
Dr. Kenny, M.P.	Maurice Bradley
Dan Malony, M.P.	Hugh Fitzmaurice
The Member for S. Dublin	J. Winter
The Member for Wexford	Fred Johnson
Harry Graham, M.P., Parnell's Secretary	John Irwin
The Vice-Chairman of the Irish Party	J. Stephenson
Anti-Parnellites:	
The Member for Belfast	Desmond Crean
The Member for Limerick	Liam Gaffney
The Member for Longford	Edward Lexy
The Member for Cork	William Charles

ACT III: 1890-91

Kate	Ria Mooney
Mary	Nora O'Mahony
Dr. Jowers	Lionel Dymoke
Charles Stewart Parnell, M.P.	Denis Carey
Harry Graham, M.P.	John Irwin
An Irish Countryman	Cyril Cusack
A Musician	T. Kiernan
A Parnellite	Michael Clarke
Richard Power, P.L.G.	Desmond Crean
Tomsy	Tom Moran
An Anti-Parnellite	William Charles
Dr. Kenny, M.P.	Maurice Bradley
Dan Malony, M.P.	Hugh Fitzmaurice
The Member for S. Dublin	J. Winter
The Member for Wexford	Fred Johnson
A Stationmaster	Don Barry
Miss Springfield	Mary Manning
A Local Enthusiast	J. Stephenson
Parnellites, Anti-Parnellites Reporters	

Produced by Lennox Robinson

25th October 1934

First Production by the Abbey Company of
MACBETH
By William Shakespeare

First Witch	Mary Manning
Second Witch	Nora O'Mahony
Third Witch	Truda Barling
Duncan	J. Stephenson
Malcolm	Cyril Cusack
Donalbain	J. Linnane
Angus	W. J. Scott
Lennox	Tom Purefoy
Ross	Denis Carey
A Wounded Sergeant	Maurice Bradley
Macbeth	Gearoid O'Lochlainn
Banquo	Tom Moran
Fleance	Marie Moylan
Lady Macbeth	Ann Clery
Seyton	Desmond Crean
A Porter	Eric Gorman
Macduff	Fred Johnson
Menteith	Maurice Bradley
A Gentlewoman	Elizabeth Plunkett
First Murderer	J. Stephenson
Second Murderer	John Irwin
Third Murderer	J. Winter
Hecate	Shelah Ward
Lady Macduff	Christine Hayden
Boy	Irene Murphy
An English Doctor	W. J. Scott
A Scotch Doctor	John Irwin
Siward	Tom Moran
Young Siward	J. Winter
A Servant	J. Linnane
Ladies in Court: S. O'Toole, D. McDonough, K. O'Brien, E. Thompson	

Produced by Bladon Peake

26th December 1934

First Production by the Abbey Company of
AT MRS. BEAM'S
A Comedy in Three Acts by C. K. Munro

Miss Shoe	Madelene Ross
Mr. Durrows	Fred Johnson
Miss Cheezle	Truda Barling
Mrs. Bebb	Christine Hayden
James Bebb	Brian Carey
Mrs. Stone	Elizabeth Plunkett
Miss Newman	Nora O'Mahony
Mrs. Beam	Madame K. Hackett
Mr. Dermott	Geoffrey Davids
Laura Pasquale	Irene Murphy
Colin Langford	Cyril Cusack

Produced by Bladon Peake

29th April 1935

THE KING OF SPAIN'S DAUGHTER
A Play in One Act by Teresa Deevy

Peter Kinsella	John Stephenson
Jim Harris	Cyril Cusack
Mrs. Marks, a neighbour	Ann Clery
Annie Kinsella, Peter's daughter	Ria Mooney
Roddy Mann, a loafer	J. Winter

Produced by Fred Johnson

12th August 1935

First Production by the Abbey Company of
THE SILVER TASSIE
A Tragi-Comedy in Four Acts
by Sean O'Casey

Sylvester Heegan	Barry Keegan
Mrs. Heegan, his wife	Ann Clery
Simon Norton	Michael J. Dolan
Susie Monican	Eileen Crowe
Mrs. Foran	May Craig
Teddy Foran, her husband	P. J. Carolan
Harry Heegan, D.C.M., Heegan's son	F. J. McCormick
Jessie Taite	Aideen O'Connor
Barney Bagnal	Fred Johnson
Soldiers: Denis O'Dea, J. Winter, Cyril Cusack, J. Hand, P. J. Carolan	
The Corporal	J. Stephenson
The Visitor	Edward Lexy
The Staff Wallah	Tom Purefoy
Stretcher-bearers: W. O'Gorman, M. Finn, M. Clarke, B. Carey	
Casualties	W. Redmond, Edward Lexy
Surgeon Forby Maxwell	Tom Purefoy
The Sister of the Ward	Truda Barling

Produced by Arthur Shields. Settings made in the Theatre from designs by Maurice McGonigal, R.H.A.

16th September 1935

A DEUCE O' JACKS
A Comedy in One Act by F. R. Higgins

Luke Gaffney	Michael J. Dolan
Harefoot Mike	Fred Johnson
Knacker Byrne	P. J. Carolan
The Nobbler	J. Stephenson
Yockle Brough	F. J. McCormick
Golden Maggie	Maureen Delany
A Melodeon Player	M. Schiff
A Tin Whistle Player	J. Davenport
Pharaoh's Daughter	Muriel Kelly

A HISTORY, 1899–1951

Jezebel . . . . . . Chris. Sheehan
Michael Moran . . . . Denis O'Dea
A Priest . . . . William Patterson
Hawkers, Ballad Singers, Corner Boys, etc.: Michael Finn, J. Winter, Michael Clarke, Cyril Cusack, W. O'Gorman, Nora O'Mahony, Ann Clery, Kathleen Murphy

Produced by Michael J. Dolan. Scene and Costumes by Tanya Moiseiwitsch.

30th September 1935

First Production by the Abbey Company of

A VILLAGE WOOING

A Comediettina for Two Voices
by G. Bernard Shaw

A . . . . F. J. McCormick
Z . . . . Ria Mooney
Steward . . . . . Michael J. Dolan

Produced by Hugh Hunt

30th September 1935

First Production by the Abbey Company of

CANDIDA

A Mystery by G. Bernard Shaw

Rev. James Mavor Morell . Arthur Shields
Miss Proserpine Garnett . . May Craig
Rev. Lexy Mill . . . . Denis O'Dea
Mr. Burgess . . . . . P. J. Carolan
Candida . . . . . . Eileen Crowe
Eugene Marchbanks . . . Cyril Cusack

Produced by Hugh Hunt

9th December 1935

SUMMER'S DAY

A Play in Three Acts and an Epilogue
by Maura Molloy

Kate Lambart . . . . . Ria Mooney
Mr. Lambart . . . . John Stephenson
Sarah Curran . . . . . Moya Devlin
Richard Curran . . . . Cyril Cusack
Robert Emmet . . . . Arthur Shields
Amelia Curren . . . . . May Craig

Produced by Hugh Hunt. Settings and costumes by Tanya Moiseiwitsch.

13th January 1936

First Production by the Abbey Company of

CORIOLANUS

By William Shakespeare

First Citizen . . . . . W. O'Gorman
Second Citizen . . . . . W. Redmond
Menenius . . . . . Barry Fitzgerald
Caius Maritus . . . . Reginald Jarman
First Senator of Rome . . Eric Gorman
Cominus . . . . . Arthur Shields
Titus Larius . . . . . Cyril Cusack
Sicinius . . . . . Michael J. Dolan
Brutus . . . . Fred Johnson
Second Senator of Rome . Desmond Crean
Tullus Aufidius . . . John Stephenson
First Volscian Senator . . F. F. Carney
Second Volscian Senator . . J. J. Henry
Volumnia . . . . . . May Carey
Virgilia . . . . . . Shelah Richards
Valeria . . . . . . Aideen O'Connor
First Aedile and Herald . . . J. Winter
Second Aedile and Herald . Maurice Bradley
First Servant to Aufidius . . P. J. Carolan
Second Servant to Aufidius F. J. McCormick
Third Servant to Aufidius Desmond Crean
Lieutenant to Aufidius . Kenneth Barton
Young Marcius . . . . Hazel Ross
Gentlewomen Shelah May, Clodagh Garrett
Citizens, Soldiers, Watchmen, Messengers, etc.: Leo Douris, James Flynn, J. A. MacMahon, P. G. Quinn, Con Sheenan, Declan Murphy, Austin Meldon, Martin Murphy, Cecil Forde, J. J. Henry, K. Barton, J. F. Carney, J. Winter
Citizenesses: N. O'Doherty, J. Fitzgerald M. Mullins

Produced by Hugh Hunt

3rd February 1936

THE GRAND HOUSE IN THE CITY

A Play in Four Acts by Brinsley MacNamara

Henry Bergan . . . . Michael J. Dolan
Massie Ward . . . . Maureen Delany
Diana Gilsenan . . . . . Eileen Crowe
Walter Gilsenan . . . . Cyril Cusack
Olivia Petit . . . . . Christine Hayden
Vincent Kelch . . . . Arthur Shields
Mary Ward . . . . . . May Craig
Brian Merriman . . . . . Fred Johnson
Richard Gilsenan . . . F. J. McCormick
Owen Lynam . . . . . P. J. Carolan
Delia Lynam . . . . Aideen O'Connor

Produced by Hugh Hunt. Settings and Ladies' Costumes by Tanya Moiseiwitsch.

24th February 1936

BOYD'S SHOP

A Comedy in Four Acts by St. John Ervine

Andy	Cyril Cusack
Andrew Boyd	P. J. Carolan
Agnes Boyd	Frolie Mulhern
Miss McClurg	Eileen Crowe
John Haslett	Arthur Shields
Mrs. McBratney	Maureen Delany
Miss Clotworthy	May Craig
Miss Logan	Ria Mooney
Rev. Ernest Dunwoody	F. J. McCormick
William Henry Doak	Barry Fitzgerald
Carrie	Ann Clery
Rev. Arthur Patterson	Michael J. Dolan

Produced by Hugh Hunt. Settings by Tanya Moiseiwitsch.

16th March 1936

KATIE ROCHE

A Play in Three Acts by Teresa Deevy

Stanislaus Gregg	F. J. McCormick
Katie Roche	Eileen Crowe
Amelia Gregg	Ria Mooney
Reuben	Michael J. Dolan
Michael McGuire	Arthur Shields
Jo Mahony	Cyril Cusack
Margaret Drybone	May Craig
Frank Lawlor	Barry Fitzgerald

Produced by Hugh Hunt. Settings by Tanya Moiseiwitsch.

13th April 1936

THE PASSING DAY

A Play in Six Scenes by George Shiels

The Doctor	F. J. McCormick
The Nurse	Eileen Crowe
Mrs. Fibbs	May Craig
Peter Fibbs	Denis O'Dea
Daw	Arthur Shields
John Fibbs	Michael J. Dolan
Black	P. J. Carolan
Samson	Eric Gorman
Looney	Barry Fitzgerald
Hind	Cyril Cusack
Old Man	Eric Gorman
Boy	W. Redmond
Old Woman	Maureen Delany

Produced by Hugh Hunt. Settings by Tanya Moiseiwitsch.

1st June 1936

First Production by the Abbey Company of

HASSAN

A Play in Five Acts by James Elroy Flecker

Hassan	Michael J. Dolan
Selim	Fred Johnson
Yasmin	Ria Mooney
Porter of Yasmin's House	Frank Carney
Haroun al Raschid	F. J. McCormick
Ishak	Arthur Shields
Jafar	John Stephenson
Marrur	P. J. Carolan
Rafi	Denis O'Dea
Alder	Aideen O'Connor
Willow	Mary O'Neill
Juniper	Phyllis Ryan
Tamarisk	Nora O'Mahony
Leader of the Beggars	W. O'Gorman
Ali	Eric Gorman
Abdu	Barry Fitzgerald
The Chief of the Police	Desmond Crean
The Captain of the Military	J. Winter
Herald	Cecil Ford
The Chinese Philosopher	Frank Carney
A Wandering Dervish	Fred Johnson
The Court Tailor	Cecil Brock
Pervaneh	Eileen Crowe

Guards, Beggars, Merchants: Messrs. Quinn, Murphy, Ford, Winter, Crean, Stephenson, Carney, Johnson, Brock

Dancing Women: C. Garret, M. Kelly, B. Boyd, I. Bushnell, Devitt.

Singers: Messrs. Murphy, O'Loughlin, Broadbent, O'Dwyer

Produced by Hugh Hunt

14th September 1936

THE SILVER JUBILEE

A Play in Three Acts by Cormac O'Daly

Rev. Michael O'Carroll, P.P.	Michael J. Dolan
Hannah	Ann Clery
Rev. William O'Dowd, P.P.	Fred Johnson
Julia Casey	May Craig
Mary Casey	Aideen O'Connor
John Joseph Barrett	Cyril Cusack
John Casey	P. J. Carolan

Produced by Hugh Hunt. Settings by Tanya Moiseiwitsch.

A HISTORY, 1899–1951

12th October 1936
THE JAILBIRD
A Comedy in Three Acts by George Shiels

Dan Farn, the jailbird	F. J. McCormick
Mary Anne, a country dressmaker	Eileen Crowe
Martha, her daughter	Shelah Richards
Lily, an apprentice	Frolie Mulhern
James Kelsey, a farmer	Michael J. Dolan
Mrs. Kelsey, his wife	May Craig
Mrs. Chesney, an American	P. J. Carolan
Charlie, a quarry-man	Arthur Shields
Mr. Bunton, a solicitor	Fred Johnson
Miss Jean	Maureen Delany
A Police Sergeant	W. O'Gorman

Produced by Hugh Hunt. Settings by Tanya Moiseiwitsch.

9th November 1936
THE WILD GOOSE
A Play in Three Acts by Teresa Deevy

Martin Shea	Fred Johnson
Mary Kavanagh	Christine Hayden
Eileen Connolly	Ria Mooney
Father Ryan	Frank Carney
Stephen Power	Eric Gorman
Hannah Power	Ann Clery
Captain de Lacey	J. Winter
Tim O'Dowd	W. O'Gorman
Soldiers: P. H. Considine, M. Keegan	

Produced by Hugh Hunt. Settings and costumes by Tanya Moiseiwitsch.

30th November 1936
WIND FROM THE WEST
A Comedy in Three Acts by Maeve O'Callaghan

Stephen Joyce	Arthur Shields
Josie Joyce	Shelah Richards
Mrs. Kelleher	Christine Hayden
David Kelleher	W. O'Gorman
Kate Kiernan	Ria Mooney
Dr. Tom Dillon	Eric Gorman
Nellie	Ann Clery
Rebecca	Frolie Mulhern
Carpet-layer	A. Meldon
Policeman	J. Winter

Produced by Hugh Hunt. Settings by Tanya Moiseiwitsch.

26th December 1936
BLIND MAN'S BUFF
A Play in Three Acts by Ernst Toller and Denis Johnston

Laura	Patsy Fitzpatrick
Mary Quirke	May Craig
Dominick Mapother	F. J. McCormick
Dr. Chavasse	Arthur Shields
Dr. Anice Hollingshead	Eileen Crowe
Sergeant Carey	P. J. Carolan
John Roche, Chavasse's Solicitor	Eric Gorman
Theobald Thin, Council for the Defence	Michael J. Dolan
Liam Poer, State Solicitor	Fred Johnson
Henry Jarrican, Crown Prosecutor	J. Muldoon
Mr. Justice Drooley	T. Purefoy
Court Registrar	Frank Carney
Seamus Ua Caoilte, Assistant State Pathologist	Denis O'Dea
Juryman	Brian Carey
Solicitors, Barristers, Clerks, Civic Guards: Messrs. Carney, Considine, Hickey, Boyd, Finn, Barror, Carey	

Produced by Hugh Hunt. Settings by Tanya Moiseiwitsch.

25th January 1937
SHADOW AND SUBSTANCE
A Play in Four Acts by Paul Vincent Carroll

Very Rev. Thomas Canon Skerritt, P.P.	Arthur Shields
Brigid, his servant	Phyllis Ryan
Father Corr, C.C.	Fred Johnson
Father Kirwan, C.C.	Austin Meldon
Dermot Francis O'Flingsley, the local schoolmaster	Cyril Cusack
Thomasina Concannon, the Canon's niece	Aideen O'Connor
Miss Jemima Cooney	Ria Mooney
Francis Ignatius O'Connor	W. O'Gorman
Martin Mullahone	P. J. Carolan
Rosey Violet	Maureen Delany

Produced by Hugh Hunt. Settings by Tanya Moiseiwitsch.

8th February 1937
THE END OF THE BEGINNING
A Comedy in One Act by Sean O'Casey

Darry Berrill	P. J. Carolan
Lizzie Berrill	Maureen Delany
Barry Derrill	F. J. McCormick

Produced by Arthur Shields

29th March 1937
QUIN'S SECRET
A Comedy in Three Acts by George Shiels

Quin	Cyril Cusack
Miss Norris	Maureen Delany
Crilly	Michael J. Dolan
Nellie	Madge Heron
Mrs. Henry	Shelah Ward
Briggs	Arthur Shields
Mrs. Dolman	Ann Clery
Cassie	Sheila Timmon
Bob Reid	Fred Johnson

Produced by Hugh Hunt. Settings by Tanya Moiseiwitsch.

19th April 1937
KILLYCREGGS IN TWILIGHT
A Play in Three Acts by Lennox Robinson

Judith De Lury	Christine Hayden
Margaret	May Craig
Sylvester Brannigan	Eric Gorman
Kit De Lury	Ria Mooney
Loftus De Lury	Cyril Cusack
Mrs. Pratt	Josephine Fitzgerald
Francis Morgan	W. O'Gorman
Dr. Pratt	Arthur Shields
Janey Fitzpatrick	Shelah Richards
Moya Fitzpatrick	Aideen O'Connor
Sir James Cotter	F. J. McCormick

Produced by Hugh Hunt. Settings by Tanya Moiseiwitsch.

17th May 1937
WHO WILL REMEMBER...?
A Melodrama in Three Acts by Maura Molloy

Charles Pommery	F. J. McCormick
Cressida Pommery, his daughter	Ria Mooney
Hugh Pommery, his grandson	Hugh Hunt
Neil Murray, the Pommery lawyer	Arthur Shields
Ned Armstrong	Denis O'Dea
Dr. John Halpin	Fred Johnson
Mary Halpin, his daughter	Shelah Richards
Andro Vanzetti, an Italian sculptor	Malachi Keegan
Pat Scanlon, a servant of the Pommerys	P. J. Carolan
Nell Scanlon, his niece	Eileen Crowe

Produced and lighting devised by Hugh Hunt. Scenery and costumes by Tanya Moiseiwitsch.

31st May 1937
IN THE TRAIN
A Play in One Act from the short story by Frank O'Connor dramatised by Hugh Hunt

Sergeant	P. J. Carolan
His wife	Eileen Crowe
Drunken Traveller	F. J. McCormick
Magner	Fred Johnson
Foley	Arthur Shields
Delancey	Denis O'Dea
Kendillon	Michael J. Dolan
Moll More	Maureen Delany
Two Countrywomen:	Shelah Ward, Josephine Fitzgerald
The Woman	Ann Clery
The Chorus:	Moya Devlin, Mary O'Neill, Maureen Jordan, Malachi Keegan, C. Barror, Frank Carney.

Produced by Hugh Hunt. Setting by Tanya Moiseiwitsch.

5th August 1937
THE PATRIOT
A Comedy in Three Acts by Maeve O'Callaghan

Dr. Cusack	Fred Johnson
Laelia Cusack	Ann Clery
Mrs. Cusack	Ann Penhallow
Lottie	Shelah Ward
Esther Cusack	Shelah Richards
Ian Cusack	Brian Carey
Dan Cusack	Cyril Cusack
Geraldine Tarquin	Nora O'Mahony
Clive Waingate	Frank Carney
Peggy Cusack	Moya Devlin
Professor Tarquin	Eric Gorman
Floor Polisher	D. Kelly
Butcher's Boy	M. Kinsella

Produced by Hugh Hunt. Settings by Tanya Moiseiwitsch.

27th September 1937
THE MAN IN THE CLOAK
A Play in Three Acts by Louis D'Alton

John Mangan	Malachi Keegan
Mick Fogarty	Eric Gorman
Bridie Gilheany	Josephine Fitzgerald
Marty Phelan	W. O'Gorman
Con Colgan	Seumas Healy
Cis Carmody	Shelah Ward
Clarence Mangan	Cyril Cusack
James Mangan	Fred Johnson
Mrs. Mangan	Ann Clery
Catherine Hayes	Shelah Richards

Blythe . . . . J. Winter
Laurence Tighe . . . . T. Purefoy
A Doctor . . . . . . C. Barror
A Messenger . . . . P. J. Considine
Produced by Hugh Hunt. Settings by Tanya Moiseiwitsch.

18th October 1937
THE INVINCIBLES
A Play in Seven Scenes
by Hugh Hunt and Frank O'Connor

First Fenian . . . . Dermot Kelly
Second Fenian . . . . . Michael Finn
Publican . . . . . . Victor Boyd
James Carey . . . . . Fred Johnson
Timothy Kelly . . . . . Cyril Cusack
P. J. Tynan (Number One) . Frank Carney
Joe Brady . . . . . . W. O'Gorman
Daniel Curley . . . . . Eric Gorman
Ned McCaffrey . . . Laurence Elyan
Maggie Fitzsimmons . . . Shelah Ward
Caretaker . . . . . . Seumas Healy
Mr. O'Leary . . . . . W. Redmond
The Publican, at Chapelizod . Brian Carey
The Angler . . . . . P. H. Considine
Michael Kavanagh . . . M. Kinsella
Dan Delaney . . . . . J. MacDarby
The Man with the Proclama-
  tions . . . . M. Kinsella
Mrs. Brady . . . . Christine Hayden
Inspector Mallon . . . . . C. Barror
The Warder . . . Malachi Keegan
The Governor of the
  Prison . . . Gearoid O hIcheadha
The Sister of Mercy . . . Ann Clery
Fenians, Citizens, etc.: Messrs. Boyd, Barror, Finn, Kelly, MacDarby, Kinsella, Keegan, O hIcheadha

Produced by Hugh Hunt. Settings by Tanya Moiseiwitsch.

22nd November 1937
COGGERERS
A Play in One Act by Paul Vincent Carroll

Eamonn O'Curry . . . Eric Gorman
Mrs. Galgoogley . . Josephine Fitzgerald
Owen, her son . . . . W. T. O'Connor
Parnell . . . . Fred Johnson
Wolfe Tone . . . . . Frank Carney
Robert Emmet . . . . W. Redmond
John Mitchel . . . . W. O'Gorman
Lord Edward Fitzgerald . P. H. Considine

Produced by Hugh Hunt. Setting by Tanya Moiseiwitsch.

27th December 1937
SHE HAD TO DO SOMETHING
A Comedy in Three Acts by Sean O'Faolain

Maxine Arnold . . . . Evelyn Bowen
Patrick Arnold, her husband . Frank Carney
Julie Arnold, her daughter . Shelah Richards
Canon Kane . . . . Liam Redmond
Neddy, his nephew . . . Cyril Cusack
Moran, a Poet . . . . Victor Boyd
Peter Petroff, a dancer . . Fred Johnson
Natasha, a dancer . . . Sara Payne
Mary, the maid . . . . . Ann Clery
Father Basil . . . . . Cecil Barror
Trench Coat . . . . Malachi Keegan
Bowler Hat . . . . D. Kelly
Dr. Beasley . . . . P. H. Considine

Produced by Hugh Hunt

17th January 1938
NEAL MAQUADE
A Play in Seven Scenes by George Shiels

Neal Maquade, a country
  innkeeper . . . . Liam Redmond
Hannah Maquade, his daughter . Ann Clery
John Lilly, a farmer . . . Fred Johnson
Adam Lilly, his son . . . Cyril Cusack
Samuel Lilly, Adam's half-
  brother . . . . . . Fred Johnson
Fanny, Lilly's servant girl . Shelah Richards
Master Magee, a retired
  schoolmaster . . . . Laurence Elyan
Specky Boyce, a pedlar . . Eric Gorman
Samuel Boyce, his brother Malachi Keegan
Mulgrew, a policeman . . . J. Winter

Produced by Hugh Hunt. Settings by Tanya Moiseiwitsch.

14th February 1938
A SPOT IN THE SUN
A Play in One Act by T. C. Murray

Denis Harman . . . . Cyril Cusack
Rose Harman . . . . Shelah Richards
Mrs. Harman . . . . Christine Hayden
Annie . . . . Ann Clery
First Man . . . . . . Fred Johnson
Second Man . . . . Malachi Keegan

Produced by Hugh Hunt. Setting by Tanya Moiseiwitsch.

28th February 1938
MOSES' ROCK
A Play in Three Acts
by Hugh Hunt and Frank O'Connor

Cady O'Leary, a merchant	W. O'Gorman
Kate O'Leary, his sister	Ann Clery
Joan O'Leary, his daughter	Shelah Richards
Shuvaun O'Leary, his mother	Shelah Ward
Ned Hegarty, a poet	Cyril Cusack
Jer Coghlan, a lawyer	Fred Johnson
Lieutenant Grant Fortescue	P. H. Considine
Dr. Corney Jackson	Liam Redmond
Biddy Lally	Christine Hayden
Sorry O'Sullivan	Evelyn MacNeice
Nelly, a maid	Gertrude Quinn

Produced by Hugh Hunt. Settings by Tanya Moiseiwitsch.

4th April 1938
THE DEAR QUEEN
A Play in One Act by Andrew Ganly

Sarah	Gertrude Quinn
Rev. Mr. Munn	Liam Redmond
Miss Sophie	Christine Hayden
Miss Lottie	Shelah Richards
Miss Nellie	Ann Clery

Produced by Hugh Hunt. Setting and costumes by Tanya Moiseiwitsch.

10th August 1938
PURGATORY
A Play in One Act by W. B. Yeats

Boy	Liam Redmond
Old Man	Michael J. Dolan

Produced by Hugh Hunt. Setting by Anne Yeats.

12th September 1938
BIRD'S NEST
A Play in Three Acts by Lennox Robinson

Joseph Fehily	F. J. McCormick
His children:	
Josie	Shelah Richards
Philip	Austin Meldon
Bob	Patrick Carey
Hyacinth	Cyril Cusack
Dollie Schofield, his sister-in-law	Ria Mooney
Con Schofield, his brother-in-law	Fred Johnson
Matt Fox	Denis O'Dea
Stanislaus O'Grady	Arthur Shields
Mickey Roche	M. Kinsella
Charlie Daly	Malachi Keegan

Produced by Hugh Hunt. Settings by Tanya Moiseiwitsch.

19th September 1938
THE GREAT ADVENTURE
A Comedy in One Act by Charles I. Foley

George Benson	Cyril Cusack
Madge Benson	Ann Clery
Tommy Ryan	Michael J. Dolan

Produced by Hugh Hunt. Setting by Tanya Moiseiwitsch.

10th October 1938
PILGRIMS
A Play in Three Acts by Mary Rynne

Nano Vaughan	Phyllis Ryan
Captain Fletcher	Michael J. Dolan
Mrs. Martin	Maureen Delany
Peter McCarthy	Austin Meldon
Desmond Morris	Cyril Cusack
Dr. George Kenny	Denis O'Dea
Kitty Brady	Frolie Mulhern
Madge McCarthy	Ann Clery
Gus Kelly	M. Kinsella
Marco	Wilfrid Brambell
Miss Cox	Ria Mooney

Produced by Hugh Hunt. Settings by Tanya Moiseiwitsch.

26th December 1938
TIME'S POCKET
A Play in Five Acts by Frank O'Connor

Abby Driscoll	Eileen Crowe
Nance	Ria Mooney
Patrick	Denis O'Dea
Denis	Austin Meldon
Martin Conlan	F. J. McCormick
Sergeant Daly	Fred Johnson
Corporal Dargan	W. O'Gorman
Red Fahy	Victor Boyd
Ned Sullivan	J. Winter
Father Costello	Michael J. Dolan
The General	Eric Gorman
The General's Wife	Shelah Ward
Mylie Dargan	Brian McAuliffe

A HISTORY, 1899–1951 167

Sergeant of Police . . . Malachi Keegan
Policemen . Michael Finn, Paud Holahan
Soldiers: Thomas O'Gorman, Gearoid O hIcheadha
Orderly . . . . . Wilfrid Brambell
Produced by Prionnsias Mac Diarmada. Settings by Tanya Moiseiwitsch.

6th February 1939
CAESAR'S IMAGE
A Tragedy in Four Acts by E. F. Carey

Maria Brady . . . . . Eileen Crowe
Dan Brady, her husband . . Fred Johnson
Katie Brady, her daughter. . Phyllis Ryan
Patsy Brady, her son . . . W. O'Gorman
"Sloper" Neale, her brother . . . . Michael J. Dolan
Neighbours:
Mrs. Hogan . . . Maureen Delany
Mrs. Behan . . . . . . May Craig
The Widow Whooley . . Christine Hayden
Chrissie Whooley, her daughter . . . . . . Ria Mooney
Coal Collectors:
Martin Powell . . . . Denis O'Dea
Young Man . . . . . Victor Boyd
Detective . . . . Malachi Keegan
Policeman . . . . Gerard Kiernan

Produced by Louis D'Alton. Settings by Anne Yeats.

13th March 1939
TO-MORROW NEVER COMES
A Play in Three Acts by Louis D'Alton

Lar Broderick . . . . . Louis D'Alton
Mary Broderick . . . . Ria Mooney
Ned Claffey . . . . . . Cyril Cusack
Mick Hennessy . . . . Denis O'Dea
Cornelius D'Arcy . . . . W. O'Gorman
Guard Bannon . . . . Seumas Healy
Sergeant Harrigan . . . Austin Meldon
James McEvelly . . . Michael J. Dolan
Mrs. Counihan . . . . . . May Craig
Neighbours

Produced by the Author. Settings by Anne Yeats.

8th April 1939
THE HERITAGE
A Comedy in Four Acts by J. K. Montgomery

Nathaniel Norton . . . Michael J. Dolan
Joshua Norton . . . . F. J. McCormick
Tom Norton . . . . . Denis O'Dea
Mrs. Norton . . . . Maureen Delany
Nancy Petticrew . . . . Eileen Crowe
James Petticrew . . . . Cyril Cusack
Ellen Soutar . . . . . . Ria Mooney
Adam Meek . . . . . W. O'Gorman
Janet Duff . . . . . Frolie Mulhern

Produced by Louis D'Alton. Settings by Anne Yeats.

31st July 1939
ILLUMINATION
A Play in Two Acts by T. C. Murray

Charles Egan, a solicitor . F. J. McCormick
Helen, his wife . . . . . Eileen Crowe
Brian, his son . . . . Joseph Linnane
Dr. Richard Moore . . Michael J. Dolan
Christina, his daughter . . Phyllis Ryan
Hugh Dwyer, a civil servant . . . . Liam Redmond
Paddy Doran, a young farmer . . . . . . W. O'Gorman
Lizzie, the Egans' maid . Maureen Delany

Produced by Lennox Robinson. Settings by Anne Yeats.

28th August 1939
FOHNAM, THE SCULPTOR
A Play in a Prelude and Three Acts by Daniel Corkery

Tethra, the King . . . F. J. McCormick
Alova, the Queen . . . Eileen Crowe
Fohnam, a sculptor . . . Fred Johnson
Fanla, a councillor . . . Michael J. Dolan
Keltar, a chronicler . . . Victor Boyd
Cormac, a herald . . . . Gerard Healy
Cunnud, Fohnam's gilly . . W. O'Gorman
Three singing maidens:
Eeving . . . . . . Phyllis Ryan
Findmor . . . . Eithne Dunne
Dectora . . . . . Cathleen Fawsitt
Ivor . . . . Austin Meldon
Delbay . . . . . . Robert Mooney
First Sailor . . . . . . Sean Colleary
Second Sailor . . . John MacDarby
First Guard . . . . . Val. Iremonger
Second Guard . . . . Michael Clarke
Lewy . . . . Frank Biggar
First Woman . . . . Patricia Clancy
Second Woman . . . . Brid Lynch
Soldiers, Servants, Attendants, etc.

Produced by Prionnsias Mac Diarmada. Settings by Anne Yeats.

25th September 1939

KINDRED

A Play in Six Scenes by Paul Vincent Carroll

Part I (Scenes 1 and 2)

Mary Griffin	Eileen Crowe
Dermot O'Regan	W. O'Gorman
Primrose Carr	Gertrude Quinn
Figure I	Gerard Healy
Figure II	J. Winter

Part II (Scenes 3, 4, 5 and 6)

Mary Fennet	Eileen Crowe
Robert Fennet, her husband	Michael J. Dolan
Michael Fennet, their son	Denis O'Dea
J. K. Keefe	F. J. McCormick
Agnes Keefe, his daughter	Shelah Richards
Dermot O'Regan	W. O'Gorman
Alice	Brid Ni Loinsigh
Sergeant Hannigan	Fred Johnson
Figure I	Gerard Healy
Figure II	J. Winter
Figure III	John MacDarby

Produced by Prionnsias Mac Diarmada. Settings designed by Austin Meldon and painted by Anne Yeats.

30th October 1939

GIVE HIM A HOUSE

A Comedy in Three Acts by George Shiels

Pat Hooey, a local revolutionary	Cyril Cusack
Dorothy, his wife	Ria Mooney
Josephine, their daughter	Brid Ni Loinsigh
Mrs. Hooey, the grandmother	Shelah Ward
Kate, her daughter	Gertrude Quinn
Gerty, Kate's student daughter	Cathleen Fawsitt
Father Hope, P.P.	Eric Gorman
Mr. Kandy, a solicitor	P. H. Considine
Joseph McGrady, an Urban Councillor	J. Winter
Sam Wilson, a labourer	Seumas Healy
Archy, a farm hand	W. O'Gorman
Danny, a lorry driver	Joseph Linnane
Henry McManus, Mrs. Hooey's brother	Frank Biggar

Produced by Prionnsias Mac Diarmada. Settings designed by Gearoid O hIcheadha and painted by Anne Yeats.

4th December 1939

THEY WENT BY THE BUS

A Play in Three Acts by Frank Carney

Jimmy Macken, hotel porter	Eric Gorman
Mr. Prescott, commercial traveller	Austin Meldon
Hannah, the hotel housekeeper	Shelah Ward
Joe Kerrigan, shop assistant	J. Linnane
John Joe Martin, rate collector	Cyril Cusack
Badger Finnigan	Gertrude Quinn
Michael Harkin	C. Barror
Sarah Harkin	Edith Lemass
Tady Finnigan	Finbar Howard
Sailor	W. O'Gorman
Joan Carroll	Cathleen Fawsitt
Thomas Carroll	J. Winter
First Man	Frank Biggar
Mrs. Sharkey	Isobel Couser
Mrs. Moloney	Maura Carroll
Second Man	Martin Conboy
Bus Driver	Wilfrid Brambell
Bus Conductor	Seumas Healy

Produced by Lennox Robinson. Scenes by Seaghan Barlow and painted by Anne Yeats.

29th January 1940

THE SPANISH SOLDIER

A Play in Three Acts by Louis D'Alton

Mrs. McMorna	Eileen Crowe
Moses Furlong, her brother	F. J. McCormick
Her sons:	
Hugh McMorna	Denis O'Dea
Kevin McMorna	Cyril Cusack
Hessy McMorna, Kevin's wife	Ria Mooney
Nanno Deasy	Phyllis Ryan
Davey Deasy, her father	Fred Johnson
Father Conn	Michael J. Dolan

Produced by Lennox Robinson

23rd March 1940

WILLIAM JOHN MAWHINNEY
Being the Story of his Bi-centenary
A Comedy in Six Scenes by St. John Ervine

John McMichael	F. J. McCormick
Sarah McMichael, his sister	May Craig
Willie Semple	Cyril Cusack
Councillor Andrew Kernaghan, Chairman of the Ballyfarland U.D.C.	W. O'Gorman
Councillor Alexander Pottinger, Vice-Chairman, Ballyfarland U.D.C.	Cecil Ford
George Larmour, Clerk to the Council	Denis O'Dea
Red Dan	John MacDarby
A Sergeant of the R.U.C.	Fred Johnson
William Gracey, M.D.	Michael J. Dolan
Mrs. Logan	Ria Mooney
Mrs. Cairnduff	Eileen Crowe
Arthur McKinstry	Finbar Howard
Councillor Joseph McGlade	Seumas Healy
Councillor Henry Harpur	Austin Meldon
Joe Stitt	Michael Kinsella
A Reporter	U. Wright
A Press Photographer	Joseph Linnane
A Telegraph Boy	Edward Stewart
A Radio Announcer	Cecil Ford

Gunmen, Policemen, Press-men, etc.

Produced by Lennox Robinson. Settings by Anne Yeats.

22nd April 1940

MOUNT PROSPECT
A Tragedy in Three Acts by Elizabeth Connor

Mrs. Kennefick	Ria Mooney
Rex, her son	Charles Blair
Her stepchildren:	
Peter	Denis O'Dea
Mary	Brid Ni Loinsigh
Mr. Horsham, a solicitor	Michael J. Dolan
Ned Cronin	F. J. McCormick
Kit, his wife, and sister of Mrs. Kennefick	Eileen Crowe
Mrs. Clancy	Christine Hayden
Miss Chapp	Gertrude Quinn
Winnie Sullivan	Kitty Thuillier
Mrs. Sullivan, her mother	May Craig
Annie, a maid	Maura Lane

Produced by Frank Dermody. Settings by Anne Yeats.

13th May 1940

BIRTH OF A GIANT
A Play in Three Acts by Nora MacAdam

Robert Watson	W. O'Gorman
Lily Watson, his daughter	Eileen Crowe
Ruth Watson, a younger daughter	Sheila Manahan
James Cathcart, a ship's carpenter	Austin Meldon
Harry Moody, an engine man	J. Prendergast
Mrs. Larkin	May Craig
Pat Larkin, her son, employed at the "yard"	J. MacDarby
Susan Larkin, her daughter	Kitty Thuillier
Tommy Mallin, out of work	C. Fitzsimons
John Myers, a young Englishman lodging in Watson's	Denis O'Dea

Produced by Michael J. Dolan. Settings by Anne Yeats.

15th July 1940

TO-DAY AND YESTERDAY
A Comedy in Three Acts by W. D. Hepenstall

Mrs. Loftus	Eileen Crowe
Major Patrick Loftus, her son	Denis O'Dea
Ellen, their parlourmaid	Kathleen Murphy
Major Loftus's daughters:	
Geraldine Loftus	Sheila Manahan
Margaret Loftus (Peggy)	Ginnette Waddell
Tony Fleming	Cecil Ford
Sylvester Spillane	W. O'Gorman
Desmond Carmody	James Dunne
Mrs. O'Callaghan	Ria Mooney
John Carmody	Michael J. Dolan
Virginia Carmody	Joan Plunkett
Sir Hiram De Frayne	F. J. McCormick
Mr. O'Callaghan	P. H. Considine

Produced by Prionnsias Mac Diarmada. Settings by Anne Yeats.

5th August 1940
THE RUGGED PATH
A Play in Three Acts by George Shiels

Michael Tansey, a farmer .	John MacDarby
Mrs. Tansey, his wife	May Craig
Sean Tansey, their son . .	Denis O'Dea
Sara Tansey, their daughter .	Ria Mooney
Mr. Adare, a schoolmaster	Michael J. Dolan
Miss Benny, a teacher . .	Brid Ni Loinsigh
Hugh Dolis, a mountaineer .	Seumas Healy
Peter Dolis, a son	James Dunne
Mrs. Dolis, wife of Hugh Dolis	Kathleen Murphy
Maggie, a neighbour . . .	Eileen Crowe
John Perrie, an old-age pensioner	Harry Brogan
Marcy, a travelling man .	F. J. McCormick
Sergeant, Civic Guard . .	Austin Meldon
Radio Announcer	Cecil Ford

Produced by Michael J. Dolan. Settings by Anne Yeats.

4th November 1940
THREE TO GO
A Play in Three Acts by Olga Fielden

Lady Helen O'Flanagan .	Ginnette Waddell
Maeve McFerran, her niece .	Ria Mooney
Hannah, her parlourmaid . .	Shelah Ward
Mrs. O'Grady, her cook .	Maureen Delany
Mr. Justice Barlow .	Rutherford Mayne
Captain Felix O'Hare . .	Edward Byrne
Hiram P. Smith . . .	Brian O'Higgins
Phyllis Smith	Bonnie Fagan
Patrick K. Dempsey . . .	J. Winter
Hugh O'Neill	W. O'Gorman
Captain Oxenham . . .	Dan O'Herlihy
District Inspector, R.U.C. .	Terry Wilson

Produced by Frank Dermody. Settings by Anne Yeats.

25th November 1940
PEEPING TOM
A Play in Three Acts by Frank Carney

Margaret Fitzgerald	May Craig
Jennifer Fitzgerald . . .	Brid Ni Loinsigh
Finula Fitzgerald	Eileen Crowe
Wilfred Burke	Michael J. Dolan
Dr. John Victor Burke . .	Eric Gorman
Rita Burke	Ria Mooney
Peter Burke	Dan O'Connell

Michael Noonan	James Dunne
Nana	Maureen Delany
Lucy Gallagher . . .	Joan Plunkett
George Mulligan . . .	F. J. McCormick

Produced by Frank Dermody. Settings by Anne Yeats.

9th December 1940
STRANGE GUEST
A Play in Three Acts by Francis Stuart

Illyria Charters	Eileen Crowe
Betty Charters	Eithne Dunne
Max Charters	Austin Meldon
Mary, a maid	Kitty Thuillier
Mairead Deruiloba	Ria Mooney
Osmond Grink	Joseph Linnane
Dr. Leonard Bond	Gerard Healy
Sir John Muller . . .	F. J. McCormick

Produced by Frank Dermody. Settings by Anne Yeats.

6th January 1941
TRIAL AT GREEN STREET COURTHOUSE
A Play in Ten Scenes by Roger McHugh

Ryan, a reporter . . .	Joseph Linnane
Jerry, the barman . . .	Finbar Howard
Old Man	John MacDarby
Counsel for the defence:	
Isaac Butt	F. J. McCormick
Frederick Falkiner . .	W. O'Gorman
Counsel for the Crown:	
Solicitor-General Dowse	Austin Meldon
Serjeant Armstrong .	Michael J. Dolan
Chief Justice Whiteside . .	Tom Purefoy
Chief Baron Pigott . . .	James Dunne
Doctor Stokes	Michael Walsh
Doctor Tufnell	Harry Brogan
Doctor McDonnell . . .	Eric Gorman
Edmund Vesey, a medical student	Denis O'Dea
Constable Mullen . . .	Seumas Healy
Constable Holland	J. Winter
Henry Talbot	U. Wright
Doctor O'Leary . . .	Edward Byrne
Rose O'Leary, his wife . .	Ria Mooney
Clerk of the Court . . .	Malachy Dooney

Produced by Frank Dermody. Settings by Michael Walsh.

A HISTORY, 1899–1951   171

10th February 1941
THE SUMMIT
A sequel to "The Rugged Path" in Three Acts by George Shiels

Michael Tansey, a farmer	John MacDarby
Mrs. Tansey, his wife	May Craig
Sean Tansey, their son . .	Denis O'Dea
Sara Tansey, their daughter	Brid Ni Loinsigh
Mr. Adare, a schoolmaster	Michael J. Dolan
Miss Benny, a teacher . .	Ria Mooney
Hugh Dolis, a mountaineer .	W. O'Gorman
Mrs. Dolis, his wife .	Kathleen Murphy
Peter Dolis, their son . . .	James Dunne
Maggie, a neighbour . . .	Eileen Crowe
Liam Cassidy, a farmer . .	Fred Johnson
Marcy, a travelling man .	F. J. McCormick
Sergeant, Civic Guard . .	Austin Meldon

Produced by Frank Dermody

10th March 1941
THE MONEY DOESN'T MATTER
A Play in Three Acts by Louis D'Alton

Tom Mannion	W. O'Gorman
His children:	
Harvey Mannion . .	Brian O'Higgins
Norah Mannion . . .	Brid Ni Loinsigh
Philip Mannion	Denis O'Dea
Veronica Hogan . .	Ria Mooney
Mick Kenirons . .	F. J. McCormick
Father Maher	Liam Redmond
Michael Harney . . .	Joseph Linnane
Mrs. Kinchella	Eileen Crowe
Robert Murtagh . . .	Michael J. Dolan
Maid	Cathleen Fawsitt

Produced by Frank Dermody. Settings by Michael Walsh and Anne Yeats.

19th May 1941
THE LADY IN THE TWILIGHT
A Play in Three Acts by Mervyn Wall

Billiard Corry	Fred Johnson
Malachy Ross	Harry Brogan
Kathlyn Ross	Ria Mooney
Verna Ross	Joan Plunkett
Patrick Egan	Denis O'Dea
Philip Vane	Michael J. Dolan
Father Gabriel Shannon, P.P.	F. J. McCormick
Edward Allen	Liam Redmond
Raymond Allen, his son . .	Gerard Healy

Produced by Frank Dermody. Settings by Seaghan Barlow.

30th June 1941
FRIENDS AND RELATIONS
A Comedy in Three Acts by St. John Ervine

Kate	May Craig
Fanny Cairns	Ria Mooney
Doreen Cairns	Brid Ni Loinsigh
Arthur Cairns	Gerard Healy
Adam Bothwell	Denis O'Dea
Jenny Conn	Eithne Dunne
Edward Scantlebury . .	F. J. McCormick
James Finlay	Michael J. Dolan
Mrs. Corken	Eileen Crowe
Gourlay	Fred Johnson

Produced by Frank Dermody. Settings by Michael Walsh.

18th August 1941
REMEMBERED FOR EVER
A Tragi-Comedy in Three Acts by Bernard McGinn

Roderick Brosnan, otherwise Mr. Kelly	Denis O'Dea
Nora	Eithne Dunne
Michael Murphy	W. O'Gorman
Christopher O'Connell .	Austin Meldon
Brian	Liam Redmond
Cassidy	Dermot Kelly
O'Keefe	Michael J. Dolan
Guard Hennessy . . .	Fred Johnson
Miss Sullivan	Eileen Crowe
A Figure	Gerard Healy

Produced by Frank Dermody. Settings by Michael Walsh.

1st September 1941
THE FIRE BURNS LATE
A Comedy in Three Acts by P. J. Fitzgibbon

Betty Flatley	Brid Ni Loinsigh
Denis Flatley	Denis O'Dea
Miss Brady	May Craig
Joan Flatley	Joan Plunkett
Mrs. Flatley	Ria Mooney
James Keely	Michael J. Dolan
Mr. O'Leary	Fred Johnson
Aunt Agatha	Eileen Crowe
Donald O'Leary	Gerard Healy
Mickey	Luke McLoughlin
Mr. O'Gorman . . .	F. J. McCormick

Produced by Frank Dermody. Settings by Seaghan Barlow.

22nd September 1941
SWANS AND GEESE
A Comedy in Three Acts by Elizabeth Connor

P. J. Wynn	F. J. McCormick
Lena Cantwell, his daughter	Ria Mooney
Robert Cantwell, her husband	Michael J. Dolan
Their children:	
John Cantwell	Denis O'Dea
Lucille Cantwell	Joan Plunkett
Tommy O'Connor, a journalist	Joseph Linnane
Tim Hannigan	W. O'Gorman
Mary, his daughter	Eithne Dunne
Simon Cusack	Gerard Healy
Beatrice Capelli	Eileen Crowe
Sergeant, Civic Guards	Liam Redmond
Maggie	Brid Ni Loinsigh

Produced by Frank Carmody. Settings by the Producer.

20th October 1941
LOVERS' MEETING
A Tragedy in Three Acts by Louis D'Alton

Tom Sheridan	W. O'Gorman
Jane Sheridan, his wife	Eileen Crowe
Mary Sheridan, his daughter	Phyllis Ryan
Jane's sisters:	
Hannie Martin	Ria Mooney
Frances Linehan	Maureen Delany
Mossy Linehan	Michael J. Dolan
Joe Hession	Denis O'Dea
Sergeant Toolin	F. J. McCormick
Batt Seery	Seumas Healy

Produced by Frank Dermody. Settings by Michael Walsh and Seaghan Barlow.

24th November 1941
THE THREE THIMBLES
A Comedy in Three Acts by Brinsley MacNamara

Maria Murray	Maureen Delany
Emily Flynn	Eileen Crowe
Edmund Flynn	F. J. McCormick
Phoebe Flynn	Eithne Dunne
George Heddigan	Fred Johnson
John Kellaghan	Austin Meldon
Martin Eivers	Denis O'Dea
Henry Sammon	W. O'Gorman
Simon Crosbie	Michael J. Dolan
Julia Heddigan	May Craig

Produced by Frank Dermody. Settings by Michael Clarke.

26th December 1941
FORGET-ME-NOT
A Play in Three Acts by Lennox Robinson

Eugene McCarthy, a country Solicitor	Michael J. Dolan
Frank McCarthy, his son	Denis O'Dea
Brannan	Fred Johnson
Fannie O'Shea	Eileen Crowe
Dan Foley	Liam Redmond
Lanty Sheridan	Gerard Healy
Margaret Harte	Shelah Richards
Kit Blennerhassett	Ria Mooney
Samuel Perrier	F. J. McCormick
Nora	Maureen Delany
Robert O'Shea	Francis Foley
Flora O'Shea	Una Collins
Kitty Blennerhassett	Cathleen Fawsitt
Poppy McCarthy	Eithne Dunne

Produced by the Author. Settings by Michael Walsh and Seaghan Barlow.

28th December 1941
BLACK FAST
A Poetic Farce by Austin Clarke

Man Servant	Harry Webster
Steward	Denis O'Dea
Girl Servant	Maureen O'Sullivan
Connal More of Ulster	Michael J. Dolan
Blanaid Fairnape, his wife	Ria Mooney
Mahan, an Adviser	W. O'Gorman
Lord Bishop Cummian	Austin Meldon
Ulster Monks:	
	Fred Johnson, Luke McLoughlin
Romanus	Michael Clarke
Munster Monks:	
	Terry Wilson, Francis Foley
Cogitosus	Liam Redmond

Produced by Liam Redmond. Settings and Costumes by Michael Clarke.

9th March 1942
THE CURSING FIELDS
A Play in Five Acts by Andrew Ganly

Mr. Henry Beaufort	Liam Redmond
Mrs. Madeline Beaufort	Eileen Crowe
Miss Ruth Beaufort	Phyllis Ryan
Miss Irene Beaufort	Joan Plunkett
Mr. Richard Dudley	F. J. McCormick
Mr. James Harnett	Fred Johnson
Mr. Tom Barry	Brian O'Higgins
Mrs. Maureen Barry	Josephine Fitzgerald
Sir George Oliver, Bart.	Harry Webster
The Nurse	Maureen Delany

A HISTORY, 1899-1951

The Maid	. . . .	Maureen O'Sullivan
Old John Herlihy	. . .	Michael J. Dolan
Kate Herlihy	. . . .	. May Craig
Peter Herlihy	. . . .	W. O'Gorman
Mag Sheridan	. . . .	Brid Ni Loinsigh
Nanny Finucan	. . . .	Ria Mooney
Johnny Finucan	. . .	Denis O'Dea
Michael Flynn	. . . .	Austin Meldon

Produced by Frank Dermody. Settings by Michael Clarke.

6th April 1942
THE SINGER
A Play in One Act by Padraic Pearse
Special Commemoration Performance

Mac Dara, the singer	. .	Michael Clarke
Colm, his brother	. . .	Denis O'Dea
Maire ni Fhiannachta, mother of Mac Dara	. .	Ria Mooney
Maoilshfachlainn, a schoolmaster	. . . .	W. O'Gorman
Cuimin Eanna	. . .	Michael J. Dolan
Diarmaid of the Bridge	.	Harry Webster
Neighbour	. . . .	Luke McLoughlin

Produced by Liam Redmond

13th April 1942
THE FORT FIELD
A Play in Three Acts by George Shiels

Henry Caven, a village shopkeeper	. . . .	Michael J. Dolan
Mrs. Caven, his wife	. . .	Ria Mooney
Bernard Caven, their son	.	Liam Redmond
Dan Caven, a farmer	. .	F. J. McCormick
Ellen Caven, his wife	. .	Eileen Crowe
Jacob, a farm servant	. . .	Fred Johnson
Lizzie, a maid	. . . . .	Phyllis Ryan
Seamus, a walking tourist	.	Brian O'Higgins
Maurya, his wife	. . .	Joan Plunkett

Produced by Frank Dermody. Settings by Michael Clarke.

3rd May 1942
LA LA NOO
A Play in Two Acts by Jack B. Yeats

Publican	. . . . . .	Brian O'Higgins
Stranger	. . . . . .	. W. O'Gorman
First Woman	. . . .	Cathleen Fawsitt
Second Woman	. . .	Florence Lynch
Third Woman	. . . .	Nellie Manning
Fourth Woman	. . .	Brid Ni Loinsigh
Fifth Woman	. . . . .	Mary O'Neill
Sixth Woman	. . .	Maureen O'Sullivan
Seventh Woman	. . .	Eve Watkinson

Produced by Ria Mooney. Settings and costumes by Michael Clarke.

6th July 1942
THE WHIP HAND
A Comedy in Three Acts by B. G. MacCarthy

Mrs. Fogarty, a widow	. .	Eileen Crowe
Paud Fogarty, her brother-in-law	. . . . .	Michael J. Dolan
John Fogarty, her elder son	.	Fred Johnson
Larry Fogarty, her younger son	. . . . . .	Brian O'Higgins
Berney Regan	. . . .	Brid Ni Loinsigh
Dan Keogh, a farmer	. .	F. J. McCormick
Maureen Keogh, his daughter	. . . .	Maureen O'Sullivan
Willie Brannigan	. . .	Liam Redmond
Peter Cavanagh, an archeologist	. . . . .	Harry Webster
Nora	. . . .	Sheila Manahan

Produced by Frank Dermody. Settings by Michael Clarke.

7th September 1942
AN APPLE A DAY
A Comedy in Three Acts by Elizabeth Connor

Dr. Burke	. . . . .	Liam Redmond
Tottie Burke, his sister	. .	Eileen Crowe
His daughters:		
Janet Burke	. . . .	Brid Ni Loinsigh
Ann Burke	. . . .	Sheila Manahan
Dr. Gavin Barry	. . . .	Cyril Cusack
Sarsfield Clancy, T.D.	. .	F. J. McCormick
Jeremiah Power	. . .	Michael J. Dolan
Lizzie Power, his wife	. .	Maureen Delany
Statia Slattery	. . . .	Ria Mooney
Jim Hannigan	. .	Ciaran O hAnnrachain
Biddy Hannigan	. .	Maureen O'Sullivan

Produced by Frank Dermody. Settings by Michael Clarke.

25th January 1943
FAUSTUS KELLY
A Play in Three Acts by Myles na gCopaleen

Kelly, Chairman of the Urban Council	. . .	F. J. McCormick
Members of the Council:		
Cullen	. . . . . .	Fred Johnson
Reilly	. . . . . .	Michael J. Dolan
Shaun Kilshaughraun	.	Brian O'Higgins
Hoop	. . . . . .	Denis O'Dea
Town Clerk	. . . .	Cyril Cusack
Mrs. Crockett	. . . .	Ria Mooney
Hannah	. . . . . .	Eileen Crowe
Capt. Shaw	. . . .	Gerard Healy
Mr. Strange	. . . .	Liam Redmond

Produced by Frank Dermody. Settings by Michael Clarke.

8th March 1943
THE O'CUDDY
A Play in Three Acts by Anthony Wharton

George Posnett	Michael J. Dolan
Clench	Fred Johnson
Countess Pilsudska	Joan Plunkett
Lord Kilfoyne	Gerard Healy
Thaddeus Cuddy	Cyril Cusack
Dr. McRoney	F. J. McCormick
Cormac O'Cuiddeach	Denis O'Dea
Michael	Brian O'Higgins
A Masked Figure	Harry Webster
Two Guards:	Ciaran O hAnnrachain, Micheal O Briain

Produced by Frank Dermody. Settings by Michael Clarke.

21st March 1943
ASSEMBLY AT DRUIM CEAT
A Poem for Players by Roibeard O Farachain

Dallan, a Poet	Michael J. Dolan
Shanahan, a Poet	Sean MacGiolla Chlaoin
King Aedh	Liam Redmond
Caltra, a King	Cecil Barror
Liuda, a King	Tomas Luibheid
St. Colmcille	Roibeard O Farachain
1st Woman Narrator	Patricia Clancy
2nd Woman Narrator	Maureen Kiely
1st Man Narrator	Gerard Healy
2nd Man Narrator	Patrick Holland
Morbhan	George Greene
Aedh's Sons:	
Connall	Harry Webster
Domhnall	Ciaran O hAnnrachain
1st Accuser	Peadar O hUllachain
Derryman	Daniel Connolly
Poets: Oliver Bradley, Michael Brady, Patrick MacMahon, Liam Gannon	
Monk	Micheal O Briain
Aedh's Queen	Marcie Collins
Caltra's Queen	Marie Judge
Boy	Robert Wilton

Produced by Ria Mooney. Costumes and Settings by Michael Clarke. Incidental music composed and directed by Dr. Arthur Duff.

24th April 1943
OLD ROAD
A Play in Three Acts by Michael J. Molloy

Patrick Walsh (alias "The Lord")	F. J. McCormick
Myles Cosgrave, farm labourer	Cyril Cusack
Luke Sweeney, a cobbler	Michael J. Dolan
William Duffy, a neighbour	Eric Gorman
Brigid McDonagh, a servant	Brid Ni Loinsigh
"Bodhagh" Merrigan, a big farmer	Brian O'Higgins
Paak Merrigan, his son	Denis O'Dea
Mary Kennedy	Maureen O'Sullivan
Mrs. Callaghan, a widow	Maureen Delany
Sergeant	Fred Johnson

Produced by Frank Dermody. Settings by Michael Clarke.

26th April 1943
LOST LIGHT
A Verse Play by Roibeard O Farachain

Dermot Daintry	Michael J. Dolan
Harriet, his wife	Ria Mooney
Major Philip Ferguson	Denis O'Dea
Imelda Carlin	Eithne Dunne
Barbara	May Craig

30th August 1943
THY DEAR FATHER
A Play in Three Acts by Gerard Healy

Eileen Walsh	Eithne Dunne
Anna Dooley	Ria Mooney
Bridie	Eileen Crowe
Mrs. Dooley	May Craig
Jack Dooley	Liam Redmond
Fr. Michael Dooley	Denis O'Dea
Fr. Tahaney	F. J. McCormick
Danny Kelly	Michael J. Dolan
Mrs. Kelly	Kathleen Murphy

Produced by Frank Dermody. Settings by Sean Barlow.

7th February 1944
THE WISE HAVE NOT SPOKEN
A Play in Three Acts by Paul Vincent Carroll

Peter MacElroy	Denis O'Dea
Francis, his brother	Cyril Cusack
His sisters:	
Una	Eithne Dunne
Catherine	Brid Ni Loinsigh
Andy Redfern	Liam Redmond
Sylvester Tiffney	Michael J. Dolan
Paddry Ardee	F. J. McCormick
Sean Mulligan	Harry Brogan
Dr. Rafferty	Fred Johnson
Martyn Langley	Brian O'Higgins

Produced by Frank Dermody. Settings by Alicia Sweetman.

A HISTORY, 1899–1951   175

6th March 1944

THE NEW REGIME
A Play in Three Acts by George Shiels

Thomas Bleacher, a factory owner	F. J. McCormick
Emma Bleacher, his wife	Eileen Crowe
Fanny Bleacher, his daughter	Eithne Dunne
Harry Bleacher, his son	Gerard Healy
Minnie Bleacher, Harry's wife	Brid Ni Loinsigh
Mr. O'Neill, a gentleman farmer	Fred Johnson
Bert Smith	Denis O'Dea
Miss Fossit	Maureen O'Sullivan
Sam Drippin	Michael J. Dolan
Jim M'Cuttack	Cyril Cusack
Susan, a maid	Maire Ni Dhomhnaill
Matt Feenix, a Labour official	Brian O hUiginn
Dooley, his chauffeur	Harry Brogan
A Detective	Harry Webster

Produced by Ria Mooney. Settings by Alicia Sweetman.

8th May 1944

THE COLOURED BALLOON
A Comedy in Three Acts by Margaret O'Leary

Jerry Joyce	F. J. McCormick
Matt Joyce	Michael J. Dolan
Mina Joyce	Ria Mooney
Sally Joyce	Maire Ni Dhomhnaill
Catherine Nolan	Eileen Crowe
Mrs. Mollie Manning	Brid Ni Loinsigh
Geoffrey Burke, N.T.	Fred Johnson
Mrs. Hannah Burke	May Craig
Philomena Burke	Eithne Dunne
Carmel	Joan Plunkett
Sonny Manning	Patrick Fay

Produced by Frank Dermody. Settings by Alicia Sweetman.

28th August 1944

THE END HOUSE
A Play in Three Acts by Joseph Tomelty

Wallace Mac Astocker	F. J. McCormick
Saralice, his wife	May Craig
Monica, their daughter	Sioghan Ni Chionnaith
Seumas, their son	Cyril Cusack
Stewartie Pullar, a lodger	Michael J. Dolan
Mrs. Griffith, a neighbour	Eileen Crowe
Constable Hanna	Harry Brogan
Insurance Visitor	Christine Hayden
Mrs. Fruin, another neighbour	Brid Ni Loinsigh
Policemen:	Brian O'Higgins, Seumas Locke
Baker, a military policeman	Denis O'Dea
Sergeant, R.U.C.	Fred Johnson

Produced by Frank Dermody. Settings by Alicia Sweetman.

20th November 1944

RAILWAY HOUSE
A Play in Three Acts by Ralph Kennedy

Willy Davro	Denis O'Dea
Nano Ross	Sioghan Nic Chionnaith
Jonathan Coyne	F. J. McCormick
Susan Ross	Brid Ni Loinsigh
Dan Shanahan	Michael J. Dolan
Martha Davro	Eileen Crowe
Dr. Edward Creagh	Brian O'Higgins
Stephen Ross	Harry Brogan
The Station Master	Fred Johnson

Produced by Frank Dermody. Settings by Alicia Sweetman.

31st March 1945

ROSSA
A Play in a Prologue, Three Acts and an Epilogue, by Roger McHugh

The Figure in Uniform	Seumas Locke
Jeremiah O'Donovan Rossa	W. O'Gorman
A Magistrate	Fred Johnson
Mary	Brid Ni Loinsigh
Parish Priest	Seumas Healy
Mrs. Luby	Eileen Crowe
Judge Keogh	Cyril Cusack
Governor	F. J. McCormick
Governor's Secretary	May Craig
First Warder	Denis O'Dea
Chaplain	Michael J. Dolan
Second Warder	Micheal O Briain
First Commissioner	Eric Gorman
Second Commissioner	Pat O'Rourke
Third Commissioner	Sean O Maonaigh
Rossa's Secretary	Sioghan Nic Chionnaith
Mr. Lanigan	Austin Meldon
Mr. Madigan	Harry Brogan
General Ryan	Michael Cosgrave

Produced by Frank Dermody. Settings by Alicia Sweetman.

6th August 1945

MARKS AND MABEL

A Comedy in Three Acts
by Brinsley MacNamara

Marks Heffernan	Denis O'Dea
Mabel Heffernan, his wife . . .	Sioghan Nic Chionnaith
Ignatius Crinnion	Fred Johnson
Alice Crinnion (*née* Heffernan), his wife. .	Brid Ni Loinsigh
Sydney Heffernan . . .	Seumas Locke
Marcella Heffernan, his wife, formerly Mrs. Marcella Molloy	Eileen Crowe
Festus Darby	F. J. McCormick
James Heffernan, father of Marks, Alice and Sydney	Michael J. Dolan
Paul Heffernan, his brother	Harry Brogan
Roseanne Heffernan, Paul's wife . .	Padraigin Ni Mhaidin
Tessie Malone . .	Maire Ni Dhomhnaill

Produced by Frank Dermody. Settings by Alicia Sweetman.

10th September 1945

TENANTS AT WILL

A Play of Rural Ireland in the Young Ireland Period by George Shiels

Sir Andrew, the landlord .	Michael J. Dolan
Dawson, his agent	Cyril Cusack
Scobey, the bailiff . . .	Fred Johnson
Noggan, under bailiff . . .	Eric Gorman
Marshall Rock, an extensive farmer . .	F. J. McCormick
Dyson, a Trinity College Perambulator	Harry Brogan
Master O'Byrne, a hedge school-master . . .	Austin Meldon
Granny Sheegan . . .	Eileen Crowe
Michael Sheegan, her son . .	Denis O'Dea
Patrick Sheegan, another son	Micheal O Briain
Nora Sheegan, his wife . .	Brid Ni Loinsigh
Peter Mohun, a labourer .	John MacDarby
Johnny Doyle, an old soldier	Sean O Maonaigh
R.I.C. Constable . . .	Seumas Locke

Produced by Frank Dermody. Settings by Alicia Sweetman.

11th February 1946

MUNGO'S MANSIONS

A Play in Three Acts by Walter Macken

Mungo King	F. J. McCormick
Mairteen, his son . . .	Micheal O Briain
Nellie, his daughter	Sioghan Nic Chionnaith
Willie Gilhealy, known as "Winnie of the Wild Duck"	Eileen Crowe
Mister Skerret, landlord's agent	Michael J. Dolan
Mowleogs Canavan . .	Harry Brogan
Jack Manders	Denis O'Dea
Mrs. Manders, his wife .	Brid Ni Loinsigh
The Doctor	Fred Johnson
Voices	

Produced by Frank Dermody. Settings by Alicia Sweetman.

25th March 1946

First Production by the Abbey Company of

THE OLD BROOM

A Comedy in Three Acts by George Shiels

Ben Broom, a retired land agent	Denis O'Dea
Barbara Broom, his daughter	Peggy Hayes
Austin Broom, his son .	Sean Mac Labhraidh
Rachel Broom, Austin's wife	Siobhan Nic Chionnaith
Archy Broom, another son	Sean O Maonaigh
Emily Broom, Archy's wife	Maire Ni Dhomhnaill
Tom Frailey, a solicitor . .	Harry Brogan
Sarah Frailey, his wife . .	Brid Ni Loinsigh
Hubert Dobie, a solicitor .	Brian O'Higgins
A Landlady	May Craig

Produced by Frank Dermody. Settings by Alicia Sweetman.

29th July 1946

THE RIGHTEOUS ARE BOLD

A Play in Three Acts by Frank Carney

Michael Martin Geraty . .	Fred Johnson
Mary Kate Geraty, his wife . .	May Craig
Patrick Geraty, his son .	Micheal O Briain
Nora Geraty, his daughter . . .	Maire Na Dhomhnaill
Nellie the Post	Brid Ni Loinsigh
Doctor Moran	Brian O'Higgins
Father O'Malley . . .	Michael J. Dolan
Anthony Costello . .	Raghnall Breathnach
Mother Benedict . . .	Christine Hayden
Sister Mary of the Rosary . . .	Mairin Ni Shuilleabhain

Produced by Frank Dermody. Settings by Alicia Sweetman.

A HISTORY, 1899–1951

18th November 1946

THE VISITING HOUSE

A Play in Three Acts by M. J. Molloy

Broc Heavy, Merryman and Master of The Visiting House	Denis O'Dea
Mary Heavy, Daughter of The Visiting House	Maire Ni Dhomhnaill
Murt King, Ganger of The Visiting House	Brian O'Higgins
Tim Corry, Newcomer to The Visiting House	Raghnall Breathnach
Mickle Conlon, The Man of Learning	F. J. McCormick
Verb To Be, the Man of Education	Harry Brogan
Kate, The Scoffer	May Craig
Beezie, The Woman of Gifts	Eileen Crowe
Julia	Brid Ni Loinsigh
Igoe	Micheal O Briain

The Haws: Rank and file of The Visiting House: Doirin Ni Mhaidin, Seathrun O Goilidhe, Labhras O Galicobhair, Liam O Laoghaire, Mairin Ni Shuilleabhain, Dermot Kelly, Maire Ni Thuathail, Padraigin Ni Mhaidin, Micheal O Duinn, R. O. Shuilleabhain

Produced by Michael J. Dolan. Settings by Alicia Sweetman.

18th February 1947

THEY GOT WHAT THEY WANTED

An Improbable Comedy by Louis D'Alton

Bartley Murnaghan	F. J. McCormick
Bessie Murnaghan, his wife	Eileen Crowe
His children:	
Sally Murnaghan	Maire Ni Thuathail
Nora Murnaghan	Doirin Ni Mhaidin
Jack Murnaghan	Seathrun O Goilidhe
Derry Murnaghan	Raghnall Breathnach
Peter Murnaghan	Micheal O Briain
Owny Tubridy	Harry Brogan
Matty McGrath	Brian O'Higgins
Joe McGrath	Sean O Maonaigh
Tom Cassidy	Padraig O Dulchonta
Lorcan	Micheal O Duinn

Produced by Michael J. Dolan. Setting by Maire Purseil.

12th May 1947

THE DARK ROAD

A Play in Three Acts with Prologue and Epilogue by Elizabeth Connor

Ignatius Ross	Harry Brogan
Julia Ross, his wife	May Craig
Katherine Ross, his daughter	Doirin Ni Mhaidin
Dr. Richard Mahon	Sean Mac Shamhrain
Nora Mahon, his wife	Brid Ni Loinsigh
Charles Mahon, his son	Seathrun O Goilidhe
John Davern:	
as a boy	Aodh Mac Giolladuinn
as a man	Raghnall Breathnach
Robert Bolger	Brian O'Higgins
Office Boy	Niall O Muineachain

Produced by Michael J. Dolan. Settings by Carl Bonn.

25th August 1947

First Production by the Abbey Company of

THE GREAT PACIFICATOR

By Sigerson Clifford

Daniel O'Connell	Brian O'Higgins
Father Miley	Donnchadha O Muiridhe
Maureen	Brid Ni Loinsigh
Muirish MacCarthy	Micheal O Briain
Dermot MacCarthy	Raghnall Breathnach
Darby Sullivan	Sean Mac Shamhrain
John Mitchel	Harry Brogan
Thomas Davis	Liam O Foghludha
Biddy Moriarty	Eileen Crowe
Captain Dardis	Padraigh O Dulchonta
Voice of Luigi	Micheal O Duinn

Produced by Michael J. Dolan. Settings by Carl Bonn.

16th February 1948

THE CARETAKERS

A Play in Three Acts by George Shiels

Mr. Brice, a solicitor	Pilib O Floinn
Mr. Hannon, an auctioneer	Raghnall Breathnach
Ned Caffer, not in business	Michael J. Dolan
Laura Caffer, his daughter	Ronnie Masterson
Robert Croobin, an old man	Harry Brogan
David Macosh, a retired official	Brian O'Higgins
Minnie Macosh, his wife	Eileen Crowe
Joss Nably, the village porter	Seumas Locke
Matty, an old servant	Brid Ni Loinsigh
Bertha, her sister	May Craig

Produced by Ria Mooney. Settings by Carl Bonn.

12th July 1948

THE DRUMS ARE OUT

A Play in Three Acts by John Coulter

Sergeant Thomas Sheridan,
  R.U.C. . . . . . Brian O'Higgins
Mrs. Sheridan, his wife . . Eileen Crowe
Jean, his daughter . Maire Ni Dhomhnaill
Constable Nixon, R.U.C. . . Pilip O Floinn
Denis Patterson . . Raghnall Breathnach
Matt McCann . . . . . Harry Brogan
Three Men: Reamonn Mac an Fhailghigh, Micheal O Duinn, Labhras O Gallchobhair

Produced by Ria Mooney. Settings by Carl Bonn.

23rd August 1948

THE LUCKY FINGER

A Comedy in Three Acts by Lennox Robinson

Statia Clancy . . . . . . May Craig
Richard Clancy, her husband . . . . . Liam O Foghlu
Their children:
  Emmy . . . . Maire Ni Thuathail
  Puck . . . . . Doirin Ni Mhaidin
  Charles . . . . Raghnall Breathnach
Julia ("Juley") Clancy,
  Richard's sister . . . . Eileen Crowe
Maurice ("Mosey") Clancy,
  Richard's younger brother . . . . Bhaitear O Maicin
Marjorie ("Marge"),
  Maurice's wife . . . Brid Ni Loinsigh
Pat, their son . . . Feilim Mac Uidhir
Honor, the Clancys'
  servant . . . . . Ite Ni Mhathuna
Sir Adrian Burke . . . . Harry Brogan
Stephen Foley . . Micheal O hAonghusa
John Twohig . . . . Brian O'Higgins
Eddie Twohig, his son . Aodh Mac Gunna
Sister Mary Francis . . . . Ita Little
Sister Sebastian . . Ronai Nic an Mhaistir
Jim, a waiter . . . Micheal O Briain
Squint Robinson . Labhras O Gallchobhair
Stuart Bingham . Reamonn Mac an Fhaili
Brennan, a Civic Guard . Seathrun O Goili
Maggie Delaney . Maire Ni Dhomhnaill
Annie Twohig . . . . Aine Ni Riain

Produced by Ria Mooney. Settings by Carl Bonn.

18th October 1948

THE KING OF FRIDAY'S MEN

A Play in Three Acts by M. J. Molloy

Gaisceen Brehony, huntsman to Caesar French . . Harry Brogan
Una Brehony, his niece . Rite Ni Fhuarain
Owen Fenigan, son of
  one of Caesar's
  tenants . . . Micheal O hAonghusa
Maura Pender, daughter
  of one of Caesar's
  tenants . . . Ronai Nic an Mhaistir
Bartley Dowd, a man
  from Tyrawley . . Bhaitear O Maicin
Boorla, Caesar's bailiff . . Micheal O Duinn
Rory Commons, son of
  Cormac Commons, last
  of the Bards . . . Brian O'Higgins
Kitty, a peasant girl from
  a neighbouring estate . Ite Ni Mhathuna
Biddy, Caesar's housekeeper . . . . . Brid Ni Loinsigh
Murty, stable hand of
  Caesar's . . . Sean Mac Shamhrain
Caesar French, Landlord
  of Kilmacreena . . . Liam O Foghlu
Crowd: Labhras O Gallchobhair, Reamonn Mac an Fhaili, Micheal O Briain, Raghnall Breathnach, Pilib O Floinn, Feilim Mac Uidhir

Produced by Ria Mooney. Settings by Carl Bonn.

14th March 1949

THE BUGLE IN THE BLOOD

A Play in Three Acts by Bryan MacMahon

Maroya Trimble, owner of a
  lodging house . . . Brid Ni Loinsigh
Joseph Trimble, her son . Brian O'Higgins
Andy Trimble, her son . Padraig O'Neill
Evelyn McCann, her
  married daughter . Maire Ni Thuathail
Botany Connell (neighbour),
  a cobbler . . . . Michael J. Dolan
Circus Jack (lodger),
  street strong man . Bhaitear O Maicin
Rab (lodger), Indian
  peddler . . . Sean Mac Shamhrain
Mrs. Monahan, a neighbour . Eileen Crowe
May Bridie Monahan,
  her daughter . . . Doirin Ni Mhaidin
Tim Sullivan, member of
  the C.I.D. . . . . . Harry Brogan
Voices of neighbouring women: Ite Ni Mhathuna, Rite Ni Fhuarain, Ronai Nic An Mhaistir

Produced by Ria Mooney. Settings by Vere Dudgeon.

A HISTORY, 1899–1951   179

16th April 1949

ALL SOULS' NIGHT

A Tragedy in Three Acts by Joseph Tomelty

Katrine Quinn . . . Maire Ni Chathain
John Quinn, her husband . Michael J. Dolan
Michael Quinn, her
  son . . . Reamonn Mac An Fhaili
Molly Trainor . . . Siobhan Ni Eaghra
Mr. Thurston, bank
  manager . . . . Bhaitear O Maicin
Tom Byers, a neighbour . . Harry Brogan
A Figure . . . Labhras O Gallchobhair

Produced by Ria Mooney. Settings by Vere Dudgeon.

3rd October 1949

ASK FOR ME TO-MORROW

A Play in Three Acts by Ralph Kennedy

Robert Browne, the bank
  manager . . . . . Michael J. Dolan
Ann Browne, his wife . . . Eileen Crowe
Betty Browne, his
  daughter . . . Maire Ni Dhomhnaill
Eva Bell, his sister . . . Brid Ni Loinsigh
Victor Moore, his
  adopted son . . . Raghnall Breathnach
Marie Wozinski, a
  Polish refugee . . Doirin Ni Mhaidin
Leo, the bank porter . . Micheal O Briain
Julia, the housekeeper . . . . May Craig
Aeneas Murphy . . Bhaitear O Maicin
Alex Driver, chief
  bank inspector Reamonn Mac An Fhaili

Produced by Ria Mooney. Settings by Vere Dudgeon.

8th April 1950

DESIGN FOR A HEADSTONE

A Play in Three Acts by Seamus Byrne

Political prisoners:
Conor Mangan . Micheal O hAonghusa
Aiden O'Leary . . . Eamon Guailli
Kevin Shields . Reamonn Mac An Fhaili
Tommy McGovern . Raghnall Breathnach
Jim O'Shea . . . Sean O Maonaigh
Ructions McGowan Bhaitear O Maicin
Bill Dunne . . . . Micheal O Duinn

Joe Fitzpatrick . . Tomas Mac Anna
Micheal Breathnach . . Micheal O Briain
P. J. Corrigan . . Aodh Mac Gunna
O'Sullivan . . Traolach O hAonghusa
Prison warders:
Pat Gerrity . . . . Pilib O Floinn
Mouth Phelan . . . Seathrun O Goili
Charles Grimes . . . . James Carty
Principal Warder . . . . Noel Guy
Criminal prisoners:
Jakey . . . . . . Brian O'Higgins
Muscles Rogan . . . . Harry Brogan
Butcher Healy . . . . Leo Keogh
Bayer . . . . . . Michael J. Dolan
Father Maguire, Prison
  Chaplain . . . . . Liam O Foghlu
Mrs. Mangan, Conor
  Mangan's wife . . . Brid Ni Loinsigh
Other prisoners, warders, etc.: Michael O'Herlihy, Colm O'Kelly, Harry O'Reilly, Tom Dullaghan, Pol O'Meara, Finbar Howard, Michael Conway, Joe Cooney, Joe Nolan

Produced by Ria Mooney. Settings by Vere Dudgeon.

10th August 1950

MOUNTAIN FLOOD

A Play in Three Acts by Jack P. Cunningham

Old Black Jameseen Brennan,
  father of Peter and Red . Harry Brogan
Mary Weir, the Faction's mid-
  wife . . . . May Craig
Kate McGuire, a neigh-
  bour . . . . . Brid Ni Loinsigh
Lame Thomaseen Sweeney,
  a poteen vendor . . Micheal O Briain
Ellen Clarke, daughter of
  Tom Clarke . . . Ite Ni Mhathuna
Sons of Old Black Jameseen Brennan:
  Red Brennan . Micheal O hAonghusa
  Peter Brennan . . Seathrun O Goili
Tom Clarke, father of Ellen Brian O'Higgins
John McGuire, husband of
  Kate McGuire . . . Pilib O Floinn
Black Antony, leader of the
  Faction . . . Bhaitear O Maicin

The action takes place in Black Jameseen Brennan's small thatched house, used as a shebeen, in a wild and boggy district in North Mayo.

Produced by Ria Mooney. Settings by Vere Dudgeon.

2nd October 1950

THE GOLDFISH IN THE SUN

A Play in Three Acts by Donal Giltinan

Civic Guard Callaghan	Pilib O Floinn
Mrs. Murphy	Brid Ni Loinsigh
Dannocks	Eamon Guailli
Mrs. Coughlan	Ite Ni Mhathuna
Statia Keaney	Maire Ni Chathain
Mrs. Sheelan	May Craig
Jimmy Sheelan	Seamus O Dubhghaill
Milly Keaney	Maire Ni Dhomhnaill
Another Guard	Micheal O Duinn
Plain Clothes Guard	Rae Mac An Aili
Bos'n Treston	Harry Brogan
Danjoe Keaney	Micheal O hAonghusa
Mr. Sheelan	Eric Gorman
Postman	Micheal O Briain
Seamus O'Neill	Labhras O Gallchobhair
Lizzie O'Neill	Siobhan Ni Eaghra
Shirley O'Neill	Doirin Ni Mhaidin
Lamp Lighter	Traolach O hAonghusa
Lorry Driver	Tomas Mac Anna
Tim Coughlan	Seathrun O Goili
Messenger	Liam O Foghlu

Others: Sean O Maonaigh, Aingeal Ni Nuamain

Produced by Ria Mooney. Settings by Vere Dudgeon.

CONCLUSION

But what an absurd word to write at the top of the final page of this History, for there is no conclusion. While I am writing these words a play by an unknown author is having its first rehearsal on our stage. Two new players, a young man and a young woman, are awkwardly moving and stuttering their words. The author of that play may be a new Synge, a new Sean O'Casey, a second Lady Gregory. These players, after years of training, may be Sara Allgoods and F. J. McCormicks. Our Theatre in size and shape is very much the same as when it opened its doors in 1904. A few years ago there was a dream of a theatre worthy of our Republic, a theatre stretching from Lower Abbey Street to the Liffey, a building which would embrace the Gate Theatre and the Gaelic Theatre. A change of Government and financial facts have postponed that lovely, grandiose idea. But only postponed it; it will come to pass, if not next year, then certainly in the near future. Meanwhile I can recall that since the curtain rose on *The Countess Cathleen* in the Antient Concert Rooms in 1899 the Irish Theatre has produced four hundred and fifty plays. Perhaps a hundred of these plays will never be heard or seen again, but all were accepted in good hope and faith, in the belief that the authors might write better given this preliminary encouragement.

"We Irish," as Bishop Berkeley might say, have for the last three centuries taken our Irish theatre with a high seriousness, not only in the theatre's tragedies but in its comedies and even in its farces. And we are jealous and resent—perhaps to an exaggerated degree—scenes and words which are critical of our country. Thus, at the first performance of *The Countess Cathleen* in 1899, certain young men made a dignified protest on religious-nationalist grounds. A less dignified protest was evoked by *The Playboy* in 1907. Norreys Connell's *The Piper* (1908) was booed and hissed, the Cork realists were disliked; and a fierce storm broke over *The Plough and the Stars* (1926). Twelve years later *The Plough's* production was objected to;

not on the ground of its subject, the criticism was of its production. Two young literary men suddenly appeared and addressed the audience, complaining that the acting and production were unworthy of such a masterpiece. Having made their protest they quietly withdrew. Whether their protest was justified or not I do not know, for I was five thousand miles away, but I rejoiced in their protest for it showed the vitality of our Theatre, that it was still held to be one of the precious things in Irish life, something still to be loved, hated, guarded. It is difficult to imagine—even in Stratford-on-Avon—an audience rising in protest at So-and-so's production of "The Dream" or Mr. Blank's "Hamlet," or an audience in the United States walking out on a trivial performance of *Mourning Becomes Electra*.

Great names sail down our fifty years: Yeats, Gregory, Synge, Colum, Fitzmaurice, Boyle, Robinson, Murray, Ray, Ervine, Shaw, MacNamara, Shiels, O'Casey, D'Alton, Carroll, Deevy, Mayne. And in players: the Fays, Maire Nic Shiubhlaigh, Sara Allgood, Maire O'Neill, Arthur Sinclair, J. M. Kerrigan, Fred O'Donovan, F. J. McCormick, Arthur Shields, Michael J. Dolan, Eric Gorman, Christine Hayden, Barry Fitzgerald, Maureen Delany, Eileen Crowe, May Craig, Shelah Richards, Brid Ni Loinsigh, Harry Brogan—I cannot remember accurately the Galaxy—"Mine eyes dazzle."

POSTSCRIPT

At 10.15 on the evening of 17th July 1951 the curtain fell at the conclusion of a brilliant performance of *The Plough and the Stars*. By 11 o'clock the players and the staff had left the Theatre. An hour and a half later two young men passing in the street saw that the building was in flames—a cigarette butt—a fused wire? We shall never know. Not everything was destroyed. The stage, the scene-dock, the green-room, wardrobe-rooms, paint-room and dressing-rooms disappeared, but the front offices and the vestibule were not injured and willing helpers from the street rescued all our lovely pictures.

Almost from the day in 1904 when the Theatre was opened it had been harshly criticised, its players derided and its plays condemned. Now, when the building was almost extinct, love, sympathy and offers of help poured in from other theatres, from cinemas, from individuals not only in Ireland but in England, in U.S.A., on the Continent. It only needed this little tragedy (for, really, the loss of the Abbey building is a small thing in its history compared with the early death of Synge, or the death of F. J. McCormick) to realise how deeply rooted is the Abbey Theatre in the national life of Ireland.

The Directors of Guinness and Co. generously put their new small theatre at our disposal, and now we have moved for a few years to the commodious Queen's Theatre.

Two new plays by new authors are under rehearsal—Ireland's Abbey Theatre is as alive as ever.

APPENDIX I

PICTURES IN A THEATRE

He enclosed a letter from Professor Merriam of Montana University, Missoula. It said that Brendan O'Neill was in the American Army and, if in luck and he survived, would come to Dublin to look up relations, and that he was interested in the theatre and could I do anything for him? I made an appointment one morning in the vestibule of the Abbey Theatre. Brendan turned out to be a strapping six-footer and he brought with him a rather weedy young man. He introduced him:

I

BRENDAN: My second cousin, David, from Sligo, or near there.

DAVID: From the borders of Sligo and Donegal, sir.

SELF: I know Sligo fairly well and a bit of Donegal.

BRENDAN: What I want to know is, about this theatre. You see my eldest brother—he's sixteen years older than me—was at a summer school once at Missoula and you were there and you lectured about Ireland and the Abbey Theatre, and you produced a play with the students, and then a few years after he saw the Abbey Players in Helena—I don't think you were with them—and he fell for them, but my dad—he's a real old Irishman—he had seen the same sort of plays in Chicago years back and he liked the acting, but he said some of the plays were terribly crude, that *Playboy*, for instance, by Synge——

SELF: Sing (*I corrected*). You singe a cat, you sing Synge.

BRENDAN: Thanks, I accept the correction. But there was one of yours he liked, something about the Back Hills.

SELF: I'm glad he liked it.

BRENDAN: He said it was all right—I mean he liked it. Now, tell me about this theatre.

SELF: There's so much to tell, lots of books have been written about it—I've written about it so often myself. Let's start by just looking at these pictures in the vestibule. Don't you think it's a lovely little gallery?

BRENDAN: It certainly is. I don't pretend to know much about pictures, but I——

SELF: Know what I like. Isn't that the best reason for liking a picture? So, let's just go quietly round, starting on our right—no, for the moment we'll skip the first one and look at the one over the gas-fire.

BRENDAN: She looks a fine, powerful old woman.

SELF: She *was* fine and powerful; that is Lady Gregory. There would be no theatre here, you and I wouldn't be standing here, if it wasn't for her. She was of the Protestant class—what some people sneeringly call "the ascendancy class"—and she was a great Irishwoman. She met Yeats, and she knew a man called Edward Martyn, a neighbour of her own, a Catholic landlord in County Galway. Martyn and Yeats had written plays and they wanted them produced, and they thought of having them done in London. Lady Gregory, who up to this had no particular interest in the drama, said they should be done in Dublin and, thanks to her energy, done in Dublin they were—this was away back in 1899. In a few years' time she became absorbed in the Irish theatre, she started to write plays herself and ended up by being one of the most important playwrights of our early days. She was a Director of our theatre and without her firm hand and her unflinching belief in our theatre's future we should have no national theatre in Ireland today. ... But let's leave her for a moment, she'll crop up again and again, for she permeates every stick and stone of this building. We'll turn back—and forward—to the two young men whose portraits hang on her right and left. Their names are Fay, Frank Fay and Willie Fay.

BRENDAN: Nice-looking fellas.

SELF: Aren't they? And so beautifully painted by J. B. Yeats. He was W. B. Yeats's father and the father of Jack B. Yeats, our finest, most original painter in Ireland today, some think one of the most exciting painters in Europe and America. But the Fays—they were brothers—were acting in small halls in Dublin, and they got to know what Yeats and Martyn were trying to do, knew they were trying to create an Irish drama, on Yeats's side a poetic, heroic drama, on Martyn's side a more psychological drama. Those early performances had been given by professional English companies, generally in some big Dublin theatre, but when the Fays and their friends joined Yeats's group a change took place. The performances were held now in small Dublin halls ill-fitted for stage purposes, the audiences were generally small and none of the players were paid. The brothers were contrasted in their gifts; Frank, a beautiful speaker of verse, Willie a comedian of genius. Can't you see the poetry in Frank's eyes?

BRENDAN: I sure can. Who's that left of the door?

SELF: That's Doctor Larchet. Not a Doctor of Medicine, a Doctor of Music. He came to the theatre, a young man, as leader of the orchestra. It was a poorly-paid job. Jack Larchet became very successful and busy; teaching, composing, university work, examinations, but he so loved the Abbey that he could not bear to leave it. He knew every play that was performed, though he would always consider the acts of a play as "the interval" and his music the *coup* of the evening. And many others agreed with him and would go out for a smoke during the acts and come back for what *we* call "the interval." It's a fine portrait, very like him, and though Jack doesn't conduct for us any more I don't think he ever misses a new play. Above the door is George Russell, better known as "AE." He had a lot to do with the theatre in the very early days before it had a theatre, but then he dropped out of the movement.

BRENDAN: But we've missed the delicate-looking chap in the corner.

SELF: Ah, that's a man called Padraic Colum. He was one of our earliest playwrights, he started to write at about the same time as Synge, that is to say, when the theatre was beginning to turn from the poetic, heroic theatre Yeats had dreamed of to a more realistic type of play—but it had not yet reached the harshly realistic plays of T. C. Murray, R. J. Ray and myself—the "three Cork realists," as Yeats called us. Colum wrote about contemporary country life, the life of the small farmer, such plays as *The Land* and *The Fiddler's House*, bringing into them a poetry of speech—not as emphasised as Synge's speech—but essentially poetry. He has lived in New York for many, many years and has a distinguished literary position there. I am sure you have heard of him.

BRENDAN: I certainly have. So that's Padraic Colum!

SELF: Yes, but a long time ago. His best play, written much later than the ones I have named, was not about the country, it was about a country-town and a workhouse-master, it is called *Thomas Muskerry*. I am proud to remember that I gave it its first production.

DAVID: Who's that above the box-office, staring down?

SELF: That's W. B. Yeats, son of the man who painted the portraits and the originator of this theatre. And yet I don't think he cared very much for plays, he told me once that the only plays he really liked were Shakespeare's. He wrote some beautiful verse-plays himself, but when our theatre grew realistic he stood aside, though late in life he wrote a very remarkable little prose play about Jonathan Swift called *The Words Upon the Window-pane*. But he was much more a poet than a dramatist and, funny to say, a hard-headed man of business. He could even understand a balance-sheet, and that's not an easy thing to do. As you say, he stares down. I like to fancy he's watching the people booking seats and wondering whether there will be a full house tonight, and whether the ladies behind the little window are giving the correct change—I bet they are.

But now let's swing to the left, to the far corner. That lovely, delicate portrait—look at the hands—is of Miss Horniman. She was an Englishwoman who got to know Yeats and to admire his work and the work of the players, who were still only an amateur company, with no theatre, not even a hall of their own. She took over this old theatre, furbished it up, made additions to it and for a number of years gave it an annual subsidy. To have a permanent home, to have a fixed income—even if a small one—meant a tremendous lot. The players could now be paid regular salaries—fantastically small salaries judged by present-day standards—but it enabled them to leave their jobs and devote all their time to the theatre. I believe she was difficult to work with—I never met her—she wrote on yellow paper in red ink, and Synge used to declare that he grew slightly ill when he saw a yellow envelope in the morning's post. But, difficult though she may have been, this theatre is deeply in her debt.

DAVID: The next is a powerful-looking chap.

SELF: Isn't he? His name was Higgins, F. R. Higgins, he was our managing-director for a few years but he wasn't, mainly, a man of the theatre. He was a poet, our best, most promising poet—no, I shouldn't say promising, for he was a poet of achievement and a great friend of Yeats. Alas, he died all too young. I can never look at that splendid portrait by Seán O'Sullivan without a deep pang of regret.

BRENDAN: It seems just too bad. And the guy beyond him, isn't that yourself?

SELF: That guy, as you say, is indeed myself. We needn't dwell on the subject of the portrait but only note the rich beauty of the painting. It is by a man called Sleator, one of our finest portrait painters; he was made President of our Hibernian Academy a few months ago. But now, before starting up the stairs, what about going out for a cup of coffee and a cigarette?

BRENDAN: Sounds O.K. by me.

DAVID: I'd like that—or a bottle of stout.

SELF: Right. Let's go.

(*And we went*)

II

SELF: Well, here we are back again. There are not many pictures left for us to look at—only five—but I've a lot to tell you about them ... just one step up the stairs and you'll see it better.

BRENDAN: I don't care a lot for it.

SELF: You're quite right, it's the only poor picture in the vestibule. It was painted by an old Irishwoman—at least she was old when she died, ninety something—her name was Sarah Purser, a rich, witty old woman and she could paint very good pictures and some not so good; and this is one of her not-so-goods, but when she offered the portrait to us we were delighted to accept it, for our gallery wouldn't be complete if there wasn't in it a portrait of Sara Allgood.

BRENDAN: Gee! Is that Sara Allgood. I've heard a lot about her.

SELF: Of course you have. I don't think we've ever had an actress to compare with her. Of course, every great player is unique and, in a sense, it is ridiculous to make comparisons, but Sara Allgood was peculiarly unique. (I speak in the past tense because it is years since she played here, but she is still very much alive, thank God.) To begin with, she had a marvellous voice. You have heard of Sarah Bernhardt's "Voice of Gold"; I only heard the French Sarah in her old age and her voice then did not particularly impress me; other things about her did, immensely. But our Sara's voice had a range, a depth, a clarity impossible to describe. It was gold and silver and, if she so wished, iron.

BRENDAN: A gift of God, I guess.

SELF: Yes, but God gave her, as it were, just the ingredients, it was for herself to fashion and mould and use them. How often have I known Sara to get to the theatre an hour before rehearsal and, standing alone on the stage, practise her vocal exercises to a theatre empty save for the chars. Consequently, eventually, she had perfect control of her voice which I admit must have begun as something wonderful, but it was her own hard work which made it unique. But don't think she was just a fine speaker, she is an actress to her finger-tips, a mistress of comedy as well as of tragedy. She created the part of "Juno" in *Juno and the Paycock*. That is a Dublin slum play and the Dublin slum accent is not very beautiful, but to that part she brought all her motherly instincts—she was always a perfect mother on the stage, a tender mother, a domineering mother, oh, she could be harsh if the part demanded harshness and she made "Juno" a thing to be long remembered. And what humour she had! I wish you could have seen her in some of Lady Gregory's early comedies, in *The Jackdaw* or *Hyacinth Halvey*. Lady Gregory loved her dearly and she adored Lady Gregory. Dear Sally! How she and I used to fight in the old days.

DAVID: About what?

BRENDAN: Yes. What did you scrap about?

SELF: Oh, the silliest little things, I've forgotten them, the things actresses *do* scrap about. But we forgave and forgot very quickly. She "made" my first two plays, so I should never have said a cross word to her.

BRENDAN: And she's not here now?

SELF: No, she's in Hollywood, worse luck. You Americans have taken so many of our good players, Barry Fitzgerald, J. M. Kerrigan, Arthur Shields—we mustn't grudge you them, they are earning what they deserve and we have as good a company as ever we had, but if Sara Allgood walked on the stage this evening what a cheer there'd be, you'd hear it down to the Liffey. One often sees her on the screen, but I have never seen her yet in a part worthy of her genius. She's happy in Hollywood, has a little house of her own and hens and she drives her car—my, I wouldn't trust myself in a car with Sally at the wheel; why, when she was trying to learn to ride a bicycle, practising behind the Custom House, her teacher advised her to give it up, he said she would be a menace to the public. I get long letters from her now and then and she sends me tea—Again, bless her.... Now, a step up.

BRENDAN: A man.

DAVID: In a sort of a fancy dress.

SELF: Yes, that's Arthur Sinclair, a contemporary of Sara Allgood's. When those two were acting together and you had Kerrigan and Fred O'Donovan and Maire O'Neill and Sydney Morgan in the other parts then you would have a performance to make you sit up and remember. The "fancy dress," David, is because the artist painted Sinclair as "King James" in a play of Lady Gregory's called *The White Cockade*. The picture was painted by her son, Robert, a beautiful painter, killed flying over Italy in the last war. Sinclair is known best to the public as a comedian, yet grand and rich as his comedy is, I like almost better to remember his tragic parts. In a little play called *The Pie-dish*, as a brutal farmer in a play of mine called *The Cross Roads*, above all as the blind man in *The Well of the Saints*. He has not Sara Allgood's lovely voice, but he has all her versatility—perhaps he is even more versatile than she is. He acts often in London and I read grand notices of his performances but I haven't seen him act for years. That striking drawing at the top of the stairs is by the English artist, Augustus John. Years ago, in 1921, when we were deep in the Anglo-Irish war things went very hard with the theatre, we had curfew at half-past eight, and to raise money to keep us alive an Irish friend of ours, J. B. Fagan, arranged a series of lectures in his great drawing-room in London. Yeats lectured, and Shaw came and read the first act—it had not yet been played or published—of *Back to Methuselah*. We made quite a lot of money and Augustus John gave us this drawing to be auctioned. Fagan said wittily enough that it depicts Sara Allgood and her sister Maire O'Neill not allowing the new actress to have a look-in. Yes, I'm afraid actresses are often like that, not always. Actors are generally much more generous. But now, look across—no, we'll go downstairs and look at them from the floor.

DAVID: Two grand women. The top one's a beauty.

SELF: You're right. Her name is Maire Nic Shiubhlaigh. She was one of the earliest and the best of our actresses. She lacked the power of Sara Allgood and she hadn't the *diablerie* of Sara's sister, Maire O'Neill, hanging below her, but she had a grace and a charm and a poetic beauty that was all her own. I never knew her well as an actress, she was a little before my time, but we meet fairly often and she doesn't seem to have lost a fraction of her delicacy and charm. Yeats painted it, oh, many years ago; it's a very poetic picture, don't you think? The portrait hanging below is by him also, painted years later in New York.

BRENDAN: I guess the girls were different.

SELF: They certainly were. Maire O'Neill—she is Sara Allgood's sister —how can I describe her? That is the heart-breaking thing about acting, it is made afresh each night, and each night perishes like a soap-bubble. Colley Cibber said it so much better than I can when he wrote two hundred years ago trying to describe the great Betterton in Shakespeare. "The animated graces of the player can live no longer than the instant breath and motion that presents them; or at best can but faintly glimmer through the memory of imperfect attestation of a few surviving spectators." Maire O'Neill doesn't "faintly glimmer" through my memory. She is as vivid as when I saw her in *The Shadow of the Glen*, the first night I was ever in this theatre, October 8th, 1908—the night of my first play here. She was beautiful, dark, very Irish-looking. Her qualities were quite different from her sister's. When I came to the theatre first there was a certain rivalry between them; there needn't have been. Sally could do things Molly couldn't touch, and vice versa. Sally's tragedy was grandiose, Molly's was intimate and personal. She could be deliciously impish. In her Pegeen Mike (in *The Playboy*, that play your father so disliked) she ran through the whole scale of the emotions, she was practical, harsh, playful, loving—everything a young girl can be, right up to her last heart-broken cry. I don't believe there will ever be such a Pegeen Mike again. She acted with every fibre of her body. I have seen her standing in the wings waiting for her cue, cigarette in her mouth, a girl, whispering gaily, raddled and dressed as an old woman but still a girl; then the cue came, the cigarette was crushed out and in an instant every muscle in her body seemed to alter, her face shaped itself exactly to those lines which had looked so absurd, the young voice cracked and she hobbled on to the stage an old Cork country-woman. She was a bit of a divil (which is not the same thing I'd have you know, Mr. MacNeill, as being a *devil*). Men were crazy after her and she went on tour one summer in England—not with our company—and vowed she'd come back with three engagement rings—and did.

BRENDAN: I'm not surprised.

SELF: Well, that's the end of our little picture-show.

BRENDAN: Is that all there is?

SELF: We haven't room to hang any more here. Of course there's a lot of stuff in the Green Room.

DAVID: Oh, couldn't we——?

BRENDAN: It would be fine—if it's not taking too much of your time.

SELF: Not at all, if you'd really care to.

BRENDAN: If we'd care!

SELF: Very well. We'll go through this door and across the stage, I don't think they're rehearsing this morning. Mind the steps. I'll go first and hold the door open. . . . I *told* you to mind the steps!

III

SELF: Well, you haven't sprained an ankle. . . . I'll switch on a light. I'm glad Dossy Wright isn't here. He hates my finger on a switch. He's always got his eye on the electric light bill, and, of course, rightly.

BRENDAN: But, gosh, this isn't the stage?

SELF: Yes, it is——

BRENDAN: But—but—it doesn't go anywhere.

SELF: No—it's only about twelve or fourteen feet deep—I've no head for figures: you see there's a lane just behind—we can't get more depth, but one of these days, and really within a few years, we'll have a new grand theatre—I suppose some of us old Abbey stagers will regret the passing of this pocket-handkerchief of a stage—I can't think without emotion of all the grand plays and the grand players who have trod these boards. Ah, there will be just as good players and plays to come. But, you see, we've quite a good deal of space here on the far side of the stage —room for props and scenery. If players were nearly always friends of mine, the stage staff were always friends; I can't remember a decent row between us. I like to dwell on their names; sometimes they must be only *in memoriam*; I mean, because they are dead, but others, thank goodness, are very much alive. But in memory, dear Barney Murphy, I think the best prompter we ever had, though once I, myself, was supposed to be a good prompter.

BRENDAN: Are there good and bad prompters? I thought you just spat out the words.

SELF: It's not quite as easy as that—you need to know when a player has really dried up. If the sentence is "I forget" you spit (as you say) "I forget, *I forget*" until at last the player says in desperation "Yes, I know I forget." But there was a time when Sally Allgood wouldn't go on in a new part unless I was crouching at the back of the fire ready to help her. But then this corner of the stage is so full of memories. But of course, topping everyone, Seaghan Barlow. How afraid of him I was 35 years ago. I think I am a bit afraid of him still. His lunch of cocoa and his study of Greek, his telling you that what you asked for was perfectly impossible, and the next day the impossible was in your hands. The scenery and furniture, you see, is only a small bit of what we use —a repertory theatre has to accumulate so much scenery—and the costumes. We won't go upstairs to see Miss Devoy—I'm not afraid of her—she has an infallible memory. I will say to her vaguely "There was that pale green silk dress—twenty-five years ago, very pale———" and Miss Devoy will go into a dream and tomorrow the dress will be there. But we haven't yet got near the Green Room. You see I could talk for hours about the workers. Come up these steps, I haven't much time.

(*We enter*)

BRENDAN (*Coming in*): It's really a Green Room?

SELF: Yes, so few theatres nowadays have a Green Room. I mean, a room where players can sit down and talk with each other, perhaps play a game of cards or darts while waiting for the third act. I think I shouldn't have bothered you to bring you around for there is really nothing very distinguished to show you. But you see those clever photographs? Those are of the players you were seeing in the play last night. Eileen Crowe I often think a better "Juno" than Sara Allgood because more "slum" without the poetry which Sara couldn't resist bringing into the part. And F. J. McCormick—of course, the best actor we ever had—yes,

I'm not forgetting Barry Fitzgerald and Fred O'Donovan and Arthur Sinclair, but one week McCormick is *Joxer* and the next week *King Lear* or *Oedipus*. Ah, "there's richness for you." Oh, now you'd be bored if I went from photograph to photograph praising every one, because I must praise them all. May Craig, Arthur Shields, Maureen Delany—all these lovely geniuses of players I have worked with so many years.

BRENDAN: But those others are four powerful photos.

SELF: Yes. They were taken by a man called Pirrie MacDonnell, a Scot of New York. He died a few years ago. He photographed Yeats, AE, Colum (you saw his portrait in the vestibule), and myself. Pirrie would only photograph men, and was independent. President Hoover commanded him to the White House. Pirrie declined the invitation as he wasn't interested in Hoover's face and he wasn't interested in his politics.

BRENDAN: The room seems so full of junk.

SELF: I suppose it *is* junk, but always important junk. Those presses are all crammed with scripts of plays and parts, as hard to keep correct as scenery and props and wardrobe. But there are a few important pictures in the room, an early one of Lady Gregory over the fire by AE, and then this grand portrait by Dermot O'Brien of Barry Fitzgerald as the King in *The Golden Apple*. It is my property but, of course, it is better it should hang here than in my small home. And round the corner, in the room where I hold my acting classes, there is a noble painting of Fred O'Donovan as Robert Emmet, painted years ago by James Sleator.

BRENDAN: I suppose there have been lots of plays about Emmet.

SELF: Not as many as you might think and perhaps none of them very good. My play about him, *The Dreamers*, wasn't the best, but it attempted to say history realistically—I mean I didn't wave a flag—of course, I was only copying the headline Lady Gregory set in her Folk-History Plays. But looking at Barry Fitzgerald, and thinking of Fred O'Donovan, I think how differently they achieved fame. Fred O'Donovan from the moment of his first appearance on the stage was an actor *par excellence*. I don't mean to say that he didn't improve and enrich himself, that he didn't go from strength to strength, but he didn't have to grope and stumble for a couple of years as so many players have to do. Barry had to grope and stumble and then suddenly shine out. I don't think McCormick had to grope, but he had some stage experience before I started to work with him. But Eileen Crowe, in her early days, nearly broke my heart.

BRENDAN: You fell for her?

SELF: No. I'd often liked to have fallen *on* her and beaten her hard. She took her work so carelessly, an hour and a half late for a rehearsal was nothing to her. How often have I not longed to tell her off fiercely, but—oh, from the first audition she gave me, I knew we had an actress and a voice, and then suddenly she knew she was an actress, pulled up her socks and worked like a demon at her profession—worked as a player must work. But now I've babbled on too long, but I could go on talking about these players, these plays, these workers for hours more—and I'm boring you.

AN INTERRUPTER: A parcel for you, Mr. Robinson; eightpence to pay.

SELF: Oh, Sloan, what is it about? Oh, I know. It is those raisins my brother is sending me from Pretoria.

SLOAN: I don't think it is from Pretoria, Mr. Robinson. It seems to me to come from Hollywood from Miss Sara Allgood and it is 2 lbs. of tea.

SELF: You see, I wasn't lying when I said that Sara Allgood sends me tea, and, of course, one of the pounds must go for Christmas to Mrs. Martin, one of our best workers, who, like all good Irishwomen, loves tea. And I'll ask to-night if Seaghan Barlow would like a pound of tea, and if he does both of them will drink it in memory of Sara Allgood and Lady Gregory. But here's Mr. Dermody coming in and he is having a rehearsal, so we must clear out.

BRENDAN: It was nice and homely you knowing Montana.

SELF: Ah, isn't it far away? You know, when I was at Missoula that summer everyone was so kind. Professor, students, everyone, but sometimes I'd get very homesick for Ireland. I'd remember about 3000 miles of sea from Ireland to New York and then about 3000 miles of train from New York to the Rockies—would I ever arrive home again? And then, in Butte, with Professor Merriam I went down a copper mine, 3000 feet down (not miles), and there in the dripping heat, the mine's lowest level, I was greeted in soft West Cork accents with "Do you know Drimoleague? Have you ever been in Clonakilty?" Household names to me. So, perhaps you, Brendan, felt a scrap of what I felt when you know that I can talk to you of Montana, ah—Mr. Dermody, we're interrupting—good-bye—good luck—remember me to Professor Merriam when you get back, and maybe next summer I'll get again to Sligo, David. . . .

1946

APPENDIX II

PLAYS IN GAELIC

9th May 1938

CASADH AN T-SUGAIN
Drama Aon-ghnimh
Leis an gCraoibhin (Dubhghlas de hIde)

Tomas O hAnnrachain, File Fain
o Chonnacht . . . . Cyril Cusack
Maire Bean Ui
Riogain . . . . Josephine Fitzgerald
Una Ni Riogain . . . Brid Ni Loinsigh
Seamus O hIarainn . . Liam Redmond
Sile . . . . Nora O'Mahony
Piobaire . . . . . . Daithi Page
Comharsain: Moya Devlin, Shelah Ward, Phyllis Ryan, Florence Lynch, W. O'Gorman, M. Kinsella, John MacDarby, Finbar Howard
Rinnceoiri: Tomas O Ruairc, Gearoid O Cianan, Maire Ni Dhubhluighe, Siobhan Ni Chaomhanagh
Leiritheoir: Hugh Hunt. Feisteas Staitse: Tanya Moiseiwitsch.

12th December 1938

BAINTIGHEARNA AN GHORTA
Le Seamus de Bhilmot

Sagart . . . . . . Micheal O Beirn
Saicriosta . . . Peadar O Donnchadha
Maire Ni Cuistealaigh . . . . . . Brid Ni Loinsigh
Seainin O Suilleabhain . Vincent Mahoney
Stroinsear . . . . . . Denis O'Dea
An Fear Og . . . Padraig O Cearnaigh
Daoine Eile: Maire Nic Giolla Mhartain, Sighle Nic Dhonnchadha, Sean O Tuama, Finbar Howard, Tomas O'Gorman, Maire Ni Thuama agus Moirin Ni Chuilleanain.
Leiritheoir: Prionnsias Mac Diarmada.
Feisteas Staitse: Tanya Moiseiwitsch.

15th May 1939

DONNCHADH RUADH
Le Seamus O hAodha

Traolach, Captain of a
fishing vessel . . . Prionnsias Bigear
Muiris, the First
Mate . . . Val Mac Giolla Iarainn

Brighid, owner of the
Tavern . . . . . Brid Ni Loinsigh
Donnchadh Ruadh, a
poet . . . . . Cathal O Ceallaigh
Henry, an English soldier . Wilfrid Brambell
George, another English
soldier . . . . . Robert Mooney
Irish Sailors: Brian O hUiginn, Sean Mac Cathal Riabhaigh, Seamus Mac hUiginn, Padhraig O hEanuigh.
Produced by Prionnsias Mac Diarmada.
Setting by Anne Yeats.

(Play bilingual)

22nd February 1942

CACH
Drama moralta de'n 15adh Aois
Earnan de Blaghd d'aistrigh

Teachtaire . . . . Sean O Siothchain
Guth De . . Aindrias O Muimheachain
Bas . . . . . Liam Mac Reamoinn
Cach . . . . Ciaran O hAnnrachain
Comhluadar . . Gearoid O Lochlainn
Gaoltas . . . . Mairin Ni Shuilleabhain
Colceathar . Eibhlin Ni Chathailriabhaigh
Colceathar eile . . Maedhbh Ni Mhathuna
Airneis . . . . Seamus O Caomhanaigh
Ghiomhartha Maithe . . Brid Ni Loinsigh
Eolas . . . . . Ide Ni Fhlaithimh
Faoistin . . . . . Brian O hUiginn
Sciamh . . . Neasa Ni Annrachain
Neart . . . Donnchadha O Deaghaidh
Cuig Ceadfai: Caitlin Ni Chathain, Cait Ni Choileain, Seamus O Tuama, Eamonn O Dubhthlaigh, Sean O Neachtain
Discreid . . . . Fionnuala Nic Ghathain
Aingeal . . . . Feardorchadh Mac Eoin
Rinnceoiri:
Scleip da dtagann
Ainmhian . . Jacqueline Robinson
Craos . . . . June Fryer
Sainnt . . . . . . Emma Walsh
Giodal . . . . . . Joan Wall
Ciocras cearrbhaigh Gearoid O hEilighthe
Meisce . . . Lucas Mac Lochlainn
Ciocras cearrbhaigh . . Emil Zlotover
Ceol an Drama ceapaithe ag Dr. Walford

Davies. An t-Amhran Oil nua-cheapaithe ag Gearoid O Lochlainn. Fuireann-cheoil agus Cor Chraobh an Cheitinnigh ag seinm agus ag amhranaiocht.

22nd February 1942

GLOINE AN IMPIRE

Bun-drama aon-mhir le
Traolach O Raithbhearthaigh

An tSeanbhean . . . . Brid Ni Loinsigh
Andre . . . . . Sean O Neachtain
Leiritheoir: Prionnsias Mac Diarmada.
Stiurthoir Ceoil: Prionnsias O Ceallaigh.
Stiurthoir Rinnce: Erina Brady.

29th November 1942

AN STOIRM

Drama Se Radharc le Alexander Ostrovsky
An leagan Gaedhilge le Aodh Mac Dhubhain

Cuiliogan . . . . . . Cyril Cusack
Seapcin . . . . . Liam O Ceallaigh
Aindrias Kuidriais . . . Brian O hUiginn
Pol Diokaoi . . Gearoid O Lochlainn
Boris Diokaoi, a nia Ciaran O hAnnrachain
Olga, ban-oilithreach . Ide Ni Fhlaithimh
Mdm. Kabanova . . Caitlin Ni Chathain
Tiochon Kabanov,
a mac . . . Donnchadha O Deaghdha
Caitriona, a bhean . . . Brid Ni Loinsigh
Bairbre, a
dHriofuir . . . Mairin Ni Shuilleabhain
Maire, seirbhiseach . . . Aine Ni Riain
Sean-Bhean . . . . . . Ria Mooney
Sean . . . . . Nicolas O Cinneide
Pol . . . Conchubhar O Shuilleabhain
Marta . . . Mairin Ni Ealuighthe
Leiritheoir: Prionnsias Mac Diarmada.
Feisteas Staitse: Micheal O Cleirigh.

31st January 1943

AN BHEAN CHRODHA

Drama Tri Gniomh le Piaras Beaslaoi

An Cornal Hunger-
ford . . . . Gearoid O Lochlainn
Ros, a bhean . . . . Eibhlin Nic Eoin
Agata . . . . Mairin Ni Shuilleabhain
Mairead de Barra . . . Brid Ni Loinsigh
Captaen Bateman . . Padraig O Nuallain
Beastun, Giuistis . . Sean O Siothchain
Domhnall O Math-
ghamhna . . Ciaran O hAnnrachain
Sorcha . . . . . Caitlin Ni Chathain
Labhras O Suilleabhain,
Sagart . . . . . Brian O hUiginn
Eoghan O Drisceoil, file Seamus O Tuama
Cait . . . . . Monica Ni Mhurchadha
Saigdiuiri, etc.
Leiritheoir: Prionnsias Mac Diarmada.
Feisteas Staitse: Micheal O Cleirigh.

21st February 1943

AR AN MBOTHAR MOR

Drama Cuig Gniomh le Jean Jacques Bernard
Liam O Briain d'aistrigh

Micheal, stat-sheirbhiseach
ar pinsean . . . . Seamus O Tuama
Prionnsin, a inghean . . Brid Ni Loinsigh
Eilie, a bhean . . Mairin Ni Shuilleabhain
Antoine Vanier, ur-
scealai cailiuil Donnchadha O Deaghdha
Roibeard Vanier, a
mhac, peinteir . Ciaran O hAnnrachain
Leiritheoir: Prionnsias Mac Diarmada.
Feisteas Staitse: Micheal O Cleirigh.

4th April 1943

AN COIMISINÉAR

Drama Grinn Tri Ghniomh
le Tomas O Suilleabhain

Mairtin O Faolain, Cathaoir-
leach Comhairle Cathrach
Chinn Golaimh Gearoid O Lochlainn
Blathnaid, a
inghean . . . Mairin Ni Shuilleabhain
Maire, seirbhiseach. . . Brid Ni Loinsigh
Micheal O hAodha, muin-
teoir Sealadach . . . . Cyril Cusack
Seamus O Murchadha,
comhairleoir . Seamus O Caomhanaigh
Feidhlim O Domh-
naill . . . Ciaran O hAnnrachain
Comhairleoiri eile: Brian O hUiginn, Micheal
O Briain, Liam O Ceal-
laigh, Seamus O Dubhda,
Micheal O hAodha, Diar-
muid O Ceallaigh
Cleireach na
Cathrach . . Donnchadha O Deaghdha
Seoirse O Maolaidhe,
fear oibre . . . . Seamus O hEilighthe
Leiritheoir: Prionnsias Mac Diarmada.
Feisteas Staitse: Micheal O Cleirigh.

198 IRELAND'S ABBEY THEATRE

30th May 1943
AN TRAONA SA MHOINFHEAR
Drama nua tri-ghniomh
le Seamus de Faoite
Fachtna O hAnnrachain d'aistrigh

Sile, cailin aimsire i
  dtigh feirme na n-
  Aodhaganach   Mairin Ni Shuilleabhain
Sean, leanan Shile   Ciaran O hAnnrachain
Seana-Thadhg O hEalaighthe,
  "buachaill" aimsire ar
  an bhfeirm .   Donnchadha O Deaghdha
An "Maistir," cara buan
  le Seana-Thadhg . . . Cyril Cusack
Tomas Mac Aodhagain,
  fear an tighe . . . . Brian O hUiginn
Maire, a bhean   . . . Brid Ni Loinsigh
Leiritheoir: Prionnsias Mac Diarmada.
Feisteas Staitse: Micheal O Cleirigh.

24th October 1943
ORDOG AN BHAIS
Duais-drama le Micheal O hAodha

Bean Ui Ghriobhtha . . Brid Ni Loinsigh
Donnchadh O Griobhtha,
  a mac . . . . Ciaran O hAnnrachain
Seamus O Griobhtha,
  mac eile . . . . Cathal MacSiomoin
Eamonn O Griobhtha, uncal
  do Sheamus is Donn-
  chadha . . . . . Brian O hUiginn
Sorcha Ni Dhuibhir   Caitriona Ni Chriothain
Bridin . . . . Maire Ni Shuilleabhain
An Dochtuir Liam O
  Linn . . . . . Cearbhall O Coisog
Comharsain: Bernie Ni Bhuadhain, Sile Ni
  Mhainin, Maire Ni Dhomhnaill
Leiritheoir: Prionnsias Mac Diarmada.
Feisteas Staitse: Alicia Sweetman.

30th January 1944
LAISTIAR DE'N EADAN
Duais-drama le Eibhlin Ni Shuilleabhain

Cait . . . . . Maire Ni Dhomhnaill
Neill . . . . Sile Ni Mhainin
Maire Ni Aodha . . . Brid Ni Loinsigh
Donnchadha Ban . . . Micheal O Briain
Blathnaid Ni
  Bhriain . . . Ronnie Nic an Mhaistir
Paidin O Maoil-
  leain . . . Donnchadha O Deaghdha
Prionnsias O Muirithe . Liam O Ceallaigh
Leiritheoir: Prionnsias Mac Diarmada

26th March 1944
STIANA
Drama tri-ghniomh le Peadar O hAnnrachain

Eoghan O hArrachtain . . Brian O hUiginn
Maire, a bhean . . . . Brid Ni Loinsigh
Eamonn, a mhac   Donnchadha O Deaghdha
Mam Chrionna . . Mairin Ni Shuilleabhain
Stiana de Brun,
  alias Daithi O
  Muireagain . . Gearoid O Lochlainn
Maitiu, a mhac . . . Tomas Studlai
Sairseant na bPoilini . Liam O Ceallaigh
1adh Poilin . . . . Padraig O Cearbhall
2adh Poilin . . Seumas Mac Conlocha
Peig Ni Shuil-
  leabhain . . . Maire Ni Dhomhnaill
Bean Stiana . . . Siobhan Nic Cionnaith
Fear og . . . . . . Micheal O Briain
Leiritheoir: Prionnsias Mac Diarmada

21st May 1944
SODAR I NDIAIDH NA NUASAL
(Le Bourgeois Gentilhomme)
Siamsa tri-ghniomh le Molière
Aistriu Gaeilge le Earnan de Blaghd

M. Jourdain . . Gearoid O Lochlainn
Madame Jourdain . . . Brid Ni Loinsigh
Lucile, a n-inghean   Mairin Ni Shuilleabhain
Cleonte . . . Donnchadha O Deaghdha
Dorimene . . . . Eibhlin Ni Bhriain
Dorante . . . . . . Cyril Cusack
Nicole . . . . Siobhan Nic Chionnaith
Covielle . . . . . Micheal O Briain
Maistir Ceoil . . Seamus O Caomhanaigh
Maistir Rinnce . . . Liam O Ceallaigh
Maistir Pionnsaireachta . Brian O hUiginn
Maistir Feallsunachta . . Sean O Maonaigh
Tailliuir . . . . Seamus O hEilighthe
Printisigh: Padraig O Ruairc, Tomas Studlai
Giollai: Micheal O Cinnsealla, Seamus O
  hEigeartaigh
Mufti . . . . Fred Johnson
Turcaigh: Eamonn O Cathain, Seosamh
  Muireachaigh, Gearoid O Suilleabhain,
  Harry Brogan, Diarmuid O Ceallaigh,
  Padraig O Cearbhaill, Padraig O Ruairc,
  Sean O Maonaigh
Amhranuithe: Micheal O hUiginn, Mairin
  Fenning, Gabriel Lyons
Rinnceoiri: Michael Matthews, Peggy Radford, Avril Graney, Mary Lydon, Olga
  Mohan, Myrtle Lampkin, Doreen Ryan,
  Valerie Ryan

Leiritheoir: Prionnsias Mac Diarmada.
Feisteas Staitse: Alicia Sweetman.

23rd October 1944

BORUMHA LAIGHEAN

Drama tri-ghniomh
le seana-Sheain O Conchubhair

Tuathal Teachtmhar, an tArd Ri	Sean O Maonaigh
Dairine, inghean leis	Brid Ni Loinsigh
Fithir, inghean eile leis	Siobhan Nic Chionnaith
Fiacha, Draoi	Gearoid O Lochlainn
Eochaidh, Ri Laighean	Donnchadha O Deaghdha
Aongus, mac Ri Uladh	Seumas Mac Conlocha
Art, File	Seumas O Tuama
Aoife, bean choimhdeachta	Maire Ni Dhomhnaill
Fearghus, Ri Uladh	Brian O hUiginn
Feidhlim, Reachtaire na Teamhrach	Micheal O Briain
Connrach, Taoiseach airm	Padraig O Dubhghaill
Ceirdne, Draoi	Feardorcha Mac Eoin
Cairbre, Freastalai	Padraig O Ruairc
Bean choimhdeachta	Mairin Ni Shuilleabhain

Saighdiuiri, Ceoltoiri, Rinnceoiri.
Leiritheoir: Prionnsias Mac Diarmada.
Feisteas Staitse: Alicia Sweetman.

7th January 1945

AN T-UBHALL OIR

Aistriu Gaeilge le Liam O Briain de *The Golden Apple* le Lady Gregory

Gairdineoir	Donnchadha O Deaghdha
Bean Feasa	Brid Ni Loinsigh
Pampog	Maire Ni Dhomhnaill
Muireann	Siobhan Nic Chionnaith
Ri	Gearoid O Lochlainn
Maor	Micheal O Briain
Dochtuir	Sean O Maonaigh
Ruairi, mac an Ri	Seumas Mac Con Locha
Fathach	Briain O hUiginn
Bean an Fhathaigh	Mairin Ni Shuilleabhain

Leiritheoir: Prionnsias Mac Diarmada

18th March 1945

GIOLLA AN TSOLUIS

Duais-drama tri-ghniomh
le Mairead Ni Ghrada

Brid, Bean Ui Dhalaigh	Brid Ni Loinsigh
Cait Ni Dhalaigh, a h-inghean	Siobhan Nic Chionnaith
Colum O Dalaigh, a mac	Padraig O Ruairc
Micheal O Dalaigh, mac eile	Seumas Mac Conlocha
Taidhgin O Cathasaigh, seana-mhairnealach	Micheal O Briain
Sean Ban, oileanach	Sean O Maonaigh
Lean, a bhean	Mairin Ni Shuilleabhain
Muiris O Cleirigh, oileanach og	Conchubhar O Seaghdha
Noirin Ni Loingsigh	Maire Ni Dhomhnaill
Giolla an tSoluis	Donnchadha O Deaghdha
Peadar O Se	Micheal O Griobhtha
Dochtuir	Liam O Ceallaigh
Cailini: Padraigin Ni Mhaidin, Ronnie Nic an Mhaistir, Sile Ni Mhainin, Cara Ni Dhonnchadha	

Leiritheoir: Prionnsias Mac Diarmada.
Feisteas Staitse: Alicia Sweetman.

13th May 1945

AN T-UDAR I N-GLEIC

Drama tri-ghniomh le Labhras Mac Bradaigh

An tUdar	Donnchadha O Deaghdha
Reasun an Udair	Conchubhar O Seaghdha
Bean Ni Chearbhaill	Mairin Ni Shuilleabhain

Carachtaerai in aigne an udair agus aisteoiri san Amharclainn:

Bean Ui Bhroin	Siobhan Nic Chionnaith
Cailin	Maire Ni Dhomhnaill
Chomharsa	Sile Ni Mhainin
Cara lei	P. Ni Mhaidin
Cara eile lei	Cara Nic Dhonnchadha
Doirseoir	C. O. Morain
Ban-Chomhairleoir	Brid Ni Loinsigh
Ban-Chomhairleoir eile	R. Nic an Mhaighistir
Comhairleoir O Floinn	Micheal O Briain
Comhairleor Mac Giolla Cearra	Seamus Mac Fhinn
Còmhairleoir Mac Gearailt	Sean O Maonaigh
Cathaoirleach an Choisde Deontas	P. O Ruairc
Oifigeach Feidhmeannach an Choisde	Liam O Ceallaigh

Freastalaithe Staitse: Gearoid O Suilleabhain, Gearoid O Maille

Cathal Piondargas	Gearoid O Lochlainn
An tAthair O Criomhthain	Seumas O hEaluighthe
An tAthair O Ruairc	Seamus Mac an Locha
Bainisteoir na hAmharclainne, Maidhc	Micheal O Cinnsealaigh

Ceathrar de 'n Daoscar-Shluagh: Feardorcha Mac Eoin, Micheal O Griobhtha, Finghin O Muineachain, A. O. Loinsigh Domhnall O Suilleabhain, cara leis an udar . . . Seamus O Tuama Fir agus Mna: P. O. Cearbhaill, Sean de Buitleir, Tomas Studlai, Vera Nic Raghnaill, P. Nic Lochlainn, A. O. Loinsigh, M. Ni Riordain, Sorcha Ni Ghuairm, Diarmuid O Ceallaigh

Leiritheoir: Prionnsias Mac Diarmada.
Feisteas Staitse: Alicia Sweetman.

27th May 1945

OIGHREACHT NA MARA

Drama tri-ghniomh le Bhaitear O Maicin
Gha leiriu ag fuireann taibhdhearc na gaillimhe

Mairtin Breathnach,
  iasgaire de chuid an
  Chladaigh . . . Sean Mac Labhraidh
Peig, a bhean . . . . Peig Ni Mhaicin
Nora, a inghean . . . Ite Ni Mhathuna
Sean, a mhac . . . Bhaitear O Maicin
Timin, leannan Nora . Domhnall O Riordain
Sorcha Ni Neachtain,
  leannan Sheain . . Eibhlin Ni Bhriain
Pat O hEigeartaigh . . Sean O hOdhrain
Tom, cara le Sean . . Gearoid O Maille
Sean O Domhnaill . Tomas Ua hEaluighthe

Leiritheoir: Bhaitear O Maicin. Feisteas Staitse: Cara Donagh.

30th September 1945

NUAIR A BHIONN FEAR MARBH

Oiriunu ar "Prenez Garde à La Peinture" Drama tri-ghniomh le René Fauchois bunaithe ar an aistriu a rinne an tOllamh Liam O Briain

An Dochtuir Seamus
  Mac Eochaidh . Gearoid O Lochlainn
Bairbre, a bhean . . . Brid Ni Loinsigh
Blathnaid, inion leis Maire Ni Dhomhnaill
Nuala, inion leis . . Doirin Ni Mhaidin
Nora, cailin aimsire Siobhan Nic Chionnaith
Ciaran O Neill . Donnchadha O Deaghdha
Ambros O Bruachain,
  leirmheastoir . . Sean Mac Labhraidh
Siobhan, a bhean . Ronnie Nic an Mhaistir
Bhaitear Puirseal . . Micheal O Briain

Breanndan O Flaithimh,
  ealadhnach og . Seamus Mac Con Locha

Leiritheoir: Prionnsias Mac Diarmada.
Feisteas Staitse: Alicia Sweetman.

26th December 1945

MUIREANN AGUS AN PRIONNSA

Bunaithe ar "An tUbhall oir"

Muireann . . . . . Doirin Mhaidin
Garadoir . . Donnchadha O Deaghdha
Bean Feasa . . . . Sean O Maonaigh
Pampog, a h-inion . Maire Ni Dhomhnaill
Saighdiuir . . . Tomas O Suilleabhain
Triur na Hatai Sioda: Gearoid O Lochlainn,
  Con O Seaghdha, Tomas Mac Coillte
Maoir: Criostoir O Morain, Donnchadha O Liathain, Seosamh O Muireadhaigh
Ruaidhri . . Seamus Mac Con Locha
Dochtuir . . . . Liam O Foghludha
Bean Ui Mhordha . . . Brid Ni Loinsigh
Mna Diolta Glasrai: Sile Ni Mhainin, Padraigin Ni Mhaidin
Beartla . . . . . Micheal O Briain
Jimin O Mordha . Siobhan Nic Chionnaith
Bollscairi Raidio: Feardorcha Mac Eoin, Siobhan Nic Chionnaith
Fathach . . . . . Sean MacLabhraidh
Bean an Fhathaigh Mairin Ni Shuilleabhain
Fear teach Gill . . Micheal O Cinnsealaigh
Amhranai ag an
  gCeilidhe . . Tomas O Suilleabhain
Stocaire . . . . . Iarla Mac an Ghoil
Rinnceoiri, Cor, etc: Aibhistin O Murchadha, Cait Ni Lannagain, Annrai O Loinsigh, Maire Ni Lionain, Eamonn Mac Gearailt, Filis Ni Bhriain, Gearoid O Suilleabhain, Mairead Nic Fhualain, Lorcan O Laimhin, Fionnghuala Ni Riain, Sean O Donnghaile, Eibhlin Ni Shuilleabhain, Sean O Murchadha, Alma Ni Sheachnasaigh, Sean O Nuallain, Treasa Ni Ghearain, Nodlaig O Mathuna, Caitlin Ni Chuilinn, Peadar Aghas, Riobaird Mac Risteaird, Padraig O Faolain, Liam O Broin, Eamonn O Maolchathail, Seumas O hEilidhe, Risteard O hUiginn, Sean O Buaidh, Eamonn Mac Aoidhe, Risteard O Dorain, Seosamh Mac an Ghabhann, Micheal O Brughain, Loreto Nic Dhonnchadha, Eithne Nic Pharthalan, Valerie de Breadun, Siubhan Ni Shioradain, Dolores de Burca, Maire Nic Mhairtin, Sile Ni Ogain, Padraigin Ni Mhaolmhuaidh, Dearbhail Ni Dhuinn, Aine Ni Mheachair

Leabhai i Sraid Ui Mhordha: Ragnhaill O
Muilleora, Iarla Mac an Ghoill, Eamonn
Mic Cuag, Nodlaig Beineid, T. O Neill.
Mna i Sraid Ui Mhordha: May Craig, Treasa
Nic Ghiollaruaidh.
Leiritheoir: Prionnsias Mac Diarmada.
Feisteas Staitse: Alicia Sweetman.

20th April 1946

CAITLIN NI UALLACHAIN
Le W. B. Yeats
Aistrithe ag Tomas Luibheid

Peadar O Gealain . . Sean Mac Labhraidh
Micheal O Gealain, a mhac,
  ata le posadh . . . Micheal O Briain
Padraig O Gealam,
  mac eile . . . Labhras O Gallchobhair
Brighid, bean Pheadar
  Ui Ghealain . . Siobhan Nic Chionnaith
Sile Ni Chathail, geallta
  do Micheal . . Maire Ni Dhomhnaill
An tSean Bhean Bhocht . Brid Ni Loinsigh
Leiritheoir: Prionnsias Mac Diarmada.
Feisteas Staitse: Alicia Sweetman.

8th September 1946

AN BUNNAN BUIDHE
Drama aon-ghnimh le Domhnall O Corcora
Aistrithe ag P. O'Domhnaill

Sean Mac Domhnaill, sean-
  duine bodhar . . . Aodh O Dubhgain
Nora Ni Dhomhnaill, a
  inion phosta, ina
  comhnai sa teach
  leis . . . Aine Nic Ghiolla Bhrighde
Aodhagan Mac Giolla
  Ghionnain, comh-
  ursa . . . . Padraig O Baoighill
Sile Ni Ghallchobhair,
  bean comhursan . Aine Nic Ghairbheach
Cathal Buidhe Mac
  Giolla Ghunna,
  an file . Eamonn Mac Giolla Easbuic
An Sagart . Domhnall Mac Giolla Easbuic
An Mhaighdean
  Mhuire . . . . Maire Ni Bhaoighill

8th September 1946

OIDHREACHT
Drama dha-ghniomh le T. C. Murray
Aistrithe ag Maire Ni Shiothchain

Padraig O Briain,
  feirmeoir . . . Aodh O Dubhgain

Maire, a bhean Aine Nic Ghiolla Bhrighde
Eamonn, an mac
  is sine . Domhnall Mac Giolla Easbuic
Sean, an mac is oige . Padraig O Baoighill
Domhnall O hOireach-
  taigh, comhursa . Niall O Maolagain
Leiritheoir: Aine Nic Ghiolla Bhrighde, le
cuidiu o Ghearoid O Lochlainn.

15th November 1946

CARA AN PHOBAIL
Aistriu Gaeilge le M. O'Droighneain de
Hyacinth Halvey le Lady Gregory

Mac Ui Ailbhe . Conchubhair O Seaghdha
Seamus O Cuirc . . Micheal O Duinn
Feardi O Fearghall . . Sean O Maonaigh
Sairsint Carden . . Labhras O Gallchobhair
Bean Ui Dhileain . Mairin Ni Shuilleabhain
Maire Seoighe . . . Maire Ni Thuathail
Leiritheoir: Liam O Laoghaire

29th December 1946

FERNANDO AGUS AN DRAGAN
An Prionnsa Fernando,
  mac Ri na Spainne . Cathal Mac Siomoin
An Bhanphrionnsa
  Caitlin, inion Ri na
  hEireann . . . Doirin Ni Mhaidin
An Dragan . . . . Seumas Mac Siomoin
Peadro, seirbhiseach
  Fhernando . . . Liam O Foghludha
Fear Feasa Spainneach . Con O Seaghdha
Banrion na hEireann . Sean O Maonaigh
Giofog . . . . . . Brid Ni Loinsigh
Poilini: Micheal O Duinn, Diarmuid O
  Ceallaigh
An Dall Glic . Donnchadha O Deaghdha
Buime Chaitlin . . Mairin Ni Shuilleabhain
Ri na nGormach . . Gearoid O Lochlainn
Conchita, a inion . Maire Ni Dhomhnaill
Gormaigh: Raghnall Breathnach, Tomas
  Studlai, Sean Mac Shamhrain
Ard-Ri na hEireann . . Brian O hUiginn
An Priomh-Fhreastalai Micheal O Maolain
Ri na bPortach . . . Micheal O Briain
Aintini Ri na bPortach: Seathrun O Goilidhe,
  Siobhan Nic Chionnaith, Padraigin Ni
  Mhaidin
Bollscaire Raidio . . Micheal O hAichir
Seanascal i dTeamhair . . Con O Seaghdha
Ban-Ostach an Chlub
  Oiche . . . Seosach Ni Shuilleabhain

Amhranaithe, Rinnceoiri, Freastalaithe, Lucht Cuirte, Gormaigh: Iarla Mac an Ghoill, Coilet Nic Reamoinn, Breandan Mac Laidhigh, Padraigin Tornoir, Micheal O Maolain, Bheara Nic Fhearadhaigh, Padraig O Dulchonta, Blaithin Ni Annrachain, Seamus Mac Siomoin, Mairin Ni Thuathail, Seosamh O Nuallain, Peig Ni Mhurchu, Risteard O Suilleabhain, Eibhlin Ni Mhainnin, Labhras O Gallchobhair, Eibhlin Ni Choiligh, Raghnall Friuin, Siobhan Ni Chearbhall, Sean O Riain, Cait Ni Lanagain, Criostair O Cadhla, Eibhlin Ni Fhlaithile, Leon Mac Eochaidh, Rite Ni Fhuarain, Tomas O Dalachain, Aine Ni Bhroin, Padraig O Broin, Coilet Nic Pheice, Peadar O Donnghaile, Maire Ni Bhroin, Traolach O Muiridhe, Roideog Ni Nuadhain, Padraig O Coitir, Sile Ni Aodhagain, Pilib O Ceallaigh, Dolores de Burca, An Sairsint Aodh MacNeill, Siobhan Ni Shioradain, An Corporal Aodh O Cuinneagain, Mairin Ni Mhairtin, An Corporal Traolach O Dubhghaill, Doirin Nic Oscar, An Corporal Sean Mac Gearailt, Peig Ni Dhubhshlaine, An Corporal Donnchadh Piolo, Eithne Nic Threinfhir, An Corporal Diarmuid O Rinn, Cleire Ni Bhuadain, Bhail Iremonger, Eibhlin Ni Shuilleabhain, Riobaird Mac Liam, Aoife Ni Bhreannain, Sean Mac Reamoinn, Sile Ni Sheachnasaigh, Gearoidin Ni Oireachtaigh, Gearoidin Ni Shuilleabhain, Eibhlin Soff, Eilis Ni Mhaoilmhiadhaigh, Sile Ni Mhainin

Leiritheoir: Prionnsias Mac Diarmada. Leas-Leiritheoir: Liam O Laoghaire. Feisteas Staitse: Carl Bonn.

19th May 1947
CAITRIONA PARR

Aistriu Gaeilge le Liam O'Laoghaire ar Drama Aon Ghnimh le Maurice Baring

Annraoi a h-Ocht,
Ri Shasana   Donnchadh O Muireadhaigh
Caitriona Parr . . . Maire Ni Thuathail
Giolla . . . . Labhras O Gallachobhair

Leiritheoir: Prionnsias Mac Diarmada

19th May 1947
OICHE MHAITH AGAT, A MHIC UI DHOMHNAILL

Aistriu Gaeilge a rinne an tOllamh
Liam O Briain
ar "Good Night, Mr. O'Donnell"
Drama Dha Ghnimh le Roibeard O Braonain
Eilis . . . . Mairin Ni Shuilleabhain

Natainiol Mac Riada . Sean O Maonaigh
Jimin O Domhnaill . Micheal O Briain
Mollai Ni Aonghusa . Doirin Ni Mhaidin
Brian O Grada . . . Raghnall Breatanach
Sean Mac Gabhann . Brian O hUiginn
Bean Ui Aonghusa . . Brid Ni Loinsigh
An Sairseant . . . Micheal O Duinn

Leiritheoir: Liam O Laoghaire. Feisteas Staitse: Carl Bonn.

3rd November 1947
DIARMUID AGUS GRAINNE
Le Micheal Mac Liammhoir

An tArd Ri . . . . Micheal O Duinn
Fionn Mac Cumhaill . . . Pilib O Floinn
Diarmuid O Duibhne Seamus Mac Con Locha
Oisin . . . . . . Liam O Foghlu
Caoilte . . . . . Raghnall Breathnach
Goll . . . . . Padraig O Dulchonta
Oscar . . . . Labhras O Gallchobhair
Diorraing Draoi . . . . . Con O Se
Ciach . . . . . . Micheal O Briain
Luan . . . . Micheal O hAonghusa
An Bhainrion . . Seosach Ni Shuilleabhain
Grainne . . . Ronai Nic an Mhaistin
Saidhbh . . . . . Brid Ni Loinsigh
Bandraoi na gCnoc . Mair Ni Dhomhnaill
Sean Bhanaltra . . . Eibhlin Ni Riain
Aonghus Dia an Ghra . Seathrun O Goili
An Chead Duine Si . Maire Ni Thuathail
An Dara Duine Si . . Rite Ni Fhurain
An Treas Duine Si . . Doirin Ni Mhaidin

1st January 1948
REALT DHIARMUDA

Aonghus an Ghra . . . Seathrun O Goili
Lasairiona, Ban-Phrionnsa
Thir na nOg . . Siubhan Nic Shiubhlaigh
Diarmuid . . . Seamus Mac an Locha
Deamhan an Dorchadais . Micheal O Duinn
Cnu . . . . . Sean Mac Shamhrain
Cnu Og . . . Diarmuid O Ceallaigh
Conan Maol . . . . Sean O Maonaigh
Sadhbh, bean Chonain . Liam O Foghlu
Triur Cocaire: Rite Ni Fhuarain, Ite Ni Mhathuna, Eibhlin Ni Riain
Smiditheoir sa Pharlus
Sceimhe . . . Padraig O Dulchonta
Grainne . . . Maire Ni Dhomhnaill
Ard-Ri na hEireann . Raghnall Breathnach
Banrion na hEireann . Maire Ni Thuathail
Fionn Mac Cumhaill . Gearoid O Lochlainn
Seascal Mac
Ronain . .Reamonn Mac an Fhailghigh

Goll Mac Morna . . . Sean O Colmain
Oisin Mac Fhinn . . . Gearoid O Colmain
Draoi . . . . . Micheal O hAonghusa
Bollscaire Thrath na
  gCeist . . . . . Brian O hUiginn
Moltoir Dornalaiochta . Pilib O Floinn
Cleasunach . . . . . Ailbhe Le Bas
Domhnall Texais . . Micheal O Maolain
Oifigigh Chustaim: Labhras O Gallchobhair,
  Ailbhe Le Bas
Rajah . . . . . . Micheal O Briain
Sineach . . Giolla Easboig O Suilleabhain
Druisin . . . . . . Brid Ni Loinsigh
Cleopatra . . . . Doirin Ni Mhaidin
Fear na Casoige Baine Padraig O Dulchonta
An Sphincs . . Ronai Nic an Mhaistir
O'Donnabhain Rossa . . Tomas Mac Anna

Indiathaigh, Eigiptigh, Buachaille Bo, Rinnceoiri, Fianna: Pearla Nic Stibhin, Caithlin Nic Chonchoille, Sile Ni Dhubhlain, Olga Ni Mhochain, Coilead Ni Dhubhthaigh, Nuala Ni Chaireallain, Peig Nic Mhaghnuis, Eithne Nic Ghrianna, Maire Ni Liodain, Siubhan Ni Chearbhaill, Padraigin Ni Dhiosca, Cairmeal Ni Eilithe, Maire Ni Fhlannagain, Eibhlin Ni Fhlaithile, Eibhlin Ni Choiligh, Caitlin Ni Cholmain, Seosach Ni Shuilleabhain, Caitlin Ni Thuathail, Olga Nic Amoinn, Geama Ni Mhuircheartaigh, Aine Nic Eoin, Maedhbh Ni Eigeartaigh, Colmnaid Nic an Bhaird, Maire Ni Bhloscaidh, Luisin Studlai, Eamonn Mac Daibhidh, Pol O hEadromain, Sean Mac Gabhann, Padraig Mac Eamoinn, Trealach O Dubhghail, Donncha Piolo, Diarmuid O Riain, Seamas O Deasunaigh, Ugo Mac Neill, Seosamh O Finn, Eamonn Mac Shitric, Cearbhall O Colmain, Seamas O Duibhne, Micheal O Mearlaigh, Seamas Mac Daibhidh, Sean Mac Gearailt, Padraig O Conchubhair, Eamonn O Cuinneagain, Sean Mac Cathail Riabhaigh, Seamas Mac Siomoin, Micheal O Connmhaigh, Sean O Riain.

Leiritheoir: Prionnsias Mac Diarmada (le caoin-chead Gabriel Pascal). Feisteas Staitse: Carl Bonn.

15th March 1948

MAIRE ROS

Drama Tri nGniomh le J. M. Barrie aistrithe ag Siobhan Nic Chionnaith

Maire Ros . . . Siobhan Nic Chionnaith
Siomon de Blaca . Micheal O hAonghusa
Harry de Blaca . . Micheal O hAonghusa

Camshron . . Donnchadha O Deaghdha
An tUasal Morlainn . . Micheal O Briain
Bean Ui Mhorlainn . . Brid Ni Loinsigh
An tOirminneach Amy . Bhaitear O Maicin
Bean Mhic Oitir . Maire Ni Dhomhnaill

Leiritheoir: Tomas Mac Anna. Feisteas Staitse agus Cultacha: Carl Bonn.

5th April 1948

MOILL NA MITHIDI

Aistriu Gaeilge le Gobnait Ni Loinsigh de "A Minute's Wait" So chluiche Aon Ghnimh le Martin J. McHugh

Domhnall O Muimh-
  neachain . . . . . Bhaitear O Maicin
Criostoir, a mhac   Reamonn Mac an Fhaili
Bean Ui Uallachain   Maire Ni Dhomhnaill
Cait, a neacht . . . Doirin Ni Mhaidin
Aindi O Ruairc, maistear
  an staisiuin . . . . Micheal O Briain
Paid Mac Muiris,
  giolla iompair . Micheal O hAonghusa
Seamai O Bhriain, garda
  na traenach . . . . Micheal O Duinn
Tomas O Cleirigh, fear
  diolta eisg . . . Sean O Maonaigh
Bean Ui Cleirigh . . . Ite Ni Mhathuna

Leiritheoir: Tomas Mac Anna. Feisteas Staitse: Carl Bonn.

16th August 1948

ARIS

Aistriu Gaeilge le Liam O Briain de "La Joyeuse Farce des 'Encore'" le Henri Ghéon

An Fear . . . . . Micheal O Briain
An Bhean . . . . . Ite Ni Mhathuna
An Comhursa . . . . Pilib O Floinn
An Sagart . . . . . Seathrun O Goili

Leiritheoir: Tomas Mac Anna. Feisteas Staitse: Carl Bonn.

11th October 1948

NA CLOIGINI

Aistriu Gaeilge le Maighread Nic Mhaicin ar "Le Juif Polonais" le Erckmann-Chatrian

Hans Mathis, Meara an
  bhaile . . . . . . Eamon Guailli
Caitriona, a bhean . . . Brid Ni Loinsigh
Annette, a inion . . Maire Ni Dhomhnaill

Ghiolla Chriost Beme,
sairsint poilini Reamonn Mac an Fhaili
An Dochtuir . . . Labhras O Gallchobhair
Henrich Schmitt, maor
coille . . . . . Micheal O Briain
Bhaitear, a chara . . Micheal O hAonghusa
Giudach Polach. . . Raghnall Breathnach
Noitear . . . . . . Seathrun O Goili
Eilis, cailin aimsire . . Maire Ni Thuathail
Nicolas, buachaill
aimsire . . . . Sean Mac Shamhrain
Uachtaran na Cuirte . . Brian O hUiginn
An Cleireach . . . Sean O Maonaigh
An Suan-Draoi . . . . Pilib O Floinn
Gardai na Cuirte: Micheal O Duinn, Eamonn Ceitinn
Poiteoiri: Liam O Foghlu, Sean O Maonaigh, Ite Ni Mhathuna, Doirin Ni Mhaidin, Ronai Nic an Mhaistir, Rite Ni Fhuarain, Feilim Mac Uidhir, Aodh Mac an Ghunna, Una Ni Loinsigh, Eithne Ni Mhathuna, Aingeal Ni Nuanain, Elmer O Deiseal

Leiriu: Tomas Mac Anna. Feisteas Staitse agus Cultacha: Carl Bonn.

27th December 1948

BRIAN AGUS AN CLAIDHEAMH SOLUIS

An Prionnsa Brian Reamonn Mac an Fhaili
Nuala . . . . . Peig Ni Mhurchadha
Bean Feasa . . . . Sean O Maonaigh
Ri na hEireann . . . . Pilib O Floinn
Bainrion na hEireann Maire Ni Dhomhnaill
An Saoi . . . . . Micheal O hAonghusa
An Priomh-Aire . . . Seathrun O Goili
Luisin, Printiseach
na Mna Feasa . Ronai Nic an Mhaistir
An Fathach . . . . . Micheal O Duinn
Domhnall, seirbhiseach an
Phrionnsa . . . . Micheal O Briain
An Bhaintreach . . . Brid Ni Loinsigh
An Priomh-Bhaille . . Liam O Foghlu
Na Ruisigh: Bhaiteir O Maicin, Raghnall Breathnach, Eamonn Guailli, Sean Mac Shamhrain
Rinnceoiri (le caoin-chead The Theatre Royal): Alys Dalgarno, Liam Mac Seain
Bean Ti an Fhathaigh . . Rite Ni Fhuarain
Ri na Frainnce . . . . Brian O hUiginn
Madame Pompadour . . Ide Ni Bheagain
Lispin, driothair an
Fhathaigh . . . Feilim Mac Uidhir
Sean Macanta . . . Gearoid O Lochlainn
Amhranai . . . Caitriona Ni Chorcrain

Triur Banostach Aer: Doirin Ni Mhaidin, Ite Ni Mhathuna, Maire Ni Thuathail
Doirseoir . . . Labhras O Gallchobhair
Bailli, Clann na Baintri, Sluaite, agus eile: Una Ni Loinsigh, Aodh Mac Gunna, Grainne Ni Sheanain, Eamonn Ceitinn, Siobhan Ni Eaghra, Liam Mac Cormaic, Aingeal Ni Nuamain, Sean O Donghaile, Eithne Ni Mhathuna, Nollaig Gui, Mairin Ni Dulchonta, Traolach O hAonghusa, Aine Ni Shiolbhroin, Nollaig O Mairtin, May Craig, Arailt O Raghallaigh, Colmin Nic an Bhaird, Traolach Mac Liaim, Nial Toibin

Leiritheoir: Tomas Mac Anna. Feisteas Staitse: Vere Dudgeon.

31st October 1949

BEAN AN MHI-GHRA

Aistriu le Paidragin Ni Neill
ar "La Malquerida" le Jacinto Benavente

Raimunda, bean cheile
Estaban . . . . . Brid Ni Loinsigh
Acacia, a h-inion . Maire Ni Dhomhnaill
Juliana, seirbhiseach an
tighe . . . . . . Ite Ni Mhathuna
Dona Isabel . . . . Maire Ni Chathain
Millagros, a h-inion, cara
do Acacia . . . Doirin Ni Mhaidin
Fidela, cara do Acacia . . Rite Ni Fhuarain
Bernabia, cara do Acacia Siubhan Ni Eaghra
Engracia, bean
chomharsan . . Ronai Nic an Mhaistir
Gaspara, fear
comharsan . . Labhras O Gallchobhair
Estaban, leas-athair
Acacia . . . . Bhaitear O Maicin
Norberto, nia do
Raimunda . Reamonn Mac an Fhaili
Faustino, geallta le
Acacia . . . Micheal O hAonghusa
Tio Eusebio, athair
Faustino . . . . Micheal O Briain
Bernabe, seirbhiseach do
Raimunda . . . Pilib O Floinn
Rubio, seirbhiseach do
Estaban . . . . Seathrun O Goili
Fir Chomharsan: Sean Mac Shamhrain, Liam O Foghlu, Micheal O Duinn
Cailini, 7rl: Aingeal Ni Nuamain, Grainne Ni Sheanain

Leiritheoir: Tomas Mac Anna. Feisteas Staitse: Vere Dudgeon.

A HISTORY, 1899–1951

26th December 1949

NIALL AGUS CARMELITA

An Prionnsa Niall,
  mac Ri na
  hEireann . .   Reamonn Mac an Fhaili
An Bhanprionnsa Car-
  melita, inion Ri na
  Spainne . . . . Peig Ni Mhurchadha
Balor . . . . . . Bhaiteir O Maicin
Na Fomhoraigh: Micheal O hAonghusa,
    Aodh Mac Gunna, Traolach
    O hAonghusa, Liam Mac
    Cormaic
Olga, an Spiaire
  Speiriuil . . . Maire Ni Dhomhnaill
Ailbhe, mac an
  Impire . . . Sean Mac Shamhrain
A Bhuime . . . . . Seathrun O Goili
Ri na Spainne . . .   Pilib O Floinn
Bainrion na Spainne . . Brid Ni Loinsigh
Sorcha, Bean na
  bPisreog . . . . Maire Ni Chathain
Don Ciochote . . . . Micheal O Briain
Sancho Panza . . Labhras O Gallchobhair
An Giolla Fada . . Raghnall Breathnach
Reics Carlo . . . . Liam O Foghlu
Jimin, a chuntoir . . . . Nollaig Gui
An Stat-Sheirbhiseach . . Padraig O Neill
An Mandairin Sineach . Sean O Maonaigh
An Dochtuir . . . . Micheal O Duinn
An Caiptin Loinge . . Eamonn Guailli
Dulcinea del Tobosa . . Ite Ni Mhatuna
An tAmhranai . . Mairtin O Diomsaigh
Maire Pheats Tamai Aindi Rite Ni Fhuarain
Roisin Bui . . . Ronai Nic An Mhaistir
Maire Aine . . . . Maire Ni Thuathail
Colaimbin . . . . Doirin Ni Mhaidin
An Bollscaire . . . . . Pol O Meara
Na Rinnceoiri: Nollaig O Mairtin, Arailt
    O Raghallaigh
Na Mairnealaigh: Seamus O Gormain,
    Eamonn Ceitinn
Banamhranui . . . . Luisin Studlai
Naomh Ruadhain Lothra . Brian O hUiginn
Eoghan Ruadh O Neill Raghnall Breathnach
Na Sinigh: Doirin Ni Mhaidin, Luisin Studlai,
    Maire Ni Thuathail, Aingeal Ni Nuamain,
    Rite Ni Fhuarain, Siobhan Ni Eaghra
Na Cailini sa Choill: Mairin Ni Dhulchonta,
    Mairin Nic Sheanlaoich, Grainne Ni
    Sheannain, Luisin Studlai, Siobhan Ni
    Eaghra, Aingeal Ni Nuamain
Ceol Nua-chumtha: Eamonn O Gallchobhair,
    Gearoid Mac an Bhuadha, Seosamh O
    Maoldhomhnaigh
Focla na nAmhran: Tomas Toibin, Caoimhin
    O Conghaile, Niall Toibin, Gearoid Mac an
    Bhuadha, Tomas Mac Anna, Eamon O
    Faolain, Eamon O Guailli
Ceol coirithe aige: Seosamh O Maoldhomh-
    naigh, Gearoid Mac an Bhuadha, Eamonn
    O Gallchobhair, Caomhin O Conghaile
An Scribhinn o: Niall Toibin, Caoimhin O
    Conghaile, Tomas Mac Anna, Pilib O
    Floinn, Micheal O Duinn, Eamon O
    Faolain
Rinnci coraithe ag: Alice Dalgarno (le caoin-
    chead na hAmharclainne Riula) agus Sean
    O Maonaigh

Leiritheoir: Tomas Mac Anna. Feisteas
Staitse: Vere Dudgeon.

22nd May 1950

TRISTAN AGUS ISIALT

Le Joseph Bedier agus Louis Artus
Donn Piatt a d'aistrigh go Gaeilg

Tristan . . . . . Raghnall Breathnach
Isial Bhan . . . . Doirin Ni Mhaidin
Brainnionn . . . Maire Ni Dhomhmaill
Irial . . . . . . Liam O Foghlu
Ri na hEireann . . . . Brian O hUiginn
Bainrion na hEireann . Maire Ni Chathain
Gairbheanal . . . . Bhaitear O Maicin
Marc, Ri Tintagel . . . Eamon Guailli
Uaisle de chuid Tintagel:
  Gondan . . . Micheal O hAonghusa
  Andrias . . . . . Seathrun O Goili
  Donnalmhain   Reamonn Mac an Fhaili
Dionas de Lidan, Priomh
  Aire . . . . . . Pilib O Floinn
Froicin, an Dronnan . . Sean O Maonaigh
Oighrin, Dithreabhach . Micheal O Briain
Isialt Chrobh-Gheal . . Ite Ni Mhatuna
Iobhan, an Lobhar . Labhras O Gallchobhair
Ceannaire na nIochtaran . Micheal O Duinn
Na hIochtarain, muinntir Tintagel: Rite Ni
    Fhurain, Siobhan Ni Eaghra, Cait Ni
    Chathain, Fionnbarr Howard, Paidraigin Ni
    Chathain, Gearoidin Nic an Bhuaidh
Ridiri Tintagel: Traolach O hAonghusa,
    Micheal O hIarfhlaithe, Nollag Gui
Sclabhuithe, Lobhair, Cleasuithe, 7rl: Cait Ni
    Bhealduin, Ailin Ni Mhiallat, Arailt O
    Raghallaigh, Nollag O Mairtin
Ridiri na hEireann, 7rl: Tomas O Dhuilleagan,
    Aodh Mac Gunna, Leo Mac Eochaidh

Leiritheoir: Tomas Mac Anna. Feisteas
Staitse: Vere Dudgeon.

15th October 1950

CLOCHA NA COIGCHRICE

Drama aon-gniomh le Aindreas O Callchobhair

Niall, fear an ti . . . . Bhaitear O Maicin
Neili, a bhean . . . . . Brid Ni Loinsigh
Domhnall, mac leo . . . Micheal O Briain
Caitlin, cailin on
  gcomharsanacht . Maire Ni Dhomhnaill
Radharc: Cistin ti bhig i dTir Chonall timpeall leath-uair tar eis a cuig maidin samhraidh, i ndiaidh siamsa oiche
Am: Fe lathair
Leiritheoir: Tomas Mac Anna. Feisteas Staitse: Vere Dudgeon.

26th December 1950

UNA AGUS JIMIN

Una . . . . Doirin Ni Mhaidin
Jimin Mhaire Thaidhg,
  fasta suas . . . . Micheal O Briain
An Seannachai, Micheal
  Mhicilin . . . . . Pilib O Floinn
Bealbeo Mac Claon-Innste Eamon Guailli
Fachna O Faisneise, An
Stat-Sheirbhiseach Traolach O hAonghusa
Seannach O Sinnire . Liam Mac Cormaic
Mairead, Aintin Una . . Brid Ni Loinsigh
Ludog Mac Ludramain, An
Leannan Si . . Sean Mac Shamhrain
Snathad Mac Breidin-Buile,
An Tailliur . . . Micheal O Duinn
An Bhainrion Maebh . . Seathrun O Goili
Oilioll, A Fear Ceile . Aodh Mac Ghunna

An Buaiciollach . . . Liam O Foghlu
Beitsin Lu . . . Maire Ni Dhomhnaill
Craoiseach O Slea . . Rae Mac An Aili
Sean Bui . . . Micheal O hAonghusa
An Moltoir . . . . Seamus O Gormain
Clann-Inion Mhaeibhe:
  Fionnfhuar . . . Siobhan Ni Eaghra
  Aidre Bhideach . . . Colette Ni Reamoinn
Cormac Cam, Ceannaire
  na nGormach . Labhras O Gallchobhair
Amhranaithe: Bhera Ni Dhubhthaigh, Roibeard O hAimhirgin
Tondeleo, Inion Chormaic . . . . . Mairin Ni Thuathail
An Sirriam . . . . . Pilib O Floinn
An Taoiseach Mor Tarbhin-a-Shui . . . . Leo Mac Eochaidh
Seosamh O Cruaigh . Sean O Maonaigh
Babs, a inion . . Aingeal Ni Nuamain
An Marascal Boris O Laoi Brian O hUiginn
Natasha Pavlova, Sonia
Petruiscea Ni Mhurchu An Bhanaltra Ronai Nic An Mhaistir
Sceitimin Ni Fhlaitheartaigh, Ban-ostach an
  Tabhairne . . . Maire Ni Chathain
Sambo, Cocaire . . Gearoid Mac Carthaigh
Rinnceoiri: Luisin Studlai, Cait Ni Bhealduin, Padraigin Ni Laoghaire, Una Ni Fhaolain, Arailt O Raghallaigh, Nollag O Mairtin
Maili Ban . . . . Ite Ni Mhathuna
An Marcach Franncach . . . Domhnall O Cruadhlaoigh
Buachaill Sreangsceil . Ailin Nic Mhilidh

Leiritheoir: Tomas Mac Anna. Feisteas Staitse: Vere Dudgeon. Bainisteoir Staitse: U. Wright.

APPENDIX III

TRANSLATIONS

16th March 1907

First Production by the Abbey Company of
INTERIOR
A Play in One Act by Maurice Maeterlinck

In the Garden:
The Old Man	F. J. Fay
The Stranger	J. M. Kerrigan
Martha	Maire O'Neill
Mary	Brigit O'Dempsey
A Peasant	J. A. O'Rourke

In the House:
The Father	Arthur Sinclair
The Mother	Sara Allgood
The Sisters: Annie Allgood, B. Warrington	

19th March 1908

TEJA
A Play by H. Sudermann
Translated from the German by Lady Gregory

Teja	J. M. Kerrigan
Bathilda	Maire O'Neill
Amalaberga	Sara Allgood
Bishop Agilla	Arthur Sinclair

Great Men of the old Gothic Kingdom:
Theodimer	Sydney Morgan
Eurich	U. Wright
Two Councillors	T. J. Fox, D. Robinson
Haribalt, a watchman	J. A. O'Rourke
Ildebad, King's spearbearer	Fred O'Donovan
Two Guards	A. Power, S. Hamilton

5th January 1911

A NATIVITY PLAY
By Douglas Hyde, LL.D.
Translated from the Irish by Lady Gregory

First Woman	Sara Allgood
Second Woman	Maire O'Neill
Kings: Fred O'Donovan, Ambrose Power, J. M. Kerrigan	
Shepherds: Arthur Sinclair, J. A. O'Rourke, Eric Gorman	
Saint Joseph	Sydney J. Morgan
Mary Mother	Maire Nic Shiubhlaigh

Produced by S. L. Robinson

20th February 1913

First Production by the Abbey Company of
HANNELE
A Dream-Play in Two Acts
by Gerhardt Hauptmann
Translated by Charles Henry Meltzer

Inmates of an almshouse:
Tulpe	Mary Roberts
Hete	Sheila O'Sullivan
Pleschke	Farrell Pelly
Hanke	Michael Conniffe
Gottwald, a schoolmaster	Philip Guiry
Seidel, a woodcutter	A. Patrick Wilson
Hannele, a poor child	Lilian Jago
Schmidt, a police official	Thomas Barrett
Berger, a magistrate	George St. John
Dr. Wachler	Sean Connolly
Sister Martha, a deaconess	Nora Desmond

The Dream figures in the order of their appearance:
Mattern, a mason (supposed to be Hannele's father)	Patrick Murphy
Hannele's Dead Mother	Nora Desmond
Three Angels of Light: Nell Byrne, Betty King, Annie Aherne	
A Great Dark Angel	Una O'Connor
Sister Martha	Nora Desmond
The Village Tailor	Charles Power
Gottwald (afterwards the Stranger)	Philip Guiry

Gottwald's Pupils
Mourners: Seidel, Pleschke and other paupers.
Numerous Bright Angels, Great and Small

Produced by Lennox Robinson

6th March 1913

THERE ARE CRIMES AND CRIMES
A Comedy in Four Acts by August Strindberg
Translated by Edwin Björkam

A Watchman	Fred Harford
Jeanne	Nell Byrne
An Abbé	Eric Gorman
Marion	Olive Ashley
Emile, a workman, Jeanne's brother	George St. John

207

Maurice Gerard, a playwright . . . . Thomas Thornhill
Madame Catherine . . . Nora Desmond
Henriette Mauclerc . . . Elizabeth Young
Adolphe, a painter . . . Charles Power
A Commissionaire . . . Sean Connolly
A Waiter . . . . . . Philip Guiry
A Guard . . . . . Thomas Barrett
A Servant Girl . . . . Peggy Buttimer

Produced by Lennox Robinson

17th April 1913
THE STRONGER
A Comedy in One Act by August Strindberg
Madame X, an actress, married . . . . . Elizabeth Young
Mdlle. Y, an actress, unmarried . . . . . Una O'Connor
A Waitress . . . . . Peggie Buttimer

Produced by Lennox Robinson

18th October 1921
A MERRY DEATH
A Harlequinade in One Act
by Nicholas Evreinov
Harlequin . . . . Ralph Brereton Barry
Pierrot . . . . . . Michael J. Dolan
Columbine . . . . . Cecile Perry
Doctor . . . . P. Kirwan
Death . . . . . . Tony Quinn

6th December 1921
THE PERFECT DAY
A Comedy in One Act by Emile Mazaud
Translated by Esther Sutro
Mr. Pique . . . . . Gabriel J. Fallon
Mr. Mouton . . . . . Peter Nolan
Mr. Trouchard . . . . Michael J. Dolan
Marie . . . . May Craig
Milkman . . . . . Gabriel J. Fallon

22nd March 1923
A DOLL'S HOUSE
A Play in Three Acts by Henrik Ibsen
Translated by R. Farquharson Sharp
Torvald Helmer . . . F. J. McCormick
Nora, his wife . . . . Eileen Crowe

Doctor Rank . . . . Michael J. Dolan
Mrs. Linde . . . . . Christine Hayden
Nils Krogstad . . . . Arthur Shields
Helen . . . . May Craig
Children . James Shields, Raymond Fardy
A Porter . . . . . P. J. McDonnell

Produced by Lennox Robinson

12th February 1924
THE TWO SHEPHERDS
A Comedy in Two Acts by G. Martinez Sierra
Translated by Helen and Harley
Granville-Barker
Dona Paquita . . . . . Sara Allgood
Lucia . . . . Eileen Crowe
Dona Gertrudis . . . Christine Hayden
The Schoolmistress . . . . May Craig
The Mayoress . . . . Maureen Delany
Rosita . . . . . . Shelah Richards
Nina . . . . Irene Murphy
A Young Lady . . . . May Kavanagh
Another Young Lady . Eveline Kavanagh
Don Antonio . . . . Michael J. Dolan
Don Francisco . . . . Gabriel J. Fallon
Don Jose Maria . . . F. J. McCormick
Don Juan de Dios . . . . Eric Gorman
Juanillo . . . . Tony Quinn
Mateo . . . . Arthur Shields
Demetrio . . . . . Maurice Esmonde
Niceto . . . . P. J. Carolan
The Mayor . . . . . . Peter Nolan
The Colonel of the Civil
Guard . . . . . . P. J. Carolan

Produced by Michael J. Dolan

3rd November 1924
First Production by the Abbey Company of
THE KINGDOM OF GOD
A Play in Three Acts by G. Martinez Sierra
Translated by Helen and Harley
Granville-Barker
ACT I
Old Man . . . . . . Tony Quinn
Gabriel . . . . P. J. Carolan
Tranjano . . . . . Michael J. Dolan
Sister Juliana . . . . . Eileen Crowe
Sister Manuela . . . . Eileen O'Kelly
Don Lorenzo . . . . Maire McIntyre
Maria Isabel . . . . . Tom Moran
Lulu . . . . . Maeve McMurrough
Liborio . . . . . . Gabriel J. Fallon

A HISTORY, 1899–1951

Act II

Candelas	Maureen Delany
Cecilia	Toni Desmond
The Dumb Girl	Shelah Richards
Sister Christina	May Craig
Sister Feliciana	Ria Mooney
Quica	Lini Doran
Sister Gracia	Eileen Crowe
Margarita	Sara Allgood
Enrique	F. J. McCormick

Act III

Sister Dionisia	Maureen Delany
Engracia	Joan Sullivan
Lorenza	Ria Mooney
The Innocent	Dolly Lynd
Morineto	U. Wright
Policarpo	Eric Gorman
Vicente	P. J. Carolan
Sister Gracia	Eileen Crowe
Paguita	Norma Joyce
Juan de Dios	Arthur Shields
Felipe	Tony Quinn
Boys	J. Breen, G. Breen, etc. etc.

Produced by Michael J. Dolan

28th April 1925

First Production by the Abbey Company of
THE PROPOSAL
By Anton Tchehov

Stepan Stepanovitch Tchubukov	Michael J. Dolan
Natalya Stepanovna	Ria Mooney
Ivan Vassilyevitch Lomov	F. J. McCormick

Produced by Michael J. Dolan

16th February 1926

First Production by the Abbey Company of
DOCTOR KNOCK
By Jules Romains
Translated by Harley Granville-Barker

Doctor Knock	F. J. McCormick
Doctor Parpalaid	Michael J. Dolan
Mosusquet	Eric Gorman
Bernard	Arthur Shields
The Town Crier	Michael Scott
A Country Fellow	P. J. Carolan
Another Country Fellow	Gabriel J. Fallon
Scipip	Tony Quinn
Madame Parpalaid	Eileen Crowe
Madame Remy	Maureen Delany
A Farmer's Wife	Christine Hayden
Madame Pons	Helena Moloney
A Nurse	Shelah Richards
Jean	Tony Quinn

3rd April 1928

JOHN GABRIEL BORKMAN
A Play in Four Acts by Henrik Ibsen
Translated by William Archer

John Gabriel Borkman, formerly Managing Director of a bank	F. J. McCormick
Mrs. Gunhild Borkman, his wife	Eileen Crowe
Erhart Borkman, their son, a student	Arthur Shields
Miss Ella Rentheim, Mrs. Borkman's twin sister	May Craig
Mrs. Fanny Wilton	Meriel Moore
Vilhelm Foldol, subordinate clerk in a Government office	Michael J. Dolan
Frida Foldol, his daughter	Kitty Curling
Mrs. Borkman's maid	Maureen Delany

Produced by Lennox Robinson

12th November 1928

First Production by the Abbey company of
THE WOMEN HAVE THEIR WAY
By Serafin and Joaquin Alvarez Quintero
Translated by Helen and Harley Granville-Barker

Don Julian	Michael J. Clarke
Sanitita	Hindel Mallard
Angela	Susan Hunt
Pilar	Ursula Dempsey
Dieguilla	Elizabeth Potter
Concha Puerto	Hester Plunket
Pepe Lora	J. B. O'Mahony
Don Cecilio	Edgar F. Keatinge
Don Adolfo Adalid	Thomas Marshall
Dona Belen	Blanaid O'Carroll
Juanita La Rosa	Gertrude Quinn
A Village Girl	May Bonass
The Sacristan of San Antonio	Patrick O'Flaherty
Guitarra	John Reynolds

31st October 1932

First Production by the Abbey Company of

THE WILD DUCK

By Henrik Ibsen

Translated by William Archer

Werle	T. Moran
George Werle	A. J. Leventhal
Old Ekdal	Eric Gorman
Hjalmar Ekdal	Geraoid O'Lochlainn
Gina Ekdal	Ann Clery
Hedvig	Shelah Richards
Mrs. Sorby	Christine Hayden
Relling	C. H. Pilkington
Molvik	Fred Johnson
Graaberg	Joseph Linnane
Jensen	J. Winter
Pettersen	H. Delamere
Waiter	Rex Mackey

Guests: C. H. Pilkington, Fred Johnson, W. O'Gorman, Gerard Kelly, G. Horgan, T. Marshall, G. Byrne, V. B. Wynburne, Denis Murray

12th November 1934

First Production by the Abbey Company of

GALLANT CASSIAN

By Arthur Schnitzler

Sophy	Shelah Richards
Martin	Cyril Cusack
Cassian	Fred Johnson
Valet	Joseph Linnane

12th November 1934

First Production by the Abbey Company of

THE SCHOOL FOR WIVES

By Molière

Translated by C. H. Wall

Chrysalde	Tom Purefoy
Arnolphe	Eric Gorman
Alain	Tom Moran
Georgette	Christine Hayden
Agnes	Nora O'Mahony
Horace	John Irwin
A Notary	J. Winter
Enrique	Joseph Linnane
Oronte	J. Stephenson

3rd December 1934

First Production by the Abbey Company of

SIX CHARACTERS IN SEARCH OF AN AUTHOR

By Luigi Pirandello

The Manager	Tom Moran
The Property Man	Desmond Crean
The Prompter	J. Winter
The Doorkeeper	Joseph Linnane

Actors and Actresses:
J. Geoffrey Davids, W. J. Scott, Tom Purefoy, Elizabeth Plunkett, Betty Holden, Elizabeth Potter

The Father	Fred Johnson
The Mother	Nora O'Mahony
The Step-daughter	Shelah Richards
The Son	Cyril Cusack
The Young Boy	Irene Murphy
The Young Girl	Mary Collins
Madame Pace	Madame Kirkwood Hackett

4th November 1935

First Production by the Abbey Company of

NOAH

By André Obey

Translated by Arthur Wilmurt

Noah	Michael J. Dolan
The Bear	John Stephenson
The Lion	J. A. MacMahon
The Monkey	Kenneth Barton
The Elephant	F. J. McCormick
The Cow	May Craig
The Tiger	W. O'Gorman
Japheth	Cyril Cusack
Shem	Barry Fitzgerald
Ham	Arthur Shields
Mrs. Noah	Maureen Delany
Ada	Sheila May
Sella	Aideen O'Connor
Naomi	Ria Mooney
The Man	P. J. Carolan

A SAINT IN A HURRY

2nd December 1935

By José Maria Penam

Translated by Hugh De Blacam

Lefevre	W. O'Gorman
Oliva	Brian Carey
Brito	J. Linnane
Francis Xavier	F. J. McCormick
Alvaro de Atayde	Barry Fitzgerald
Violette	Cathleen Murphy
Ignatius de Loyola	Michael J. Dolan
Father Broet	James J. Henry
Father Salmeron	J. Winter
Don Mascarenas	Fred Johnson
A Lay Brother, Mansilla	W. Redmond
Don Martin	P. J. Carolan
Count de Castaneda	Peter Nolan
A Lady	Nora O'Mahony
A Page	Kenneth Barton
Dona Leonor	Eileen Crowe
Father Rodriguez	Declan Murphy
The King of Portugal	John Stephenson
First Lady	Christine Hayden
Second Lady	May Craig
Father Cosme de Torres	Brian Carey
Matthew	Cyril Cusack
The Patamar	U. Wright
The Mother	Cathleen Murphy
The Chamberlain	James J. Henry
The Chief	P. J. Carolan
The Brahman	Eric Gorman
Don Duarte	Fred Johnson
Father Juan Fernandez	J. F. Carney
Yagiro, afterwards Brother Paul	J. Linnane
The Vicar-General	W. O'Gorman
Don Miguel, brother to Francis Xavier	Desmond Crean

His Brother	Brian Carey
His Sister	Christine Hayden
A Beggar	Kenneth Barton

Negroes and children

Produced by Lennox Robinson. Scenery and dresses by Tanya Moiseiwitsch.

27th December 1943

POOR MAN'S MIRACLE

A Play in Three Acts by Marian Hemar

Translated from the Polish by F. B. Czarnomski

Elizabeth, widow of George Majewski	May Craig
Her daughters:	
Anna	Eithne Dunne
Teresa	Brid Ni Loinsigh
Michael, a shoemaker, Anna's husband	Denis O'Dea
Joseph, an electrician, Teresa's husband	Cyril Cusack
A Neighbour	Ria Mooney
The Caretaker	Eileen Crowe
Dr. Szulc, M.D.	Harry Webster
Policemen: Michael Cosgrave, Micheal O Briain	
The Magistrate	Eric Gorman
The Verger	Brian O'Higgins
Magistrate's Secretary	Sean O Maonaigh
The Minister of Justice	Gerard Healy
The Rector	Liam Redmond
The Warder	U. Wright
The President of the Court	Fred Johnson
Counsel for the Defendant	Harry Brogan
The Psychologist	F. J. McCormick

Court Warders, Policemen, Neighbours

Produced by Frank Dermody. Settings by Alicia Sweetman.

APPENDIX IV

EXPERIMENTAL THEATRE

5th April 1937

THE PHOENIX
A Play in One Act by N. O. B.

Edward Mills	Cecil Ford
Jack Beatty	Austin Meldon
Oliver Goldsmith	Cecil Barror
Dr. Theaker Wilder	Brian Carey
Peggy O'Shaughnessy	Mary O'Neill
Catty Kiernan	Aine Cox
O'Reilly	Dermot Kelly

Produced by Frank Carney

5th April 1937

ALARM AMONG THE CLERKS
A Play in Three Acts by Mervyn Wall

Harkin	Michael Kinsella
Mr. Plus	Cecil Barror
Miss Noone	Anne Potter
Mr. Fox	Gearoid O hIceadha
Mr. Ireton	Austin Meldon
Mr. Finn	Brian Carey
Mr. Mullin	Malachi Keegan
Mr. Doody	John McDarby
Miss Boyd	Shelah Ward
Mr. Selskar	Frank Carney
Publican	Victor Boyd
Street Singer	Dermot Kelly

Produced by Cecil Ford

5th June 1939

HARLEQUIN'S POSITIONS
A Play in Five Acts by Jack B. Yeats

Madame Rose Bosanquet	Evelyn MacNeice
Claire Gillane, her sister	Sheila Maguire
Johnnie Gillane, their nephew	Robert Mooney
Annie Jennings	Anne Potter
Alfred Clonboise	Wilfrid Brambell
Kate	Moira McSwiggan
Guard	Gearoid O hIceadha
First Porter	Michael Kinsella
Second Porter	Dermot Kelly
Apple Woman	Sarah O'Kelly
Boy	Finbar Howard
First Pilot	Victor Boyd
Second Pilot	John McDarby

Produced by Ria Mooney and Cecil Ford

25th October 1948

THE BRIERY GAP
A Play in One Act by T. C. Murray

Joan	Angela Newman
Morgan	Pat Nolan
Father Coyne	Pilib O Floinn

Produced by Tomas Mac Anna. Setting by Tomas Mac Anna.

25th October 1948

LIGHT FALLING
A Play in One Act by Teresa Deevy

Pat Scully	Micheal O Briain
Mary, his daughter-in-law	Ita Little
John, his son	Eamonn Ceitinn
Kenneth Leslie	William McCormick
Ismay, his wife	Margaret Dunne

Produced by Sean Mac Shamhrain. Setting by Seathrun O Goili. Dance sequence by Sean O Maonaigh. Music for song by Gerard Victory and Joseph Maloney.

25th October 1948

CAVALIERO (The Life of a Hawk)
A One-Act Play in Four Scenes by Terence Smith

His Honour	Eamon Guailli
Dinny, a country lad	Raghnall Breathnach

Produced by H. L. Morrow. Settings by Anne Yeats.

A HISTORY, 1899–1951

29th November 1948

NICOLAS FLAMEL

A Play in Four Scenes from the French of Gerard de Nerval by Seamus O'Sullivan

(The first three scenes are translated from fragments left unfinished by Gerard de Nerval at the time of his death, 1855. The fourth scene is new.)

Nicolas Flamel, Scribe and
  Student of Alchemy .   Eamon Guailli
Pernelle, his wife . . Peig Ni Mhurchadha
Stranger. . . . . . Pilib O Floinn
Bailiff . . . . Noel Guy
Creditor. . . . . William McCormick

Produced by Sean Mac Shamhrain. Settings by Vere Dudgeon.

29th November 1948

THE BARN DANCE

A Fragment by Arthur Power

Old Donnelly . . Feidhlim Mac Uidhir
Lizzie . . . . . . Angela Newman
Janie . . . . Eithne McMahon
Patsy . . . . . Margaret Dunne
Kitty . . . . Siobhan Ni Eaghra
Peg . . . . Maire Ni Thuathail
Sheila . . . . . . Una Ni Loinsigh
Maureen . . . Doirin Ni Mhaidin
Kate Donnelly . . . Maire Ni Dhomhnail
Shaun Kinsella . . Reamon Mac an Fhaili
Dick Sheedy . . . . . J. O'Rourke

Produced by Sean Mac Shamhrain. Setting by Seathrun O Goili.

29th November 1948

THE DREAMING OF THE BONES

A Play in One Act by W. B. Yeats

First Musician . . . . Eamon Guailli
Second Musician . . . . . Ita Little
Third Musician . Doirin Ni Mhaidin
A Young Man . . Raghnall Breathnach
A Stranger . . . . . . Pilib O Floinn
A Young Girl . . . . Wendy Fowler

Produced by Ria Mooney. Music by Gerard Victory. Setting and Costumes by Vere Dudgeon.

7th March 1949

BLOOD WEDDING

A Tragedy in Three Acts
by Federico Garcia Lorca

Translated by Richard L. O'Connell and James Graham-Lujan

Bridegroom . . . Eamon Keating
His Mother . . . . Peggy Hayes
Neighbour . . . . Ita Little
Leonardo . . . Reamon Mac An Fhaili
His Mother-in-Law . . . Molly Griffin
His Wife . . . . Peig Ni Mhurchadha
Little Girl . . . . Grania O'Shannon
Servant . . . . . . Ite Ni Mhathuna
Bride . . . . Angela Newman
Her Father . . . . . Pilib O Floinn
Wedding Guests: Molly Hammond, Maire Ni Thuathail, Eithne McMahon, Denis O'Donovan, Micheal O Duinn
Woodcutters: William McCormick, Noel Guy, Traolach O hAonghusa
Moon . . . . Joan Stynes
Beggarwoman (Death) . Siobhan Ni Eaghra

Produced by Eamon Guailli. Settings by Vere Dudgeon.

19th April 1949

IN SAND

A Play in Three Acts by Jack B. Yeats

Anthony Larcson . . . Pilib O Floinn
John Aldgrove . . . . . . Noel Guy
The Mayor . . . Traolach O hAonghusa
Editor . . . . . . Denis O'Donovan
Town Councillor . . . Bill McCormick
Alice . . . . . Grania O'Shannon
Her Mother . . . . Mollie Griffen
Her Father . . . . . . Bill Shawn
Maurice . . . . . . Liam O Foghlu
Kitchen Maid . . . . Rite Ni Fhuairain
Chauffeur . . . Sean Mac Shamhrain
Old Sailor . . . . . Brian O'Higgins
Tourist . . . . . Raghnall Breathnach
Governor . . . . . Eamon Guailli
Hotel Boy . . . . . Brendan Clegg
Brown Boy . . . Micheal O hAonghusa
Brown Girl . . . . . Angela Newman

Produced by Sean Mac Shamhrain. Settings by Gene Martin assisted by Leslie Scott.

17th October 1949

THE HARD MAN

A Play in One Act by Michael J. Murphy

Padge Hanlon, nephew of
Jemmy Hanlon . . . Pilib O Floinn
Rosh Mulholland, Padge's
betrothed . . . Maire Ni Chathain
Micky Phelimy, a neighbour . James Carty
Jemmy Hanlon, known as
"The Bulker" . . . The Hard Man

Produced by Liam O Foghlu. Setting by Seathrun O Goili.

The Individual . . . . Patrick Nolan
Patriotism . . . . William McCormick
Bravery . . . . Sean Mac Shamhrain
The People on one side: Ronai Nic An Mhaistir, Siobhan Ni Eaghra, Peig Ni Mhurchadha, Eamonn Keane, Donn Fanning, Hugh Gunne, Harold O'Reilly, Tom Dullaghan
The People on the other side: Grania O'Shannon, Aingeal Ni Nuamain, Paul O'Mara, Noel Martin, Jim Monaghan, Joseph Martin, Michael Conway

Produced by Tomas Mac Anna. Setting and costumes by Tomas Mac Anna.

17th October 1949

THE LINK

A Tragedy in One Act by August Strindberg

Baron . . . . . . Liam O Foghlu
Baroness . . . . Aingeal Ni Nuamain
Judge . . . . Micheal O hAonghusa
Pastor . . . . Sean Mac Shamhrain
Lawyer . . . . Jim Carty
Sheriff . . . . . . Tomas Mac Anna
Constable . . . Labhras O Gallchobhair
Alexandersson . . . . Micheal O Duinn
Jury: Pat Nolan, Padraig O Neill, Noel Guy, Hugh Gunne, Harry Edmonds
Alma Johnson . . . Peig Ni Mhurchadha
Serving Girl . . . Siobhan Ni Eaghra
Serving Man . . . William McCormick

Produced by Charles McCarty. Setting by Seathrun O Goili.

17th October 1949

WAR, THE MONSTER

A Verse Play by Mary Davenport O'Neill

The Voice of the
Monster . . . Traolach O hAonghusa
The Leaders of Men: Padraig O Neill, Eamonn Cietinn, Noel Guy, Micheal O hAonghusa

3rd April 1950

THE HOUSE OF BERNARDA ALBA

A Play in Three Acts by Garcia Lorca

Translated by Richard L. O'Connell and James Graham-Lujan

Bernarda . . . . . . Peggy Hayes
Augustias, her eldest
daughter . . . . Maire Ni Chathain
Her other daughters:
Magdalena . . . . . Ite Ni Mhathuna
Amelia . . . Maire Ni Dhomhnaill
Martirio . . . . Doirin Ni Mhaidin
Adela . . . . Aingeal Ni Nuamain
Maria Josefa, her mother . Brid Ni Loinsigh
La Poncia, housekeeper . . Eileen Crowe
Servant . . . . Shelah Ward
Prudencia, a neighbour . . . May Craig
Beggar Woman . . Siobhan Ni Eaghra
Child . . . . . . Moya Jacob
First Woman . . . . Rite Ni Fhuarain
Second Woman . Roni Nic An Mhaistir
Third Woman . . . Peig Ni Mhurchadha
Fourth Woman . . . Anna Manahan
Other Women: Grainne Ni Sheannain, Pat Plunkett, Sheila Doyle, Nuala Bigger, Mary Willoughby

Produced by Eric Bentley. Settings by Vere Dudgeon.

APPENDIX V

BALLETS

30th January 1928

Part I

VENETIAN SUITE — *Respighi*
The Romantic Lady . . Ninette de Valois
The Sophisticated Lady . Vivienne Bennett
Two Unsophisticated Ladies:
 Marie Neilson and Freda Bamford
The Minstrel . . . Eileen Murray

"PASTORAL" — *Schubert*
 Cepta Cullen, Doreen Cuthbert

"A DAUGHTER OF EVE" — *Arensky*
 Ninette de Valois

"BEAUTY AND THE BEAST" — *Ravel*
Beauty . . . . . Marie Neilson
The Beast . . . Vivienne Bennett

"PRIDE" — *Scriabin*
 Ninette de Valois

Part II

"RHYTHM" — *Beethoven*
 Marie Neilson, Vivienne Bennett, Freda Bamford, Michael O'Sullivan, Rachel Law, Eileen Murray, Margaret Horgan

"DANCE OF THE PEASANT" — *Liadov*
 Ninette de Valois

MEXICAN DANCE — *Valverde*
 Vivienne Bennett

"FANTAISIE RUSSE" — *Rebikov*
 Ninette de Valois, Marie Neilson

Part III

"THE CURSE OF THE ASPEN TREE"
 arr. *Kennedy-Frazer*
 Freda Bamford, Michael O'Sullivan, S. Spratt, Kate Curling, Freda Beckett, Eileen Murray, Margaret Horgan

16th April 1928

Part I

1. THÈME CLASSIQUE — *Chopin*
 Ninette de Valois, Marie Neilson, Frances James, Chris Sheehan, May Kiernan, Margaret Horgan, Doris Nolan

2. "SILHOUETTE" — *Grieg*
 Doreen Cuthbert, Cepta Cullen, Toni Repetto-Butler

3. "THE GOLDFISH" — *Debussy*
 Marie Neilson, Frances James, Sara Patrick, Doreen Cuthbert
 Solo Piano: Hilda Shea

Part II

4. "SERENADE" — *Boccherini*
 Ninette de Valois

5. PRÉLUDE ORIENTALE — *Gliere*
 Frances James

6. "LES BUFFONS" — *Liadov*
 Sara Patrick, Cepta Cullen, Rachel Law, Eileen Murray, Freda Beckett

7. "YARABE TAPATTO" (Mexican)
 arr. *A. Partichela*
 Ninette de Valois

8. "THE AWAKENING" — *Ravel*
 Marie Neilson

Part III

9. "RITUELLE DE FEU" — *Manuel de Falla*
 The Maiden . . Ninette de Valois
 Chorus of Sun Worshippers: Marie Neilson, Frances James, Sara Patrick, Chris Sheehan, May Kiernan, Margaret Horgan, Doris Nolan, Eileen Murray, Rachel Law, Freda Beckett
 Solo Piano: Hilda Shea

24th September 1928

THÈME CLASSIQUE — *Chopin*
 Ninette de Valois, Sara Patrick, Doreen Cuthbert, Margaret Horgan, Chris Sheehan, May Kiernan, Doris Nolan

DIVERTISSEMENT

1. "A DAUGHTER OF EVE" — *Arensky*
 Ninette de Valois

2. "IDYLL" — *Schubert*
 Doreen Cuthbert, Cepta Cullen

3. DANCE OF THE RUSSIAN PEASANT — *Liadov*
 Ninette de Valois

4. "LES BUFFONS" *Liadov*
Arthur Hamilton, Rachel Law, Thelma Murphy, Muriel Kelly, Mariequita Langton

5. "THE FAUN"
The Faun . . . *Arthur Hamilton*
Elves: Doreen Cuthbert, Cepta Cullen, Toni Repetto-Butler, Jill Gregory, Anne Clarke, Geraldine Byrne
Shades: Ninette de Valois, Sara Patrick, Margaret Horgan, Chris Sheehan, May Kiernan, Doris Nolan, Rachel Law
Music by Harold R. White
Costumes designed by Rosalind Patrick
Choreography by Ninette de Valois

22nd April 1929
DIVERTISSEMENT

1. "TURKISH BALLET SUITE" (The Would-be Gentleman) *Lulley*
Sara Patrick, May Kiernan, Margaret Horgan, Doris Nolan
Choreography by Sara Patrick

2. "PRIDE" *Scriabin*
Ninette de Valois

3. "JACK AND JILL"
Jack . . . Toni Repetto-Butler
Jill . . (Mon. Tues. Wed) Eileen Hare
(Thurs. Fri. Sat.) Muriel Kelly

4. "FANTAISIE RUSSE" *Rebikov*
Ninette de Valois, Sara Patrick

5. "PRELUDE" *Chopin*
Chris Sheehan, Doreen Cuthbert, Cepta Cullen
Choreography by Sara Patrick

6. "SERENADE" *Boccherini*
Ninette de Valois

7. "IDYLL" *Schubert*
Jill Gregory, Geraldine Byrne

8. "ROUT" *Arthur Bliss*
Poem by Ernst Toller, translated by Ashley Dukes
Ninette de Valois, Sara Patrick, Chris Sheehan, Margaret Horgan, May Kiernan, Doreen Cuthbert, Cepta Cullen, Thelma Murphy
At the piano: Julia Gray, Hilda Shea
Vocalist: May Doyle
Costumes and Setting arranged by Hedley Briggs
Choreography (unless otherwise stated) by **Ninette de Valois**

14th May 1929

1. "LES SYLPHIDES" *Chopin*
Chris Sheehan, Cepta Cullen, Doreen Cuthbert, Eileen Murray, Rachel Law, Muriel Kelly, Mariequita Langton
Choreography by Ninette de Valois

2. "PRELUDE" *Chopin*
Sara Patrick, Margaret Horgan, May Kiernan
Choreography by Sara Patrick

13th August 1929

1. "TAMBOURINE" ——
Chris Sheehan, May Kiernan

2. (*a*) WALTZ *Johann Strauss*
(*b*) POLKA
Thelma Murphy, Muriel Kelly, Rachel Law, Ninette de Valois, Hedley Briggs

3. "PAVANE" ——
Margaret Horgan, Doreen Cuthbert, Mariequita Langton
Singer: John Stevenson

4. "TYROLESE" *Schubert*
Ninette de Valois, Sara Patrick, Hedley Briggs
Choreography by Ninette de Valois

19th November 1929

1. "WALTZ" *Strauss*
Thelma Murphy, Doreen Cuthbert, Cepta Cullen

2. "JEUNE PAYSANNE" *Dunhill*
Sara Patrick
Choreography by Sara Patrick

3. "MOVEMENT PERPÉTUEL" *Poulenc*
Ninette de Valois, Chris Sheehan, Cepta Cullen
At the Piano: Julia Gray, Hilda Shea
Vocalist: May Doyle
Choreography (unless otherwise stated) by Ninette de Valois

9th February 1931

1. "LES JEUNES PAYSANNES" *Dunhill*
Doreen Cuthbert, Muriel Kelly, Evelyn Murphy

2. AIR ON G-STRING *Bach*
   Thelma Murphy, Margaret Horgan, Doris Nolan
3. RUSSIAN COURT DANCE —
   Ninette de Valois
4. PAS DE TROIS CLASSIQUE *Tschaikowsky*
   Jill Gregory, Eileen Kane, Toni Repetto-Butler
5. "SUNDAY AFTERNOON" *Somerville*
   Doreen Cuthbert, Cepta Cullen
6. PRÉLUDE ORIENTALE *Gliere*
   Ninette de Valois
7. "WHEN PHILLIDA FLOUTS HIM"
   Julia Gray
   Sara Patrick, Frances Robert, Thelma Murphy, Doreen Cuthbert, Joan Crofton, Muriel Kelly, Evelyn Murphy, Eileen Kane

Numbers 2, 3, 4, 6, Choreography by Ninette de Valois
Numbers 1, 5, 7, Choreography by Sara Patrick

6th December 1931

THÈME CLASSIQUE *Chopin*
   Thelma Murphy
   Doreen Cuthbert, Cepta Cullen, Eileen Kane, Jill Gregory, Muriel Kelly, Audrey Smith

DANCE STUDIES

1. "THE NEW HAT" *Grieg*
   Geraldine Byrne
2. "AT THE BALL" *Strauss*
   Ginette Waddell
   Choreography by Nesta Brooking
3. "SOLITUDE" *Grieg*
   Cepta Cullen
4. "HE LOVES ME, HE LOVES ME NOT"
   MacDowell
   Eileen Kane
5. "VARIATION" *J. S. Bach*
   Thelma Murphy
6. TYROLESE DANCE *Schubert*
   Victor Wynburne, Cepta Cullen, Audrey Smith
7. "THE WATER LILY" *MacDowell*
   Muriel Kelly
8. "SERENADE" *Boccherin*
   Jill Gregory
9. "RUSSIAN COURT DANCE" *Zwerkov*
   Doreen Cuthbert

FEDELMA

A Mime Ballet in One Scene

Fedelma . . . . . . Doreen Cuthbert
The Son of the King of
   Ireland . . . . Victor B. Wynburne
The Hag . . . . . Nesta Brookling
Doves: Molly Furley, Muriel Kelly, Eileen Kane, Audrey Smith
Ravens: N. Curtin, R. Francis, J. Reynolds

Choreography for Dances and Ballets, unless otherwise stated, by Ninette de Valois
Music by William Alwyn
Costumes designed by D. Travers Smith

25th July 1933

THE DRINKING-HORN

A Ballet by Arthur Duff

The Elf . . . . Vera Bryans
The Knight of the Well . Robert Francis
The Flute Player . . Bartholomew Lynch
Dancers: Christine Kane, Mabel Rockett, Marjorie Pearce, Eileen Mayne, Fanny O'Meara, Tess Dillon Kelly
The Youth . . . . Toni Repetto-Butler
The Girl . . . . . . Jill Gregory

Choreography by Ninette de Valois
Conducted by the Composer

BLUEBEARD

A Ballet Poem by Mary Davenport O'Neill

Sister Ann, Ilina's sister . . Ria Mooney
Cyril, a manservant . . Joseph O'Neill
Ilina, Bluebeard's seventh
   wife . . . . . . Ninette de Valois
Baron Bluebeard . . . J. V. Wynburne
Attendant . . . . Toni Repetto-Butler
Ilina's Two Brothers: Robert Francis, Bartholomew Lynch
The Ghosts of Bluebeard's six former wives: Chris Sheehan, Doreen Cuthbert, Muriel Kelly, Cepta Cullen, Thelma Murphy, Margaret Horgan
Choir: Misses K. Roddy, C. Kenny, Betty Burne, M. Fanning

Programme produced under the direction of Arthur Shields
Music by J. F. Larchet
Choreography by Ninette de Valois

GENERAL INDEX

(See also Index of Casts of First Productions and Index of Plays referred to in Text. Plays in Gaelic, Translations, Experimental Theatre, Ballets, have not been indexed; details will be found in the respective Appendices, see Contents, page xii.)

Abbey Theatre Company, visits abroad, 52, 95, 127
Abbey Theatre, The, named, 43; first State-subsidised Theatre in English-speaking world, 126; fire at, 183
AE (George Russell), and the Fays, literary activities, 26, 27, 84
Ainley, Henry, 20
Alcott, Chauncey, 96, 98
Allgood, Sara, 25, 46, 52, 55, 58, 85, 98, 100, 182
All-Ireland Review, quoted, 27
D'Alton, Louis, 149
Anglo-Irish War, 120; effect of curfew on theatres, 120
d'Annunzio, 119, 121
Antient Concert Rooms, 5, 29, 39
Avenue Theatre, London, 3, 39

Bailey, W. F., 100
Barlow, Seaghan, 52, 66; personal reminiscence, 69-76, 153
Barry, Dr., 7
Benson, Mrs., 21
Benson, Sir Frank, 20, 21, 93
" Black-and-Tans," 29, 120
Blythe, Ernest, letter to Lennox Robinson on Government grant to Abbey Theatre, 126; joined Board of Directors, 149, 150
Bonn, Carl, 153
Boucicault, 1, 13, 96, 98
Bould, James, 152
Boyle, William, 14, 49, 50, 85
Brogan, Harry, 182
Brown-Potter, Mrs., 93
Byrne, Seamus, 149

Camden Street Hall, 28, 29
Campbell, Mrs. Patrick, 21
Carney, Frank, 149
Carroll, Paul Vincent, 149
Casey, W. F., 59
City Morgue, Dublin, 43
Clarke, Austin, 149
Coffee Palace, Dublin, 25
Colum, Padraic, 37, 38, 39, 49, 84, 85

Connell, Norreys, 181
Connor, Elizabeth, 149
" Cork Realists, The," discussed, 83
Cosgrave, President, written to by Abbey Directors, 125
Coulter, John, 149
Cousins, J. H., 26
Craig, Gordon, 152
Craig, May, 182
Crowe, Eileen, 182
Cumann na nGaedeal, 29
Curran, C. P., quoted, 154

Daily Express, quoted, 15
Daily Independent and Nation, quoted, 36
Daily Nation, quoted, 6
Darley, Arthur, 51
Darragh, Miss, 55, 56
Delany, Maureen, 120, 182
Dermody, Frank, 152
Diggles, Dudley, 25, 52
Dolan, Michael J., 152, 182
Dublin, Drama League, founded, 121
Duffy, Bernard, 100
Dunsany, Lord, 121

Edwards, Hilton, 121
Edwards-MacLiammoir Co., 121, 153
Elgar, Sir Edward, 20
Ervine, St. John, 91, 100
Evening Mail, quoted, 8, 10, 54
Evening Telegraph, quoted, 89, 93
Experimental Theatre, 154-155. (See also Appendix IV, page 212.)

Fagan, J. B., lectures in his Chelsea house, 123
Farr, Florence, 5
Farren, Robert, 149; joined Board of Directors, 150
Fay, Frank, 25; special interests, 26, 58
Fay, the brothers (see also Fay, Frank and W. G.), 29; start of theatrical careers, 25; education, 25; meeting with W. B. Yeats, 26, 27; foundations of Abbey Theatre, 29, 30, 51, 55, 58

GENERAL INDEX

Fay, W. ("Willie") G., and Irish National Theatre Society, 27, 28, 40, 42, 51, 52; resignation from Abbey Theatre, 56, 57, 98
Fitzgerald, Barry, 58; Broadbent in *John Bull's Other Island*, 59, 120, 182
Fitzmaurice, George, 59
Forbes-Robertson, Sir Johnston, 13, 93, 119
Freeman's Journal, quoted, 9, 47, 84

Gaiety Theatre, Dublin, 13, 20
Gaiety Theatre, Manchester, 87
Ganly, Andrew, 149
Gonne, Maud, 27, 52
Gorman, Eric, 182
Gregory, Lady, *Our Irish Theatre*, quoted, 1-2, 3, 4; marriage, 4, 11; and Douglas Hyde, quoted, 22; her first play produced, 28; and *The Rising of the Moon*, 29, 45, 46, 49, 50; and the finances of the theatre, 52; and *The Playboy*, quoted, 53, 57, 59; quoted, 59; and Mrs. Martin, 66, 86, 88, 93; and American tour, 96, 97, 98, 100, 119-124 *passim*; Journals, quoted, 125; death of, 149
Guinness and Co., Directors of, 183

Harvey, Sir John Martin-, 20, 92
Hayden, Christine, 100, 182
Healy, Gerard, 149
Henderson, W. A., quoted, 29
Higgins, F. R., joined Board of Directors, 149
Hone, J. M., 88
Horniman, Miss A. E. F., at Camden Street Hall, 28, 39; secretary to Yeats, 40; interests, 40; and The Mechanics' Institute, 42-45, 47-49, 55; controversy over opening of theatre on day of funeral of King Edward VII, 86; decision to withdraw her support of Abbey Theatre, 86, 90; appraisal, 87-89, 153
Hunt, Hugh, 50, 149, 152
Hyde, Douglas, 16, 20, 21; career, 21-23, 27

Ibsen, 1, 4, 14
Irish Literary Theatre, guarantors, 3, 13, 15, 16, 18, 20, 23, 98
Irish National Theatre, 3, 25
Irish National Theatre Society, founded, 27, 98
Irish Statesman, quoted, 154
Irish Times, quoted, 8, 9, 46
Irving, Sir Henry, 20

Johnston, Denis, 121, 149

Keating, Sean, 152
Kelly, P. J., 25
Kennedy, Ralph, 149

Keogh, J. Augustus, 100
Kerrigan, J. M., 52, 85, 182
Kettle, T. M., 8
King Edward VII, death of, 85; controversy over opening of theatre, 86

Larchet, J. F., 51, 187
Logue, Cardinal, 6
Loinsigh, Brid Ni, 182

McCormick, F. J., 120; portrait, 155; death of, 156, 182
MacDonagh, Thomas, 94, 99, 122
McGuinness, Norah, 152
McHugh, Roger, 149
MacLiammoir, Michael, 121
MacNamara, Brinsley, 119, 149
MacSwiney, Terence, 99; his *The Revolutionist* produced, 122
Macken, Walter, 149
Mair, G. H., 86
Malone, Andrew, quoted, 54
Markievicz, Countess de, 29, 69
Martin, Mrs., 66; personal reminiscence, 67-69
Martyn, Edward, 2, 3; and Ibsen, 4, 5, 9, 11; quoted, 13; his plays commented on, 11-16, 99
Maxine Elliot Theatre, 97
Maxwell, Sir John, 100
Mayne, Rutherford, 149
Mechanics' Institute, The, 42
Milligan, Alice, 13, 15
Mitchell, Susan, 18
Moiseiwitsch, Tanya, 152
Molesworth Hall, 28, 29, 32, 40
Molloy, M. J., 149
Montague, C. E., 86
Mooney, Ria, appointed Producer, 153; and Experimental Theatre, 154
Moore, George, 4-5, 11; collaboration with Edward Martyn, 13-14; speech to Irish Literary Theatre, 16; letter to Press, 18; collaboration with W. B. Yeats, 20, 21, 25, 52
Morgan, Sydney J., 52, 85
Murray, T. C., 83, 90-91

O'Casey, Sean, 120-122, 127; *The Silver Tassie* rejected by Abbey, 152
O'Connor, Frank, 149; joined Board of Directors, 149
O'Donnell, Frank Hugh, 6
O'Donovan, Fred, 58, 85, 100, 182
O'Kelly, Seumas, 14
O'Neill, Eugene, 121
O'Neill, Maire, 52, 58, 85, 182
Ormonde Dramatic Society, 25

O'Rourke, J. A., 52
O'Sullivan, Seamus, 47, 84

Payne, Iden, 55
Peacock Theatre, The, described, 153
Peake, Blandon, 152
Plunkett, Joseph, 99
Power, A., 52
Purser, Sarah, and vestibule windows, 155. (See also List of Illustrations, page xiii.)

Queen's Theatre, Dublin, 183
Quinn, Mary, 99
Quinteros, The, 121

Ray, R. J., 83, 90
Richards, Shelah, 182
Ricketts, Charles, 87, 152
Roberts, George, 47
Robinson, S. L. (Lennox Robinson), 85
Ryan, Fred, 27, 28, 29, 50

St. Teresa's Hall, 27
Salkeld, Cecil, 155-156
Scott, C. P., asked to arbitrate in the King Edward VII controversy, 86
Shaw, George Bernard, 3; lecture in Antient Concert Rooms, 5; mother, 5; *John Bull's Other Island* refused by Abbey, 59; *The Shewing-up of Blanco Posnet* accepted by Abbey, 59 *et seq.*; quoted, 65, 100; lecture, 123
Shiels, George, his plays discussed, 121-122
Shields, Arthur, 100, 119, 182
Shiubhlaigh, Maire Nic, 47, 52, 58, 94, 100, 182
Sinclair, Arthur, 46, 52, 58, 59, 85, 98, 182
Smith, Dorothy Travers, 152
Stuart, Francis, 149
Symonds, Arthur, 39; letter to W. G. Fay, 57
Synge, John Hatch, 34

Synge, John Millington, meeting with Yeats in Paris, 34; early days, 34-35; his plays, 34-37, 49; death, 65

The Countess Cathleen, controversy concerning plot, 6-9
The Saturday Review, quoted, 37
Tomelty, Joseph, 149
Tynan, Katherine, 84

Ulster Literary Theatre, 149
United Irishman, quoted, 15
Unnamed newspapers, quoted, 10, 14, 37

Vaughan, Ernest, 25
Vernon, Miss, 47

Walker, Frank, 47
Walker, Marie (Maire Nic Shiubhlaigh), 25
Walkley, A. B., 14, 39
Wall, Mervyn, 149
White, Dudley, 93
Whitty, Dame May, 5, 8
Wright, Udolphus, 52, 66; personal reminiscence, 76-77, 92

Yeats, Jack B., 42, 186
Yeats, J. B., 186
Yeats, William Butler, 2 *et seq.*; dislike of Ibsen, 4; influences on, 4; letter to Edward Martyn, 6; letter to Dr. Barry, 7, 8, 11, 16, 20, 25; and the Fays, 26; and Irish National Theatre Society, 27; and letter from F. J. Fay, 28, 30; lecture quoted, 32; and Irish Legends, 34; and Miss Horniman, 39-40; and letter from Miss Horniman, 44, 46, 49; debate after *Playboy* incident, 54, 55, 56, 57, 83-88 *passim*, 93, 119, 121; lecture on "The Irish Theatre," 123, 124, 149; death of, 152

INDEX OF CASTS OF FIRST PRODUCTIONS

A Deuce o' Jacks, 160
A Disciple, 146
Aftermath, 133
A Leprecaun in the Tenement, 134
Aliens, 117
A Little Bit of Youth, 117
A Little Christmas Miracle, 108
All Souls' Night, 179
All's Over, Then, 147

A Minute's Wait, 111
An Apple a Day, 173
Androcles and the Lion, 129
A Night at an Inn, 128
An Imaginary Conversation, 102
Ann Kavanagh, 133
Anti-Christ, 137
An Tincear Agus an tSidheog, 106
Apartments, 135

Aristotle's Bellows, 132
Arms and the Man, 114
A Royal Alliance, 131
A Serious Thing, 128
Ask for Me To-morrow, 179
A Spot in the Sun, 165
Assembly at Druim Ceat, 174
At Mrs. Beam's, 160
Atonement, 118
Autumn Fire, 137
A Village Wooing, 161

INDEX OF CASTS OF FIRST PRODUCTIONS

Bedmates, 132
Before Midnight, 142
Bird's Nest, 166
Birth of a Giant, 169
Birthright, 104
Black Fast, 172
Black Oliver, 141
Blight, 116
Blind Man's Buff, 163
Boyd's Shop, 162
Brady, 128
Bridgehead, 158
Broken Faith, 109
By Word of Mouth, 112

Caesar and Cleopatra, 141
Caesar's Image, 167
Candida, 161
Candle and Crib, 132
Cartney and Kevney, 142
Cathleen Listens In, 135
Cathleen ni Houlihan, 31
Church Street, 158
Coats, 105
Coggerers, 165
Coriolanus, 161
Crabbed Youth and Age, 134
Crusaders, 115

Damer's Gold, 108
Dark Isle, 144
Dave, 141
David Mahony, 110
Days Without End, 158
Deirdre (AE), 31
Deirdre (Yeats), 79
Deirdre of the Sorrows, 103
Dervorgilla, 80
Design for a Headstone, 179
Diarmuid and Grania, 24
Drama at Inish, 157
Duty, 110

Ever the Twain, 143

Family Failing, 107
Fand, 80
Fanny's First Play, 138
Faustus Kelly, 173
Fighting the Waves, 143
First Aid, 136
Fohnam, The Sculptor, 167
Forget-Me-Not, 172
Fox and Geese, 115
Fraternity, 113
Friends, 116
Friends and Relations, 171
Full Measure, 142

Give Him a House, 168
Grasshopper, 134
Grogan and the Ferret, 158

Hanrahan's Oath, 117
Harvest, 104
Hassan, 162
Hyacinth Halvey, 79

Illumination, 167
Insurance Money, 133
In the Train, 164

John Bull's Other Island, 114
John Ferguson, 113
Judgement, 107
Juno and the "Paycock," 136

Katie Roche, 162
Killycreggs in Twilight, 164
Kincora, 78
Kindred, 168
King Argimenes and the Unknown Warrior, 105
King Lear, 143
Kinship, 111

La La Noo, 173
Let the Credit Go, 145
Look at the Heffernans!, 139
Lost Light, 174
Lovers' Meeting, 172

Macbeth, 160
Macdaragh's Wife, 106
Maeve, 19
Man and Superman, 115
Margaret Gillan, 157
Marks and Mabel, 176
Maurice Harte, 107
Meadowsweet, 129
Men Crowd Me Round, 157
Michaelmas Eve, 147
Mirandolina, 104
Mixed Marriage, 105
Money, 146
Moses' Rock, 166
Mountain Dew, 143
Mountain Flood, 179
Mount Prospect, 169
Mr. Murphy's Island, 139
Mungo's Mansions, 176
My Lord, 110

Nannie's Night Out, 137
Neal Maquade, 165

Never the Time and the Place, 136
Nic, 114
1920, 157

Oedipus at Colonus, 141
Oedipus the King, 140
Old Mag, 137
Old Road, 174
On the Rocks, 159

Parnell of Avondale, 159
Parted, 141
Partition, 114
Patriots, 107
Paul Twyning, 134
Peeping Tom, 170
Peter, 144
Peter the Liar, 145
Pilgrims, 166
Portrait, 138
Professor Tim, 138
Purgatory, 166

Queer Ones, 129
Quin's Secret, 164

Railway House, 175
Red Turf, 106
Remembered for Ever, 171
Rossa, 175

Sable and Gold, 117
Sancho's Master, 140
Scrap, 146
Shadow and Substance, 163
Shanwalla, 113
She Had to Do Something, 165
Sheridan's Mills, 148
She Stoops to Conquer, 135
Sovereign Love, 109
Spring, 117
Stephen Grey, 102
Strange Guest, 170
Summer's Day, 161
Swans and Geese, 172

Temporal Powers, 147
Tenants at Will, 176
The Admirable Bashville, 146
The Annunciation, 106
The Bacac, 116
The Bargain, 113
The Bending of the Bough, 19
The Big House, 139

222   IRELAND'S ABBEY THEATRE

The Big Sweep, 147
The Blind Wolf, 142
The Bogie Man, 107
The Bribe, 110
The Bugle in the Blood, 178
The Building Fund, 78
The Canavans, 79
The Caretakers, 177
The Casting-out of Martin Whelan, 104
The Cat and the Moon, 146
The Challenge, 103
The Clancy Name, 82
The Cobbler, 111
The Cobweb, 111
The Coiner, 113
The Coloured Balloon, 175
The Counter Charm, 115
The Countess Cathleen, 12
The Country Dressmaker, 80
The Courting of Mary Doyle, 132
The Critic, 112
The Critic, 145
The Critics, 110
The Crossing, 111
The Cross Roads, 102
The Cuckoo's Nest, 108
The Cursing Fields, 172
The Dark Hour, 111
The Dark Road, 177
The Deaman in the House, 130
The Dean of St. Patrick's, 108
The Dear Queen, 166
The Deliverer, 105
The Devil's Disciple, 130
The Doctor in Spite of Himself, 79
The Doctor's Dilemma, 116
The Dragon, 128
The Drapier Letters, 141
The Dreamers, 112
The Dreaming of the Bones, 146
The Drifters, 131
The Drinking Horn, 157
The Drums are Out, 178
The Eloquent Dempsey, 78
The Emperor Jones, 140
The Enchanted Trousers, 129
The End House, 175
The End of the Beginning, 163
The Eyes of the Blind, 80
The Far-off Hills, 142

The Fiddler's House, 128
The Fire Burns Late, 171
The Flight into Egypt, 106
The Fort Field, 173
The Full Moon, 105
The Gaol Gate, 79
The Glittering Gate, 102
The Glorious Uncertainty, 135
The Gods of the Mountain, 144
The Golden Apple, 130
The Golden Helmet, 81
The Goldfish in the Sun, 180
The Gombeen Man, 109
The Good-natur'd Man, 130
The Grabber, 118
The Grand House in the City, 161
The Great Adventure, 166
The Great Pacificator, 177
The Green Helmet, 103
The Heather Field, 12
The Heritage, 167
The Home-coming, 108
The Image, 103
The Importance of Being Earnest, 140
The Inca of Perusalem, 115
The Interlude of Youth, 106
The Invincibles, 165
The Island of Saints and How to Get Out of It, 131
The Jackdaw, 80
The Jailbird, 163
The Jezebel, 157
The Jug of Sorrow, 112
The King of Friday's Men, 178
The King of Spain's Daughter, 160
The King of the Great Clock Tower, 159
The Labour Leader, 129
The Lady in the Twilight, 171
The Land for the People, 132
The Land of Heart's Desire, 105
The Last Feast of the Fianna, 19
The Laying of the Foundations, 31
The Long Road to Garranbraher, 134
The Lord Mayor, 110
The Lost Leader, 117

The Lucky Finger, 178
The Magic Glasses, 109
The Magnanimous Lover, 108
The Man in the Cloak, 164
The Man of Destiny, 133
The Man Who Missed the Tide, 81
The Marriage, 106
The Marriage Packet, 158
The Master, 142
The Mating of Shan McGhie, 147
The Mine Land, 109
The Mineral Workers, 79
The Miser, 102
The Money Doesn't Matter, 171
The Moon in the Yellow River, 146
The Moral Law, 134
The New Gossoon, 144
The New Regime, 175
The O'Cuddy, 174
The Old Broom, 176
The Old Man, 137
The Old Woman Remembers, 136
The Orangeman, 110
The Parnellite, 116
The Passing, 137
The Passing Day, 162
The Patriot, 164
The Philosopher, 113
The Pie-dish, 81
The Pipe in the Fields, 141
The Piper, 81
The Piper of Tavran, 133
The Playboy of the Western World, 79
The Player Queen, 130
The Plough and the Stars, 139
The Plough-lifters, 114
The Poorhouse, 80
The Post Office, 109
The Pot of Broth, 31
The Prodigal, 111
The Racing Lug, 31
The Reapers, 144
The Rebellion in Ballycullen, 128
The Resurrection, 159
The Retrievers, 136
The Revolutionist, 132
The Righteous are Bold, 176
The Rising of the Moon, 80
The Rogueries of Scapin, 81
The Round Table, 133

INDEX OF CASTS OF FIRST PRODUCTIONS   223

The Rugged Path, 170
The Rune of Healing, 145
The Saint, 128
The Scheming Lieutenant, 81
The Second Shepherd's Play, 106
The Serf, 131
The Shadow of a Gunman, 135
The Shadowy Waters, 41
The Shewing-up of Blanco Posnet, 103
The Shuiler's Child, 105
The Silver Jubilee, 162
The Silver Tassie, 160
The Singer, 173
The Sleep of the King, 31
The Slough, 112
The Spanish Soldier, 168
The Spoiling of Wilson, 116
The Story brought by Brigit, 136
The Strong Hand, 116
The Suburban Groove, 82
The Summit, 171
The Supplanter, 111
The Tents of the Arabs, 131
The Three Thimbles, 172
The Townland of Tamney, 41

The Travelling Man, 104
The Twisting of the Rope, 24
The Unicorn from the Stars, 80
The Visiting House, 177
The Well of the Saints, 78
The Whip Hand, 173
The White Blackbird, 138
The White Cockade, 78
The White Feather, 103
The Whiteheaded Boy, 115
The Wild Goose, 163
The Wise Have Not Spoken, 174
The Woman, 143
The Words upon the Window Pane, 145
The Workhouse Ward, 81
The Worlde and the Chylde, 107
The Would-be Gentleman, 139
The Yellow Bittern, 131
The Young Man from Rathmines, 133
They Got What They Wanted, 177
They Went by the Bus, 168
Things That Are Caesar's, 147

Thomas Muskerry, 104
Three to Go, 170
Thy Dear Father, 174
Time, 102
Time's Pocket, 166
To-day and Yesterday, 169
Tommy Tom Tom, 115
To-morrow Never Comes, 167
Trial at Greenstone Courthouse, 170
Trifles, 140
'Twixt the Giltinans and the Carmodys, 135

Vigil, 147

When Love Came Over the Hills, 117
When the Dawn Is Come, 82
Widowers' Houses, 114
William John Mawhinney, 169
Wind from the West, 163
Who Will Remember . . .? 164
Wrack, 148

You Never Can Tell, 158

INDEX OF PLAYS REFERRED TO IN TEXT

Asterisk denotes cast given in text

Aftermath, 91, 125
A Minute's Wait, 66
An Enemy of the People, 14
An Imaginary Conversation, 76
Aristotle's Bellows, 120
Arms and the Man, 3, 39
Arrah-na-Pogue, 13
Autumn Fire, 91, 127

Back to Methuselah, 123
Bedmates, 121
Birthright, 91, 95, 96
Boyd's Shop, 149
Bridgehead, 149
* Broken Soil, 37, 38

Casadh an tSugain, 20, 57, 150
Cathleen ni Houlihan, 26, 27, 39, 69, 72, 74, 99, 100
Church Street, 149
Cock-a-doodle Dandy, 121
Comedy of Sighs, 3
Crabbed Youth and Age, 121

Deirdre (AE), 26, 69
Deirdre (Yeats), 49, 56
Deirdre of the Sorrows, 65, 152
Dervorgilla, 50
Diarmuid and Grania, 16, 18, 20, 22

Drama at Inish, 149

East Lynne, 13
Eilis Agus an Bhean Deirce, 29, 150

Fand, 56
Forget-Me-Not, 149
Friends and Relations, 149

Gallant Cassian, 152

Hamlet, 1
Hanrahan's Oath, 100
His Lost Legs, 25, 69
Hyacinth Halvey, 49, 51, 69, 75, 95

Illumination, 91
Insurance Money, 121
Interior, 55, 75
* In the Shadow of the Glen, 34, 36, 37, 52, 73, 95

John Bull's Other Island, 59, 100, 152
John Ferguson, 100
John Gabriel Borkman, 1
Juno and the "Paycock," 121, 127

Kincora, 47, 50, 75

Little Eyolf, 1, 91
Look at the Heffernans!, 127

Macbeth, 152
Maeve, 13, 14, 15
Margaret Gillan, 149
Maurice Harte, 91
Mice and Men, 13
Michaelmas Eve, 91
Mixed Marriage, 91
Mourning Becomes Electra, 182

* On Baile's Strand, 46, 70

Paul Twyning, 122
Peer Gynt, 153
Purple Dust, 121

Red Roses for Me, 121
* Riders to the Sea, 36, 37, 52, 74

School for Wives, 152
Shanwalla, 100
* Spreading the News, 46, 50, 51, 52, 66, 73, 74
Spring, 91, 100

The Bending of the Bough, 13, 14, 50
The Blind Wolf, 91
The Bribe, 14
The Building Fund, 47, 49, 50, 73
The Canavans, 49, 50, 152, 156
The Casting-out of Martin Whelan, 90

The Clancy Name, 84
The Colleen Bawn, 13
The Countess Cathleen, 3, 4, 5, 6, 7, 8, 9, 10, 16, 23, 39, 74, 181
The Country Dressmaker, 59
The Cross Roads, 68, 85
The Doctor in Spite of Himself, 49, 50
The Dragon, 120
The Dreamers, 100
The Eloquent Dempsey, 14, 49, 50, 72, 73, 85
The Face at the Window, 13
The Father, 14
The Fiddler's House, 39
The Gaol Gate, 49
The Golden Apple, 120, 151
The Gombeen Man, 90
The Heather Field, 2, 4, 5, 9, 10, 14, 15, 23
* The Hour Glass, 2, 10, 32, 33, 39, 58, 70
The Image, 71
The Jackdaw, 50
* The King's Threshold, 28, 33, 34, 40, 76, 87, 152
* The Land, 38
The Land of Heart's Desire, 3, 9, 17, 21, 39, 87
The Last Feast of the Fianna, 13
The Laying of the Foundations, 29, 39, 50
The Lord Mayor, 14
The Lost Leader, 100
The Lucky Finger, 149
The Magnanimous Lover, 91
The Man Who Missed the Tide, 59
The Memory of the Dead, 69
The Mineral Workers, 49
The Miser, 50, 51
The Orangeman, 68
The Passing Day, 122
The Pie-dish, 58, 59
The Pipe in the Fields, 91
The Piper, 181
The Playboy of the Western World, 52, 53, 54, 55, 58, 61, 65, 67, 88, 95, 96, 97, 98, 127, 152, 181

The Player Queen, 121
The Plough and the Stars, 121, 127, 156, 181, 183
The Pot of Broth, 28, 29, 39, 74
The Racing Lug, 29
The Rebellion in Ballycullen, 119
The Revolutionist, 99, 122
The Rising of the Moon, 29, 99
The Rogueries of Scapin, 50, 51
The Round Table, 121
The Rugged Path, 122
The Saxon Shilling, 38
The Second, 25
The Shadow of a Gunman, 121
The Shadow of the Glen, 95, 100
The Shadowy Waters, 1, 40, 49, 70, 75
The Shewing-up of Blanco Posnet, 59, 60, 61, 62, 63, 64, 65, 98, 100
The Silver Tassie, 152
The Sleep of the King, 29
The Star Turns Red, 121
The Suburban Groove, 51, 59
The Summit, 122
The Tale of a Town, 13, 14
The Tinker and the Fairy, 150
The Townland of Tamney, 40
The Twisting of the Rope, 18, 150
The Well of the Saints, 47, 52, 58, 71
The White Cockade, 47, 50
The White Feather, 90
The Whiteheaded Boy, 100, 123, 124
The Would-be Gentleman, 50
Thomas Muskerry, 39, 85
Time, 76
* Twenty-Five, 28, 32, 33, 39, 46, 50, 76

When the Dawn Is Come, 99, 122
When We Dead Awaken, 1